Laurence Oliphant

Haifa

Life in modern Palestine

Laurence Oliphant

Haifa
Life in modern Palestine

ISBN/EAN: 9783337282622

Printed in Europe, USA, Canada, Australia, Japan

Cover: Foto ©Andreas Hilbeck / pixelio.de

More available books at **www.hansebooks.com**

HAIFA

OR

LIFE IN MODERN PALESTINE

BY

LAURENCE OLIPHANT

AUTHOR OF 'THE LAND OF GILEAD,' 'ALTIORA PETO,'
'PICCADILLY,' ETC.

SECOND EDITION

PREFACE.

THE expectations which have been excited in the minds of men by the prophecies contained in Scripture, and the hopes which have been roused by them, have ever invested Palestine with an exceptional interest to Biblical students; while its sacred conditions, historical associations, and existing remains prove an attraction to crowds of pilgrims and tourists, who annually flock to the Holy Land. As, however, the impressions of a resident and those of a visitor are apt to differ widely in regard to the conditions which actually exist there, and the former has opportunities of researches denied to the latter, I have ventured to think that a series of letters originally addressed to the New York 'Sun,' and extending over a period of three years passed in the country, might not be without interest to the general reader. Many of these will be found to deal chiefly with archæological subjects, which must, indeed, form the main subject of attraction to any one living in the country, and conversant with its history.

A flood of light has been thrown of recent years

upon its topography, its ancient sites, and the extensive ruins which still exist to testify to its once teeming population, by the prolonged and valuable researches of the " Palestine Exploration Fund " of London.

As, however, these are embodied in volumes so expensive that they are beyond the reach of the general public, and are too technical in their character to suit the taste of the ordinary reader, I have in many instances endeavoured to popularise them, availing myself extensively of the information contained in them and in Captain Conder's excellent 'Tent Work in Palestine,' and quoting freely such passages as tended to the elucidation of the subject under consideration, more especially with regard to recent discovery at Jerusalem ; but which, as I was grubbing about, I have not been able to define as exactly as I should have liked to do had all the publications been beside me at the moment.

The experience and investigation of the last three years, however, have only served to convince me that the field of research is far from being exhausted, and that, should the day ever come when excavation on a large scale is possible, the Holy Land will yield treasures of infinite interest and value, alike to the archæologist and the historian.

HAIFA, 1886.

CONTENTS.

INTRODUCTION.

The chapters which compose this volume originally formed a series of letters, all of which passed through my hands. I prepared them for their first appearance in print, and corrected the proofs afterwards. Finally, it was at my suggestion and advice that they were gathered together in a book.

The deep interest which the land of Palestine possesses for every thoughtful mind makes us all greedy for fresh and truthful information, alike concerning its present condition and the discoveries which now researches add to our knowledge of the past. From this point of view, many of the pages which follow are of exceeding importance. Every Christian will read with deep attention the author's description of the present state of places connected with momentous events of New-Testament history; and when, as in the present instance, the traveller and investigator is one whose judgment and whose accuracy may be entirely relied upon, the value of the report surpasses every careless estimate.

It is with this feeling that I have urged my friend to complete his work for publication, and with this feeling I earnestly commend it to the reader. Nor is its interest confined to historical and Biblical questions alone; the ethnologist examining the races of modern Syria, and the philosopher contemplating the marvellous processes of Asiatic transformation, will also find here material which will repay their most careful study.

C. A. DANA.

NEW YORK, November, 1886.

HAIFA.

A VISIT TO EPHESUS.

Smyrna, Nov. 4, 1882. — There are two ways of doing Ephesus: you may either go there and, like the Apostle, "fight with beasts," in the shape of donkeys and donkey boys, or you may wear yourself to death under the blazing sun, alternately scrambling over its rocks, and sinking ankle deep in the mire of its marshes. In old days it was an easy two days' ride from Smyrna to Ephesus, the distance being about fifty miles, but the Smyrna and Aiden Railway speeds you to the ruins in about two hours now, first through the romantic little gorge from whose rocky ledge rises the hill crowned by the ruined castle which overlooks the town, past a modern and an ancient aqueduct, the latter moss-grown and picturesque, with its double sets of arches rising one above the other ; through orange and pomegranate groves, and vineyards yellow and languishing at this season of the year from the drought ; across fertile plains from which the cereals and corn crops have been removed, and where flocks of sheep and goats are scattered on distant hill slopes, or follow in long lines the striking figures of the shepherds in their broad-shouldered felt coats ; past the black tents of the Yourouks, a nomadic tribe of Turcomans, whose kindred extend from here to the great wall of China, and who vary their pastoral operations from one end of Asia to the other with predatory raids upon unsuspecting travellers ; and so on into a wilder country, where the mountains close in upon us, and the Western tourist begins to realize that he is really in Asia, as groups of grunting camels, collected at the little railway stations, and their wild-looking owners, tell of journeys into the far interior, and excite a longing in his Cock-

1

ney breast to emancipate himself from the guidance of Cook, and plunge into the remote recesses of Asia Minor or Kurdistan.

As we approach Ephesus the country again becomes more fertile, and groves of fig-trees, surpassing all preconceived notions of the size ordinarily attained by these trees, reveal one of the principal sources of supply of those " fine fresh figs " which find their way in such abundance to American railway cars. As the modern Ephesus is a miserable little village, containing only a few huts and a very limited supply of donkeys, the wary traveller will see that his are sent on from Smyrna beforehand, and will probably find some consolation for the absence of any competent guide or decent accommodation, or appliances for seeing the ruins, in the evidence which this fact affords of the comparative rareness of tourist visitors.

So far from being assailed by shouts for backsheesh, or bombarded by sellers of sham antiques, or struggled for by rival guides, one is left entirely to one's own devices on that desolate little platform. There is an apology for a hotel, it is true, where cold potted meats are to be obtained, and, by dint of much searching, a guide, himself an antique, turns up, but we are very sceptical of his competency. A row of columns still standing, which once supported an aqueduct, and the crumbling ruins of a castle on a conical little hill immediately behind the railway station, suggest the mistaken idea that these are the ruins of Ephesus. They are very decent ruins, as ruins go, but the castle is a comparatively modern Seljük stronghold, and there is nothing certain about the antiquity of the aqueduct. In exploring the castle we find that the blocks of stone of old Ephesus have been built into its walls, and that a still more ancient gateway, dating from the early period of the Byzantine Empire, is also largely composed of these antique fragments, upon which inscriptions are to be deciphered, proving that they formed part of a Greek temple. So, in the old mosque of Sultan Selim, which is at the base of the hill, we find that the magnificent monolith columns of a still more ancient edifice have been used in the construction of what must in its day have been a fine specimen of Saracenic architecture; but we have not yet reached the site of ancient Ephesus. As we stand on the steps of the old mosque we look over a level and marshy plain, about a mile broad, which extends to the foot of two rocky hills, each about two hundred feet high, and divided from each other by what appears to be a chasm. Behind these is a higher ridge, backed by the mountain chain. It is on these two rocky eminences, and on their farther slopes, now hidden from view, that the ancient Ephesus stood ; but the problem which has for many years vexed antiquarians is the site, until recently undiscovered, of what gave the town its chief notoriety.

The temple of the great goddess Diana, about a quarter of the way across the plain, was a wide, low mound, and here it is that the recent excavations of Mr. Wood have laid bare one of the most interesting archæological discoveries of modern times. We eagerly tramp across the mud and over the corn-stalks of this year's crop to the débris, and, climbing up it, look down upon a vast depressed area, filled with fragments of magnificent marble columns, and with carved blocks on which are inscriptions so fresh that they seem to have been engraved yesterday, all jumbled together in a hopeless confusion, but from amid which Mr. Wood, who has had a force of three hundred men excavating here for the three previous years, has unearthed many valuable memorials. At the time of our visit the work was suspended and Mr. Wood was away, nor was it possible to obtain from the utterly dilapidated old Arab who called himself a guide, any coherent account of the last results, beyond the fact that a ship had come to take them away.

I made out one inscription, which was apparently a votive tablet to the daughter of the Emperor Aurelius Antoninus, but in most cases, though the engraving, as far as it went, was clear, the fragments were too small to contain more than a few words. In places the marble pavement of the temple was clearly defined, and its size was well worthy the fame which ranked it among the seven wonders of the world. From here a long, muddy trudge took us to the base of the hill, or mount, called Pion, on the flank of which is the cave of the Seven Sleepers, and attached to it is the well-known legend of the seven young men who went to sleep here, and awoke, after two hundred years, to find matters so changed that they were overcome by the shock. When I surmounted the hill and looked down upon the Stadium, the Agora, the Odeon, and other ruins, I was conscious of two predominating sentiments. One was surprise and the other disappointment: surprise, that one of the most populous and celebrated cities in the world should have arisen on such a site; and disappointment, that so little of its magnificence remained.

From an architectural point of view there is absolutely nothing left worth looking at. Lines of broken stone mark the limits of the principal buildings. The Stadium, which accommodated 76,000 persons, and one of the theatres, which accommodated over 56,000, are almost shapeless mounds. The whole scene is one of most complete desolation, and we are driven to our imagination to realize what Ephesus once must have been. In the case of Palmyra and Baalbec no such effort is necessary; enough is left for us to repeople without difficulty those splendid solitudes; but in Ephesus all is savage and dreary in the extreme; deep fissures run into the rock, which must have formed nearly the centre of the town; huge boulders of natural stone suggest the wild character of some portion of the city in its palmiest days. It is difficult to conceive to what use the citizens devoted this Mount Pion, with its crags and caverns and fissures. The lines of the old port are clearly defined by the limits of a marsh, from which a sluggish stream, formerly a canal, runs to the sea, about three miles distant, not far from the debouchure of the Meander. No doubt the mass of the city surrounded the port, but there is a marvellous lack of débris in this direction. Between the Temple of Diana and the foot of Mount Pion there is not a stone, so that the probability is that the temple was situated amid groves of trees. On the hill there are stones, or, rather, rocks, enough, but they are of huge size, and for the most part natural. Of actual city comparatively few remains still exist. No doubt its columns and monuments and slabs have supplied materials for the ornamentation and construction of many cities, and the convenience of getting to it by sea has materially aided the spoilers. Still, the site of ancient Ephesus affords abundant material for conjecture, and the more one studies the local topography the more difficult is it to picture to one's self what the ancient city was like.

From historical association it must ever remain one of the most interesting spots in the East, while, even from a purely picturesque point of view, the wild and rugged grandeur of the scenery amid which it is situated cannot fail to stamp it upon the memory. As I believe it is intended to continue excavations, we may hope for still further results, and there can be no doubt that, when once the obstacles which are now thrown in the way by the present government, to all scientific or antiquarian research in Turkey, are removed by the political changes now pending in the East, a rich field of exploration will be opened, not at Ephesus alone, but throughout the little-known ruined cities of Asia Minor.

THE RUINS OF ATHLIT.

HAIFA, Nov. 27, 1882.—The more you examine the countries most frequented by tourists, the more you are perplexed to comprehend the reasons which decide them to confine themselves to certain specified routes, arranged apparently by guides and dragomans, with a view of concealing from them the principal objects of interest. There is certainly not one tourist in a hundred who visits the Holy Land who has ever heard of Athlit, much less been there, and yet I know of few finer ruins to the west of the Jordan. To the east the magnificent remains of Jerash, Amman, and Arak-el Emir are incomparably more interesting, and these, of course, are also almost ignored by tourists ; but that may be accounted for by the fact that special permission from the government is required to visit them, while an impression still exists that the journey is attended with some risk. Practically this is not the case. It takes a long time to remove an impression of this kind, and it is the interest of a large class of persons who live on blackmail to keep it up. But in the case of Athlit there is no such drawback. Probably the neglect with which it is treated is due largely to the fact that no scriptural association attaches to the locality, and people would rather go to Nazareth than examine the majestic remains of Roman civilization, or the ruder superstructures of crusading warfare.

The easiest way to reach Athlit is to go to it from Carmel. As the monastery there is a most modern structure, about fifty years old, tourists often get as far as that, because the guide takes them there; but they know nothing of the mysteries of this sacred mountain, second only to Sinai, in the estimation of the modern Jew, in the sanctity of its reputation, and they turn back when, by riding a few miles down the coast, they would follow a route full of interest. The road traverses a plain about two miles in width. On the left, the rugged limestone slopes of the mountain are perforated with caves—in the earliest ages of Christianity the resorts of hermits, from whom the order of the Carmelites subsequently arose. Here tradition still points out the spot where the crusading king, St. Louis of France, was shipwrecked; and in a gorge of the mountains may still be seen the foundations of the first monastery, near a copious spring of clearest water, where the pious monarch was entertained by the first monks, whom, out of gratitude, he enabled subsequently to establish themselves upon the site occupied by the present monastery, and to found an order which has since become celebrated. Along this line of coast there is an uninterrupted stretch of sandy beach, upon which the full force of the Mediterranean breaks in long lines of rollers, and which would afford an interesting field of study to the conchologist. Among the most curious shells are the *Murex brandaris* and the *Murex trunculus*, the prickly shells of the fish which in ancient times yielded the far-famed Tyrian purple. The Phœnicians obtained the precious dye from a vessel in the throat of the fish.

Instead of following closely the line of coast, I kept near the base of the Carmel range, reaching in about two hours from Carmel the village of El Tireh, where the mosque is part of an old Benedictine monastery, the massive walls of which have been utilized for religious purposes by the Moslems. Their worship has had little effect upon the inhabitants, who are the most notorious thieves and turbulent rogues in the whole country side. They are rich enough to indulge their taste for violence with comparative impunity, as they can always square it with the authorities. Their village is surrounded with a grove of thirty thousand olive-trees and the rich plain, extending to the sea, is nearly all owned by them. Indeed, their evil reputation keeps other would-be proprietors at a distance. Here the plain begins to slope backward from the sea, so as to prevent the water from the mountains from finding a natural outlet, and in summer the country becomes miasmatic and feverish.

From El Tireh, where the inhabitants treated me with great civility, I crossed the plain, and in an hour more reached an insignificant ruin called El Dustrey, a corruption of the crusading name "*Les Destroits*," or "The Straights," so called from a gorge in the limestone ridge, which here separates the plain from the sea. This very remarkable formation extends for many miles down the coast. It is a rugged ridge, varying from twenty to fifty feet in height, and completely cutting off the sea beach from the fertile plain behind. Here and there it is split by fissures, through which the winter torrents find their way to the sea. Skirting this ridge, we suddenly come upon an artificial cutting, just wide enough to allow the passage of a chariot. At the entrance, holes were cut into the rock on both sides, evidently used in ancient times for closing and barring a passage-way. The cutting through the rock was from six to eight feet deep and from sixty to eighty yards in length. The deep ruts of the chariot-wheels were distinctly visible. Here and there on the sides steps had been cut leading to the ridge, which had been fortified.

Passing through this cutting, we debouch upon a sandy plain and a reedy marsh, in which my companion had the year before killed a wild boar; and here we were in the presence of a majestic ruin. Immediately facing us was a fragment of wall, eighty feet high, sixteen feet thick, and thirty-five yards long. It towers to a height of one hundred and twenty feet above the sea, and is a conspicuous landmark. It has been partially stripped of the external layer of carved stone blocks, and has furnished a quarry to the inhabitants for some centuries. The wall had evidently once continued across the base of the promontory upon which the ancient fortress and town were built. Passing up a rocky passage and under an archway of comparatively modern date, and which could still be closed by means of massive wooden doors, we enter the *enceinte*, and discover that the whole promontory is underlaid with huge vaults. It became also evident that the immense fragment I have described was the outer wall of a large building, for on the inside were three ribbed, pointed arches, supported on corbels, representing on the left a bearded head, on the right a head shaven on the crown, with curling hair on the sides; in the centre a cantalever, with three lilies in low relief. As the roof had fallen in, the spring of the arches alone remained. The whole was constructed of blocks of stone about three feet long, two feet high, and two feet wide. The promontory upon which all this solid masonry had been erected was washed on three sides by the sea. It rose above it precipitously to a height of about fifty feet. The area was occupied by a miserable population of possibly a hundred squalid, half-clad Arabs, whose huts were built among the ruins, thus preventing any effectual examination of them. It would be difficult to conceive a greater contrast than is presented by these wretched fellahin and their burrowing habitations with the splendour of the edifices and the opulence which must have characterized the former inhabitants. Here and there we see a fragment of a granite column, while, when we reach the brink of the cliff which forms the sea-face of the promontory, we are again surprised at the stupendous scale of these ancient works, and of the sea-wall built out upon a ledge of rocks, exposed to the full fury of the waves, and still standing to a height of forty or fifty feet.

To the right of the promontory, a wall, the base of which is washed by the waves, is perforated by three arches. It presents a most picturesque appearance. The southern face is, however, the most perfect. Here there were evidently two tiers of walls, one upon the sea-level and one upon the face of the cliff. Descending into the space between these I perceived an opening in the side of the rock, and found myself in a vaulted chamber, which was sufficiently lighted by apertures in the rock for me to measure it roughly. I estimated the length at a hundred and twenty feet, the breadth at thirty-six, and the height at thirty. It so happened that on the occasion of my visit it was blowing half a gale of wind from the seaward. The breakers were rolling in upon the reefs at the base of the promontory, throwing their spray high up on the ruined walls, and producing an effect which, with the grandeur of the surroundings, was indescribably impressive. This chamber was the handsomest of a series of vaults, several others of which I have explored under the guidance of the shick, by means of candles and torches. They are altogether six in number, running round a rectangle measuring about five hundred feet by three

hundred. They are of different sizes, varying from fifty to
three hundred feet in length, from thirty to fifty in breadth,
and from twenty-five to thirty in height.

The name of the town which stood here in ancient times
has never been discovered. This is the more singular as it
must evidently have been a place of considerable importance in the time of the Romans, more probably as a fortress
than as a place of commerce. Its natural advantages for
defence suggest themselves at once. It is important in the
history of the crusades as being the last spot held in Palestine by the crusaders, who evacuated it in 1291. It was
then destroyed by the Sultan Melik el Ashraf, so that the
most modern parts of the ruins are only six hundred years
old. But the crusaders must have entered into possession
of what was then an ancient fortress in a high state of preservation. When they took it, it became celebrated as Cas-
tellum Peregrinorum, or the Castle of the Pilgrims. It is
also spoken of in the crusading records as Petra Incisa,
from the fact that it was entered through the cutting in the
rock which I have described. In 1218 the Knights Templars restored the castle, and constituted it the chief seat of
their order. They found "a number of strange, unknown
coins." That it was a place of great strength may be in-
ferred from the fact that it was chosen by such good judges as the Knights Templars as their chief stronghold; that
it was successfully besieged by one of the sultans of Egypt,
and that it was finally abandoned only because every other
crusading possession in Palestine had succumbed.

A JEWISH COLONY IN ITS INFANCY.

HAIFA, Dec. 10.—About sixteen miles to the south of the projecting point of Carmel, upon which the celebrated monastery is perched above the sea, there lies a tract of land which has suddenly acquired an interest owing to the fact of its having been purchased by the Central Jewish Colonization Society of Roumania, with a view of placing upon it emigrants of the Hebrew persuasion who have been compelled to quit the country of their adoption in consequence of the legal disabilities to which they are subjected in it, and who have determined upon making a *bona fide* attempt to change the habits of their lives and engage in agricultural pursuits. I was invited by the local agent in charge of this enterprise to accompany him on a visit to the new property, whither he was bound with a view of making arrangements for housing and placing upon it the first settlers. Traversing the northern portion of the fertile plain of Sharon, which extends from Jaffa to Carmel, we enter by a gorge into the lower spurs of the Carmel range, which is distant at this point about three miles from the seacoast, and, winding up a steep path, find ourselves upon a fertile plateau about four hundred feet above the level of the sea. Here over a thousand acres of pasture and arable land have been purchased, on which a small hamlet of half a dozen native houses and a storehouse belonging to the late proprietor compose the existing accommodation. This hamlet is at present occupied by the fellahin who worked the land for its former owner, and it is proposed to retain their services as laborers and copartners in the cultivation of the soil until the new-comers shall have become sufficiently indoctrinated in the art of agriculture to be able to do for themselves.

The experiment of associating Jews and Moslem fellahin

in field labor will be an interesting one to watch, and the
preliminary discussions on the subject were more picturesque than satisfactory. The meeting took place in the
storehouse, where Jews and Arabs squatted promiscuously
amid the heaps of grain, and chaffered over the terms of
their mutual copartnership. It would be difficult to imagine anything more utterly incongruous than the spectacle
thus presented — the stalwart fellahin, with their wild,
shaggy, black beards, the brass hilts of their pistols projecting from their waistbands, their tasselled kufeihahs drawn
tightly over their heads and girdled with coarse black
cords, their loose, flowing abbas, and sturdy bare legs and
feet ; and the ringleted, effeminate - looking Jews, in caf-
tans reaching almost to their ankles, as oily as their red or
sandy locks, or the expression of their countenances—the
former inured to hard labor on the burning hillsides of
Palestine, the latter fresh from the Ghetto of some Roumanian town, unaccustomed to any other description of exercise than that of their wits, but already quite convinced
that they knew more about agriculture than the people of
the country, full of suspicion of all advice tendered to them,
and animated by a pleasing self-confidence which I fear the
first practical experience will rudely belie. In strange contrast with these Roumanian Jews was the Arab Jew who
acted as interpreter — a stout, handsome man, in Oriental
garb, as unlike his European coreligionists as the fellahin
themselves. My friend and myself, in the ordinary costume
of the British or American tourist, completed the party.

The discussion was protracted beyond midnight—the native peasants screaming in Arabic, the Roumanian Israelites endeavoring to outtalk them in German jargon, the
interpreter vainly trying to make himself heard, everybody
at cross - purposes because no one was patient enough to
listen till another had finished, or modest enough to wish to
hear anybody speak but himself. Tired out, I curled myself on an Arab coverlet, which seemed principally stuffed
with fleas, but sought repose in vain. At last a final rup-
ture was arrived at, and the fellahin left us, quivering with
indignation at the terms proposed by the new - comers.
Sleep brought better counsel to both sides, and an arrange-

ment was finally arrived at next morning which I am afraid
has only to be put into operation to fail signally. There is
nothing more simple than farming in co-operation with the
fellahin of Palestine if you go the right way to work about
it, and nothing more hopeless if attempted upon a system
to which they are unaccustomed. Probably, after a considerable loss of time, money, and especially of temper, a more
practical *modus operandi* will be arrived at. I am bound to
say that I did not discover any aversion on the part of the
Moslem fellahin to the proprietorship by Israelites of their
land, on religious grounds. The only difficulty lay in the
division of labor and of profit, where the owners of the
land were entirely ignorant of agriculture, and therefore dependent on the co-operation of the peasants, on terms to
be decided between them.

I eagerly welcomed the first streaks of dawn to get out
of the close atmosphere in which three had been sleeping besides myself, and watch the sun rise over the eastern mountains of Palestine. Ascending to the top of the hill in rear
of the hamlet, I enjoyed a magnificent view. To the south
the eye followed the coast-line to a point where the ruins of
Cæsarea, plainly visible through a glass, bounded the prospect. From the plain of Sharon, behind it, the hills rose in
swelling undulations, unusually well-wooded for Palestine, to
a height of about two thousand feet, the smoke of numerous
villages mingling with the morning haze. In the extreme
distance to the northeast might be discerned the lofty summits of Hermon, and in the middle distance the rounded
top of Tabor; while northward, in immediate proximity,
was the range of Carmel, with the Mediterranean bounding
the western horizon. While exploring the newly purchased
tract and examining its agricultural capabilities, I came
upon what were evidently the traces—they could hardly be
called the ruins—of an ancient town. They were on a
rocky hillside, not far from the hamlet. My attention was
first attracted by what had evidently been an old Roman
road, the worn ruts of the chariot-wheels being plainly
visible in the rock. Farther on were the marks of ancient
quarrying, the spaces in the rock, about two feet square,
showing where massive blocks had been hewn. The former

owners of the property, observing the interest with which I
examined these traces, took me to a spot where the natives,
in quarrying, had unearthed a piece of wall composed of
stone blocks of the same size, neatly fitted, and approached
by steps carved in the rock. In close proximity to this was
a monument, the meaning of which I was for some time at
a loss to conjecture. It consisted of three sides of a square
excavation hewn out of the solid rock of the hillside, uncovered, and the depth of which it was difficult to determine, on account of the débris which had accumulated.
Upon the faces of the chamber thus formed, rows of small
niches had been carved, each niche about a foot high, six
inches wide, and six inches deep. The niches were about
two inches apart, and on one face I counted six rows or
tiers of eighteen niches each. The other sides were not so
perfect, and the rock had broken away in places. I finally
decided that the whole had probably in ancient times been
a vault appropriated to the reception of cinerary urns, but
the matter is one which I must leave to some more experienced antiquarian than I am to determine definitely.
It is not to be wondered at that this obscure and partially
concealed ruin should have escaped the notice of the Palestine Exploration Survey.

One of the fellahin now told us of a marvel in the neighbourhood. It was a hole in the rock, to which, by applying one's ear, one could hear the roar of a mighty river.
Attracted by the prospect of so singular a phenomenon, we
scrambled through the prickly underwood with which the
hillsides are thickly covered, and finally emerged upon a
small valley, at the head of which was an open grassy space,
and near it a table of flat limestone rock. In the centre
of it was an oblong hole, about two inches by three, the
sides of which had been worn smooth by the curious or
superstitious, who had probably visited the spot for ages.
First, the Arab stretched himself at full length, and laid
his ear upon the aperture. I followed suit, and became
conscious not only of a strong draught rushing upward
from subterranean depths, but of a distant roaring sound,
as of a remote Niagara. For a moment I was puzzled,
and the Arab was triumphant, for I had treated his rush-

ing subterranean river with a contemptuous scepticism ; yet here were undeniably the sounds of roaring water. Had it been a distant gurgle or trickle it would have been ex-plicable, but it was manifestly impossible that any river could exist large enough to produce the sounds I heard. Though the day was perfectly still, the draught upward was strong enough to blow away the corner of a hand-kerchief held over the mouth of the hole. At last I solved the problem to my own satisfaction. By ascending the hill on the right the roar of "the loud-voiced neighbouring ocean," distant between two and three miles, was distinctly audible. It had been blowing the day before, and the rollers were breaking upon the long line of coast. I now conjectured that the crack in the rock must extend to some cavern on the seashore, and form a sort of whispering-gal-lery, conducting the sound of the breakers with great dis-tinctness to the top of the hills, but blending them so much that it seemed at first a continuous rushing noise. This was an explanation contrary to all tradition, and it was re-ceived by the Arab with incredulity.

We now descended once more to the plains, and, cross-ing them, reached the village of Tantura, where we arrived about midday, passing first, however, the ruined fortress of Muzraâ, a massive block of masonry about fifty yards square, the walls of which are standing to a height of about ten feet ; then turning aside to the old Roman bridge, which spans in a single high arch the artificial cutting through the limestone rocks by which the ancients facilitated the egress of a winter-torrent to the sea. The inhabitants of Tantura have the reputation of being very bad people, and three years ago I saw a party of French tourists at Jeru-salem who had been attacked and robbed by them. We were, however, entertained with the greatest hospitality, having a levée of the sheik and village notables, and with difficulty escaping from a banquet which they were prepar-ing for us. They live in a miserable collection of hovels amid the almost defaced ruins of the old town, traces of which, however, are abundant in the neighbourhood. A lofty fragment of wall on a projecting promontory half a mile to the north of the town is all that remains of what must have been a castle of grand dimensions. A chain of small, rocky islets, a few hundred yards from the shore, forms a sort of natural breakwater, and at very little expense Tantura could be converted into a good port. As it is, when the weather is smooth, native craft run in here, and when once at their anchorage can defy any gale. Tantura, or Dor, was one of the towns assigned to the half tribe of Manasseh, but we read that they failed to expel the Canaanites from it, though when Israel "became strong they put them to tribute, but did not utterly drive them out."

In the time of the Romans Dor was a mercantile town of some importance, and, though in the wars of the Diadochi it was besieged and partly destroyed, the Roman general Gabinius restored the town and harbor, and its architectural beauty was such that we read that even in the time of St. Jerome its ruins were still an object of admiration. Unfortunately, since the Turkish occupation, all these coast cities have been used as quarries for the construction of mosques and fortifications. The marble and granite pillars and columns, and the carved blocks of stone which formed the outside casings of the walls, have been carried away, leaving nothing but the mere skeletons of ruins as forlorn and desolate as the peasantry who find shelter beneath them.

THE TEMPLE SOCIETY.

HAIFA, Dec. 25.—There are probably not many of your readers who have ever heard of "The Temple Society," and yet it is a religious body numbering over 5000 members, of whom more than 300 are in America, 1000 in Palestine, and the remainder scattered over Europe, principally in Germany, Russia, and Switzerland.

The founder of the sect, if sect it can be called, is a certain Prof. Christophe Hoffman of Würtemberg, who, after studying at the University of Tübingen about thirty-five years ago, became a minister of the Lutheran Church and the principal of the College of Crischona, not far from Basle, in Switzerland. Here he became known as entertaining certain theological opinions which soon acquired some notoriety, as they consisted mainly of a criticism on the action of the Church with reference to the rationalistic opinions then becoming prevalent in Germany, and which found their culminating expression in the writings of the late Dr. Strauss. Mr. Hoffman, who was an ardent opponent of the modern and sceptical tendency of German thought, attributed its growing influence to the feeble opposition offered to it by the Church, and maintained that its impotency to arrest the evil arose from the inconsistent practice of its members with the moral teaching which they professed. Under the influence of this conviction he abandoned his charge at Crischona, and with his brothers-in-law founded a college at "Salon," not far from Stuttgart, and commenced an agitation in favour of church reform, both in written publications and by his personal influence. He was shortly after elected to the Diet at Frankfort, where he presented a petition signed by 12,000 persons in favour of reform of the Lutheran Church.

His Biblical studies at this time, especially of the book of

2

Revelations, led him to the conclusion that the period of
the second advent of the Messiah was approaching, but that
Christ could only be received by a Church which had attempted to embody his moral teaching in daily life; in fact,
that he could only recognize those as his own at his second
coming who had succeeded in practically applying the ethi-
cal code which he had taught when he came first; and he
reproached the Church with failing to inaugurate a social
reconstruction which should render possible a Christ life
in the true acceptation of the term. A doctrine based on
Scripture, and directed against the ecclesiastical system to
which he belonged, naturally brought him into direct collision with it; and as an interpretation of the New Testament
which strikes at the root of all compromise between pro-
fession and practice must ever be an inconvenient doctrine
to churches which are based upon such compromise, Mr.
Hoffman was summarily expelled, carrying with him, however, a large body of followers.

He now, with a few friends, established a sort of colony
in Würtemberg, where an effort was made to put into daily
practice these high aspirations, and the number of adherents throughout Europe and in America grew as his views
began to be more widely promulgated and understood. In
1867 the more prominent members of the society held a
meeting, at which it was decided that as the second advent
of the Messiah was expected to occur in Palestine, the Holy
Land was the fitting place for the establishment of the central point of the Church which was preparing itself to receive him; that there should be laid the corner-stone of the
new spiritual temple which gave the name of the society;
and that it was the first duty of those who were waiting
for his coming to restore the land to which so many Biblical promises especially attached. While they considered
that the new kingdom which was to own Christ as its king
was to embrace all those who were prepared to receive him,
in all lands and from among all races, yet the spiritual throne
would be erected in Palestine, and its material restoration
must be a necessary preliminary to its final and ultimate re-
demption. It was therefore decided that while the great
majority of the members of the society should remain in

Europe to witness for the truth, and to contribute to the
support of the attempt to be made in the Holy Land, a certain number should proceed thither to establish themselves
in trade and agriculture, and endeavour by the example of
honest industry to elevate the native population and redeem
the land from its present waste and desolate condition.

In 1868 Mr. Hoffman, Mr. Hartegg, and some others went
to Constantinople with a view of obtaining a firman from
the Porte, but, failing in this, they proceeded in the following year to Palestine, where, attracted by the great advantages of soil, climate, and position offered by the lands at
the foot of Mount Carmel, in the neighbourhood of Haifa,
they fixed upon that locality as the initial point of the enterprise. Hither shortly flocked agriculturists and handi-
craftsmen representing all the important industries, and they
proceeded to lay out their village and build their houses on
the slope between the foot of the mount and the sea, about
a mile to the westward of the native town; but they soon
found that it was impossible to do this without meeting
with the most strenuous opposition on the part of the native government, and incurring the covert hostility of the
monks who have for seven hundred years enjoyed a spiritual
monopoly of Mount Carmel. As the colonists were almost
without exception men of very moderate means, and believed in the responsibilities of individual ownership, and
not in any communistic system, they soon found themselves
engaged in a severe and unequal struggle.

Ignorant of the language, the country, the methods of
agriculture, the manners and customs of the inhabitants,
who regarded them askance, and unused to the climate, their
faith and powers of endurance were taxed to the utmost.
Not only did they persevere with the most unflinching resolution at Haifa, but extended their operations to Jaffa, where
at that time a colony of American Adventists, whom some
of your readers may remember, and who had emigrated
there about twenty years ago, was in process of dissolution.
Purchasing the remains of their settlement, a new group of
the Temple Society established themselves there. Since
then two more colonies have been formed, one at Sarona,
about an hour distant from Jaffa, and one in the immediate

neighbourhood of Jerusalem, where the leader, Mr. Hoffman, at present resides.

The united population of these four colonies amounts to about one thousand souls, besides which a few families are also established at Beyrout and Nazareth. But the largest settlement is at Haifa, where the society numbers over three hundred. These now, after fourteen years of vicissitudes, appear to be entering upon a period of comparative prosperity. They have not long since completed a twelve years' struggle with the government for the legalization of the titles to their land, which the authorities endeavoured to prevent by throwing every possible obstacle in the way ; and while the question was pending they were compelled to pay their taxes through the nominal native owners, who assessed the lands at four times their actual value, putting the balance into their own pockets. All these difficulties have, however, at last been surmounted. They now hold their seven hundred acres of fine arable and vine land free of all encumbrance, and their well-cultivated fields, trim gardens, and substantial white stone mansions form a most agreeable and unexpected picture of civilization upon this semi-barbarous coast.

Meanwhile, the influence of three hundred industrious, simple, honest farmers and artificers has already made its mark upon the surrounding Arab population, who have adopted their improved methods of agriculture, and whose own industries have received a stimulus which bids fair to make Haifa one of the most prosperous towns on the coast. Already, since the advent of the Germans, the native population has largely increased. New stone houses have sprung up in all directions, and many are in course of construction. The value of land has increased threefold, and the statistics of the port show a large increase in the exports and imports. Perhaps the most remarkable innovation is the introduction of wheeled vehicles. Fifteen years ago a cart had never been seen by the inhabitants of Haifa. Omnibuses, owned and driven by natives, now run four or five times a day between Haifa and Acre, the capital of the province, distant about ten miles. It is true that the road is the smooth sea beach, and that its excellence varies according to the state of the tide, but in this country carts come before roads, and

fortunately its topographical features have been favourable
to the employment of wheeled vehicles. On one side of
Carmel, extending southward, is the plain of Sharon, and
over this one may drive to Jaffa without the necessity of
road-making, so level and free from natural obstacle is it.
On the other we may cross with equal ease the plain of Esdraelon to the Sea of Tiberias—the experiment having been
made recently—and a road has been constructed to Nazareth,
distant about twenty-two miles. This involved an expenditure
on the part of the colonists of about one thousand dollars.
It is used largely by the Arabs, who have contributed
nothing towards it; but the effect on their minds, as they
drive over it in their own carts, and remember that they
owe both cart and road to the colonists, whom at first they
mistrusted and disliked, is a sound moral investment, and
bears its fruit in many ways.

Fifteen years ago no one could venture outside the town
gates to the westward after nightfall, for fear of being waylaid and robbed by the lawless inhabitants of Tireh—a village noted for its bad character, about seven miles distant—
who used to come marauding up to the outskirts of Haifa.
Now one can ride and walk with safety in all directions and
at all hours. The Germans have most of them learned to
talk Arabic, and many an Arab that one meets salutes you
with a *guten morgen* or *guten abend*, though that is probably
the limit of their linguistic accomplishments; but they respect and like the colonists, and a good deal of land is now
cultivated on shares by Germans and Arabs, who seem to
arrange their business and agricultural operations to their
mutual satisfaction and in perfect harmony. When we remember that the Carmelite monks have held the mountain
for seven hundred years, and compare their influence over
the native population with that which these honest Germans
have acquired by simple example during less than fifteen,
we have a striking illustration of the superiority of practice
to preaching, for it should be remarked that any attempt at
proselytism is entirely foreign to their principles. Their
whole effort has been to commend their Christianity by
scrupulous honesty in their dealings, by the harmony and
simplicity of their conduct, and by the active industry of
their lives.

THE TEMPLE COLONIES IN PALESTINE.

HAIFA, Jan. 20, 1883.—In a former letter I gave you a sketch of the origin of the Temple Society and of the religious motives which have led to the establishment of four agricultural colonies in the Holy Land by emigrants from Germany, America, Russia, and Switzerland. As I have taken up my winter residence in the principal one of these, situated beneath the shadow of Mount Carmel, some description of the place and its resources may not be without interest for your readers. I know of no locality in the East which offers greater attractions of position, climate, and association than this spot. Thanks to the efforts of the colonists, it has become an oasis of civilization in the wilderness of Oriental barbarism, where the invalid in search of health, or the tourist on the lookout for a comfortable resting-place on his travels, will find good accommodation, and all the necessaries, if not the luxuries, of civilized life.

Throughout the whole length of the coast of Palestine from Tyre to Gaza, only one deep indentation occurs. This is where it sweeps in a curve around the old fortress of St. Jean d'Acre, and terminates in the projecting precipice upon whose ledge the monastery of Carmel is situated. The bay thus formed is nine miles across from Acre to Carmel, and about four miles broad. It is bordered the whole distance by a smooth, hard beach, at the southeastern and most sheltered extremity of which is situated the town of Haifa, a modern native town, squeezed in between an overhanging bluff, on which are the ruins of an old castle, and the sea. It owes its origin to the arbitrary act of a pacha who, about a century ago, had rendered himself quasi-independent of the Porte, and established the seat of his government at Acre. The population of old Haifa, situated near the point, having rebelled against him, he punished them by razing it to the ground, and transported the inhabitants to the edge of the bay under the rock, on which he put a castle, while he surrounded them with a wall, thus keeping them prisoners. When he died, his successor was suppressed, the garrison of the castle was removed, and the wall was allowed to fall into disrepair. The inhabitants, who thus were restored to liberty, accustomed to their new location, began to cultivate the surrounding land and to increase in wealth and prosperity. Their gardens spread to the eastward, where the brook Kishon, winding through a fertile plain, struggles to debouch into the sea, but only succeeds at certain seasons, owing to the huge sand-bars which form at its mouth. These dam it back into small lakes, which are surrounded by date-groves, thus forming a most agreeable feature in the scenery. Behind the plain rises the low, wooded range which is traversed by the road leading to Nazareth.

Though Haifa is comparatively modern, there are some traces of old ruins in the town, the walls of an old crusading castle, one or two caverns, which bear marks of having been inhabited in the rocks immediately behind them, and the crumbling remains of an archway, dating, probably, from a period anterior to the crusades. Prior to the arrival of the colonists of the Temple Society, Haifa was as dirty as most Arab villages. It is now well paved throughout. The houses, all constructed of white limestone, quarries of which abound in the immediate vicinity, give it a clean and substantial appearance, and contain a bustling and thriving population of about six thousand inhabitants. Under the high cactus hedges at its eastern gateway are usually to be seen, squatting amid sacks of grain, hundreds of camels, which, attended by wild-looking Arabs, have arrived with their loads of cereals from the Hauran, on the other side of the Jordan; for Haifa is gradually becoming one of the great grain-exporting ports of the country, and one or two steamers are generally to be seen loading in the harbour.

Leaving the town by the western gateway, we ride for about a mile parallel to the seashore between high cactus hedges, and suddenly find ourselves apparently transported into the heart of Europe. Running straight back from the beach for about half a mile, and sloping upward for about a hundred feet in that distance, to the base of the rocky sides of Carmel, runs the village street. On each side of it is a pathway, with a double row of shade-trees, and behind them a series of white stone houses, of one and two stories, generally with tiled roofs, each surrounded with its garden, and each with a text in German engraved over the doorway. There is another, smaller, parallel street. The whole settlement contains about sixty houses and three hundred inhabitants. The English, American, and German vice-consuls are all colonists. There is a skilled physician, an architect, and engineer in the colony, an excellent hotel, a school, and meeting-house. The German government subscribes two thirds and the colonists one third of the funds required for the school. Some of the colonists are in business, and have stores in Haifa. There is also a good store in the colony, where all the most important trades are represented. There is one wind grist, and one steam mill, the latter in process of erection. There is a manufactory of olive-oil soap, the export of which to America is yearly increasing, and now amounts to 50,000 pounds, and which may be purchased in New York by such of your readers as have a fancy to wash their hands with soap direct from the Holy Land, made from the oil of the olives of Carmel, at F. B. Nichols's, 62 William Street. There is also a factory for the manufacture of articles from olive wood.

Where Carmel rises abruptly from the upper end of the street, its rocky sides have been terraced to the summit, and about a hundred acres are devoted to the cultivation of the vine. Unfortunately, the varieties which have been imported from Germany all suffer severely from mildew. I have therefore sent to the United States for Concords and some of the hardier American varieties. Along the lower slopes are thick groves of olives. Scarped along the rugged mountain-side leads the road to the monastery, distant about a mile and a half. Situated about five hundred feet above the sea, it forms a conspicuous object in the landscape as seen from the colony.

The views from the house in which I am living are a never-ending source of delight. To the east I look over

the native town and harbour, with the date-groves and the
plain of the Kishon beyond, backed by the wooded range
which separates it from the plain of Esdraelon. To the
northeast the eye rests on the picturesque outline of the
mountains of northern Palestine, with the rounded top of
Jebel Jermink rising to a height of 4000 feet in the middle
distance, and snow-clad Hermon towering behind to a height
of 9000 feet. Immediately to the north, across the blue
waters of the bay, the white walls and minarets of Acre
rise from the margin of the sea, and beyond it the coast-
line, terminating in the white projecting cliff known as
"The Ladder of Tyre." To the northwestward we look
across a plain about a mile wide, containing the colony
lands, and beyond is the sea horizon, till we turn sufficiently
to meet Carmel bluff and monastery. Behind us the mountain rises precipitously, throwing us at this time of the year
into shade by three in the afternoon. But even on New-Year's
Day we do not grudge the early absence of the sun, for as
I write the thermometer is standing at 66°in the shade. It
is not, however, the features of the scenery which constitute
its chief beauty, but the wonderful variations of light and
shade, and the atmospheric effects peculiar to the climate,
which invest it with a special charm. On the plain to the
west of the colony, which is bounded on two sides by the
sea, on one by the mountain, and on one by the colony, are
the traces of the old town of Haifa, mentioned in the Talmud, but not in the Bible, which was besieged and taken
by storm by Tancred, the crusader, in 1100, with a massive
ruin of sea-wall and other remains, from which I have already dug out fragments of glass and pottery. Behind are
the almost obliterated remains of an old fort, with here and
there a piece of limestone cropping up, bearing the marks of
man's handiwork.

Everywhere in Palestine we come upon the evidences of
its antiquity. This plain, now made to yield of its abundance under the skilful labour of the German colonists, is no
exception, for in the time of the Romans it was the site of
the city of Sycaminum, and in the groovings of rocks upon
which the sea now breaks we see the traces of what were
its baths; in the mounds we find fragments of old masonry

and cement; in the depressions we see signs of wells, and in the rock cuttings of tombs. Only the other day I found, while digging in the garden for the prosaic purpose of planting cabbages, a fragment of polished agate which probably formed a part of the tessellated pavement of some Roman villa.

So the process of decay and reconstruction goes on, and man is ever trying to rear something new on the ruins of the old. Let us hope that the sixty or seventy substantial houses of the new colony are but the outward and visible signs of that moral edifice which these good people have come to Palestine to erect, and that from the ruins of a crumbling ecclesiasticism they may build a temple worthy the worship of the future.

EXPLORING MOUNT CARMEL.

HAIFA, Feb. 7.—It was my fate as a child to live in a country-house in Scotland, of which one half was some centuries old, with stone walls several feet thick, and circular stone steps leading up into a mysterious tower, which was supposed to be haunted, and in which it was rumoured that a secret chamber existed, built in the wall, and I remember perfectly that certain places seemed to sound hollow to blows of a crowbar, which as I got older, I used to apply to suspected localities. It is more years than I care to think of since those days, but I can trace a resemblance to that childish feeling in the sensations by which I am animated when I wander over the gloomiest recesses of Carmel alone in search of caverns.

It is called in some ancient Jewish record "the mountain of the thousand caves," and has been inhabited from time immemorial by hermits and religious devotees. Independently of the Biblical record, we have historical traces of its holy character. According to the most ancient Persian traditions, sacred fire burned at the extreme western point of Carmel. Suetonius speaks of the oracles of the god of Carmel, and Alexander the Great repeats the saying. The Syrian city, Ecbatana, alluded to by Pliny, was situated on this mountain. Pythagoras lived here in retreat for some time because it had a reputation for superior sanctity, but Strabo mentions the caves as being haunts of pirates. They were doubtless used as places of refuge for bad characters, as well as of seclusion for pious ones. Others were used for tombs, others for crusaders' sentry-boxes, and now they are the retreat of flocks and herds, and in some instances storehouses for grain.

Those, however, thus utilized are comparatively few in number; I believe many to be unknown even to the natives, while others are invested by them with a mysterious character, and their dimensions are probably exaggerated. I have received accounts of some, which I hope to visit, which are said to extend beyond any known exploration, of others which bear traces of carving and inscriptions, but nothing can be more uncertain or unsatisfactory than native accounts upon all matters where definite information is required. I have tried exploring with guides and exploring alone, and have been almost as successful one way as the other.

One of my first visits was to a ruin which I had observed crowning a summit of the range, but which was only visible from certain points, so shut in was it by the intervening mountain-tops. I started on horseback, determined to find my way alone, and struck into a valley where the narrow path followed a ledge of limestone rock, often not more than two feet wide. I soon found myself diving into a sombre gorge, the precipitous sides of which rose abruptly from the bed of the winter torrent. As I proceeded it became more and more uncanny; the path was so narrow I could no longer venture to risk my horse's footing, as a slip would have involved a fall of at least two hundred feet. My ruin disappeared, and my gorge seemed to trend away from it, the sun sank behind the range, and the deep gloom of the solitary valley, hemmed in on all sides by terraces of limestone, with here and there a fissure indicating some cavernous recess, was becoming depressing.

I tried to turn, but the ledge was too narrow, so I was obliged to creep cautiously on in the wrong direction. I began now rather to fear lest I should meet some one, not merely because passing would have been impossible, but because the spot was eminently well calculated for an act of violence, and, while I always go about unarmed, I find that my neighbours seldom go out riding alone without carrying revolvers. The aspect of a wild-looking Arab, with a gun slung behind him, suddenly turning a corner and coming straight towards me, was, under these circumstances, not reassuring. Fortunately, at the moment I saw him I had reached a spot where a huge rock had been displaced, and had left a vacant space large enough to enable me to

turn comfortably, and I retraced my steps, amply repaid for
my failure in not reaching the ruin, by the solemn grandeur
of the part of the mountain into which I had been penetrat-
ing, and by finding my Arab, when he overtook me, to be a
communicative and harmless individual, who was on his way
home from a cave in which he stored his grain, and which
he assured me I should have reached if I had continued a
few hundred yards farther. Beyond this, he said, the path
led nowhere.

My next attempt was made with a friend who knew the
way, and who led me along a corresponding ledge upon the
opposite side of the valley, into a side gorge, which we followed past a wall of rock, in which were two or three small
caverns, which I entered, the largest not more than twelve
or fourteen feet square, and showing no signs of having been
inhabited. A huge rock detached from the mountain-side,
and hollowed into a sort of gallery, is so celebrated among
the natives that it has a name of its own. Just behind it we
turned to scramble almost straight up the mountain-side,
covered with a scrub composed of camelthorn, odoriferous
thyme, sage, marjoram, and arbutus, and then found we
were at the foot of seven clearly defined terraces, completely encircling the rounded hill, upon the top of which
stood the crumbling walls of an old fort, and which formed
portions of its defences. On one of these stood a shepherd's
hut, and inside the enclosure made of bushes was the entrance to a cavern, about thirty yards long, four feet high,
and twenty or thirty feet across. In it, when they were
not out feeding, the shepherd kept his flock of long-eared
goats.

Ascending to the ruin, I found it to consist of the remains
of what had evidently been a fort, the walls of which, enclosing a space of about sixty yards long by forty broad, were
standing to a height of eight or ten feet, and were composed
of blocks of limestone. At one angle a portion of the fortress
had at a later period been converted into a church, the apse,
with its arches, being in a tolerable state of preservation.
The name of this ruin is Rushmea, and according to the
most reliable sources of information to which I have had
access, it was used by Saladin to watch the progress of the

siege of Acre when that place was held by the crusaders.
Prior to the crusades and the formation of the order of the
Carmelite monks, the mountain was inhabited by anchorites,
some of whom claimed to have inherited the sacred character of Elijah and Elisha. For some time seven of them
seem to have divided the claim between them, and one of
them is reported to have lived in a cave at Rushmea, which
is said to contain carving and inscriptions. It was for this cave
I was especially in search; but though I have visited the locality three times in all, twice with guides, and have found
some seven or eight caves, one of which had a carved limestone entrance, none of them seemed of sufficient importance
to answer the traditional description. A magnificent view
is obtained from the ruin over the Bay of Acre, with the
town in the distance and the plain of Kishon beneath, and
plainly visible the famous well for the possession of which
Saladin and Richard Cœur de Lion fought. I have visited
this celebrated source, with its massive masonry and crumbling cistern, in the centre of which there is now a flourishing
fig-tree. During the siege which Haifa then withstood, the
town was completely destroyed, so that the crusading army
had to remain in tents, and here it was that the lion-hearted
king caught that severe fever which gave rise to reports of
his death, and which resulted in his remaining for four weeks
at Haifa to recover his health. That plain is as unhealthy
now as it was then, and the date-groves, which are its most
striking feature, must have existed then, for they are mentioned in the records of the year 1230, when King Amalrich
II. died of a surfeit of sea-fish, for which the place is celebrated.

To return to Rushmea. The whole hill-top is covered with
the traces of remains far anterior to the ruins of crusading
times. Everywhere we come upon the solid limestone foundations of what must have been large buildings; there are
flights of steps hewn in the rock, large square cuttings from
which blocks have been taken, places where circular holes
have been drilled, grooves, niches, and excavations. On a
plateau about a hundred yards to the west is a series of massive stone arches in a very fair state of preservation. I
found the elevation of Rushmea, by my aneroid, to be as

nearly as possible seven hundred feet above the sea. In a valley behind it, and a hundred feet below it, are a dozen olive-trees of immense age, and near them a celebrated spring, called the Well of Elisha. It is not above twelve feet deep, and, on descending into it, I found that it was in fact not a spring, but a subterranean stream which enters a receptacle formed for it in the rock, from a cave at the side, and from which it disappears again. Instead of returning from Rushmea by the way I had come, I pushed up to the head of the valley in which the spring is situated. On two of the hills which rise from it I found terraces and the foundations of stone edifices. Indeed, wherever one wanders in Carmel, one is apt to stumble upon these substantial records of its bygone history. As the mountain is about thirteen miles long and nine miles wide at its southeastern extremity, and as every valley and hillside and plateau has at one time or other been inhabited, and as many of these remain still to be explored for the first time, there is abundant field for investigation, and it is impossible to take a ride or a scramble in any direction without coming upon some object of interest. Nor is it possible to lose one's way when alone, except to a limited extent, for the nearest hill-top, if you can get to it, is sure to let you know where you are.

Thus leaving Rushmea without a guide, and soon without a path, I pushed through the scrub, now dismounting and driving my horse before me, now forcing him, much to his discomfort, through the prickly bushes. Even at this time of year the hills are bright with scarlet anemones, and the delicate pink or white cyclamen, and fragrant with aromatic odours as we crush through the shrubs. Suddenly I came upon the foundations of a wall, which I followed for about a hundred yards, and which was about four feet in thickness. Near it, half hidden by the bushes, was a circular block of limestone about five feet high and the same in diameter, in the centre of which had been drilled a hole. It looked like the section of some gigantic column such as we see in some of the temples of Upper Egypt; but it stood alone, and I fail to imagine its design. Possibly it may have been used for sacrificial purposes. Shortly after I found myself on a high, level plateau, where the soil was so excellent, and the rocks had so far disappeared, that it would do admirably for farming purposes. It seemed to extend over some hundreds of acres. Formerly, the whole of these fertile tracts of Carmel were covered with magnificent forests—even in the memory of man—but of late years the demand for charcoal has so much increased that the mountain has been almost completely denuded of trees, and although a strict order has been issued by the government against the felling of timber, it still continues, and, thanks to the system of backsheesh, the export of charcoal from Haifa last year exceeded that of any previous year. Keeping westward by my compass I soon after struck a path, and finally dropped down upon the German colony near Haifa, after a day's ramble through the most delightful scenery, every step of which was replete with historical association and antiquarian interest.

HAIFA, Feb. 12.—A more thorough examination of the rocky hillsides of the Carmel promontory in the vicinity of the celebrated monastery than I have been hitherto able to give it, has revealed many spots of interest, and one in particular, which seems to have escaped the observation of the Palestine Exploration Fund Survey. About two miles and a half from Haifa the road to Jaffa passes between a projecting spur of the range and a mound about a hundred feet high, which formed the centre of the ancient city of Sycaminum, and which probably conceals some interesting remains, which I hope some day to be able to unearth.

It projects out into the sea, and on the flat rocks at its base, over which the waves break in stormy weather, there is a large circular bath excavated by the Romans, about twenty feet in circumference, with a channel cut through the rock, which admits the rising tide. All round this mound are fragments of columns, carved capitals, and blocks of polished marble, some of the lightest of which I have carried away; but it is upon the unknown contents of the mound itself that my imagination is prone to speculate. On the left of the road are caverns and rock-cut tombs, some containing the remains of loculi; and the surface of the smooth limestone rock leaves traces of ancient steps, and cuttings, showing that in old times the hand of man had been actively employed upon it. I had often examined these, and thought I had reached their limit, when, pushing my exploration farther up the steep hillside a few days ago, through the low brush by which it is covered, I unexpectedly came upon a plateau eight or ten acres in area, and about two hundred feet above the level of the sea, covered with the débris of ancient ruins. It was evidently the upper part of the old city of Sycaminum, and commanded a

3

magnificent view of the coast-line southward, and of what
was formerly the lower town, which has heretofore been
supposed to be all that there was of the city.

This upper town, from its cool and delightful position,
was probably the residence of the wealthier inhabitants;
here, too, were fragments of marble columns and carved
capitals, and conspicuous among them two gigantic old
olive millstones, one about eight feet in diameter and two
feet thick, and the other of less diameter, but of more
than three feet in thickness. There were, moreover, many
rock tombs with loculi, the foundations of ancient walls
of immense thickness, and here and there fragments of
the wall itself standing, in one place to a height of about
five feet. But the most interesting find was a triangular
piece of marble, on which was an inscription in a character
which may possibly be ancient Syriac. It is certainly not
Greek, Roman, or Hebrew, though at the first glance I
thought it was the former. Unfortunately, the stone has
been cut since the inscription was engraved, and there are
only a few letters of each word, one below the other, but it
was evidently originally a long one, consisting of many
lines. I also discovered here a cistern, with four circular
apertures; causing myself to be lowered into it, I found
it to be seventy feet long, supported by four pillars hewn
from the living rock, lined with cement, and twenty feet
high, from the débris with which it was partially choked.
Altogether the place is well worth a fuller and more careful
investigation, which I hope to give it.

About an hour's ride farther south is an interesting spot
called the Valley of the Martyrs, which, though rarely visited, is well worth an excursion, not merely on account of
its peculiar geological features and its great scenic attractions, but from the historical associations which attach to it.
It was towards the close of the twelfth century that Father
Brocard was elected vicar-general of the order "of the
Blessed Virgin Mary of Mount Carmel," whose sanctuary
had been long established upon the mountain, though the
members of the order had their homes in its numerous caverns, resorting to the shrine only for purposes of worship,
while they lived as scattered ascetics in the surrounding

valleys. Father Brocard conceived the idea of collecting them in a monastery, and placing them under certain fixed regulations, which have ever since been the rules of the order, and which were sanctioned in A.D. 1207 by Saint Albert, Patriarch at Jerusalem, Pope's Legate, and then resident at Acre.

It was in this gorge, which subsequently became known as the Valley of the Martyrs, that Father Brocard decided to build the first monastery, attracted thither, probably, by its beauty of situation and the copiousness of its springs, one of which is called after Elijah, as tradition has it that the inhabitants in his time complained of a lack of water, and he touched the rock and caused the present stream to gush forth. It wells up from under the limestone rock, and flows through a channel cut for it, for a few yards, into a basin hollowed out of the solid rock, about twelve feet square and six feet deep; from here it flows down the narrow gorge, and speedily expends itself in fertilizing some small gardens of figs, oranges, and pomegranates, which are wedged in between the rocky hillsides, and are tended by one or two poor families who live in caves. These gardens are now claimed by the present monastery, but there seems much doubt as to the validity of their title.

It is safer to dismount after passing this spring, as we now have to cross the smooth surface of the limestone rock as we follow the steep path that leads up to the ruin of the old monastery, the position of which is indicated by the remains of an enormous wall which nearly reaches across the gorge, looking from below like some huge dam, and which must have concealed the monastery itself from public gaze, except from the hills above. We are now struck by the extraordinary petrifactions over which we are passing. The path is worn deep by centuries into the soft limestone, in the sides of which appear layers of petrified twigs and branches of the bushes of a bygone period. They are perfectly white, except where fractures exhibit the black flint core; but in some instances the form of the branch is perfect with all its twigs. Passing under the projecting buttress of the dam-like wall, we suddenly open on a terrace covered with vines and fruit-trees on one side, and find ourselves at the mouth of a large cave on the other. Entering this, if we are willing to brave the fleas—for, as it is generally inhabited by an Arab family, they abound—we find that we are in a spacious apartment supported by a column of solid rock, while all around are mangers for horses, cut out of the stone. Of these we count fourteen, which will give some idea of the size of the cave. Probably in crusading times it was a cavalry outpost, affording, from its strong natural position and proximity to the plain of Sharon, a splendid point of vantage from which to pounce upon an unsuspecting enemy.

Ascending from the cave by some steps to the terrace, we come unexpectedly upon a delicious spring overshadowed by spreading fig-trees, which fills with crystal water a basin that has been hollowed out of the overhanging rock; from this it trickles into another stone-cut reservoir, from whence it is led by a stone channel, hollowed by the monks, to the monastery itself, one small room of which is still standing. The rock rises perpendicularly behind, and is scooped here and there into recesses, which were formerly, doubtless, the cells of monks, while the cool shade of spreading fruit-trees, the beauty of the view, the presence of running water, and the ever-blowing southwest wind, of which they got the full benefit, must have modified to a considerable extent the austerities of their existence.

There came a day, however, when their peaceful solitude was rudely disturbed. In 1238 the Saracens came upon them unexpectedly, and massacred them all, not leaving one to tell the bloody tale. There seems to be no record of the actual number who fell victims upon this occasion, but they must have been very numerous, as the Monastery of St. Brocard had become a refuge for monks from all parts of Palestine, who fled hither to escape the persecution to which they were being subjected in other parts of the country. Not content with putting them to death, the Saracens dragged their bodies down to the Spring of Elijah, and flung them into the square reservoir there, which I have already described. According to the pious chronicler of this tragic event, the spring immediately refused to flow, and when the Christians of Acre, hearing the news, came to bury their coreligionists, they found it dry. When they had completed their melancholy task, they prayed that the water might commence to run once more, which it immediately did, and has never ceased since.

The result of this tragedy was the practical expulsion of the order of the Carmelites from Palestine. The Monastery of St. Brocard, after its short-lived existence, fell into ruins, and more than four hundred years elapsed before the order once more secured a footing on Mount Carmel, and built a monastery upon it at the end of the promontory, which served as a hospital for the French soldiers during Napoleon's occupation of this part of the country. His hurried evacuation of Palestine involved the destruction of the monastery and the massacre of all the wounded, to whose memory a monument has since been erected in the garden attached to the present edifice. But there can be no doubt that both for picturesqueness and historical association the old ruin of the Monastery of Saint Brocard, which altogether escapes the attention of the tourist and the pilgrim, is far more interesting than the modern monastery, which is not fifty years old, and which is about two miles distant from this old site.

On the top of the hill above the ruins of the Monastery of St. Brocard is a plateau, called the Garden of Elijah, or the field of melons, which is abundantly strewn with geodes, or fragments of calcareous stone, having all the shape and appearance in many cases of petrified fruit, the crystallization of the centres when they are split open having confirmed this idea, thus doubtless giving rise to the legend that Elijah on one occasion, passing through the gardens which were once situated here, asked the proprietor for some fruit. He replied, not wishing to comply with the request, that they were stones, on which the prophet, apparently in a fit of temper, said, "Well, stones let them remain," and stones they have remained ever since. I found some curious specimens so like small melons that one can well understand how this fable may have originated among an ignorant population.

THE ROCK-HEWN CEMETERY OF SHEIK ABREIK.

NAZARETH, Feb. 18.—There is a low range of hills, about five hundred feet above the sea-level, half-way between Haifa and Nazareth. It is beautifully timbered with oak-trees, and cut up into the most charming valleys. Running almost due north and south, it divides the plain of Esdraelon from that of Acre. Its southern extremity, terminating abruptly, forms a small gorge with the Carmel range, through which the Kishon forces its way to the sea. It was during a heavy rain-storm a week ago that I approached the ford of this river from Haifa. It was not without trepidation, for the stream had been so swollen by recent rains that communication with the interior had been interrupted. It was doubtful whether the passage of this river, which almost dries up in summer, would not involve a ducking. I therefore prudently requested my companion to precede me into the yellow, swirling stream, and although the water came up to our saddle-bags, the horses managed to get across without losing their footing. Then we galloped into the oak-woods. The sun broke out from behind the clouds, and we determined to prosecute our search for certain caves, of the existence of which we had heard, and which, owing to the state of the weather, we had almost decided to abandon.

Leaving the high-road to Nazareth to the right, we followed a path for about half an hour which took us to the village of Sheik Abreik. It was a miserable collection of mud hovels, in the muddiest of which dwelt the sheik. After much palaver and promises of abundant backsheesh we got him to admit the existence of the caverns of which we were in search, and persuaded him to be our guide to them. The first was called by the Arabs "The Cave of

Hell." Its entrance seemed to justify the ill-omened appellation. It was a steep, sloping tunnel into the bowels of
the earth, just large enough to admit the passage of a man's
body. To slide into this feet foremost after a heavy rain
involved a coating of mud from top to toe. After going
down a few yards we found a chamber in which we could
stand erect. Here we lighted our candle and looked about
us. We found that it was the first of a series of similar
chambers opening one into another. Each contained loculi,
hewn out of the solid rock. The entrances to these chambers were arched. The pilasters on each side of the entrance
were in some cases ornamented with rude sculptures and
decorated with designs in a yellow pigment. These were in
the form of curves, scrolls, and circles, and were carried over
the roof. Each chamber was about ten feet long by six
feet wide, and on an average contained three tombs or loculi,
one across the chamber, facing the entrance, and one on
each side. There do not seem ever to have been lids to
these stone receptacles for the corpses.

The bodies were embalmed, wrapped in cloths, as we read
in Scriptural accounts of burials, notably in that of our
Saviour. "Each in his narrow cell forever laid," they remained undisturbed until rude hands, ages afterwards,
"rolled away the stone from the mouth of the cave" and
rifled the contents.

Some of the entrances to the chambers had been completely filled up. In such cases the partition wall of rock
had been broken through. Some of the chambers were
larger than others, and there were two tiers of loculi. In
order to get from one chamber to another it was often necessary to drag yourself along at full length upon the ground.
In one case the roof had been broken through into a chamber above, and this probably led to more.

I had not time fully to explore this most curious and interesting spot. Examinations of this sort in the middle of a
long day's ride are very fatiguing. The effort of scrambling about on all fours, or after the fashion of the serpent,
is very great, and makes you very dirty. In the absence of a
string you are haunted by the idea of not being able to find
your way back, to say nothing of the chance of sticking in

one of these narrow passages. Altogether, I entered about
fifteen different chambers, and doubtless the others did not
differ in any important particulars. I am afraid, however,
that I was not the first to discover them, but that this honour
rests with Captain Conder, Royal Engineers, of the Palestine Exploration Fund. The sheik told us he had once before guided a foreigner to this locality, and on the next cave
we visited we found the letters R. E. scratched in red paint
on the rock, which under these circumstances can only mean
Royal Engineers.

The next cave was a much more comfortable one to examine, though not nearly so interesting. You could walk about
it comfortably, but there was no ornamentation. The chambers were larger, but there were only five or six of them.
The stone coffins had, in many instances, been completely
destroyed, but the massive stone columns, or rather blocks,
of living rock which supported the roof were finer than
those in the "Cave of Hell." Perhaps it owed its more
dilapidated condition to the largeness of its entry, and its
proximity to another huge cave which had evidently in
crusading times been converted into a Christian place of
worship. According to a rough measurement obtained by
pacing it, the nave was seventy feet by thirty, the apse
eighteen by twenty-one, and two apse-shaped transepts
about twenty by eighteen ; but these were very much filled
with rubbish. The height of the cave was about thirty
feet. The whole formed a subterranean church, which, in
its perfect condition, when entered from the hillside, must
have presented a very imposing appearance. On the slope
of the hill, not far from this cave, was the carved pedestal
of a granite column, and near it a handsome stone sarcophagus.

Instead of going back to the Nazareth road after finish-
ing our examination of this interesting spot, we made for a
hill on the summit of which we saw some large blocks of
stone betokening ruins. Here we came upon a native excavation, evidently very recent. Indeed, we heard later that
it had only been abandoned the week before. The natives occasionally find an unopened tomb, and dig into it
for treasure. It was useless to attempt to disabuse their

minds of the idea that we were treasure-hunters. On asking them what they had found, they said, some red glass
bottles, which they had broken to discover what they contained. They had also found three jars, one containing
ashes, one earth, and one was empty. These they had also
smashed. It was enough to make one's mouth water to
hear of the destruction of these curiosities so very recently.
I implored them if they found any more not to break them,
but to bring them to me. They laughed, and promised to
do so, saying, at the same time, "They are so very old that
they are not worth anything." This cave was evidently an
important one, but the natives, finding nothing but the glass
and the jars, had blocked up the entrance again, and I had
to put off the examination of it to some future time. On
the top of the hill there were several sarcophagi, some coffins hewn out of the living rock on the surface, with the
stone lid at the side. At one place I saw a huge stone lid
about eight feet long, two feet six inches broad at its base,
and the same in height, but coming up to a ridge, which was
evidently still covering the mortal remains which had originally been placed beneath it. The position of this I have
also marked, and propose, at some future time, to remove it
by gunpowder and see what is below.

Had it not been necessary to push on in order to reach
Nazareth before night, I would have lingered longer at
these ruins, which are called Zebda by the natives. They
are worthy of a full examination. The whole rocky summit of the hill is evidently honeycombed with cave tombs,
many of which had not yet been opened. One of these, some
miles farther on towards Nazareth, especially attracted my
attention. A huge circular stone about two feet in diameter had been rolled into the carved stone entrance to the
cave, and become tightly wedged. All the efforts of the natives to remove it, and the marks of such efforts were visible, had evidently been unavailing. It needed a very small
charge of dynamite to remove the obstacle which had so
successfully resisted the barbarian ingenuity of ages. This
I had arranged to do, but on the day fixed for the purpose
persistent rain disappointed me. However, it is a treat in
store.

The first entrance into one of these old Jewish tomb-caverns will be an exciting episode, but there is an amount of suspicion and jealousy on the part of the natives which will render prudence and circumspection necessary if any attempt of this sort is to be carried out with success.

The whole plain of Esdraelon, on the verge of which this ruin is situated, as well as part of the hills behind, is now all owned by one rich firm of Syrian bankers, who draw an annual income of about $200,000 a year from it. They own practically about five thousand human beings as well, who form the population of thirty villages, which are in their hands. I found no more potent talisman in inducing the natives to comply with my request than to mention the name of "Sursuk," and imply that I had the honour of his acquaintance. No despot exercises a more autocratic power over the liberties or the lives of his subjects than does this millionaire landed proprietor, who continues annually to add to his territory till the whole of Galilee seems in danger of falling into his hands. This part of the country, however, is at present beginning to attract the attention of foreigners, and it is to be hoped that before long he may find rivals in the field who will do more to improve the condition of the peasantry, and introduce methods of agriculture which may make them more independent of the money-lenders who now make their profit by sucking their very life-blood.

EASTER AMONG THE MELCHITES.

HAIFA, April 2.—The population of Haifa, which amounts to about six thousand souls, consists, so far as religious distinctions are concerned, of Moslems, Roman Catholics—here called "Latins"—orthodox Greeks, and Greek Catholics, or Melchites. Of these the latter are the most numerous. This town may be considered the stronghold of the Melchite schismatics. They are more influential here than in any other town in Syria. They compose two thirds of its entire population. Originally orthodox Greek, they owe their origin to the missionary efforts of Romish priests and Jesuits during the last two centuries. As the object has been to gain partisans, more pains have been taken to obtain nominal submission to the authority of the pope than any real change of doctrine or ritual. To this day, Lazarists, Franciscans, Carmelites, and Jesuits are active in their efforts to make proselytes to this sect from the orthodox Greek Church. They allow them to retain their independence of Rome in many particulars. Thus it is governed by a patriarch at Damascus who owes allegiance to the pope. Mass is celebrated in Arabic, they administer the sacrament in both kinds, they retain their Oriental calendar, and their priests may be married men, though they may not marry after ordination. They differ from the orthodox Greek Church in this, that they take the Romanist view of the procession of the Holy Spirit. They believe in Purgatory, they eat fish in Lent, and acknowledge the papal supremacy. Otherwise they have made no change in passing from one jurisdiction to the other. As perverts they are naturally intensely hated by the orthodox Greeks, and when disturbances take place between Moslems and Christians, the Greek orthodox are generally to be found siding with the Moslems against Roman Catholics and Melchites.

To this sect belong some of the wealthiest and most aristocratic families in Syria. As the ordinary traveller is not often brought into contact with them, I was not sorry for the opportunity which my residence furnished me of witnessing their Easter observances. At midnight on the Saturday preceding Easter Sunday the festival is announced by a great consumption of gunpowder. An uproar which would do credit to a prolonged skirmish lasts till the early mass. The Melchite church is the largest and most imposing in Haifa. It is enclosed in a courtyard, round one side of which runs a balcony. At an early hour on Sunday morning the whole population turns out in its grandest attire. The men wear short embroidered jackets, with long sleeves slashed to the elbow, waistcoats of brilliant colours and innumerable buttons, bright-coloured sashes, and baggy trousers. The women are in flowing white robes, which, drawn over their heads, are held under their chins, only partially concealing their gay head-dresses sparkling with coins, and their low-cut vests, gaudy with gold or silver embroidery. The children are especially subjects of decoration in costume, and strut about in the brightest of garments, plentifully ornamented with gold lace and flowers.

The narrow street leading to the church is tolerably crowded as we force our way along until we suddenly meet a loud-voiced procession, the priests, accompanied by choristers, keeping up a discordant nasal chant as they march round the church with the image of the Saviour on a crucifix, with red and green banners, and with swinging censers, followed by a miscellaneous crowd, all carrying tapers. This occurs three times. Afterwards the church square fills with a noisy crowd of men. The windows and housetops which command a view of it are filled with female spectators, who are not allowed to mingle freely with the men. On the stairs leading to the housetops are clustered the tawdrily dressed little girls, upon whom no such restriction is imposed, and then, if I may be pardoned the expression, the religious fun may be said to begin. It consists in letting off squibs, crackers, pistols, and guns till the spectator is almost deafened. The men form themselves in a circle so large that it fills the whole courtyard, each man throwing his arms right and left round his neighbour's neck, and, lifting up his voice in a discordant scream, which is supposed to have some musical connection with the screams of all his neighbours. It is a dull dance, although noisy. Everybody makes ungainly steps in time, yelling and leering at each other in an idiotic manner, and letting off their guns when impelled to do so by excitement. As far as I could make out, their songs were rather of an amorous than a religious character.

When this entertainment came to an end a seedy-looking character entered the arena with an open Bible in his hand. He proceeded up the stairs to the open balcony, whither he was followed by the armed crowd who had been dancing. These ranged themselves right and left beside him, and he commenced in Arabic to read in a loud voice a chapter from the Gospel of St. John. When he had read a certain number of verses he paused, and about a hundred guns went off in a sort of *feu de joie.* Then he read on, while his audience loaded their guns. Then he paused again. They fired again, and so on all through the chapter, thus emphasizing as it were the most striking passages by periodical explosions of gunpowder. When this was over the church bell rang, and some priests with round, high-crowned hats and locks flowing over their shoulders made their appearance. I was told by a Melchite friend that there was no use in going to church now, as everybody intended to go and get drunk and pay visits, and indulge in more dancing of a less restrained character, but that there would be a better mass on the following day, because the French consul was going to attend in full uniform, and everybody would be there.

This Easter festival lasts three days. The merriment increases and culminates on the last day, at the expiration of which everybody has given proof of his religious devotion by arriving at a blind state of intoxication. When in this sanctified condition disturbances not unfrequently occur between these Christian worshippers and the Moslems, in whose mind Christian religious ceremonial is inseparably connected with drunken riots and wild orgies. The Caïmakam or Turkish governor of the town, fearing that the strict observance of Easter according to their custom on the part of

the Melchites might lead to these results, issued an order
that on Easter Monday and the day following no firing was
to be allowed, but the Melchites replied to the police officer
charged with enforcing this order, that they had no intention of obeying it. A serious difficulty might have occurred
were it not for the intervention of the English and French
vice-consuls, who gave the Melchites to understand that the
Turkish authority must be respected. It was a curious illustration of the state of Turkish administration here that a
Turkish governor should have to appeal to foreign consuls
in order to secure compliance on the part of Turkish subjects with his own orders. When I attended mass on the
following day there was no firing. With the exception of
the French consul, my friends, and myself, the whole congregation stood. Three priests officiated at an altar unusually tawdry, and a group of men and boys kept up a stentorian nasal chant from first to last. They were accompanied by an orchestra of two men, each of whom had a
pair of common steel table knives, with which they kept up
a most ear-splitting clatter on the rim of a copper bowl,
that might on ordinary occasions have been used for salad.
The incense-swingers puffed fumes of incense into the faces
of the French consul and myself as being honoured guests,
and a priest brought him an open Bible to kiss, but ab-
stained from offering it to me—on religious grounds best
known to himself. Then he painted a good many people
with holy water, using a piece of cotton put on the end of
a wire. Then there was the usual procession and elevation
of the Host, and the more devout members prostrated themselves and kissed the flagstones of the church. The sacrament was administered, the bread and wine being mixed together in a silver cup, which was held over an embroidered
napkin stretched between two boys, so that none of the
contents fell to the ground as the priest put the teaspoon-
ful into the mouths of those who knelt before him. The
women did not seem to need it, as they were all bottled up
in a gallery, and could only see or be seen through a lat-
tice-work.

The service came to an end, and the people divided to allow the French consul, who, with his cocked hat and gold

lace, had been the figurehead of the ceremony, to march out
in state. These French consuls are all very pious men in
Syria. The French government, which has been ejecting
monks and nuns and closing religious establishments, and
making laws against religious instruction in France, is very
particular about the religious principles of their representatives in Syria; as a member of the French government recently remarked, "Religion is only useful as an article of
export." Thus, the French consul-general at Beyrout goes
to mass on Easter Sunday with the Roman Catholics. On
Easter Monday he attends mass with the Maronites, and on
Tuesday he worships with the Melchites, thus dividing his
favours equally, and patronizing with great impartiality any
heresies he may happen to come across.

As the correct thing among the Melchites after being at
church is to go and "have something to drink," I followed
the usual custom and paid a visit to my Melchite friend's
family. The ladies of his establishment, in gorgeous attire,
pressed beer and wine and raki, and sweetmeats and cakes
and coffee, upon our enfeebled digestion. We smoked nar-
ghilès, and enlightened our minds upon Melchite manners
and customs. As I passed through the outskirts of the town
on my return home, I came upon the male Melchite population indulging in their circular dance and their discordant
chants. They continued on the following day, stimulated
by a plentiful indulgence in intoxicating liquors, thus to
glorify God, and to celebrate the resurrection of the Saviour
among men.

THE JEWISH QUESTION IN PALESTINE.

HAIFA, April 17.—The exceptional interest which, in the minds of many people, attaches to the Jewish question in Palestine must be my excuse for now alluding to it. Although, in consequence of the strenuous opposition of the Turkish government, the tide of emigration into the country has been checked, the desire of the Russian and Roumanian Jews to escape from the persecution to which they are subjected in Europe to the Holy Land has in no degree diminished. On the contrary, colonization societies continue to be formed and funds collected both in Russia and Roumania, and the English government has lately remonstrated with the Porte on the breach of treaty which the prohibition of Jews to settle in Palestine involves, with what success remains to be seen. The diplomatic action of the present government of England is by no means of a robust kind. Curiously enough, the Russian policy on this interesting question appears to be undergoing a change. The Russian government seems disposed to espouse in Turkey the cause of the race which it oppresses so unmercifully at home. M. de Nelidoff, the Russian Minister at Constantinople, has lately addressed a note to the Porte, in which he complains that the imperial authorities at Jaffa place every possible obstacle in the way of Jewish pilgrims from Russia who wish to disembark there in order to proceed to Jerusalem. The Porte has replied that no restriction whatever has been placed upon pilgrimages to the Holy City, and that the Jews, like everybody else, are free to go there. The Porte, however, draws attention to the imperial decree, recently published, which strictly prohibits the provincial authorities from allowing Jews, under any condition whatsoever, to settle in Palestine, and states that should any

Jews, in spite of such express prohibition, seek to establish themselves there, the law of exclusion would be rigorously enforced. But all foreigners, of any nationality whatsoever, have a treaty right to settle in Palestine. The proof of which is that American and German colonists have established themselves here; that a society has been formed in Petersburg for promoting colonization in Palestine by Russian Christian subjects. A Jew, therefore, who is a Russian subject has manifestly as good a right to buy a piece of land in the country and settle upon it as a Christian. At this moment the Russian Consul - General at Beyrout is warmly espousing the cause of a Russian Jew colonist, who forms one of a colony of twenty-five Russian and Roumanian Jew families who have bought land and settled not far from the Lake of Tiberias. A Moslem youth wishing to examine his revolver, which the Jew refused to allow him to do, the weapon accidentally went off in the struggle, and mortally wounded the Moslem. The whole Mussulman village was up in arms, and it was only by the exercise of much tact on the part of the native Arab Jews that a general massacre was averted. The young Jew was thrown into prison, although it was recognized as an accident, and has been confined in a filthy cell for more than four months. His case was warmly taken up by the Russian authorities, and the plea of the Porte is that he had already signed a paper declaring himself an Ottoman subject. The Russian officials reply to this that he has since travelled under his Russian passport, has been recognized as a Russian subject by the authorities, and that the Arabic paper he signed was erroneously represented to him as being only a permission from the local authority to buy land and build a house. There the matter stands at present, and a warm correspondence is taking place on the subject. It is significant as showing the attitude which the Russians are assuming in the matter. The Russian vice-consul here not long since brought some Russian immigrant Jews on shore in spite of the remonstrances of the local authorities. It is evident that if the Russian government adopts the policy of encouraging Jewish immigration into Palestine, and of protecting the immigrants when here, they will have obtained an excellent

4

excuse for political interference in the country. This was
always the danger, and might have been avoided by a more
enlightened and far-sighted policy on the part of the Porte.
Had the Turkish government encouraged Jewish immigration
on the condition of every immigrant becoming a Turkish subject, they would have added to the population by an industrious class of people, who would speedily have increased
its material prosperity, while the government might have
so controlled and regulated the immigration and the colonization that there would have been nothing to fear from it.
By adopting this policy they would avoid possible complications with foreign powers, while they would at the same
time gain the sympathy of the most enlightened among
them, by affording to a suffering and persecuted race an
asylum where their presence would not only be harmless,
but in the highest degree advantageous to the Turkish province they had chosen for their home.   Of late the prospects of both the Jewish agricultural colonies which have
been established in Galilee have improved.   The assiduity
and perseverance with which, in spite of their inexperience,
of the obstacles thrown in their way, and of the hardships
inseparable from settlement in a new country, they have la-
boured on the soil, the progress they have made, and their
prospects for the future, all go to show that under favourable auspices colonies of this nature cannot but succeed; and
this belief has taken too firm a hold on the Jewish mind
both in Russia and Roumania for it to be lightly abandoned.
At present the pressure on the part of the Roumanian Jews
to emigrate hither is greater than in Russia, where there
has been a lull in the persecution; but unfortunately the
Roumanian government has no diplomatic agents in these
parts, and is indifferent to the fate of the Jews who leave
their country.   In former times the British government had
a habit of taking waifs and strays of this description under
its protection.   Thus, nearly the whole Jewish community
at Tiberias were originally Russian refugees who emigrated
to Palestine thirty years ago, and applied for British protection, a privilege which Lord Palmerston promptly granted
them, and to this day they travel with British passports,
and pay five shillings a year to renew their registration,

which secures them the protection of the British consul. If
any government were philanthropic enough to adopt a similar plan now, there would be no difficulty in these poor
Roumanians entering the country and settling here; but
it is a course which naturally involves responsibilities, and
opens a door to possible complications, and in these practical days people's sufferings, unless something is to be made
out of them, do not furnish a sufficient justification to compensate for the amount of trouble which they might involve.
Meantime the agricultural enterprise of the Jews in Palestine has to contend not merely with local opposition, but
with the unaccountable indifference with which their efforts
in this direction are regarded, with a few brilliant exceptions, by their Western coreligionists. At present the
seven or eight colonies which exist are all composed of
Russian or Roumanian refugees, but the best material for
farmers is to be found among those Jews who have been
bred and born in the country, who are already Turkish subjects, who speak the language, and are familiar with all the
local conditions, and who are now mendicants, subsisting on
that most pernicious institution, the Haluka, which, while it
is a tax upon the whole Jewish nation outside of Palestine,
is a fruitful source of pillage, contention, and sloth, among
its recipients at Jerusalem and Safed. Out of some seven
thousand Jews resident at the latter place, many are willing
to give up all claim to the Haluka, and establish themselves
as agriculturists, if they could be assisted in the first instance with the necessary capital. With some of these the
experiment has been tried on a small scale, and they have
proved more successful farmers in every way than the foreign immigrants, while, as they are natives of the country
and subjects of the government, the latter does not interfere
with their operations, as in the case of the foreigners. Under these circumstances, it is a thousand pities that Western
Jews do not come to their assistance. They would confer
thereby a twofold benefit upon their race. They would assist the industry and enterprise of their coreligionists, while
they would undermine that system of religious mendicancy
which is a disgrace to any religion, and they would deprive thereby their adversaries of the right to say, as

they do now, that the success which attends missionary
efforts at proselytism is due chiefly to the fact that Jews
abroad are indifferent to the best interests of such of their
race as have chosen for their home the land of their ancestors.

Nazareth, May 1.—Talking the other day to a Franciscan monk on the prospects of his religion and of the propaganda for the faith which his order is making in these parts, he informed me that much depended upon the restoration of "holy places," with a view to increasing their importance and popularity, for practically the most effective agent for the conversion of infidels is hard cash, and the increase of expenditure means the increase of converts. Of course he did not put it in this undisguised language, but it is distinctly a great pecuniary advantage to a native village that it should become a centre of religious attraction to pilgrims and tourists, and that money should be spent in building churches and monasteries, and otherwise civilizing remote and outlying localities where the inhabitants would remain paupers but for the sanctity of the spot upon which they are fortunate enough to live. Indeed, the latter are acute enough to understand that they can frequently make a good thing of it by the exploitation of the rivalries of opposing creeds, and they cleverly change from one to the other, when they perceive that it would be to their advantage to do so. Thus, not long ago, no fewer than a hundred and twenty of the inhabitants of the village of Kefr Kenna, situated only a few miles from this place, who belonged to the orthodox Greek Church, became Roman Catholics, and as a reward for this proof of their spiritual intelligence a Franciscan monastery is now in process of construction. The small village is deriving no little profit in consequence, to say nothing of the fact that it will draw pilgrims to visit the historic locality now that they will be received there by the holy fathers. For both the Greek and the Catholic churches have hitherto assumed the truth of a tradition to the effect that Kefr Kenna was the village

in which the miracle took place of the conversion of water
into wine—that it is none other, indeed, than the Cana of
Galilee—and they show you the house where the marriage
took place, and the stone water-pots, to prove it. The fact
that it is a matter of great doubt whether it be Cana of
Galilee at all, does not affect the question where religious
faith is concerned, but it seems a pity that the inhabitants
of Kâna el Jelil, commonly called Khurbet Kâna, should
not be put up to the fact that they are possibly the pos-
sessors of the site of the veritable Cana, and may have got
a " holy place " worth thousands of dollars to them if turned
to proper account.

I will not trouble my readers with quotations from Scewelf
(A.D. 1102), from Marinus Sanutus in the fourteenth century,
from Andrichomius, and from De Vogue and Dr. Robin-
son in later times, to prove that this may be so. The fact
that it is admitted by many modern geographers would be
enough for the inhabitants of Khurbet Kâna or for the
Greek Church, if they wished to revenge themselves upon
their Catholic rivals. These latter have made another still
more happy hit quite lately at Sefurieh, the ancient Sepphoris, distant about three miles from Khurbet Kâna, in
reviving there an almost forgotten "holy place." The
merit of its discovery seems to rest with Saint Helena, who
made a pilgrimage to Palestine in the fourth century, and
to whose ardent piety, vivid imagination, and energetic
exertions are due most of those traditional spots connected
with the life of Christ which attract pilgrims to the Holy
Land. On what authority she decided that a certain house
in Sepphoris—called in those days Diocæsarea—had been
the abode of Joachim and Anna, the parents of the Virgin,
we are not told, nor how, upon descending into details, she
was further enabled to identify the exact spot upon which
the Virgin received the salutation of the angel; suffice it to
say that the proofs were so convincing to her devout and
august mind that she stamped it with her sanction, and a
cathedral was afterwards erected upon it. In the course of
centuries this edifice crumbled away, the site, curiously
enough, became the manure and rubbish heap of the village,
and under the mound thus formed was buried nearly all

that remained of this ancient cathedral.   Only the high
arch of the middle aisle and the lower ones of the side aisles
still testified to the modern tourist the ancient proportions
of the edifice.

Within the last two years, however, it has occurred to the
Franciscans to make excavations here, with the view of re-
storing the ancient cathedral and of renewing its fame as a
holy place, for, to all good Catholics, it must ever be a matter of the deepest interest to see where the angel saluted
the Virgin, and where her parents lived, and to press their
lips to the ancient stones thus hallowed.   Moreover, an influx of pilgrims to this point will have a threefold effect.
It will bring money to the Franciscan treasury; it will
probably be the means of converting the resident local population, who have been fanatic Moslems, but who, I was assured by my ecclesiastical informant, had benefited so much
by the money already spent, that they were only deterred
by fear, and by its not being quite enough, from declaring
their conversion to Christianity to-morrow; and, thirdly, it
would give the French government another holy place to
protect.   For it is by the manufacture and protection of
holy places that republican France extends and consoli-
dates her influence in these parts.

It was with a view of seeing what had been done that I
determined to ride over to Sefurieh and from there take a
line of my own through the woods to the Bay of Acre, instead of returning to the coast by the regular road across
the plain of Esdraelon.   Passing Cana and the Christian village of Reineh, where there is an old well with a sculptured
sarcophagus, we leave to our right a Moslem "holy place,"
called Mashad, where there is a conspicuous wely, or Moslem
shrine.   This spot Moslem as well as Christian tradition de-
clares to be the tomb of Jonah.   This tradition is based on
the fact that the prophet is said in the Bible to be of
Gath—Hepher—and this site is pretty well identified with
that of the modern Mashad.   There can be little doubt that
these Moslem welies are the modern representatives of those
"high places" which the ancient Jews were so constantly
punished for erecting.   They seem, indeed, to differ in no very
marked degree from the "holy places" of the present day.

In an hour more we are galloping up the grassy slope on the side of which are the mud hovels of the modern population, whose conversion is so imminent, and the summit of which is crowned with the picturesque ruins of a crusading castle, reared upon foundations which are evidently of a far anterior date. This building is about fifty feet square, and from the top, which we reach by a dilapidated stair, we have a magnificent view of the surrounding country, the Buttauf, formerly the plain of Zebulon, at our feet—at this time of year a sheet of water—with the high range of the Jebel Safed behind, and bounding the horizon westward the sea-line of the Bay of Acre, with the wooded hills, through which lies my proposed route, intervening. On the side of the hill near the village is the church in process of restoration, and in the courtyard which has been recently built in front of it, where the rubbish mound lately stood, are no less than a dozen syenite columns, some standing to a height of twelve or fifteen feet, some prostrate, while their capitals and entablatures are strewn around. A small chapel has been fitted up in one of the side aisles, where a priest from Nazareth comes every Sunday to perform mass to the Arab and his wife who are left in charge during the week, and who at present form the whole congregation. The priest told me that many more handsome columns were in a subterranean part of the church which had recently been discovered, but which I could not visit, on account of débris. He also pointed out the fact that the pillars which supported the arches were divided into five sections, so built that they might actually enclose the ancient walls of the house of Joachim and Anna.

What renders this excavation interesting is, that as Sepphoris was, at the time of Christ, the principal Roman city and fortress of Galilee, some relics of a date anterior to that of the church itself may very likely be discovered. The former importance of the town may be fairly estimated by the extent of its ancient rock cemetery, which lies about a mile to the eastward, and which I visited. Here abound caves with loculi for the dead, sarcophagi, either cut into the living rock, with their stone lids still upon them, or else detached and strewn like huge water-troughs over the

rocky area, immense cisterns, and rock-cut steps, and a
quarter of a mile distant is a wonderful work of Roman
engineering skill in the shape of an aqueduct many miles
long, which supplied the citadel with water, which it is
supposed continues to Sheik Abreik, a distance of ten
miles, and which here tunnels through the hill for a quarter
of a mile. The roof has in places fallen in, and exposes to
view the canal itself, which is about twenty feet deep, with
sides beautifully cemented. This subterranean aqueduct
has only been recently discovered by the Palestine Exploration Fund Survey, and is quite unknown to tourists,
though the whole place is well worth visiting.

Leaving it with regret, for it required a longer examination than I was able to give it, I struck off past the lovely
springs of Sefurieh, where a copious stream gushes out full-
blown from its source, to fertilize a valley rich with olive
and fig gardens—a spot celebrated in crusading annals as the
scene of many skirmishes, in some of which Richard Cœur
de Lion distinguished himself so much that his name is still
handed down in tradition among the natives. Crossing
wooded hills, we find that every step opens new surprises
upon us of scenery and of discovery, for these wild forest
recesses have never been thoroughly explored. First we
came upon a group of prostrate columns on which we found
inscriptions, so worn, however, that we were unable to decipher them, but the native who was with us told us that
the clump of old trees which overhung them bore the name
of "Trees of the Bridegroom," suggestive of Baal-worship
and a holy place of antiquity. Then we examined two hill-
tops covered with cave tombs, and strewn with massive and
overgrown remains hitherto undiscovered. One of these
was called Jissy and the other Hamitz. The largest of the
caves contained three chambers with loculi. The entrances
were carved. Not far from them I found another group of
columns, and on them managed to trace the letters IMP.
AVR., evidently standing for Imperator Aurelian, which
would make them date from the third century after Christ.
So, winding through rocky, wooded dells, we reached Bethlehem of Galilee, the modern Beit Lahm, where there were the
remains of an ancient subterranean aqueduct or sarcophagus

and the fragment of a column, and on through more glassy
glades, finding our way by instinct, for we were without a
guide; but we had a better chance of stumbling upon undiscovered ruins this way, and whatever path we followed
was sure in the end to lead us somewhere; moreover, the
view guided us from the hill-tops, and our compass when
we were in the valleys. I quite regretted when at last we
suddenly emerged from these old oak woods — alas! so
rapidly being destroyed by the charcoal burners — and
found ourselves on the edge of a hill overlooking the plain
of the Kishon, across which a rapid ride of three hours
brought us to our journey's end, and completed one of the
most delightful rides it has ever been my fortune to make
in this country.

PROGRESS IN PALESTINE.

Haifa, May 16. — Considering the number of tourists, both American and English, who annually visit the Holy Land, I have been much struck with the erroneous impression which still continues to prevail in regard to its availability as a field of colonization, and as an opening for foreign enterprise and capital.

For some time past a discussion has been taking place in the Jewish papers on both sides of the Atlantic, in which the merits of Palestine from this point of view have been canvassed, and I can only account for the extraordinary inaccuracies which have characterized the arguments of the disputants, by the supposition that they have derived their information from sources which, owing to the changes which have taken place in the country during the last few years, may now be considered obsolete.

Readers will be surprised to learn that almost every acre of the plain of Esdraelon is at this moment in the highest state of cultivation; that it is perfectly safe to ride across it unarmed in any direction, as I can testify; that, so far from plundering and despoiling villages, the few Bedouins, whose "black tabernacles" are now confined to the southern margin of the plain, have, in their turn, become the plundered and despoiled, for they are all reduced to the position of being subject to inexorable landlords, who charge them exorbitantly for the land which they occupy, and for which they pay in hard cash, under penalty of instant ejection, which is ruthlessly enforced, so that the inhabitants of the villages, with which the plain is now dotted, live in perfect security, though more than twenty years have elapsed since it was predicted that "in ten years more there will not be an inhabited village in Esdraelon." It looks to-day like a huge green lake of waving

wheat, with its village-crowned mounds rising from it like
islands; and it presents one of the most striking pictures of
luxuriant fertility which it is possible to conceive.

When, therefore, I read the other day, as an argument why
colonies should not be established in this part of Galilee, a
description of the dangers which would attend any such experiment, I was amazed at the temerity of the assertion. But
as so much attention is just now devoted to the consideration
of the agricultural capabilities of Palestine, I think it only
right that the delusions which evidently continue to exist on
the subject should be dissipated with as little delay as possible.
The fact is, that nearly the whole plain of Esdraelon is divided between two great proprietors, the Sultan himself, who
has recently acquired a great part of the eastern portion of
it, and the Sursocks, the richest bankers in Syria, who are
resident in Beyrout, and who own nearly all the villages extending from the foot of the Nazareth hills to the sea.
Some idea of the amount of the grain which is annually
grown on their portion of the plain of Esdraelon alone may
be gathered from the fact that Mr. Sursock himself told me
a few weeks ago that the cost of transporting his last year's
crop to Haifa and Acre amounted to $50,000. This was
said as illustrating the necessity of a railway across the
plain, with a view of cheapening the cost of transport, as,
owing to the Sultan having property here, it has become desirable in his majesty's interest. A concession has
recently been granted to these Beyrout capitalists for the
purpose of constructing a line which shall connect the Bay
of Acre and the two ports upon it with the great grain-
growing province to the east of the Jordan, called the
Hauran, from which region thousands of camels loaded with
cereals come annually to Acre and Haifa.

As I write the engineers are starting to commence the
surveys of this line, which will run right through to the centre of the plain of Esdraelon, and open up a great extent of
new country lying in the hills behind it, which will now find
an easier access to the sea, while the whole of Galilee will
benefit from so important a means of communication. Indeed, it is a remarkable fact that while every province in
Turkey has been steadily retrograding during the last few

years, Palestine alone has been rapidly developing in agricultural and material prosperity. In Haifa and its neighbourhood land has risen threefold in value during the last five years, while the export and import trade has increased with a remarkable rapidity, and the population has doubled within ten years. Indeed, the population of the whole of Palestine shows an increase during that period, more particularly owing to immigration within the last year or two. The consequence is that although, so far as security for life and property is concerned, there is still much to be desired, great progress has been made, and with a more energetic government the country might be rendered as safe as any in the world.

As it is, the Bedouins are being gradually pushed east of the Jordan, and it is now becoming more and more rare for an Arab encampment to be seen in the neighbourhood of the more settled and prosperous part of the country. There are, of course, villages where the inhabitants have a bad reputation, and, as a rule in the establishment of new colonies, proximity to these should be avoided; but fertile lands, near peaceable villages, removed from all risk of Arab incursion, and which can be purchased at a low price, abound; and I know of no more profitable investment of money, were the government favorable to it, whether by Jew or Gentile, than is furnished by a judiciously selected tract of this description. In proof of which may be cited the extraordinary wealth which has been accumulated by the Sursocks alone, who now own thousands of acres of the finest land in Palestine, and who purchase numerous new villages every year.

At the same time it must be admitted that, practically, the purchase of land in this country is attended with many difficulties. It is either held by villages in a communal manner, or in very small patches, many of which have several owners. In the first case the whole village, with its lands, must be purchased, an operation involving many official formalities, or the co-proprietors of the small patches have to agree upon the amount of the purchase-money, and then to show a clear title and the payment of all arrears of taxes. As a rule the purchase of any considerable extent of land involves negotiations extending over several months, and strangers unused to the ways of the country and the methods by which official routine may be expedited and obstacles removed are apt to meet with many disappointments. On the other hand, owing to official corruption, immense tracts of land fit for cultivation, but which are unoccupied owing to the sparseness of the population generally, may, through favouritism and backsheesh, be obtained at an almost nominal price.

The same erroneous impression prevails in regard to the barrenness of the country, as in regard to its insecurity. Few travellers see more than the beaten routes, where the hills happen to be unusually stony and barren; but the extent of the population which once inhabited the country furnishes the best evidence of what it is capable of supporting, and its capacities in this respect have been most forcibly dwelt upon by the officers engaged in the survey of the country for the Palestine Exploration Fund, who have enjoyed unequalled opportunities of judging upon the question. The fact that the resident Jewish agricultural population of Galilee alone amounts to over a thousand souls, is probably one which will astonish Western Jews more than any one else; but I have verified it by actually visiting myself the localities in which they are engaged in their farming operations, and am not giving the number without having arrived at it upon sure data.

There are three prejudices which have operated against the colonization of Palestine by Jews, and which are all absolutely unsound, and these are, first, that the Jew cannot become an agriculturist; secondly, that the country is barren, and, thirdly, that it is unsafe. The real obstacle in the way to Palestine colonization does not lie in any of these directions, but in the fact that the government is most determinedly opposed to it.

THE FIRST PALESTINE RAILWAY.

Haifa, June 13.—When Thackeray foretold that the day would come when the scream of the locomotive would awake the echoes in the Holy Land, and the voice of the conductor be heard shouting, "Ease her, stop her! Any passengers for Joppa?" he probably did so very much in the spirit in which Macaulay prophesied the New-Zealander sitting on the ruins of London Bridge, as an event in the dim future, and as a part of some distant impending social revolution; but the realization of the prediction is becoming imminent. The preliminary survey has just been completed as far as the Jordan, of the Hamidié, or Acre and Damascus Railway, which bids fair to be the first Palestine railway.

It is called the Hamidié line because it is named after his present majesty the Sultan Abdul Hamid, and probably one reason why the firman has been granted so easily lies in the fact that it passes through a great extent of property which he has recently acquired to the east of the plain of Esdraelon. The concession is held by ten or twelve gentlemen, some of whom are Moslems and some Christians, but all are Ottoman subjects resident in Syria. Among the most influential are the Messrs. Sursock, bankers, who own the greater part of the plain of Esdraelon, and who have therefore a large interest in the success of the line. From which it will appear that this is no speculation of Western promoters or financiers, but a real, bona-fide enterprise, and one which is likely to become a large source of profit to the holders of the concession and to the shareholders, for it will tap one of the richest grain-producing districts in the East.

I have myself ridden over the line for the first twenty miles, and have just seen the surveying party, who have returned well satisfied with the facilities which it offers from an engineering point of view. Starting from Acre, it will follow the curve of the bay for ten miles in a southerly direction at a distance of about two miles from the beach. Crossing the Kishon by a sixty-foot bridge, it will turn east at the junction of a short branch line, two miles long, at Haifa. Hugging the foot of the Carmel range, so as to avoid the Kishon marshes, it will pass through the gorge which separates that mountain from the lower ranges of the Galilee hills, and debouch into the plain of Esdraelon. This plain it will traverse in its entire length. The station for Nazareth will be distant about twelve miles from that town; there may, however, be a short branch to the foot of the hills.

So far there has only been a rise from the sea-level in twenty miles of two hundred and ten feet, so that the grade is imperceptible. It now crosses the watershed, and commences to descend across the plain of Jezreel to the valley of the Jordan. Here the Wady Jalud offers an easy incline as far as Beisan, the ancient Bethshean, and every mile of the country it has traversed so far is private property, and fairly cultivated. At Beisan it enters upon a region which has, partly owing to malaria and partly to its insecurity, been abandoned to the Arabs, but it is the tract of all others which the passage of a railway is likely to transfigure, for the abundance of the water, which is now allowed to stagnate in marshes, and which causes its unhealthiness, is destined to attract attention to its great fertility and natural advantages, which would, with proper drainage, render it the most profitable region in Palestine. Owing to the elevation of the springs, which send their copious streams across the site of Beisan, the rich plain which descends to the Jordan, five hundred feet below, can be abundantly irrigated. "In fact," says Dr. Thomson, describing this place in his "Land and the Book," "few spots on earth, and none in this country, possess greater agricultural and manufacturing advantages than this valley, and yet it is utterly desolate."

It needs only a more satisfactory administration on the part of the government, and the connection of this district with the sea by rail, to make Beisan an important commercial and manufacturing centre. All kinds of machinery might be driven at small expense by its abounding brooks, and then the lovely valley of Jezreel above it, irrigated by the Jalud, and the Ghor Beisan below, watered in every part by many fertilizing streams, are capable of sustaining a little nation in and of themselves. There is a little bit of engineering required to carry the line down to the valley of the Jordan, here eight hundred feet below the level of the sea, which it then follows north as far as the Djisr el-Medjamieh. Near this ancient Roman bridge of three arches, which is used to this day by the caravans of camels which bring the produce of the Hauran to the coast, the new railway bridge will cross the Jordan, probably the only one in the world which will have for its neighbour an actual bridge in use which was built by the Romans, thus, in this now semi-barbarous country, bringing into close contact an ancient and a modern civilization. After crossing the Jordan, the line will still follow the banks of that river to its junction with the Yarmuk, which it will also cross, and then traverse a fertile plain of rich alluvium, about five miles long by four wide, to the base of the ridge which overlooks the eastern margin of the Sea of Tiberias.

This is the extent to which the survey has been completed. It is not decided whether to rise from the valley by the shoulder of the ridge which overlooks the Yarmuk, or to follow the east shore of the Lake of Tiberias to the Wady Semakh, which offers great advantages for a grade by which to ascend nearly three thousand feet in about fifteen miles. This is the toughest bit of engineering on the line, and is in close proximity to the steep place down which the swine possessed by devils are said to have rushed into the sea. Once on the plateau it will traverse the magnificent pasture-lands of Jaulan, across which I rode four years ago in the spring, when the numerous streams by which it was watered were flowing copiously, and the tall, waving grass reached nearly up to my horse's belly.

This rich tract was the one on which it is probable that Job pastured his flocks and herds—at least, all the local tradition points to this. It was well populated until comparatively recent times, but the sedentary inhabitants, the ruins of whose villages dot the country, were driven out by the

5

Arabs, who now pasture vast herds of cattle upon it, and droves of horses which are fattened here after their journey from Mesopotamia previous to being exported to Egypt. The course of the line across this region has not been definitely fixed, but it will probably take as southern a direction as possible, so as to tap the grain-growing country of the Hauran. There may possibly be a short branch to Mezrib, which is the principal grain emporium, and one of the most important halting-places on the great pilgrimage road from Damascus to Mecca. It is calculated that the transport of grain alone from this region to the coast will suffice to pay a large dividend upon the capital required for the construction of the road, which will be about one hundred and thirty miles in length. I do not remember the number of tons annually conveyed on the backs of camels to Acre and Haifa, but I have seen thousands of these ungainly animals collected at the gates of both those towns during the season, and the amount must be something enormous. This does not include the whole of the Damascus trade, which now finds its way by the French carriage road across the Lebanon to Beyrout, and which will all be diverted to the railway, or the produce of the rich country it traverses between the seacoast and the Jordan.

The grantees have also secured the right to put steam-tugs upon the Lake of Tiberias, and under the influence of this new means of transportation the desolate shores will undergo transformation. The great plain of Genesareth, across which I rode a month ago, is now a waste of the most luxuriant wild vegetation, watered by three fine streams, besides being well supplied with springs. It was celebrated of old for the amount and variety of its produce, and I have no doubt is again destined to be so. The plains in which Bethsaida and Capernaum stood formerly are all covered with heavy vegetation which conceals the extensive ruins of the cities which once adorned them; and there is a fine back country within easy reach of the lake which will send its produce to it as soon as means of transportation are provided. At present there are only half a dozen sailing-boats on the lake, rather a contrast from the time when Josephus collected no fewer than two hundred and thirty war-ships with which to attack Tiberius in the war against the Romans; and the fish with which it abounded in the days of the miraculous draught are more miraculously numerous than ever, for fishing as an industry has almost ceased to exist, and the finny tribe are left undisturbed. There are some celebrated sulphur baths also on the shores of the lake and within two miles of the town, which are visited annually by thousands of patients. I was there during the bathing season, and found them camped in tents on the margin of the lake, or sweltering in the fetid atmosphere of the one large bathing-room, in which a crowd of naked and more or less cutaneous patients were disporting themselves.

The surveying party tell me that they received the greatest kindness and hospitality from the Arabs in the Jordan valley, who were of a sedentary tribe, and cultivated the land, and who looked forward with pleasure to the advent of a railway, and to the chances of employment which it afforded them. Indeed, both natives and foreigners are not a little excited at the prospect which is now being opened to them, and which promises to be the dawn of a new era of prosperity for the country.

Note.—Since the above was written, the concession has lapsed in consequence of difficulties which arose at the last moment in the formation of the company for carrying out the enterprise; but it is again in process of renewal, and I have little doubt but that it will be ultimately accomplished.

SAFED.

HAIFA, July 10.—Next to Jerusalem, the city most highly venerated by the Jews in Palestine is Safed. I had occasion to visit it a few weeks ago on my way to a colony of Russian and Roumanian Jews which has been established in the neighbourhood. Perched on the summit of a mountain nearly three thousand feet high, it is one of the most picturesquely situated towns in the country; and there is a tradition to the effect that it was alluded to by Christ as "the city that is set on a hill, and cannot be hid," when he preached the Sermon on the Mount, the mount being supposed to be one of the Horns of Hattin, a remarkably shaped hill.

The whole of this district is indeed full of romantic scenery. It is a country of wild gorges and huge precipices, which escape the attention of the traveller following the beaten routes, and to most of them associations are attached, investing them with an interest beyond that of a mere scenic character. There is, for instance, the Wady Hammam, where the bluffs are about twelve hundred feet high, perforated with caves, communicating with each other by passages concealed in the rock, once the abode of bands of robbers who lived like eagles in their eyries. Looking up at these holes in the cliff some seven or eight hundred feet above me, I tried to picture the terrible battle which was once fought in mid-air between the denizens of these caves and the soldiers whom Herod let down the face of the cliff in baskets to attack them. The desperate nature of the struggle, as the soldiers strove to make good their foothold on the edge of the caves, and the frenzy with which the robbers, who had no loophole of escape, must have defended themselves as they endeavoured to hurl their assailants from their baskets, suggested a scene which was quite in keeping with the gloomy character of the surroundings. Some of the more accessible of these caves have been occupied at a later period by hermits, and they may have been utilized for military purposes at the time of the crusades, but they have never been thoroughly explored.

Just before reaching Safed there is a rock called Akhbera, which rises five hundred feet shéer up from the path, and is also full of similar caves. Josephus mentions having fortified it. However prepossessing Safed may look from a distance, it does not bear a close acquaintance. Down the centre of every street runs an open sewer, which renders it the most odoriferous and pestiferous place that it has ever been my fate to sleep in. The aspect of the population is in keeping with the general smell. One seems transported into the ghetto of some Roumanian or Russian town, with a few Eastern disagreeables added. The population here have not adopted the Oriental costume as they have at Tiberias, but wear the high hats, greasy gabardines, and ear-curls of the Jews of Europe. Instead of Arabic, one hears nothing in the streets but "jargon," as the dialect used by the Jews in eastern Europe is called. The total population of *Ashkenazim*, or German Jews, who are hived in this unenviable locality, is between five and six thousand; besides these there are about twelve hundred *Sephardim*, or Spanish Jews, who wear Oriental costumes, and in the other quarter of the town from six to seven thousand Moslems, making the total number of inhabitants about fourteen thousand.

As there is nothing approaching to a hotel or boardinghouse in the place, I was of course dependent on the native hospitality for board and lodging, and thus able to acquire an insight into the mode of life of rather a curious section of the human family. The majority of the Jews here are supported by a charitable fund called the Haluka, which is subscribed to by pious Jews all over the world as a sacred duty, for the purpose of providing support to those of their coreligionists who come here or to Jerusalem to pass the last years of their lives in devotional exercises, and to die on the sacred soil. The practical result of this system is to maintain in idleness and mendicancy a set of useless bigots, who combine superstitious observance with im-

moral practice, and who, as a rule, are opposed to every
project which has for its object the real progress of the
Jewish nation. Hence they regard with alarm the establish
ment of agricultural colonies, or the inauguration of an era
of any kind of labour by Jews in Palestine. They are bit
terly hostile to schools in which any secular teaching is car
ried on, and agree with those Western Jews who consider
that any scheme for developing the material resources of
Palestine by means of Jewish industry is fantastic and
visionary. It is due to the Jewish population of Safed to
say that this spirit does not prevail among the younger
members of it. There are about a hundred young Safed
Jews who actually work as day labourers on the farms of
Moslems and Christians, and I was informed by one of the
most liberal of the rabbis, the only one, in fact, who was in
clined to promote Jewish agriculture, that about two hun
dred families in Safed were desirous of being established on
farms, while several had owned land and cultivated it, and
only abandoned it at last for want of protection against the
extortionate demands of Turkish tax gatherers. It is true
that most of the Jews at Safed are under the protection of
some European power, but until lately no power has taken
sufficient interest in the race to raise a Jewish question with
the Turkish government. Now that important political in
terests are to be subserved by doing so, and the destiny of
Palestine is likely to become a crucial point in the Eastern
question, both Russia and France are seizing every excuse
for interference and complaint, and the questions which are
constantly arising in regard to their Jewish *protégés*, both in
Tiberias and Safed, are likely to furnish them with the pre
texts they desire.

When I was in Safed, Russia was actively espousing the
cause of a young Jew who had accidentally shot a Moslem,
and over whom the Turkish government claimed jurisdic
tion, on the ground that, though a Russian, he had repudi
ated his allegiance to Russia. As the youth was not of age
at the time, the Russian government still claimed the right
to protect him in Turkey, though it had not exercised this
right in Russia itself, from which country he had been com
pelled to flee for his life. As I rode through the village

where the accident had taken place, in company with some Jews, we were pelted by the Moslem population, and, although the release of the boy is now certain, he will probably be compelled to leave the country, unless the relatives of the deceased Moslem can be pacified with the blood money that has been offered them.

Jauna, which was the name of the village to which I was bound, was situated about three miles from Safed, in a gorge, from which, as we descended it, a magnificent view was obtained over the Jordan valley, with the Lake of Tiberias lying three thousand feet below us on the right, and the waters of Merom, or the Lake of Huleh, on the left. The intervening plain was a rich expanse of country, only waiting development. The new colony had been established about eight months, the land having been purchased from the Moslem villagers, of whom twenty families remained, who lived on terms of perfect amity with the Jews. These consisted of twenty-three Roumanian and four Russian families, numbering in all one hundred and forty souls. The greater number were hard at work on their potato-patches when I arrived, and I was pleased to find evidences of thrift and industry. A row of sixteen neat little houses had been built, and more were in process of erection. Altogether this is the most hopeful attempt at a colony which I have seen in Palestine. The colonists own about a thousand acres of excellent land, which they were able to purchase at from three to four dollars an acre. The Russians are establishing themselves about half a mile from the Roumanians, as Jews of different nationalities easily get on well together. They call the colony Rosch Pina, or "Head of the Corner," the word occurring in the verse, "The stone which the builders rejected, the same is become the head of the corner."

HAIFA, July 20.—One of the most interesting and little-known spots in Palestine is the famous shrine of Jewish pilgrimage called Meiron. Hither, in the latter part of the month of May, Hebrews resort in vast numbers from all parts, especially of the East, and as many as two thousand are often encamped there at a time. It is situated in a wild part of the mountains of central Galilee, on the edge of the most fertile plateau in the whole district, where the villages are surrounded by the most luxuriant gardens and groves, and the peasantry are in a more prosperous condition than I have seen elsewhere. Meiron itself is a wonderfully romantic spot; perched at an elevation of twenty five hundred feet above the sea, upon the northeastern flank of a high spur of the Jebel Jermuk range, it commands a magnificent view of the surrounding country, with the town of Safed, towering on its mountain-top, distant about five miles. A clear, brawling stream tumbles in a series of small cascades down the narrow gorge, which expands just here sufficiently to allow of some orchards of apricots, figs, and pomegranates; and near a spreading weeping-willow there is a picturesque old flour-mill, which turns to advantage so unusual a supply of water-power. A hundred yards or so above it is the spot sacred to Jewish devotees. A large, oblong courtyard, around which runs a broad stone balcony, upon which open chambers crowned with domes, marks the site of the burial-places of some of the most celebrated rabbis of Jewish history, and forms a sort of caravansary for the pilgrims. It was not the moment of the pilgrimage at the time of my visit, and I had a choice of chambers. Two of these had been fitted up most comfortably for my benefit, with beds and tables, by the Safed Jews who accompanied me, and who did the honours of the place. It was no doubt the sacredness of the tombs at Meiron which was the cause of Safed being constituted a Jewish colony and a holy city. Here are situated the tombs of the Rabbi Jochanan Sandelar, of the celebrated Rabbi Simeon ben Jochai, the reputed author of the book of the Sohar, and the Father of the Cabalists. Here repose the remains of his son, the Rabbi Eleazer; but more celebrated than all are the sepulchres of the great saints and doctors, Shammai and Hillel. The thirty-six pupils of the latter were buried with him. He founded a school of morals immediately prior to the birth of Christ; and, indeed, it is maintained by Jews that all the ethics of Christianity are to be found in the teaching of Hillel, to which Christ simply gave a more forcible expression than it had hitherto received.

Of all the tombs that of Hillel is the most remarkable. It is a huge cavern on the steep hillside, situated about half-way between the Courtyard of Shrines above, and the stream below. We first enter a chamber with loculi hewn out of the solid rock on each side. Passing through a doorway cut in the rock, we enter a chamber eighteen feet by twenty-five, with seven loculi in recess on the right, and the same number on the left, while facing us is a recess eighteen feet deep and seven wide, containing four sarcophagi hewn out of the rock. On each side of this recess is a smaller one, each containing four loculi. Most of them are covered by stone lids with raised corners, making in all thirty-six rock tombs in this one cave. The rocks all around are much cut in places into steps, cisterns, and olive-presses. There are also three dolmens on the north side of Meiron; they are not far apart, and are quite distinct, though of small dimensions; there are no traces or marks of any kind on the stones. In the shrine above these are chambers which are pointed out as traditional tombs. Near one of these was the synagogue, in which, when I visited it, there were an old man and his son engaged in their devotions. The old man had never left the room day or night for seven years, having lived the whole of that time on one meal a day of bread and water, while he slept on a mat on the stones. He had thus become invested with the odour of sanctity in the eyes of my Jewish companions.

His son, a boy of fifteen, was rapidly praying himself into the state of imbecility at which his venerable parent, by dint of swaying his body to and fro, and his unceasing chanting, had already arrived. He reminded me of the Buddhist hermits whom I have seen in China on their way to Nirvana, and was a sight more painful than edifying. At the corners of the courtyard are stone erections like fonts, and some of these are also near the rock tombs; these, when the Jewish festival of "the burning" takes place, are filled with oil, which is set on fire, and rich Jews, desirous of showing their devotion, offer to the flames the most costly articles in their possession. The richest shawls, scarfs, handkerchiefs, and the rarest books are dipped in oil and consumed, and when any article of special value is burned, the spectators, who are already intoxicated with wine and excitement, burst forth with frantic plaudits of delight. Such was the account given to me by eye-witnesses, but possibly next year I may be able to give you a description of this unique and little-known festival from personal observation.

About fifty yards higher up the hill is one of the most interesting Jewish ruins existing in Palestine. It is the remains of a synagogue, which, according to Jewish tradition, dates from fifty years after the destruction of Jerusalem.

It was about this time, or a little later, that the Jews presented the extraordinary spectacle of two regular and organized communities, one under a sort of spiritual head, the Patriarch of Tiberias, comprehending all of Israelitish descent who inhabited the Roman Empire; the other under the Prince of the Captivity, to whom all the Eastern Jews paid their allegiance. The Romans recognized the Patriarchship of Tiberias, granted it special privileges, and the Jewish colony round Tiberias under its auspices became very powerful. Schools of Talmudic learning were established, and the most celebrated rabbis wrote, and, in fact, stamped with their learning the Judaism which has felt their influence to the present day. Then it was that Meiron became their place of burial, and that the largest and most ancient synagogue of which we have any traces was built at Meiron. The site of the synagogue was chosen on the eastern side of a rocky mound, and the western side and floor were excavated

out of the solid rock. The whole of the area is ninety feet
by fifty. Pieces of columns are lying about, with pedestals
and capitals, but many of the finest fragments have rolled
down the eastern slope. The edifice fronted the south, and
here the façade remains, with a fine portal of large hewn
blocks of stone, and a side door. Some of the stones are
four and a half feet long by two and a half thick. The
portal is ten and a half feet high by five and a half
wide. Its side-posts are each of a single stone elaborately
sculptured. The sculptured lintel projects somewhat above
the side-posts, but I could see nothing of the Hebrew inscription which some of the old writers mention as being
over the door. The centre stone was shaken out of its place
by the earthquake of 1837. Altogether, the situation and general aspect of this singular ruin, projecting as it does out of
the overhanging solid rock, is full of picturesque as well as
of historical interest. Meiron is probably mentioned by
Josephus as Meroth, a place fortified by him in Upper Galilee. Dr. Thomson identifies it with the Meroz, so bitterly
cursed by Deborah because the inhabitants would not join
the expedition of Barak. And, in confirmation of this, there
is a fountain near Meiron called to this day by the Jews
Deborah's fountain, but the Sephardim rabbi, who was my
guide, philosopher, and friend at Meiron, identified it with
Shimrom-Meron, whose king was one of the thirty-one
mentioned in the Book of Joshua as having been smitten by
him on entering Canaan.

A great part of the village belonged to the rabbi, and,
with a view of encouraging agriculture among his coreligionists, he had put six Jewish families from Morocco on
the land, who were accustomed to farming, and were doing
well. Besides these there were twelve Moslem families,
which completed the population of the village. I was much
struck by the good-feeling which existed between them and
the Jews, the sheik whom I visited speaking in the highest
terms of the latter, as being hard-working and excellent agriculturists. Indeed, in walking over the village lands,
those which were cultivated by Jewish labour compared fa-
vourably with the crops of the Fellahin. Altogether, I was
so much attracted by Meiron and its neighbourhood, which

is full of interesting remains that have not yet been thoroughly examined, from an antiquarian point of view, that I propose paying it another visit.

Behind Meiron rises Jebel Jermuk, the highest mountain in western Palestine. I scrambled up it one day, finding myself as I did so in the midst of the wildest scenery to the west of the Jordan. Here villages were few and far between. Nothing was to be seen but rocky gorges and wild hillsides, trackless, excepting where the goats follow each other in search of herbage, but with a grand and savage beauty which it is difficult to reconcile with the idea that they ever supported a large population. Probably, even in the most flourishing days of Palestine, these highlands were always its wildest parts, and there are comparatively few ancient sites or traces of ruins in the remote recesses of these mountains. Jebel Jermuk rears its rounded summit to a height of four thousand feet above the sea-level, and about three hundred feet below the top are the ruins of a village which was abandoned about twenty years ago by twelve Jewish families, which formed its entire population, and who were all cultivators of the soil and owners of flocks and herds. In those days it was the highest inhabited spot in Palestine, and it is wonderful to think its pure mountain air should not have protected the inhabitants against cholera, which was then decimating the country. So far from such being the case, nearly the whole male population was carried off, and the village was abandoned, and finally became the property of a Druse village about three miles distant. The stone walls of the houses are still standing, and there is a well of delicious water, shaded by trees, making the spot altogether a desirable retreat from the summer heats and a healthy locality for a colony, if it were not so inaccessible. These mountains are not frequented by Bedouin Arabs, and need nothing but roads and cultivation to make many now barren spots fertile and profitable. The more one travels over the less-frequented parts of the country, the more one is struck with the extent of its undeveloped resources and with the possible future which is in store for it.

THE FEAST OF ST. ELIAS.

HAIFA, July 31.—The greatest religious festival of the year in these parts takes place on the 20th of July at the Monastery of Mount Carmel, and is called the Feast of St. Elias. It does not rank in the Roman Catholic Church generally as one of the highest importance, but among the Maronites, Melchites, and the Latin Oriental Church, as well as among the Carmelites themselves, it is par excellence the great annual ecclesiastical event. From all parts of Palestine worshippers of all ranks flock to the sacred grotto, and on the evening before the saint's day as many as five or six thousand souls are often assembled on the rugged promontory and in the enclosures surrounding the monastery. Hither I repaired about six o'clock on the evening of the 19th, and sipped coffee, smoked cigarettes, and chatted with the reverend fathers, while I looked out of the iron-barred windows on the multitude assembling beneath them. It was composed for the most part of venders of fruit, sweetmeats, and refreshments of all sorts, who were establishing their stalls for the night in sheltered nooks, for the feast begins at midnight, and is carried on till nine o'clock next day, being, in fact, a species of religious orgy, which appears to have great fascination for the native Christian mind. It must be admitted that devotions which consist chiefly in dancing and drinking, with an occasional free fight, all through the small hours of the morning, are religious exercises of a kind not unlikely to attract the country people, who go in for a sort of holy spree on a scale of large proportions. This year, however, a general panic which pervaded the country in consequence of the cholera in Egypt reduced the numbers materially, especially of the Fellahin, among whom all kinds of absurd rumours were prevalent that the disease had spread to Haifa, and that the monastery itself was in quarantine. After watching the picturesque arrivals for some time, I declined an invitation to spend the night in the monastery, and determined to return next morning at five o'clock, when I was assured that the fun would be fast and furious.

As I approached at that hour my expectations were excited by the reports of the discharge of pistols and guns, and the sounds of the discordant chorus-chanting which forms the usual accompaniment to the native dances. Passing under the archway and entering the large courtyard of the monastery, I found it nearly full of excited groups in large circles, their arms clasped around each other's necks, swaying their bodies to and fro, and keeping time with their feet to their songs, while they occasionally waved their arms aloft and fired in the air. This is the regular Syrian dance of the towns, and it is sufficiently monotonous. The Fellahin, however, have a far more picturesque performance, in which the girls, in bright-coloured garments, join, dancing singly, or in twos and threes. Of these, unfortunately, there were very few. No doubt it was in consequence of the small attendance that there had not been so much drinking as usual, and I only saw one man captured by half a dozen Turkish soldiers, who must have a curious idea of Christian devotions, for an improper use of his fist.

About this time the guest-chambers and corridors of the monastery—where families of the better class who had come from Acre, Tyre, Nazareth, Jaffa, and other towns had passed the night, in the lodging provided for them—began to disgorge, and the variety of costume displayed by the shouting, singing, and dancing multitude formed a scene sufficiently picturesque and animated. Sometimes processions are formed, where offerings are made to the miracle-working statue of Notre Dame de Mont Carmel, in return for a child that has been prayed for, or a sick person who has been healed, but on this occasion her protection did not seem to have been invoked, or, at all events, there was no public display of gratitude. There is a large terrace in front of the monastery, and here a dozen horsemen or so were throwing the djerrid and exhibiting their equestrian skill, much to the detriment of the unfortunate animals they bestrode, whose flanks were bleeding profusely from the pointed angles of the iron stirrups which serve as spurs, and from the cruel bits by which, when going at full speed, they were jerked back upon their haunches.

While all this was going on outside, mass was being performed in the church for those who wished to vary the entertainment. This is a spacious, vaulted building in the form of a Greek cross, with a fine-toned organ in one transept, and a statue of the miraculous Lady of Mount Carmel, between four Corinthian columns, seated on a sort of throne in a richly decorated dress of white satin, in the other. Both the Virgin and the Infant in her arms had golden crowns on their heads, the result of a miracle, for when the Frère Jean Baptiste undertook the reconstruction of the monastery fifty years ago, he intrusted the carving of the statue to Caraventa, a sculptor of Genoa, and, not having money enough to buy her a crown suitable to her position, procured her one of silver, and one of copper gilt for the Child, saying as he did so, " You will know how to procure yourself a better one;" and this she achieved shortly after at Naples, where a rich nobleman presented her with two in return for a miraculous cure of which he was the subject. There is a book sold in the monastery containing a list of the miracles that have been performed by this statue, which was gazed upon with the greatest awe and veneration by the country people. They prostrate themselves before her, touching the ground with their foreheads, and offering up their supplications after a fashion that would shock an enlightened Buddhist by the superstition and credulity thus suggested. On each side of the figure are two altars, one dedicated to St. Jean Baptiste, and the other to St. Simon Stock, an Englishman, who was made Prior-General of the Order of Carmelites in 1245, and who in his day did more than any other to increase their renown. On the right of this is the statue of Elijah slaying a prophet of Baal, which was sculptured at Barcelona by Dom Amédéo. The prophet has got his false rival on the ground between his feet, and, with uplifted sword, is in the act of cutting his head off. He is hung round with votive offerings, and worshippers crowd around to touch some part of the statue, and then kiss the finger

that has touched it.   On a table in front a monk was selling
engravings to the worshippers.   I bought one of these, representing Elijah sending Elisha to look for the sign of rain.
In the distance is the small cloud, no bigger than a man's
hand, and emerging from it is the figure of the Virgin and
Child, for the Roman Catholic tradition has it that in this
cloud was revealed to the prophet the dogma of the immac-
ulate conception, in which he was a firm believer from that
time forward.

Descending a few rock-cut steps close to this image, we
find ourselves in the cave of Elijah, a small grotto about ten
feet by fifteen, at one end of which is an altar, which the
devotees firmly believe is the actual rock that he used as
his bed.   Here a priest was performing mass.   The body of
the church was full of devotees, for the most part women
in white burnooses, who squatted on the ground, and seemed
principally engaged in suckling their babies.

The monastery derives a considerable revenue from these
celebrations, as in good seasons votive offerings to a large
value are brought; but the chief source of its wealth is derived from the sale of indulgences, or at least what virtually
amounts to this.   By these means it exercises a very powerful
moral as well as financial influence all through the country,
and as the Christian population, which is subject to it, is very
large in proportion to the Moslem in the neighbourhood, and
as it is under the exclusive protectorate of France, this influence partakes also of a very distinct political character.   In
fact, the Christians of the whole of this district enjoy a far
more efficient protection against the oppression of the Turkish government than do the Moslems themselves.

The monastery is a modern building, and if it only had
a tall chimney instead of a cupola it would look more like a
manufactory than a religious edifice.   The top of the cupola
is five hundred and fifty feet above the level of the sea, which
is immediately beneath, and commands a magnificent view.
When Napoleon besieged Acre in 1799, and was compelled
to raise the siege and retreat, the Turks fell upon the wounded
French soldiers who were left in hospital here and massacred them to a man.   The convent was, of course, deserted,
and soon after fell into ruin.   For twenty-seven years this

much venerated spot was abandoned, but the order to which
it had given its name never ceased to agitate for the restoration of its sanctuary, and the work of reconstruction was
finally undertaken in 1826, by Jean Baptiste, and completed
in 1853. So the present building is only thirty years old.
In front of the main terrace is a flower-garden and some
trellised vines, in the centre of which is a pyramid surmounted by a cross, with an inscription to the effect that it
commemorates the resting-place of the bones of the French
soldiers. It was not till five years after their massacre that
Father Jules du St. Sauveur ventured back to the mountain, where he found these melancholy traces of the tragedy
scattered among the ruins, and, collecting them, hid them
in a cave until, under more auspicious circumstances, they
could receive a Christian burial. There can be no doubt
that the order is now increasing in wealth and influence, and
expectation runs high that the day is not far distant when
northern Palestine will become a French province, and when
its prosperity will be still further secured.

G

A SUMMER CAMP ON CARMEL.

Esfia, Aug. 20.—The fact that the cholera was raging in Egypt, that in the ordinary course of events it was certain to visit Syria, that even if it did not, the months of July, August, and September are disagreeably hot at Haifa, determined me to make the experiment of camping out on the highest point of Carmel, and I am at this moment sitting under a Bedouin tent, arranged after a fashion of my own, at an altitude of eighteen hundred feet above the level of the sea, upon which I look down in two opposite directions.

On the northwest, distant six miles, curves the Bay of Acre, with the town itself glistening white in the distance; and on the southwest, distant seven miles, the Mediterranean breaks upon the beach that bounds the plain of Sharon, and with a good glass I can make out the outlines of the ruins of the old port of Cæsarea. Southward are the confused hills known as the mountains of Samaria; beyond them, in the blue haze, I can indistinctly see the highlands of Gilead; while nearer still, Mount Gilboa, Mount Tabor, the Nazareth range, with a house or two of that town visible, and Mount Hermon, rising behind the high ranges of northern Galilee, are all comprised in a prospect unrivalled in its panoramic extent and in the interest attached to the localities upon which the eye rests in every direction. I was some time picking out just the spot on which to camp, so many advantageous sites suggested themselves, but the paramount necessity of being near a village for security and supplies, and, above all, near a good spring, decided me in favour of my present location; and as the conditions under which I have brought a large party up to the top of this somewhat inaccessible mountain and planted them upon it are novel, I venture to think that an account of our experience may prove interesting.

In the first place, the village itself was out of the question, partly because Arab houses, as a rule, do not consist of more than one room, and even when one has turned out their human inhabitants, it still remains tenanted by so many others of a carnivorous character, though minute in size, that existence becomes a burden; and partly because they are pervaded with a singular odour of burnt manure, which the natives use as fuel for the ovens in which they bake their bread, and which is too pungent to be agreeable to unsophisticated nostrils. After inhaling it for a month I have got rather to like it than otherwise. As I suspected that such might be the case, and believed that a successful war might be waged against the insects, I decided on hiring one of these rooms as a guest-chamber and a place of resort from the midday sun, in case the camp did not prove a sufficient protection. This room was nothing more nor less than a vault like a cellar, with stone walls and a stone roof, supported by cross arches, about twenty feet by thirty; and I may here mention that the precaution turned out wise, for we got fairly rid of the fleas, and the temperature in the middle of the day, when we usually repair to it for our *siesta*, has never been over 80°. But how to make a camp which should accommodate three ladies and four gentlemen was a serious question. We had one European tent capable of holding two people, and a smaller one for a bachelor of modest requirements in the way of standing-room, and these we supplemented with a tent which we hired of some neighbouring Bedouins, which was thirty feet long, but which, when pitched according to their fashion, was an impossible habitation for civilized beings, as it had no walls. Indeed, the whole breadth of the black camel's-hair cloth of which it was composed was only ten feet. We therefore decided on using it merely as a roof, and sent down to Haifa for a camel load of light lumber in order to make a frame on which to stretch it. We also got up two dozen cheap mats, six feet square, at twenty-five cents apiece. With these we made front and back walls and partitions for sleeping cribs. Finally our erection, on which we proudly hoisted the national flag, was thirty-four feet long, ten feet wide, seven feet high in front and five feet in rear. These mats can be

triced up in front and rear in the daytime so as to allow a
free circulation of air. On the roof, in order to keep the
sun from beating too fiercely upon us, we spread branches
of the odorous bay-tree, with which the scrubby woods of
the mountain abound, and of these same branches we erected
a kitchen, and stable for the horse and three donkeys which
composed our establishment. The thermometer usually fell
to 70° at night, and there were heavy morning dews and
fogs.

It was no slight task selecting the furniture, bedding,
cooking-utensils, and comestibles for a party of seven, and
it took eight camels, besides sundry donkeys, to carry all our
necessaries. In order to understand the nature of the path
over which we had to travel, the reader must get rid of the
popular notion conveyed by the word "Mount," which is
usually applied to Carmel, that it is a solitary hill. So far
from such being the case, it is a mountainous district about
fourteen miles long and twelve wide at its base. It culminates in a promontory, which projects into the sea at its
apex, but we are established ten miles from Haifa, the path
ascending abruptly from that town, and following for nearly three hours' travel the backbone of the ridge, disclosing
views of wondrous beauty down gorges on the right and
left. It is "a rocky road to travel" for a delicate lady,
involving steep, precipitous ascents, for which sure-footed
donkeys are best; but we were obliged to resort to a chair
and a litter, each carried by four bearers, who, as they stumbled and clambered up the narrow path, seemed bent upon
capsizing their human burdens. Now, however, that we
have safely endured the perils of the way, we are amply repaid for them.

The nights and mornings are of ideal beauty. The effects of sunrise and sunset, ever varying, over the vast landscape that stretches around and beneath us, are a constant
source of wonder and delight. From the vine-covered terrace on which our camp is situated we look down a wild,
rocky, precipitous gorge eighteen hundred feet upon the
plain of the Kishon, scarce a mile distant, so steep is it. To
the right this gorge widens into an amphitheatre, and the
hillsides, sloping more gently, are terraced with vines, figs,

and pomegranates, and at its head is the copious spring which supplies us with water, to which one of our donkeys makes several pilgrimages a day with a large earthen jar slung in a straw cradle on each side. Here, morning and evening, files of Druse women resort, and stand and gossip round the cistern into which the water gushes from the rock, their bright-coloured dresses forming a charming contrast with the dark-green foliage of the gardens and orchards that are irrigated in the immediate vicinity. Besides about five hundred Druses there are fifty Christians in the village, who do not harmonize with the Druses very well, and there is a hot rivalry for our favour, so that we have to exercise a considerable amount of diplomacy to keep on good terms with all.

We have hired the vault from a Christian, and his family next door consists of his stepmother and four half-sisters, strapping, good-looking wenches, who are not yet married, for lack of the necessary dowers. With them is staying a cousin from Acre, one of the most beautiful women I have ever seen, quite Caucasian in type and complexion, which is white and transparent as that of any Western beauty. We have great difficulty in keeping this bevy of damsels out of our room, as Arabs have no idea of privacy, and they imagine that politeness consists in squatting round in a circle and asking silly questions. Excepting for the practice it gives one in Arabic, and for a certain insight which one thus gains into the manners and customs of the natives, these visits would be intolerable, and, indeed, we have found it necessary to take stringent measures to limit them. It is more interesting to go and sit in the cool veranda outside of the little Druse place of worship, and talk to the bright young man who is passing most of his time in studying the abstruse metaphysical system of his religion, and who is far more intelligent than the Syrian Catholic priest, who also comes and sits and smokes with us with the view of obtaining, which he has not yet succeeded in doing, some knowledge of our own religious belief. Now and then an episode occurs illustrating the conditions of native existence in these parts. One day I found the village excited at an outrage which a native mounted policeman had perpetrated. On learning that he had assaulted not merely one of the villagers, but my own servant, who had refused him access to our vault, I inflicted a little corporal punishment upon him, when his officer and the village notables interfered, and interceded in his behalf. I asked the latter why they were not glad to see a man punished who, like the rest of his class, was forever persecuting them; they said that when I was gone he would come back and take his revenge upon them. I finally made the man apologize to the Druse he had assaulted, and to my servant, all which he did very humbly, fearing that unless he did so I should insist upon his receiving a still severer punishment from the Caimacan, or local governor, at Haifa. The villagers were very grateful to see one of this arrogant and overbearing class humbled, but they say that unless one can stay and protect them their last state will be worse than their first.

THE DRUSES OF MOUNT CARMEL.

In Camp, Mount Carmel, Sept. 10.—It is not generally known that the Druse nation extends as far south as Carmel. The most southern village occupied by them in Syria is at Dalieh, about two miles from my present camp; their most northern home is at Aleppo. When, nine hundred years ago, Duruzi, the teacher from whom they take their name, came from Egypt to spread his new teaching, it was accepted by a tribe of people who lived in the neighbourhood of Aleppo, whither they had originally migrated from the province of Yemen, in Arabia. Adopting the new and mysterious faith, which, while it is a most interesting metaphysical and theological study, is too recondite to enter upon here, the body of the tribe migrated south, took possession of the valleys of the southern Lebanon, and made their headquarters at the foot of Mount Hermon. Spreading east from there, they crossed the tract known in ancient times as Iturea, and found a natural fortress in the volcanic region anciently called Trachonitis, the Biblical Argob, and in the mountains now called the Jebel Druse. Here they increased and multiplied, and in the early part of the seventeenth century produced that most remarkable warrior Fakr-Eddin, the only man of note of whom the Druses can boast. He conquered Beyrout and the southern coast towns, extending his sway as far south as Carmel, and as far east as Tiberias; and under his auspices the mountains of Galilee and Carmel became settled by Druses.

It is, therefore, not much more than two hundred and fifty years since the Druses first came to Carmel, and it is probable that when they did so they found the mountain wholly unoccupied, excepting by a few Christian hermits and devotees who lived in its caves — for the Carmelite monks had been driven away and their monastery destroyed

three hundred years before; and, indeed, it was only at the
time of the Druse occupation that the first attempt was
made to restore it. For the two centuries during which
the crusaders held the Holy Land prior to the end of the
thirteenth century, Carmel was occupied by them, and the
remains of their military posts are still to be found on
many of the summits of the mountain; indeed, many of
the old stones of which the village of Esfia is built, near
which my camp is situated, bear their devices carved on
them. Before the time of the crusaders there may have
been Moslem villages on Carmel, but its glory departed
when Palestine was conquered by the Saracens in the
seventh century, and the last remains of Roman civilization,
the traces of which still cover the mountain, were destroyed.

About the time of Christ, and for four or five centuries
afterwards, it must have been in its full loveliness, its hillsides terraced with vineyards or clothed with magnificent
forests, and its summits crowned with towns adorned with
the grace and beauty of the architecture of the period.
The discoveries I have made in proof of this I will post-
pone to another letter, as my intention now is to describe
the present population by which the mountain is inhabited.

It is a curious fact that to this day there are no Moslems
on Carmel proper. There are five or six Moslem villages
at its base, on the various sides of the triangle which com-
prises the district, and they have lands running up into the
mountain; but the actual population consists of two Druse
villages, numbering together about eight hundred souls, and
about fifty Christians, besides the twenty-five monks who
inhabit the monastery. The mountain is nevertheless capable of containing a population of many thousands, as it evidently did in old times, and is a much larger district than is
popularly supposed.

The eastern side, from the apex of the triangle, is thirteen
miles in length, the western twelve, and the base nine, giving a total circumference to this highland region of thirty-
four miles. The tract comprised in this area is beautifully
diversified by wild gorges, grassy valleys, level or undulating plateaus covered with underwood, and rocky summits;

and the scenery in places is as romantic as can well be imagined. The two Druse villages of Esfia and Dalieh are situated two miles apart, about three quarters of the way down the triangle from its apex (the projecting promontory on which the monastery is built), and occupy the most fertile part of the mountain.

When the Druses first settled here they founded no fewer than eight villages, but when, forty years ago, this country was conquered by Egypt and governed by Ibrahim Pacha, his rule was distasteful to the majority of Druses, and the inhabitants of six villages abandoned them, and migrated to the Jebel Druse. All these villages occupied the sites of ancient Roman towns, and were constructed of the ancient stones. In the course of my rambles I have visited them all. Of the two villages which remained, one, Dalieh, was occupied by some families which had migrated direct from Aleppo; the other, Esfia, is peopled by Druses from the Lebanon. There is a marked difference between the two, and the people of Dalieh are far superior to those of Esfia.

I went over there the other day, and spent the day and night as the guest of the sheik—or, I should rather say, of the sheiks, for there are two—one is the temporal and the other the spiritual head of the village—and I divided my attentions and my meals equally between them. They are very reluctant to talk about their religion, always turning the subject when any attempt is made to induce them to converse about it; but there is one question which they always ask, and that is whether there are any Druses in England. As it is an accepted fact among them that there are, any denial of it is considered a discreet reticence, and rather a proof than otherwise that one is somewhat of a Druse one's self. They also believe that the majority of Chinamen are, unconsciously to themselves, Druses; and they are firmly convinced that the world is drawing to a close, and that the appearance of Hakim, a divine incarnation, which was prophesied to take place nine hundred years after his last manifestation and translation, is now imminent, as the time is just about expiring.

The Druses are a sober, fairly honest, and industrious people, and have their own notions of morality, to which they rigidly adhere. They have only one wife, but they have great facilities of divorce. An amusing illustration of this came under my immediate notice while I was the sheik's guest. His son, a fine young man, had been my guide among some neighbouring ruins the day before. I had also made the acquaintance of the wife of the latter, a remarkably pretty woman, with a baby. Indeed, I was much struck with the beauty of the type of all the Dalieh women. Suddenly a tremendous uproar took place in the village. My host rushed out to restore order. While I looked down on the scene from an upper window, I saw his son, bareheaded, brandishing a huge stone in the air, and vehemently gesticulating, apparently in reply to a bevy of women who were screaming at him at the top of their voices. Indeed, all the women in the place seemed to have conspired to drive him to frenzy by their abuse. When the sheik appeared in the midst of them order was somewhat restored, for, to my surprise, he seemed to take part with the women, and dealt his son one or two sound blows. Then there was some palavering, and during the whole time I saw the wife of the enraged young man looking calmly on as a spectator. She had put her child in its cradle and was rocking it. Two or three old women were crying and still vociferating. Presently I saw a man come and lift the cradle with the baby, and the mother rose and followed him. They went into a neighbouring house, and were followed by the sheik and as many as could crowd in. Then ensued a long pause, until the sheik reappeared, with a document which he had been writing, in his hand, and the village population gathered around. At this time I could not see his son anywhere, but the wife was among the audience. When he had finished reading, the audience broke up and the sheik returned to me. When I asked what had been the matter, he replied, "Oh, foolish people quarrelling." So I applied elsewhere for information, and was told that for some time past the sheik's son had been tired of his wife and in love with another woman, and had been seeking a cause of quarrel. He had apparently found it in some dispute he had just been having with his wife, and had uttered in his rage the formula of divorce, by which he dismissed her and sent her back to her family. Hence the feminine outbreak against him. The sheik had disapproved his son's conduct, as the wife was his own niece, and, therefore, her husband's first cousin, and he considered it a family disgrace; but, after what had happened, patching up the matter had become impossible, and he had nothing for it but, according to Druse law, to pronounce the divorce. I must say that the entire indifference manifested by the wife, when she followed her baby's cradle away from her husband's house, deprived her of the sympathy I should otherwise have felt.

From what I have been able to gather, the Druse women, if they are pretty, are a heartless lot. Another characteristic incident was a procession of Esfia Druses to the cave of Elijah, below the monastery, in fulfilment of a vow, when a child was dedicated to a religious life, and a goat was sacrificed to God, as in the times of old. After being sacrificed, it was nevertheless eaten, which seems somewhat to deprive the performance of its merit, as the share of the Deity was the bones. There was a great clanging of discordant instruments and loud singing as they came back, some of the men caracoling around on horseback, and others, with arms clasped, dancing in a measured step, followed by a group of dancing women, in dark-blue garments, with gaudy borders and fringes and sashes, and flowing white head-dresses bound with bright-coloured scarfs. They formed a most picturesque tableau, chanting their way to their home on this wild mountain hill-top.

One day a magnificent figure of a man, armed with sword and pistol, suddenly entered my tent. I asked him where he had come from. He said from the Jebel Druse, and, seeing a foreign tent, he had turned in to see who I was. So we exchanged confidences. He was, in fact, an outlaw. He had been fighting against the government, and was wandering from one Druse village to another, not daring to go back to his own, which was in the Lebanon. He said that at this moment the Druses of the Jebel Druse were in full revolt against the Turkish government; that no Druse dare show himself in Damascus, and no Turk dare show himself in the Jebel Druse. They had defied the Governor-General, who knew that it would be useless in their wild mountains to attempt to conquer them. He offered to take me to the Jebel Druse, if I would avoid all places where there were any Turks. He had a profound contempt for his coreligionists of Dalieh and Esfia. "I am ashamed of such Druses," he said. "Why, I saw a Moslem insult one, the other day, and, instead of killing him, he walked away. Why don't they leave a place where they dare not punish insult, and come to the mountain?" I have rarely seen a finer specimen of humanity than this man was, and, with all the defiant recklessness and daring of his expression, there was the charm of entire frankness and good-nature combined with it.

Besides the two villages on Carmel, there are fourteen Druse villages, nearly all within sight of it, on the southern slopes of the mountains of Galilee. It is not improbable that, unable to support the military conscription and taxation which presses upon them, the inhabitants may, before long, abandon their present homes, and go to swell the numbers of their brethren in the Jebel Druse. The whole population of the Druse nation is about 120,000; they can put into the field 25,000 men of the best fighting material in Turkey; they are slowly migrating to the Jebel Druse, where about two thirds of the nation have already asserted their semi-independence.

HAIFA, Sept. 24.—During the two months that I have been camped on the highest summit of Mount Carmel, I have visited no fewer than twenty ruins of ancient towns and villages. Of these I have discovered six which were heretofore unknown, the others having been found ten years ago by the officers of the Royal Engineers sent out to survey Palestine by the Society for Palestine Exploration.

Prior to that time, this historic locality was a *terra incognita*. The tourists who visited the mountain, like the pilgrims who journeyed thither for devotional reasons, satisfied themselves with a short stay at the convent, and even then did not understand that they were only on one mountain spur of a highland region thirty-five miles in circumference, where almost every hilltop was crowned with a ruin, and every gorge might open up new and unexpected beauties of scenery.

It is only after so exhaustive an examination as I have just accomplished that any idea can be formed of the extent of the population by which Carmel was once inhabited, of the high state of civilization which must have prevailed here, and of the extent to which its lovely hills and valleys were cultivated. These ruins bear a great resemblance to each other; and although they none of them cover a very great extent of ground, they were built of most solid materials, and, to judge by some of the architectural remains, and the elaborate carvings and devices, they must have contained some handsome buildings.

The houses were built of blocks of drafted stone, usually four feet long by two and a half high, and two thick. The door-jambs and lintels, which in some instances are still *in situ*, were often seven or eight feet long by two feet six by two feet. In these were holes or sockets, in which the pivots worked. Some of the lintels over the doors were ornamented with devices; these were usually hexagons and circles, in the centre of which were ovals or other ornamental scrolls. Sometimes there was a bird or an animal, such as an eagle or a leopard, or seven-branched candlesticks, or raised bosses or crosses; here and there was a cornice with a florid carving, evidently of the Roman period, with fragments of columns or capitals. But some of these ruins have been inhabited by later inhabitants, who used the old stones for their modern constructions, and too often chipped off the carving. Indeed, they are the ready-made quarries of the country people of the present day, who come and carry off the stones to build their houses.

A notable and melancholy instance of this has occurred in the case of a place called Khurbet Semmaka. This was the most interesting ruin in Carmel, and was discovered ten years ago by the officers of the Palestine Exploration Survey. Here they found the portal of what once had been an ancient Jewish synagogue still standing, its door-jambs and lintels elaborately carved, part of the walls and fragments of the columns which formed an enclosing colonnade were in position, and formed the subject of much speculation, as it was the only specimen of Jewish architecture in this part of the country, and presented some features which were different from anything hitherto discovered; and it was therefore suggested that the building must have been built at a different period from any of those the remains of which still exist. Judge of my disappointment on visiting this spot to find that, with the exception of three feet of one door-jamb, all had disappeared; there was scarcely a stone left. The inhabitants of a Moslem village about two miles distant had within the last decade made a clean sweep of all these most interesting remains. Fortunately they still exist in the Palestine Society's Memoirs in the shape of most elaborate drawings and measurements, which were made by the Survey and have since been published.

Apart from the actual stones themselves and the carvings which are to be found upon them, the objects of interest which mainly characterize all these Carmel ruins are ancient olive-mills and wine-presses, often in a very perfect state of

preservation, tombs and cisterns. First, in regard to the
olive-mills. I found more than a dozen of these. On two
occasions they were hewn out of the living rock. The lower
stone, which was circular, had usually a diameter of eight
feet, with a raised rim outside nine or ten inches high,
and a raised socket in the centre, in which was a hole a foot
square, where the upright was fitted to hold the lateral beam
which worked the upper stone. This was usually five feet
in diameter and eighteen inches thick, and had a hole pierced
through the centre. Through this the long beam was passed,
to which, as it extended far beyond the circumference of the
lower stone, the horse was attached which worked the mill,
the upper stone travelling on its broad edge around the lower
stone, over the olives. From the lower stone a gutter was
carved into the vat, also hewn out of the living rock, into
which trickled the oil. I often found near these mills huge
limestone rollers about three feet in diameter and seven feet
long. On the sides of these were four vertical lines of sunk
grooves, four or five grooves in each line. Taking 2.7 as
the specific gravity of the stone, they must have weighed
about two tons each. What their functions were, or whether
they had anything to do with the olive-crushing process, I am
at a loss to conjecture. The wine-presses were nothing more
than huge vats, also hewn out of the living rock, sometimes
above ground, in the shape of sarcophagi, sometimes pits
eight or nine feet square and the same in depth.

The limestone hillsides in the neighbourhood of these ruins
were almost invariably honeycombed with cave tombs, whose
doorways were often rudely ornamented with devices, and
in one instance I found an inscription in Greek characters so
much defaced that I could not decipher it. They usually
consisted of only one chamber, eight or ten feet square, but
were sometimes larger, and contained either kokim or loculi
under arcosolia, sometimes both. The kokim are tunnel-
shaped excavations, usually seven feet long, two feet six
wide, and the same in height—in other words, just large
enough to contain a corpse. The loculus is an oblong tomb,
with sides about two feet high, also large enough conveniently to contain a body. It is cut out of the living rock, as well
as the arch which overspans it. Sometimes there is a large,

arched recess opening out of the central chamber, containing several loculi. On more than one occasion I found a circular stone like a millstone in a groove in the doorway, which only required to be rolled a couple of feet to close the tomb completely, but the tombs are generally closed by an oblong stone slab, not unfrequently ornamented with devices. I also found several sarcophagi.

The cisterns are of two kinds, bell-mouthed and of demijohn shape, or open rock-hewn reservoirs or tanks. At one ruin I found an extensive system of these latter. There were no fewer than six, of which the largest was forty feet square, all close together, divided only by narrow ledges of the solid rock out of which they had been hewn. They were from fifteen to twenty feet to the soil at the bottom, now overgrown with shrubs, so that in reality they are probably much deeper. In some cases stone steps lead to the bottom, and on the sides were deep niches from which evidently sprang arches to form the roof, for there can be little doubt that the most of them were originally covered. From the great number and extent of these cisterns it is manifest that the inhabitants were, in some instances, entirely dependent upon them for their water supply.

At the southeastern extremity of the mountain is the spot known as "the place of burning," or sacrifice, because tradition assigns it as the locality where Elijah had his controversy with the prophets of Baal, and in commemoration thereof the Carmelite monks are at this moment building a church there, and using, by the way, some of the carved stones of a neighbouring ruin, regardless of all antiquarian considerations. I feel, therefore, a malignant satisfaction in the conviction at which I have arrived that they are building their church on a spot which is indisputably not the place on which the altar of Elijah was erected, if we are to believe the Biblical record, for it is in full view of the Mediterranean, and it would have been quite unnecessary for Elijah to tell his servant to "go up and look toward the sea," for there is no higher point to go up to, and he could see the sea himself. But about a mile from this spot there stands, curiously enough, a pile of stones in a locality which would exactly fulfil the required conditions. I came upon it unexpectedly, almost concealed in a thicket of underwood. The stones are placed one upon the other without cement, and average eighteen inches square and eight or nine thick, forming a rude altar about twelve feet long and four high. The breadth varies, as they have been broken away, but there is a large artificial slab, six feet square, lying at the base. Though I do not for a moment mean to imply that this was the original altar, the unusual shape and position of this pile suggests that it may have been the result of some sacred tradition connected with the Biblical event, or it may be the remains of an ancient vineyard watch-tower. From it the ground swells back and upward in every direction, so that a vast host might have been assembled around and witnessed whatever was going forward, which would have been impossible at the traditional locality. A ten minutes' walk would have taken Elijah's servant to a neighbouring summit which commanded a full view of the sea, and the twelve barrels of water required to drench the altar could have been obtained from some rock-hewn tanks in the immediate vicinity, while the path that passes the pile leads straight down to the hill on the bank of the Kishon, where tradition has it that the priests were massacred. Moreover, it was in the centre of the most populous part of the mountain. Within a radius of two miles and a half from this pile of stones there are no fewer than twelve ruins of ancient towns and villages on the various hill-tops and mountain-spurs which surround it.

No fact could give a better idea than this of the populous character of Carmel in the days of the prophet. Not very far from this I discovered, half-way down the steep flank of the mountain, a fortress of a most ancient race, the stones which were piled one above another three high to form the rampart being immense natural unhewn boulders weighing from two to three tons each. I am not aware of anything of the kind having yet been found in Palestine, and as carrying one back to a period probably anterior to Jewish occupation, I regard it as the most interesting discovery I have made on Carmel.

7

A PLACE FAMOUS IN HISTORY.

St. Jean d'Acre, Oct. 14.—Of all the towns on the Syrian coast, from Antioch to Gaza, none has had a more eventful history than Acre, or one which more directly affected the fortunes of the rest of the country at large. Napoleon I. called it the key of Palestine, and it is doubtless owing to its important strategical position that it has undergone so many vicissitudes, and been the scene of so many sanguinary battles. There is, indeed, probably no similar area on the face of the globe on which so much blood has been shed.

I was at some trouble the other day to add up the list of sieges it has undergone, and the total was fifteen, not counting doubtful ones in the earliest history of the country, when it was invaded and conquered by the ancient Egyptians; but beginning with the siege of Acre by Shalmaneser, 721 B.C., when the fortress belonged to the Tyrians, and ending with its bombardment, in A.D. 1840, by the English Admiral Sir Charles Napier, the list is one which suggests a record of blood unparalleled in history. Its worst time was undoubtedly during the two hundred years when it was taken and retaken several times by Crusaders and Saracens successively. On one of these occasions when, after a two years' siege, the town fell into the hands of the Saracens, sixty thousand Christians are said to have fallen by the sword. The place is still shown, at the northeast salient of the outer wall, where stood the English tower, which was guarded by the troops of Richard Cœur de Lion.

The town now contains only about nine thousand inhabitants, cooped up by the fortifications in the very limited area of about fifty acres; and it is more picturesque than agreeable to live in. There is no more characteristic bazaar in the East than that of Acre, with its motley crowd of wild Bedouins from the desert, Persian devotees gathering

around a Persian holy man who has taken up his residence
here, Turkish soldiers who form its garrison, Druses, with
their white turbans and striped abeihs, or overcoats, Meta-
walis, who are wild and gipsy-looking Moslem schismatics,
Syrian Christians, and Moslem peasantry; add to these veiled
women, long strings of camels, with an occasional foreigner,
or sailor from a merchant-ship in the harbour, and you get
a population as varied as any town in the country can show.
Acre, therefore, is a most interesting place to spend a day
in, apart from any antiquarian attraction it may possess, or
monuments of more modern architecture which are worthy
of attention.

There are few finer mosques in Syria than that of Jezzar
Pacha, which stands within a large rectangular area, where
there are vaulted galleries, supported by ancient columns
ornamented by capitals brought from the ruins of Tyre and
Cæsarea. Along these galleries have been built cells, destined for the people employed at the mosque, or the pilgrims who came to visit it. They surround a magnificent
court, under which are cisterns, and upon which are palms,
cypress, and other trees. Among them are white marble
tombs, notably those of Jezzar and Suleiman Pacha. The
town contains three other mosques, the columns in which
and the pavement have certainly belonged to more ancient
buildings. There are four Christian churches in the city,
which belong to the Roman Catholics, the Schismatic Greeks,
the Maronites, and the United Greeks respectively. Under
the house of the Sisters of Nazareth and the neighbouring
houses extend vast vaulted cellars which are now divided
by walls of separation, and belong to different proprietors;
they are doubtless of crusading origin. Deep cisterns also
date from that period. Of the same date also are certain
remains of walls and vaults near the convent, which are the
ruins of a church almost completely destroyed. The most
remarkable khan is near the port, called the Khan el Aurid
on account of its columns, the galleries surrounding it being
built on pillars of gray or red granite, covered by capitals
of different orders, brought from more ancient monuments.

The citadel, as may be imagined, has often been destroyed
and rebuilt. On one side is the military hospital, the lower

part of which belongs entirely to crusaders' work, and consists of large subterranean magazines. In the middle is a great court, shaded by fig, palm, and other trees, under which are vaulted galleries and cisterns. Under the ramparts also extend immense ogival vaults, many of which belong to the time of the crusades. These have furnished magazines for later defenders of the fortress, and, during the bombardment by the English in 1840, the principal one exploded, with a loss to the defenders of 1600 men, 30 camels, 50 asses, besides horses, cows, and a great store of arms. Some of the guns lying about the ramparts are of old French manufacture, with the dates 1785, '86, '87. They are those which were sent by sea, for the use of Napoleon, but were captured by Sir Sydney Smith, and brought here to serve for the defence of the city. About half a mile from the city walls is an artificial hill or tumulus, called Napoleon's Hill, from the fact that he used it as his headquarters during one of the sieges of Acre. It was occupied for the same purpose six hundred years before by Richard Cœur de Lion.

In ancient times Acre was the most populous and flourishing port on the sea-coast after the decline of Tyre and Sidon, and contained an immense population; the town must have extended over the plain to the east of the city, which is still rich in ancient débris, fragments of pottery, and marble carvings. A great part of the modern fortification has been built from the ruins of Athlit, which I have described in a former letter, and which, before it was thus despoiled at the beginning of this century, must have been an ancient crusading fortress in almost perfect condition. When one thinks how lately it has been destroyed, one is all the more inclined to regret the disappearance of a monument which would have been the most interesting relic of its kind in existence. Acre possesses little Biblical interest. It is only mentioned once in the Old Testament, where it is alluded to as being a town from which the tribe of Asher, in whose territory it was situated, did not succeed in driving the Canaanites, but seemed to have lived with them in it upon friendly terms; and once in the New Testament, where, under the name of Ptolemais, it was visited by Paul on his way from Greece to Jerusalem.

There are many old people now in Acre who tell thrilling stories of the episodes which occurred here during the years when it was occupied by the Egyptians, between 1830 and 1840, and when it became necessary not merely to conciliate the conquerors, but to play a double game of keeping on good terms with the Turks, to whom it was ultimately, and, as it now turns out, foolishly, restored by the British; but none so thrilling as those which they have heard from their fathers, of the incidents which marked the reigns of Jezzar and Abdullah Pacha, especially the former. The following story was told me by the son of the man who was the confidential secretary of this fiend in human shape, who gloried in the name of "The Butcher." In youth he sold himself to a slave-merchant in Constantinople, and, being purchased by Ali Bey of Egypt, he rose from the humble station of a mameluke to be Governor of Cairo. In 1773 he was placed by the Emir of the Druses in command at Beyrout. There his first act was to seize 50,000 piastres, the property of the emir, and the second to declare that he acknowledged no superior but the sultan. The emir, by the aid of a Russian fleet, drove Jezzar from Beyrout, but he was soon after made Pacha of Acre and Sidon. Under his vigorous rule the pachalik extended from Baalbec on the north to Jerusalem on the south. My informant told me that he was not originally a cruel man, but that one day he was playing with a little daughter who pulled his beard. "This is very wrong," he said; "how did you learn to play with men's beards?" "Oh," she replied, "I always play with the beards of the mamelukes when they visit the ladies of the harem in your absence." This excited a fit of frenzied jealousy. Taking an escort, he announced that he was going on an official visit to a distant part of his pachalik. When he was a stage out of Acre, he told his escort to remain where they were, disguised himself, and returned rapidly and secretly to his harem. Here he found all his favourite wives disporting themselves with his mamelukes or military body-guard. Instantly he drew his cimeter and fell, not upon the men, but upon the women. Fifteen of these he is said to have killed with his own hand, and then, growing tired of the effort, he called in some soldiers to complete the massacre, not leaving one alive. My informant did not remember the total number slain. The mamelukes rushed to the great magazines, and swore they would blow themselves up and the whole town if a hair of their heads was touched. They were allowed, therefore, to saddle their horses and ride off in peace; but from that day the whole character of Jezzar Pacha was changed, and he made it a rule never to allow a week to pass without executions. His Jew banker was a handsome man. One day Jezzar complimented him on his looks, and then, calling a servant, ordered him to put out one of the Jew's eyes. Some time after Jezzar observed that the banker had arranged his turban so as almost to hide the lost eye, and he then, without a moment's hesitation, had his nose cut off. The poor Jew finally lost his head. The family of this man are still among the chief bankers of Damascus.

This butcher also employed his own leisure moments in unexpectedly drawing his sword and cutting off the ears and noses of his favourites and the people about him, and sometimes their heads, with his own hand. This was the man whom Napoleon besieged in Acre, and with whom British troops were unfortunately compelled to ally themselves to prevent the fortress from falling into French hands. My informant told me that during the latter years of Jezzar Pacha's life his character again changed for the better, and he gradually gave up his cruel practices. In fact, he described his cruelty as a monomania produced by a fit of jealousy, which it took him some years to get over.

THE BABS AND THEIR PROPHET.

Haifa, Nov. 7.—The Nahr N'aman, called by the ancients the river Belus, rises in a large marsh at the base of a mound in the plain of Acre called the Tell Kurdany, and, after a short course of four miles, fed by the swampy ground through which it passes, it attains considerable dimensions. Before falling into the sea it winds through an extensive date-grove, and then, twisting its way between banks of fine sand, falls into the ocean scarcely two miles from the walls of Acre. Pliny tells us that glass was first made by the ancients from the sands of this river, and the numerous specimens of old glass which I found in grubbing bear testimony to the extensive usage of this material in the neighbourhood. The beach at its mouth was also celebrated as a locality where the shells which yielded the Tyrian purple were to be found in great abundance, and I have succeeded in extracting the dye from some of those I have collected here. It was also renowned for a colossal statue of Memnon, which, according to Pliny, was upon its banks, but the site of this has not been accurately identified. The only point of attraction now upon its waters is a garden belonging to an eminent Persian, whose residence at Acre is invested with such peculiar interest that I made an expedition to his pleasure-ground on the chance of discovering something more in regard to him than it was possible to do at Haifa.

Turning sharply to the right before reaching Acre, and passing beneath the mound upon which Napoleon planted his batteries in 1799, we enter a grove of date-trees by a road bordered with high cactus hedges, and finally reach a causeway which traverses a small lake formed by the waters of the Belus, and which, crossing one arm of the river, lands us upon an island which it encircles. This island, which is

about two hundred yards long by scarcely a hundred wide,
is all laid out in flower-beds and planted with ornamental
shrubs and with fruit-trees. Coming upon it suddenly it is
like a scene in fairy land. In the centre is a plashing fountain from which the water is conveyed to all parts of the
garden. The flower-beds are all bordered with neat edges
of stone-work, and are sunk below the irrigating channels.
Over a marble bed the waters from the fountain come rip-
pling down in a broad stream to a bower of bliss, where two
immense and venerable mulberry-trees cast an impenetrable
shade over a platform with seats along the entire length
of one side, protected by a balustrade projecting over the
waters of the Belus, which here runs in a clear stream, fourteen or fifteen feet wide and two or three deep, over a pebbly bottom, where fish of considerable size, and evidently
preserved, are darting fearlessly about, or coming up to the
steps to be fed. The stream is fringed with weeping wil-
lows, and the spot, with its wealth of water, its thick shade,
and air fragrant with jasmine and orange blossoms, forms
an ideal retreat from the heats of summer. The sights and
sounds are all suggestive of langour and *dolce far niente*, of
that peculiar condition known to Orientals as *kief*, when the
senses are lulled by the sounds of murmuring water, the
odours of fragrant plants, the flickering shadows of foliage,
or the gorgeous tints of flowers and the fumes of the narghileh.

The gardener, a sedate Persian in a tall cap, who kept
the place in scrupulous order, gave us a dignified welcome.
His master, he said, would not come till the afternoon, and
if we disappeared before his arrival we were welcome to
spread our luncheon on his table under the mulberry-trees,
and sit round it on his chairs; nay, further, he even extended his hospitality to providing us with hot water.

Thus it was that we took possession of Abbas Effendi's
garden before I had the honour of making that gentleman's
acquaintance, an act of no little audacity, when I inform
you that he claims to be the eldest son of the last incarnation of the Deity. As his father is alive and resident at
Acre—if one may venture to talk of such a being as resident anywhere—my anxiety to see the son was only ex-

ceeded by my curiosity to investigate the father. But this, as I shall presently explain, seems a hope that is not likely to be realized. Meantime I shall proceed to give you, so far as I have been able to learn, an account of who Abbas Effendi's father is, and all that I know about him, premising always that I only do so subject to any modification which further investigation may suggest.

It is now forty-eight years since a young man of three-and-twenty appeared at the shrine of Hussein, the grandson of the Prophet, who was made a martyr at Kerbela. He was said to have been born at Shiraz, the son of a merchant there, and his name was Ali Mohammed. It is supposed that he derived his religious opinions from a certain Indian Mussulman, called Achsai, who instituted a system of reform, and made many disciples. Whether this is so or not, the young Persian soon acquired a pre-eminent reputation for sanctity, and the boldness and enthusiasm of his preaching and the revolutionary sentiments he uttered attracted many to his teaching. So far as I have been able to judge, he preached a pure morality of the loftiest character, denouncing the abuses of existing Islam as Christ did the Judaism of his day, and fearlessly incurring the hostility of Persian Phariseeism. A member himself of the Shiite sect of Moslems, he sought to reform it, as being the state religion of Persia, and finally went so far as to proclaim himself at Kufa the *bab*, or door, through which alone man could approach God. At the same time he announced that he was the Mahdi, or last Imaum, who was descended from Ali, the son-in-law of the Prophet, and whom the Shiites believe to have been an incarnation of the Deity. Mahdi is supposed by all Persian Moslems not to have died, but to be awaiting in concealment the coming of the last day.

As may be imagined, the sudden appearance after so many centuries of a reformer who claimed to be none other than the long-expected divine manifestation, created no little consternation throughout Persia, more especially as, according to tradition, the time had arrived when such a manifestation was to be looked for, and men's minds were prepared for the event. The Persian enthusiast, as soon as his preaching became popular and his pretensions vast, roused the most violent hostility, and he was executed at Tabriz in 1849, after a brief career of fourteen years, at the early age of thirty-seven. The tragic circumstances attending his death enhanced his glory, for he was repeatedly offered his life if he would consent to abate his claims, or even leave the country. He preferred, however, a martyr's crown, and was executed in the presence of a vast multitude, leaving behind him a numerous and fanatic sect, who have since then been known as the Babs, and whose belief in the founder subsequent persecutions on the part of the government have only served to confirm.

The Bab before his execution gave it to be understood that though he was apparently about to die, he, or rather the divine incarnation of which he was the subject, would shortly reappear in the person of his successor, whom, I believe, he named secretly. I do not exactly know when the present claimant first made known his pretensions to be that successor, but, at all events, he was universally acknowledged by the Bab sect, now numbering some hundreds of thousands, and became so formidable a personage, being a man of high lineage—indeed, it is whispered that he is a relative of the Shah himself—that he was made prisoner by the government and sent into exile. The Sultan of Turkey kindly undertook to provide for his incarceration, and for some years he was a state prisoner at Adrianople. Finally he was transported from that place to Acre, on giving his parole to remain quietly there and not return to Persia, and here he has been living ever since, an object of adoration to his countrymen, who flock hither to visit him, who load him with gifts, and over two hundred of whom remain here as a sort of permanent body-guard.

He is visible only to women or men of the poorest class, and obstinately refuses to let his face be seen by any man above the rank of a fellah or peasant. Indeed, his own disciples who visit him are only allowed a glimpse of his august back, and in retiring from that they have to back out with their faces towards it. I have seen a lady who has been honoured with an interview, during which he said nothing beyond giving her his blessing, and after about three minutes motioned to her to retire. She describes him as a man of probably about seventy years of age, but much younger-looking, as he dyes both his hair and his beard black, but of a very mild and benevolent cast of countenance. He lives at a villa in the plain, about two two miles beyond Acre, which he has rented from a Syrian gentleman of my acquaintance, who tells me that once or twice he has seen him walking in his garden, but that he always turns away so that his face shall not be seen. Indeed, the most profound secrecy is maintained in regard to him and the religious tenets of his sect.

Not long ago, however, public curiosity was gratified, for one of his Persian followers stabbed another for having been unworthy of some religious trust, and the great man himself was summoned as a witness.

"Will you tell the court who and what you are?" was the first question put.

"I will begin," he replied, "by telling you who I am not. I am not a camel driver"—this was an allusion to the Prophet Mohammed — "nor am I the son of a carpenter"—this in allusion to Christ. "This is as much as I can tell you to-day. If you will now let me retire, I will tell you to-morrow who I am."

Upon this promise he was let go; but the morrow never came. With an enormous bribe he had in the interval purchased an exemption from all further attendance at court.

That his wealth is fabulous may be gathered from the fact that not long since a Persian emir or prince, possessing large estates, came and offered them all, if in return he would only allow him to fill his water jars. The offer was considered worthy of acceptance, and the emir is at this moment a gardener in the grounds which I saw over the wall of my friend's villa. This is only one instance of the devotion with which he is regarded, and of the honours which are paid to him: indeed, when we remember that he is believed to possess the attributes of Deity, this is not to be wondered at. Meantime his disciples are patiently waiting for his turn to come, which will be on the last day, when his divine character will be recognized by unbelievers.

AN ANCIENT JEWISH COMMUNITY.

Haifa, Nov. 25.—In one of the most remote and secluded valleys in the mountains of northern Galilee lies a village, the small population of which possesses an interest altogether unique. As I looked down upon it from the precipitous and dangerous path by means of which I was skirting the flank of the mountain, I thought I had rarely seen a spot of such ideal beauty. It was an oasis, not actually in a desert—for the rocky mountain ranges were covered with wild herbage —but in a savage wilderness of desolation, in the midst of which the village nestled in a forest of orange, almond, fig, and pomegranate trees, the tiny rills of water by which they were irrigated glistening like silver threads in the sunlight, and the yellow crops beyond contrasting with the dull green of the hill verdure, long deprived of water, and the gray rocks which reared their craggy pinnacles above it.

The name of this village was Bukeia. I had heard vaguely of the existence of a spot in Galilee where a community of Jews lived who claimed to be the descendants of families who had tilled the land in this same locality prior to the destruction of Jerusalem and the subsequent dispersion of the race; as it had never been suspected that any remnant of the nation had clung to the soil of their fathers from time immemorial, and as it is certain that this is the only remnant that has, I took some trouble to ascertain the name of the village, and felt that it was worth a pilgrimage to visit it. Although hitherto unknown to Europeans and tourists, it has been for many years a spot much frequented by the Jews of Safed and Tiberias, and this summer especially, when the cholera panic prevailed in the country, there was a perfect rush of the wealthier Jews and rabbis of those towns to its pure air and bracing climate. In a small way it is a sort of Jewish sanatorium.

But the village does not consist altogether of Jews. In fact, they form the minority of the population, which is composed of eighty Druse, forty Greek-Christian, and twenty Jewish families, the latter numbering about one hundred and twenty souls in all. Refusing the invitation of the Druse and Christian sheiks to accept their hospitality, I listened rather to the solicitations of the elderly Hebrew who eagerly placed his house at my disposal, and was the patriarch of his coreligionists, his local title being, like those of the heads of the other communities, that of sheik. His house was a stone erection with a court-yard, and contained a single large room, which, as is common in Arab houses, afforded eating and sleeping accommodation for the whole family. On this occasion it soon became crowded to excess.

First appeared the Druse sheik, with white turban, and composed and dignified bearing. Then the sheik of the Christians, a man in no way to be distinguished from the ordinary type of native fellahin; then the Greek priest, in his high, round-topped black hat and long black coat, reaching nearly to his feet; then the Jewish rabbi, who officiates at the synagogue, in flowing Eastern robe; then some village notables of all three religions, who all squatted on mats, forming a semicircle, of which my friends and I were the centre, and which involved a large demand upon our host for coffee, for on these occasions it is a great breach of politeness not to furnish all the uninvited guests who flock in to see distinguished strangers with that invariable beverage. When one or two Moslems, who were temporary visitors to the village, dropped in from curiosity, I could not fail to be struck with the singular ethnological and theological compound by which I was surrounded. Here, in these Christian and Moslem peasants, were the descendants of those ancient Canaanites whom the conquering Jews failed to drive out of the country during the entire period of their occupation of it, though they doubtless served their conquerors as hewers of wood and drawers of water, and as farm-servants generally; for the result of the most recent and exhaustive research proves, I think, incontestably that the fellahin of Palestine, taken as a whole, are the modern representatives of those old tribes which the Israelites found settled in the country, such as the Canaanites, Hivites, Jebusites, Amorites, Philistines, Edomites. In what proportion these various tribes are now represented, whether they were preceded by a still older autochthonous population, namely, the Anakim, Horites, and so forth, are questions which have so far been beyond the reach of scientific research. But though this race, or rather conglomeration of races, which may be designated for want of a better by the vague title of pre-Israelite, still survives beneath the Mohammedan or Christian exterior, it has not remained uninfluenced during the lapse of centuries by the many events and circumstances that have happened in Palestine.

Each successive change in the social and political condition of the country has more or less affected it in various ways, and we must not be surprised when studying the fellahin at finding Jewish, Hellenic, Rabbinic, Christian, and Mussulman reminiscences mingled pell-mell, and in the quaintest combinations, with traits which may bring us back to the most remote and obscure periods of pre-Israelite existence. Indeed, for anything one could say to the contrary, the Christian fellahin of this village, though they had resisted the proselytizing efforts of the Saracen conquest in the sixth century, may, before they were converted to Christianity, have worshipped the gods of the Græco-Roman period; before that they may have been Jews, for there can be little question that the aboriginal population, to some extent, adopted the Jewish faith after the conquest, and before that were worshippers of the Syro-Phœnician deities, Baal and Ashtaroth. They may in those old times, when Jewish power was supreme, have been in this very village the servants of the ancestors of these very Jews who now share its land with them, as they had, according to their traditions, done from the most ancient period; and this means, in a country where genealogies are preserved for centuries upon centuries, a very long time ago. I have a friend at Haifa who says he can trace his ancestry back to the crusades, when his family was resident at the old town of the same name; and, as a grotesque illustration of their pretensions, a story is told of a Bedouin sheik who, being asked whether he was descended from Abraham, said that he could trace further back, and that, in fact, Abraham was not a sheik of a very good family.

The only really modern intruders in the group by which I was surrounded were the Druses, who only settled in the village about three hundred years ago, and whose origin prior to nine hundred years ago, when we know that they were settled at Aleppo, is rather obscure; but it is generally believed that they were originally a tribe inhabiting the province of Yemen. Here, too, in this small group of Arabic-speaking people, were represented four of the most widely divergent religions. There were the two Moslems, whose ancestors, probably, prior to the conquest of Palestine by the Saracens, had been Christians, but had then adopted the faith of the Prophet. There was the priest of the Greek Church, still clinging to the dogmas which he inherited from the first Christians—the descendant, possibly, of one who had actually listened to the words of Christ and his disciples, in the country which their posterity has never left. And indeed it is a curious reflection in looking at these fellahin to think that they may be the direct descendants of some of those thousands who were influenced at the time by the teaching which has since swayed the moral sentiment of civilized humanity. Then there were the Jews—the only group of Jews existing in the world whose ancestors have clung to the soil ever since that Teacher's tragic death, and whose fathers may have shared in the general hostility to him at the time—representing still the faith which was the repository of the highest moral teaching prior to Christianity, prior to Mohammedanism. Lastly, there were the Druses, in whose esoteric religion is to be found the most extraordinary confusion of metaphysical notions, gnostic and pagan, the outcome of a mystical interweaving of ideas derived from the most divergent faiths, with a Magian or Zoroastrian basis, upon which Hindoo and Buddhist, Jewish and Platonic, Christian and Moslem dogmas have been successively grafted, forming a system so recondite and abstruse that only the initiated can comprehend it, if indeed they can.

Such were the mixed religious and race conditions by which I was surrounded, and I was much struck by the ap-

parent tolerance and amiability with which all the members
of these different religions regarded each other. The Jewish rabbi told me privately that he much preferred Druses
to Christians; but he lived on good terms with all. And
when I went to see the synagogue the Greek priest strolled
round with me, and the rabbi returned the compliment by
accompanying us when I went to visit the little Greek
church. Meantime, the Hebrew sheik had summoned all
the Jewish population, and they came trooping in to perform
the usual Eastern salutation of kissing the hand. Old men
and maidens, young men and married women and children,
I saw them all, nor, so far as dress and facial type were
concerned, was it possible to distinguish them from the fellahin of the country generally. These twenty families
seemed all to have descended from one stock, they all had
the same name, Cohen, and they have never intermarried
either with the people of the country or even with other
Jews. I afterwards had some conversation with the Christian and Druse sheiks in regard to them. They said that
formerly more of the village lands belonged to them, but
owing to the wars, pestilences, and other misfortunes which
had overtaken the country at various times, their property
had become diminished; indeed, there can be little doubt
that the Druses themselves, when Fakr Eddin conquered
this part of the country, appropriated some of it; so that now,
so far as their worldly circumstances go, the Jews are badly off. Nevertheless they do not complain, and are skilful,
hard-working, and persevering agriculturists, to my mind
more deserving of sympathy than many of their coreligionists who have come to settle in the country as colonists, de-
pending more upon the assistance which they derive from
without than upon their own efforts. The experience and
example of their coreligionists at Bukeia would make the
neighbourhood of that place a desirable locality for a colony.

From Bukeia I followed a northwesterly direction, by a
most picturesque mountain path, and in a few hours reached
the romantically situated town of Tershiha, where I was
most hospitably entertained by the Cadi, a dignified Arab
gentleman of a true old Oriental type which is now becom-

ing rare. This place contains about two thousand inhabitants. They are nearly all the adherents of a certain sheik, Ali el-Mograbi, a Moslem reformer, who emigrated to this place from the north of Africa many years ago, and whose preaching has been attended with remarkable success. As his fame grew he moved to Acre, where he exercises an extraordinary influence. The tenets of the sect of which he is the head are kept a profound secret, though there is nothing to distinguish the worship of the initiated from that of any ordinary sect of howling dervishes, to the outside observer, except the sparing use of the name of Mohammed. It is said, however, that their views are latitudinarian, and, that, so far from being exclusive or fanatic, are rather in the sense of extreme toleration for other religions. Whatever be the nature of their heterodoxy, it is not now interfered with. Indeed, it is hinted that the sheik counts among his followers some of the most highly placed officials in the empire, and there can be little doubt that his doctrines are spreading rapidly among Moslems, while even Christians have joined the society. A large new mosque is now in progress of erection at Haifa. The sheik himself, whose acquaintance I made subsequently, is now a very old man, regarded with the most extreme veneration by his followers, and the results of his teaching prove that he must be endowed with gifts of a very high order.

8

DOMESTIC LIFE AMONG THE SYRIANS.

HAIFA, March 1, 1884.—The ordinary tourists in Palestine who write books of their experience have so little opportunity of knowing the conditions which surround the daily life of a resident in a small country town, that a few details of domestic existence here, as contrasted with those of more civilized countries, may not be uninteresting. As a general rule, the foreigner who comes to a native town to settle down as a permanent inhabitant finds himself compelled more or less to adopt the manners and customs of the richer class of Syrians, which gives him an opportunity of becoming acquainted with their home life. Some of these are wealthy merchants or large landed proprietors, with incomes varying from $5000 to $15,000, though a man whose yearly revenue reached the latter amount, of which he would not spend half, would be considered a millionaire, and few small towns can boast of so great a capitalist. As, owing to the march of civilization, the richer classes have of late years taken to travel and the study of languages, persons occupying this position generally speak either French or Italian, have visited Paris, Constantinople, or Alexandria, and have a thin varnish of European civilization overlaying their native barbarism.

The rich families of the Syrian aristocracy are almost invariably Christians, but they have only recently shaken off the manners of their Mohammedan neighbours and conquerors. The women associate far more freely than they used to do with the men. They now no longer cover their faces, and although they still wear the "fustan," or white winding-sheet, which serves as cloak and head-dress in one, it nearly always conceals a dress of European make, while, instead of bare feet thrust into slippers, they have Paris bottines and stockings. The men of this class also dress in European garments, wearing, however, the red fez cap.

The domestic arrangements of a family of this description are by no means so refined in character as the external aspect of the house and its proprietor, when he is taking his exercise on a gorgeously caparisoned Arab horse, would suggest. If we are on sufficiently intimate terms with him to stay as a guest in his house, we find that his pretty wife, with her Paris dress and dainty chaussure, walks about in the privacy of the domestic home with bare, or at best stockinged, feet, thrust into high wooden pattens, with which she clatters over the handsome marble hall that forms the central chamber of the house, slipping out her feet and leaving the pattens at the door of any of the rooms she may be about to enter. She wears a loose morning-wrapper, which she is not particular about buttoning, but in this respect she is outdone by sundry dishevelled maid-servants, who also clatter about the house in pattens and in light garments that seem to require very little fastening in front. As for the husband, who, when he called upon you, might have come off the boulevards of Paris, barring always the red cap, he has now reverted absolutely into the Oriental. He wears a long white and not unbecoming garment that reaches from his throat to his heels, and his feet are thrust into red slippers. As he sips his matutinal cup of coffee and smokes his first narghileh of the day, there is nothing about him to remind you that he knows a word of any other language than Arabic, or has ever worn any other costume than that of his Eastern ancestors. He is sitting in his own little den, with his feet tucked under him on the divan which runs around the room, and with his wife in close proximity, her feet tucked under her, and also smoking a narghileh and sipping coffee.

Yet, if you call upon this worthy couple as a distinguished foreigner, in the afternoon, accompanied by your wife, and are not on intimate terms, you are received in a room which they never enter, except upon such state occasions, by the same gentleman, in a perfectly fitting black frock-coat and trousers, varnished boots, and a white waistcoat, and by the same lady, in a dress which has been made in Paris.

The furniture consists of massive tables with marble tops, and handsome arm-chairs and couches covered with costly satins. The walls are resplendent with gilt mirrors and with heavy hanging curtains. The floors are covered with rich carpets. There is a three-hundred-dollar piano, on which the lady never plays; and there are pictures, of which the frames are more artistic than the subjects—the whole having the air of a show repository of some sort. Indeed, if your host is at all taken by surprise, the first thing he does is to open all the shutters, as, except upon such occasions, the apartment is one of silent and absolute gloom. He has a guest-chamber, also furnished after a civilized style, in which he puts you, if you are going to stay with him, and he has so far adopted civilized habits that he sleeps on a bed himself, and not on mats on the floor, like his forefathers. His dinner is served on a table, which is spread as he has seen it spread in the houses of foreigners, but he retains the native cooking, the huge pillaw of rice, the chicken stew with rich and greasy gravy, the lamb stuffed with pistachio nuts, the leben or sour milk, the indescribable sweet dishes, crisp, sticky, and nutty, the delicious preserves of citrons, dates, and figs, the flat bread and the goat cheese, and the wine of the country.

Altogether, he gives you plenty to eat, drink, and smoke, but his conversational powers and ideas are limited, which is not to be wondered at, considering that there is not a book in the house. He tells you that the house cost him $9000, which does not seem likely to be an exaggeration when we look at the handsome marble floors and staircase, massive arches, and the extent of ground which is covered by spacious halls and ample courts.

The kitchen and offices, if you have the curiosity to look into them, are filthy in the extreme, and the process of cooking the dinner, performed by a slovenly female, had better not be too closely examined. His domestic establishment probably consists of four women and two or three men who look after the stables, in which are three or four handsome horses, and a garden requiring constant attention. He has no wheeled vehicle, for there are no roads. The women rarely take any other exercise than that of waddling on gossiping visits to each other, when their conversation turns entirely on domestic subjects, on the marital traits of their respective husbands, on congratulations on the arrival of children, if they are boys, and condolences if they are girls, and on hopeful speculation and encouragement if there are none at all; for of all misfortunes which can befall a Syrian lady, to be childless is the greatest. If there are grown-up daughters they are carefully protected from intimacy with young men, and marriages are arranged by the parents. The chances of making a good match depend more on the amount of the marriage-settlement than on their looks. If the family happens to be a large one it is not uncommon to see a young lady who has been brought up in what, in Syria, is considered luxury, married to some poor and distant connection, whose family live in the humblest manner. In such a case the contrast is greater than can be imagined in our country. She is transferred from the palatial residence I have described to a one-storied house which probably does not consist of more than two rooms, and where her husband's family live in the old style. Here she is received, perhaps, by his mother and sister, with whom she is to live; who wear the pure native costume; who have never had a shoe or stocking on in their lives; who sleep on mats on the floor, for there are no bedsteads; who partake of their meals squatting on their heels, for there are no chairs or tables; and who eat with their fingers, for there are no knives and forks.

If the newly married couple do not occupy the same room with the rest of the family, they share the other one with the domestic animals. These probably consist of a horse, a cow, and a donkey. For the sake of security they are stabled in the room of the master of the house. Their manger is on a level with the floor on which he and his bride sleep. I have before now shared such a room with a young married couple—she, the daughter of a wealthy man who lived in civilized style—and all night I have been disturbed by the crunching of the animals feeding within a few feet of where I was lying; with their constant rising up and lying down; with the movements of my host and hostess, who would get up constantly in the night, sometimes to feed the animals, which were required for work before sunrise, sometimes to replenish the charcoal fire, sometimes to attend to the baby, or to open the door and hold a whispered conference with some nocturnal visitor. As there is no undressing on going to bed, among these people, and as they indulge in long snoozes during the day, the night does not seem to be so especially devoted to sleep as with us. They appear to think that, as going to bed simply consists in lying down on the floor in your clothes, one part of the twenty-four hours will do as well for sleep as another, and their nights are restless accordingly. As a general rule, for persons who have not been long enough in the country to get used to insects, the nights are made restless from other causes.

It is curious, in the case of such a marriage as I have described, to see the change which takes place when the young wife leaves the retired village to which she has been banished, owing to the impoverished circumstances of her husband, to pay a visit to her own family. I scarcely recognize her when I meet her again. When last I saw her in her humble home her costume consisted of a thin sort of chemisette, a pair of full, baggy trousers fastened at the knee, leaving the legs and feet bare, and over these a skirt, and we were dipping our fingers amicably into the same dish of rice. Now I would walk down Broadway with her on my arm, and be rather proud of her fashionable " get up " than otherwise; and she handles her knife and fork with far greater dexterity than I did my fingers.

The wave of civilization is, however, rapidly encroaching upon these humbler classes. It is only natural that a girl brought up in this way should endeavour to introduce innovations into her husband's home. Within the last few years there has been a marked change in this respect, particularly in a town like Haifa, where the Christian population largely predominates. A veiled face is rarely to be seen, while women, even of the poorer classes, are introducing the fashion of wearing gowns, adding a table and a few chairs to their domestic furniture, and have even gone the length of sleeping on bedsteads, though I have not yet pried sufficiently into nocturnal mysteries to know whether, when they go to bed, they have progressed in civilization so far as to undress.

FISHING ON LAKE TIBERIAS.

HAIFA, April 2.—I have just returned from a trip into the interior, during which I have been exploring some new and interesting country. Instead of following the usual road to the eastward by way of the valley of Esdraelon, I struck in a northeasterly direction across the fertile plain of Acre, fording the Kishon at the point of its debouchure into the sea, where, after the winter rains, we are generally obliged to swim the horses, while we cross ourselves in a ferry-boat. In two hours from this point we strike the first low range of the Galilee hills, at a depression from which, in the times of the crusaders, the armies of Saladin used to issue forth to give them battle. Indeed, the whole ground over which we ride has been from time immemorial the scene of bloody warfare, and it is not impossible, considering how events are shaping themselves in the East, that it may become so again. Rising gently, by grassy vales carpeted with wild flowers, to a height of about five hundred feet, we shortly reach the picturesquely situated town of Shefr Amr, dominated by the extensive walls of its ruined castle.

This has been a place of considerable importance ever since, shortly after the destruction of Jerusalem, it was the seat of the Jewish sanhedrim. It was then called Shefaram, and is probably identical with the Kefraim which Eusebius says was six miles north of Legio, and with Hapraim, which we read in the Bible was assigned to the tribe of Issachar. Since then its name has been changed to Shefr Amr, or "the healing of Omar," from a tradition that Daher el-Amr, a prince who governed this country about a hundred and sixty years ago, recovered here from a severe illness. The fortress is said to have been built by his son Othman in 1761, and it does not appear to be older, though probably it occupies the site of a much more ancient castle. It covers a very extensive area of ground, with crenellated battlements, and contains stalls for four hundred horses. It is now partly ruined, but a portion of it is still sufficiently well preserved to be the residence of the Mudir, or local governor.

I scrambled by a most dilapidated stone stair to the top of the walls, and had a magnificent view over the surrounding country. The position is so commanding that I could well understand why Saladin chose it as a point from which he could harass the Franks who were besieging Acre, which town was plainly visible in the distance. I was informed that the whole of this extensive fortress was offered by the government for sale for $1500. The stones alone would be worth more than this amount, if it were not for the cost of transport, to say nothing of the area of land which they cover. But, as a matter of speculation, Barnum's pink-and-white elephant would be about as convenient a possession for a private individual. It is no wonder that it has been for some time in the market, or that the town itself, when capital is so scarce, should be a sleepy looking, stagnant place. Still, it is better built than the average; the houses are generally constructed of stone—many of them are of two stories—there is a fair bazaar, and a population of about two thousand five hundred inhabitants, of which fifteen hundred are Greek Christians, three hundred Moslems, six hundred Druses, and the remainder Jews. Some thirty families of Morocco Jews settled here as agriculturists about the year 1850, but after struggling against extortion for twenty years they had to give it up, and the colony is now extinct, the Jews now here being natives of the country. The Druse population is also rapidly diminishing from the same cause; a slow but steady migration takes place annually to the Druse mountains to the east of the Hauran, where they are practically independent of government control; there are also a few Protestants here, with a school-house, besides a convent and church of the Roman Catholic nuns (Dames de Nazareth), built in 1866, with a girls' school.

The only other interesting building at Shefr Amr is the

Greek church, which has been rebuilt on old foundations. The remains were evidently Byzantine work, dating probably from the fifth or sixth century. Many interesting tombs are to be found both north and south of the town. The most noteworthy has a handsome façade, covered with a design of a vine with grapes in bold relief, and with small figures of birds introduced. Each vine-plant grows out of a pot. On each side of the door is an effaced Greek inscription, with rosettes in lozenges below and birds above. Here, also, are fragments of Greek inscriptions, and on the left side-wall of the vestibule is a bas-relief of a lion and a small animal, perhaps a cub; on the right a lion, a cub, and a bird. The drawing is very primitive, and has a Byzantine appearance. Inside this tomb, which contains three loculi, there are mouldings round the principal arch, with tracery of vines and carvings of birds. These tombs are interesting because both the inscriptions and ornamentation belong to the Byzantine period, thus proving that the mode of sepulture practised by the Jews from the most remote date was continued by the Christians up to the fifth or sixth century after Christ.

Our way from Shefr Amr led through the beautiful oak woods which belong to that town, but which seem doomed to destruction, for I observed that many of the handsomest trees were girdled near the base, while numerous stumps bore testimony to this lamentable work of denudation. In a country where wood is becoming so rare it was heart-breaking to ride through this beautiful, park-like scenery and witness the work of destruction going on in spite of the government prohibition against felling timber. Emerging from these grassy glades we descend into the magnificent plain of the Buttauf, now a sheet of emerald green, as the young crops extend before us as far as the eye can reach. Traversing this fertile country one is more and more impressed with the incorrectness of the judgment of the ordinary tourist, who, confining himself to the route prescribed by Cook, is taken through the barren hills of Judea, and to one or two holy places in Galilee, and then goes home and talks about the waste and desolation of Palestine. The trite saying recurred to my mind as I looked on this wealth of grain:

"I pity the man who can go from Dan to Beersheba and
say that all is barren;" or, as my travelling - companion,
who was an American, more forcibly put it: "If ever I
meet a tourist who tells me that Palestine is barren, I'll
lick him."

But we were not on the tourist track, and it was not till we
reached Tiberias that we found specimens, and they were
too discreet in their remarks to give my friend an opportunity of expressing his views in the manner contemplated.
Here we took a boat and crossed the lake. I wanted to investigate the present fishing capabilities of these waters, but
I soon found that I had not the appropriate tackle. The
natives either fish with circular hand-nets, which they throw
with great dexterity, or with long hand-lines, which they
bait with small dead fish and haul in, thus trawling in a
rough way. They have no idea of fishing with a rod, and
mine came to grief, so that I had no opportunity of casting
a fly, but I think it not unlikely, from the way I saw the
fish jumping towards evening, that they would rise to it.
The natives catch their bait by poisoning the water with
pinches of a powder which they throw in near the margin.
In a few moments the minnows and small fish are to be seen
swimming lazily along the surface, completely stupefied, and
one has only to put one's hand in and take them out. The
fish we caught were principally of the bass or perch species,
averaging half a pound or more each. One of the boatmen
caught a dozen with two or three casts of the hand-net, but
it was useless to try with a rod without proper tackle. I
am convinced that a spinning artificial minnow, or a copper
spoon, would be very killing; so, of course, would be trawling live bait, but the natives know only their own primitive
style of fishing, and the idea of a rod and line, even with
the common angle-worm at one end and a fool at the other,
was entirely new to them. Indeed, scarcely any fish are
taken from the lake. There are only four boats on it, but
these are used more for transport than fishing purposes, and
the population is so sparse on the shores that there is no demand. We were assured by our boatmen, however, that
they occasionally took fish over five feet in length, and I
have seen enough of what may be done to decide me to go

there again some day properly provided, instead of relying
on native appliances.

The spot at which we were moored on the eastern shore
of the lake was immediately under a precipitous conical-
shaped hill, which rose abruptly to a height of twelve hundred feet from the waters. Its summit was crowned with
the ruins of the ancient city of Gamala. The modern name
for it is Kalat el-Hosn, but it owes its ancient appellation
to its shape, which is exactly that of a camel's hump. It is
interesting as having been a purely Jewish fortification, the
last that was sacked by Vespasian and Titus before the
siege of Jerusalem, and it has remained to this day exactly
as they left it. Josephus gives a very graphic account of
the siege, which took place in the last days of September,
sixty-nine years after the birth of Christ. Owing to the
precipices by which it was surrounded it was supposed to
be impregnable, and when, at last, after a twenty-nine
days' siege, it was found not to be so, the whole population who had survived its horrors, consisting of five thousand men, women, and children, flung themselves into the
yawning gulf below the ramparts, thus perishing by their
own act. Of the entire population only two women escaped alive.

When we compare the fighting of those days with the
siege of Paris, for instance, where the population surren-
dered because there was a little too much sawdust in the
bread, the results of modern as contrasted with ancient civilization suggest some curious reflections. That the civilization of those days was of a high order is attested by the
magnificent remains which still exist in Gamala. Here are
to be found, strewn over the ground, some thirty huge
granite columns, which must have been transported from
Egypt to this giddy height by engineering contrivances
which would puzzle the science of these days, and Corinthian capitals neatly cut in hard, black basalt, and sarcophagi and other monuments, all evidencing a high state
of art.

These ruins have hitherto been only superficially examined, and there can be no doubt that the investigations of
the Palestine Exploration Fund, when the society is per-

mitted by the Turkish government to prosecute their researches to the east of the Jordan, will bring many interesting treasures to light. I only regretted that I had no time to give to these ruins, as my objective point lay farther to the south and east.

A VISIT TO THE SULPHUR SPRINGS OF AMATHA.

HAIFA, April 15.—At the spot where the Jordan issues from Lake Tiberias there are two large mounds, a fragment of sea-wall, and a causeway on arches which projects into the river, dividing it from the waters of the lake, and suggesting that it may possibly, in ancient times, have formed the approach to a bridge. There is no bridge there now. The river swirls round the arches, which are choked with ruins and reeds, and in a broad, swift stream winds its way to the Dead Sea. Here, in old time, stood the Roman city of Tarichæa, built on the site of a Phœnician fortress of still older date. Nothing remains but heaps of rubbish covered with broken pottery, and fragments of sculpture; but it offers, probably, a rich field for future excavation. The modern name Kerak signifies in Syriac "fortress," and its natural position was remarkably strong, as the Jordan, after leaving the lake, takes a sharp bend to the westward and flows almost parallel with it, thus leaving an intervening peninsula on which the town was situated. It was defended on the westward by a broad ditch, traces of which still remain, connecting the Jordan with the lake, thus making the peninsula an island approached only by a causeway.

Josephus mentions Tarichæa as having been an important military post in the wars of his time. When I visited it the lake was unusually high, and the Jordan was unfordable, so we were obliged to ferry over, swimming our horses and mules a distance of seventy or eighty yards across the rapid current. Then we mounted, and galloped in a southeasterly direction, over a fertile plain, waving at this season of the year with luxuriant crops. I was so much struck with the fertility and agricultural capacity of this region that I made inquiry as to its ownership, and found that it had been presented by a former sultan to one of the principal Bedouin sheiks of this

Eastern country, and that he was exempt from all taxation. His lands extend to the foothills, where the Yarmuk issues from the mountains of Gilead and Jaulan, which we were now approaching. We had ascended these but a little way when a scene burst upon us which surprised and delighted us by its wild and unexpected grandeur. The Yarmuk here enters the plain of the Jordan on its way to join that river, with a volume of water fully equal to the latter, pouring its swollen torrent between two perfectly perpendicular precipices of basalt, which are about two hundred yards apart, and look like some majestic gateway expressly designed by nature to afford the river a fitting outlet to the plain after its wild course through the mountains.

On each side of these cliffs the country swells back abruptly to a height of seventeen hundred feet above the stream. At their base, here and there, the limestone or basalt rock, for the two formations are curiously intermixed, crops out sharply, forming terraces with precipitous sides. The more distant summits are fringed with oak forests. The general effect of the landscape, as you first burst upon it after leaving the Jordan valley, is in the highest degree impressive. The path, gradually ascending, winds along the edge of cliffs, rising to a sheer height of three hundred feet from the torrent which foams beneath. We are so close to their margin on the right that it makes us giddy to look down, while on the left hand grassy slopes, covered with wild flowers, rise to the base of other cliffs above us. For an hour we wind along these dizzy ledges. In one place I observed a hundred feet of limestone superimposed upon two hundred of basalt, the whole forming a black-and-white precipice very remarkable to look upon. In fact, my further investigations of this valley of the Yarmuk, some portion of which, I believe, we were the first to explore, have convinced me that it affords finer scenery than is to be found in any other part of Palestine. It is astonishing that it should have remained until now almost entirely unknown. Where the valley opened a little we saw beneath us a small plain, almost encircled by the river, and on it about twenty Bedouin tents. Our unexpected and novel appearance on the cliff above evidently caused some little stir and amazement, but they were too far

below us to communicate with, so we pushed on to a point
where the path suddenly plunged down by a series of steps
between walls of black basalt, making a very steep descent
for loaded mules, and one not altogether pleasant for mounted
men. It had the advantage of bringing us soon to the bottom, however, but not before my eyes were gladdened by
the sight of one of the objects for which I had undertaken
the trip.

At my feet, and separated from the river by a narrow
strip of land covered with bushes, was a long pool of bluish-
gray water, in marked contrast with the yellow stream.
Above it floated a very light mist, or, rather, haze. Following with the eye a little stream of the same coloured water
which entered it, past a primitive mill, I saw that it de-
bouched from another pond similar in colour, and evidently
its source, and to this our path was conducting us. It was
the first of the hot sulphur springs of Amatha, celebrated
by Eusebius as being much frequented in the time of the
Romans, and famous for their healing qualities. We soon
reached its margin, and, dismounting, tethered our horses
under the shade of a large tree, and stretched ourselves for
a rest after our ride, preparatory to a slight repast and a
more minute investigation of the springs and the ruins by.
which they are surrounded. Our nostrils were regaled by a
strong odour of rotten eggs, which left no doubt in our
minds as to the quality of the water in the immediate neighborhood. We were here at a depression of five hundred and
fifty feet below the surface of the sea, but the climate, which
must be intolerably hot in summer, was at this time of year
delightful. We were soon sufficiently rested to scramble
down to the pool, only a few yards below us, which was about
fifty yards long by thirty broad, and apparently five or six feet
deep. The temperature was 98°; and the taste of the water
very strongly sulphurous. Then we ascended a mound behind, covered with ruins, consisting principally of fragments
of columns, carved stone seats, and drafted blocks which
had been used for building purposes. Immediately behind
this mound was an extensive ruin, consisting of three arches
in a fair state of preservation. Two of the arches were fifteen or twenty feet high, and enclosed a semicircular space

or hall for bathers. On the other side was a vaulted building which partly enclosed what is at this day the only frequented spring. This is a circular pool. Part of the old masonry which enclosed it still remains. The pool is about twenty-five feet wide, with a temperature so high that I found it impossible to keep my hand in it. To my great astonishment, and to theirs also when they saw me suddenly appear, four or five Arabs were bathing in it. How their bodies could support the heat was to me a mystery. They did not support it long. They were no sooner in than out, their bodies looking as much like lobsters as the complexion of their skins would permit. They laughed, and invited me to join them. One or two were stretched full length on the identical stone slabs under the building on which, doubtless, two thousand years ago, the bathers of that date used to repose after having been half boiled alive.

This spring must be of immense volume, to judge by the size of the torrent which gushed from it, and which was crossed on stepping-stones, flowing away in what would be considered a good-sized trout stream, to mingle its waters with the Yarmuk after a course of a few hundred yards. We determined, when our tents arrived, to pitch them near this spring, on the brink of another stream which flowed in from the eastward, and which, though slightly sulphurous, was drinkable. Indeed, we did not object to taking a moderate amount of this wholesome medicament into our organisms. We found another strong spring, not quite so hot as the one in use, a little above our tents, so that there is no lack of water. Indeed, I doubt whether sulphur springs of so much volume exist anywhere else in the world. Not far from this, with its back to another mound, were the ruins of an old Roman theatre, some of the rows of seats still clearly discernible.

These springs are situated on a plain about a mile long and half a mile broad, semicircular in shape, the chord of the arc consisting of a line of basalt precipices, from which it slopes gradually to the river, which forms the bow. It is watered by a good fresh-water spring, which rushes from the base of the cliffs. The hot sulphur stream which issues from the pool we first visited turns a mill and then flows into the long, oblong pond I first saw from above. Here, after the exertions of the day, I determined to bathe. I never enjoyed a swim more than the one in this soft sulphur water, with a temperature of 95°. The pool was about one hundred yards long and ten wide, and out of my depth nearly throughout its length. The rocks, upon which I could sit comfortably up to my neck, where the stream entered the pool were covered with a heavy white deposit. The sensation afterwards was one of delicious languor; but my full enjoyment of the bath was a little marred by the fact that I had to walk a quarter of a mile back to the tents afterwards. I had a long talk on my way, to the miller, the solitary resident of this lonely but enchanting spot, and tried to induce him to desert the mill, of which he was the guardian, and act as my guide up the river on the following day; but he was either too conscientious, too lazy, or too ignorant—I suspect the latter, as I found by experience that all the information he gave me of a topographical nature was utterly erroneous. It was, therefore, with a pleasing sense of anticipation that we retired to rest, determined to trust to our own geographical instincts alone for our proposed exploration.

9

EXPLORATION OF THE VALLEY OF THE YARMUK.

HAIFA, April 30.—In my last letter I described the little-known hot sulphur springs of Amatha, with their extensive ruins, which indicate the celebrity they must have acquired in the days of the Romans. As the river Yarmuk above this point had, so far as I know, never been explored, I determined to push up the gorges through which it cleaves its way from the highlands of the Hauran to the valley of the Jordan.

Some years ago I had crossed it about thirty miles higher up, where it flows across a plateau at an elevation of 1800 feet above the sea. I was now standing on its margin, 550 feet below the sea. In the course of this thirty miles, therefore, it has a fall of 2350 feet. In other words, it was a fair presumption that there was a waterfall somewhere between those two points which had never been visited. The inquiries which I made from the natives on the point were unsatisfactory in their result. They seemed unable to discriminate between a rapid and a waterfall, and although they told me of many places where the water rushed with great violence, they seemed to know of none where it was precipitous. Upon one point they were, unfortunately, all agreed, which was that there was no path up the river-side, and that it would be found impossible at this time of year, when the stream was flooded, to force a way up. However, we determined to try. We thought we should be more free in our movements if we were unhampered by a guide, and directed only by our topographical instincts.

We therefore left our tents standing, as a sort of home on which to retreat in case of need, and struck across the small plain upon which the springs are situated, to a ford, which four days previously had been impracticable, but which we were assured we might now risk with safety. The stream was here a hundred yards broad, full of large rocks, and with a swift, turbid current that was by no means reassuring. The water came high up on our saddle-flaps, but we reached the other bank without mishap, and found ourselves skirting a dense thicket of tropical underwood, above which a grove of· at least three hundred date-trees reared their tufted crests. It was a spot unlike any other to be found in Palestine, for, although the heat in the valley of the Jordan, owing to its depression below the sea, is as great as this, and at its southern extremity greater, nowhere throughout its length is to be found a spot where the vegetation is so dense and luxuriant. Here were wild orange, lemon, fig, almond, and mulberry trees, oleanders growing to a gigantic size, besides butm, sidr, carob, and other trees peculiar to the country, and thickets of cane twenty feet high, forming a splendid cover for the wild boars with which we were assured this jungle abounds.

The Arabs come here at certain seasons to gather the dates, weave mats from the reeds, and harvest the crops of the slopes behind, which were now all waving with young grain. During that time they live in mud hovels, partly excavated in the ground, which were now deserted. There was only one inhabitant, and he ran a small mill, picturesquely situated under some date-trees, which was turned by a stream of hot sulphur water issuing from a copious spring, with a temperature of 112°. The Yarmuk, which flows beneath a cliff of black basalt three hundred feet high, half encircles this unique spot, and I regretted that I had not time to explore it thoroughly; but the jungle was so impenetrable that it was impossible to make any impression upon it without an axe, and then it would have been a work of time.

We now followed a track which approached the river bank. The hills, fortunately, on our side sloped back gradually. Midway up the sheer face of the cliff opposite we saw here and there caves, which, from their regular shape, appear at one time to have been inhabited, but if so, the only approach could have been from above, by baskets lowered to the mouths, similar to the method used by the

robbers who inhabited the Wady Hamam, behind the plain
of Gennesareth, in days of old. Now, instead of robbers in
baskets, we saw immense eagles sailing in front of the cliff,
in the crevices of which they had placed their nests. Crossing a spur which jutted into the river from the mountains
on our right, and which prevented our following it closely,
we obtained a splendid view of its course for some miles.
To our left were basalt and limestone cliffs, and above them
steep, sloping grass lands, now carpeted with wild flowers.
Above them again were more crags and cliffs, and then the
rim which marked the edge of the plateau, fifteen hundred feet above us. To the right the hills sloped back
more slowly, cleft here and there by wild, rocky valleys,
while their summits were fringed with oak forests. Here
and there the river foamed between precipices on both sides,
and we began to perceive that the task of exploration was
by no means easy. But it was perhaps all the more interesting. We made our horses scramble where only goats had
been before, now along the base of the cliff over huge boulders, now half-way up its precipitous side, when prudence
suggested that horse and rider should separate, and each be
responsible for his own life and limbs. Now we forced our
way through tangled thickets of flowering shrubs that clung
to the rocky sides where they were less steep, and now, utterly baffled, diverging from the river and toiling up a steep
grassy slope, only to slip and scramble down it again on the
other side so as to regain the margin of the stream.

Our progress was necessarily slow, not only owing to the
natural obstacles we encountered, but to the fact that we
were mapping the country as we advanced; but the scenery
by which we were surrounded was too romantic to be hurried over, and too interesting, from its novelty, not to be
carefully noted. At last we reached a point where there
had been a land-slide, leaving bare one precipice a thousand
feet high, while it formed another above the stream, which
it had displaced. Nothing remained for it but to attempt
another ford, and try our luck on the opposite bank. This,
to the amazement of some Bedouins, who watched us from
it and waved us back, we succeeded in accomplishing, not
without a narrow escape on the part of one of our party who,

boldly leading the way, got entangled among the rocks and eddies. We were cordially welcomed by an Arab sheik, as we scrambled like half-drowned rats up the bank. He invited us to his tents, which were pitched a few hundred yards back from the stream, on a small plain. Here mats were spread for us, coffee roasted, pounded, and prepared, and, the young men gathering around, we proceeded, under the influence of an abundant distribution of cigarettes on my part, to exchange ideas. They told us they belonged to a village two and a half hours distant, and were therefore not nomads. They came hither at this season of the year to pasture their herds and look after their crops. I hardly like to report the conversation of these poor people as they came to confide their grievances to us, without our in any way inviting their confidence. Suffice it to say that the recent measure of the government by which it has been decided to substitute for the dime, which has heretofore been the share of the government in the entire produce of every village, an assessment based on the highest five years' average, has produced the greatest discontent among the rural population, whose poverty and distress, already extreme, owing to the extortion of the tax-gatherers even under the old system, and the withdrawal of the bone and sinew of the country by conscription, especially during the recent Russo-Turkish war, will thus be intensified. In fact, these poor people were driven to such desperation that they were most unreserved in their language, and although they are the most long-suffering and much-enduring of races, there is a point where the crushed worm will turn. However great the financial exigencies of the empire may be, they would better be met by a thorough reorganization and reform in the whole system of tax-collecting, than in adding to the burdens of the people, which are already greater than they can bear.

Our hosts assured us that we should find any further attempt to ascend the river impracticable, and that there was a place where the water fell for a considerable height, but we could only reach it by making a circuit, which would take a day. However, we determined to judge for ourselves, and succeeded in getting about a mile farther, when we found the river shut in by precipices on both sides. It was impossible to descend to it from the brow of the cliff on which we stood, much less to ford it afterwards, or to scramble up the precipice on the other side. There was nothing for it but to make an ascent of at least fifteen hundred feet, either to the high plateau of Jaulan, on the right, or to recross the river where we had already forded it, and scramble up the steep, wooded hillsides of Ajlun until we could find a path leading in the desired direction. This latter course we determined to adopt; so we returned to the Arab tents, crossed the river more successfully than before, warned by our previous experience, and braced ourselves for a twelve-hundred-feet climb up the best track we could find, under the guidance of one of our recent Arab acquaintances. I had been on the lookout all through the day for ruins, and I was now cheered by the intelligence that I should find some on the summit of the hill we were climbing. Such proved to be the case. The situation, at an elevation by my aneroid of about eleven hundred feet above the sea, would indicate that in old time it was a fortress. It was supplied with water by cisterns, the remains of which still exist, some of them demijohn-shaped, and one about ten feet square and twenty feet to the bottom, which, however, was much filled up. There were many piles of huge blocks of drafted stone, but I did not observe any columns or carving, and I think the remains date from a period anterior to the Roman occupation. The modern name of the place is Tel el-Hösn, but its existence has heretofore been unknown, except to the Arabs of the neighborhood, and its discovery was some compensation to me for the effort I had made to reach it.

EXPLORATION ON THE YARMUK.

Haifa, May 15.—From the ancient fortress of El-Hösn
we crossed a spur to a high projecting point, from which
we could look down a sheer precipice one thousand feet
high, which had been formed by a land-slip, to the bed of
the river. Forcing their way impetuously through a gorge
opposite, the tributary waters of the Rukkad mingled their
clear stream with the turbid Yarmuk, after a rapid course
from their source in the highlands of Jaulan, from which elevated plateau they are precipitated in a magnificent waterfall eight hundred feet high. All this scenery is as yet absolutely unknown and unexplored, this fall having only recently been discovered, by my travelling companion on this
occasion. I regretted being unable to visit it, but we were
limited for time, and although it was only hidden from
view by a projecting spur of the valley, so broken up is this
country by precipitous ravines and gorges, that it would
have taken us a day's hard riding to reach it.

It was with regret that we found ourselves compelled
to leave the elevated position on which we now stood, and
which commanded an extensive view, limited in the extreme
east by the lofty mountains of the Jebel Druze; and, steering
our way by compass, struck a southeasterly direction, over
a park-like, undulating country, covered with oak forest,
with occasional patches of cultivation. This part of the
country to the east of the Jordan, which is called the Kefe-
rat, is thinly inhabited, the villages being very small,
squalid, and far apart, but it is a country all waiting to
yield of its abundance to some future race who may turn
its magnificent resources to good account. In many places
the trees were festooned with vines, the grapes of this district being celebrated, but the population pay little heed to
their cultivation, for it is impossible to protect them from

robbers. The Bedouins consider the sedentary inhabitants
as lawful spoil, and raid over these lands at will, practically
almost unchecked by the authorities, whose administrative
hold on the country is of the slenderest description. It is,
in fact, chiefly exercised at those times when it is necessary
to send the mounted police into the villages to collect the
taxes, and they clear up all that the Bedouins may have
left, so that these poor people are engaged in a perpetual
struggle to keep body and soul together, and although they
are surrounded by a fertile country which, if it were properly cultivated, would make them wealthy, they only cultivate enough for their barest necessities, and have not the
heart to attempt to accumulate wealth which they would
not be permitted to keep. Situated at an elevation of about
eighteen hundred feet above the sea, these high, wooded,
fertile table-lands form a district which, should this country ever come to be occupied under more favourable conditions than now exist, will certainly be among the first to
attract an agricultural population. The wild, rocky gorges
by which it is intersected render the task of exploration,
without a guide, one attended with some uncertainty. We
take our bearings by compass, gallop under the vine-trel-
lised trees, over green, level slopes, or along inviting glades,
till we are suddenly brought up by a precipice down which
it is impossible to scramble, which opens unexpectedly in a
gulf at our feet. The spot we are making for is not half a
mile distant, but we have to follow the edge of the gorge in
the opposite direction. Then we come upon another at
right angles, which forces us to double back still farther; so
at last we wind round the head, first of one ravine and then
of another, till we find two hours have elapsed since we
were driven back on our tracks; the half-mile has now extended over five or six, the sun is declining with a rapidity
which seems accelerated because the daylight has become
so precious to us that we cannot bear to anticipate the prospect of its vanishing. At last we reach the head of the
valley which has baffled us so long, and are compensated by
discovering a ruin. Here are sarcophagi, rock tombs and
cisterns, and carved fragments. Fortunately we come across
a peasant, the only one we have seen since leaving the

river, and he tells us that its name is Halcebna. We write it down and take its bearings as well as we can, for it is unknown heretofore, but the day is too far spent for us to linger for minute examination. The peasant tells us that the best thing we can do, if we would get back to our tents, is to go down the valley we had intended to cross. We follow his advice and have no reason to regret it. It is a *Wâdi Mâla* of grandeur and beauty, though on a small scale. We pass between curved limestone cliffs, the fissures in which are filled with underwood, the shrubs cling to the rocks, from which at one place gushes a copious stream of water, by the side of which we hurry with it down the valley, till we get back to the Yarmuk once more, and, wearied and exhausted, reach our tents in the gathering darkness. Here we find a picturesque-looking Kurd waiting to receive us; he is an old soldier, and shows us the scars of five wounds—not all, however, received in military service, but for the most part in Arab skirmishes. He is the agent of the government in these parts, and also of the native capitalist who is the practical owner of the land, which is cultivated by an Arab tribe whose tents are pitched near us; they are heavily indebted to the capitalist aforesaid, who allows them enough of the crops to keep them from starving and takes all the rest himself. And our Kurdish visitor is his collector of revenue. He seems to have some difficulty in protecting his employer's interests, and tells us triumphantly that only a few nights before he has shot an Arab whom he caught plundering. He says that during the bathing season as many as a hundred tents may be seen pitched round the sulphur springs of Amatha, and that their fame is so great that they are visited by invalids from Aleppo and Damascus. The fact, however, that Tiberias, which is five hours distant, is the nearest place in which supplies of any sort can be procured, and that the only accommodation to be obtained is the patient's own tent, must operate as a serious obstacle to the use of these springs, about whose curative value, however, there can be no doubt.

Our way from Amatha lay back across the Jordan valley, which at this season of the year is a sheet of waving grain, cultivated by a branch of the Beni Sukkr Arabs, whose large encampment, with the handsome tent of the sheik in the centre, we pass without stopping, for we are in full pursuit at the moment of five gazelles, which scamper across country, giving us a good run, in which we should have certainly overtaken them had we not been checked by a ravine. We cross the Yarmuk at a point near its junction with the Jordan, and where it carries a volume of water certainly equal to that stream. The Jordan here falls in a fine rapid of about thirty feet in a distance of less than a hundred yards, and would furnish splendid water-power for mills in a part of the country which is much in want of them. The ancient Jisr el-Medjamich spans the stream at this point, guarded by a government toll-house. Crossing it, we determined to try a short-cut up the little-known Wady Bireh, which is watered by a clear, purling brook, which, if it were utilized, would make this valley one of the most fertile and attractive in this part of the country. After following its winding course for some miles, we found it finally narrowing into a crooked gorge, the sides of which approach so closely as scarcely to admit the passage of a loaded camel between the overhanging rocks. Indeed, when we afterwards described our route to the natives they said it was never used by them. However, it gave us an opportunity of seeing some most romantic scenery, and by shortening the way enabled us to reach Nazareth, jaded and worn out, it is true, the same night.

Haifa, May 27.—Travellers who have gone from Nazareth to Tiberias must be familiar with the singular outline of a mountain which they perceive to the left of the road, with its two rocky crests separated from each other by a hog's back about a quarter of a mile long, and called the Horns of Hattin. The summit of the higher peak, one thousand feet above the sea, and about three hundred feet above the plain across which they are riding, forms a conspicuous object in a landscape which, at this point, is one of singular interest and beauty. Rising like a gigantic natural pulpit, tradition has since declared it to be the Mount of the Beatitudes, and asserts that it was from this picturesque elevation that Christ delivered that sermon which has exercised so vast an influence on mankind ever since.

Whether this be so or not, it is certain that the plain on which the audience was supposed to have gathered which listened to it, was the scene, about eleven hundred and fifty-seven years afterwards, of the most memorable conflict in which the Crusaders ever engaged, for it was the one which lost them Palestine, and which resulted in the triumph of Saladin, the Saracen, and the slaughter or capture of the most powerful and celebrated of the Crusading chiefs. At the extremity of the plain, and immediately beneath one of the horns of the mountain, there is a precipitous gorge, down which some of the hardly pressed Crusaders vainly attempted flight, the horses and their riders, heavily panoplied with armour, only escaping the spear of the Arab to meet an even more terrible fate, as they hurled themselves headlong down the rocky precipice. As, dismounting from my active steed, I allowed him to pick his own way down this dangerous defile, I looked with interest at the scene of the disaster, and listened to the story of my guide, who narrated how, only twenty years ago, a fight had taken place here between a celebrated Bedouin chief and a Kurdish tribe, in which the latter were signally defeated on the old Crusading battle-ground, and, seeking safety, like the Christian warriors, in the direction of this treacherous gorge, left sixty dead men and horses at the bottom.

These traditions and associations served to enhance the novelty and picturesqueness of the view before me as I entered the gorge, for it was now the scene of a great gathering of the sheiks and chiefs of the Druse nation, who come here annually on a pilgrimage to the shrine of one of their most celebrated saints, at which I was fortunate enough to be allowed to assist, a privilege which, so far as I am aware, had not before been granted to a foreigner. The building which forms this sacred resort has been erected by the Druses over the tomb of a certain holy man called Schaib, but exactly who Schaib was my utmost endeavours failed to discover. The Moslems say that he is Jethro, the father-in-law of Moses; but when I asked the Druses whether Moses had married Schaib's daughter, they denied it. Then a Jew of the country, familiar with the Druses, suggested that Schaib was Balaam, but they refused altogether to admit that an ass had ever spoken to their holy man. He had crossed the Red Sea with Moses, they said, and after Moses' death had been ordered by God to bury him, and had done so, and had fought against a mighty king and prevailed against him, and had himself been buried here, and he was the Father of all Prophets and the elect of God, and there were none greater or more sacred than he. I thought possibly he might be Joshua, but him they knew by his own name, so I have given up the personality of Schaib as an insoluble mystery. He is one of those Druse characters whom their tradition has interwoven with Biblical history, but the tomb which they thus honour is undoubtedly considered by Moslems to be the tomb of Jethro, who is known among them as Schaib; and the Rabbi Bar Simeon, writing in 1210 A.D., mentions the tomb of Jethro as being at Hattin. Considering that Jethro lived in Midian, on the shores of the Red Sea, it seems rather unlikely that he should be buried here. However, that is a detail. The fact remains that the spot is one of great sanctity, but is infinitely more venerated by the Druses than by the Moslems. Indeed, I met a Moslem who laughed at the Druses' superstitions in regard to it, and who was as much surprised and puzzled as I was when he heard them deny that Moses was the son-in-law of the buried saint.

The building which the Druses have erected over the old, dilapidated Moslem shrine, which still stands here, has already cost more than $5000, all subscribed by the Druses among themselves, and it is not yet completed. It consists of a courtyard, one side of which is formed by the solid rock, while the other contains chambers. The roof forms a terrace, and above it, also partly faced by rock, is a large upper chamber surmounted by a dome. The scene as we approached was very striking. The Druse sheiks, desirous of doing honour to their guest, formed in two lines to receive me, while guns were fired off and songs of welcome were sung. The white building, with its terraces crowded by men and women in bright-coloured garments, harmonized well with the romantic character of the scenery, and formed a picture calculated to impress the imagination.

I was ushered by my hosts into an anteroom, after exchanging cordial greetings with those I knew, and being introduced to those who were still strangers to me; and then we all squatted on carpets, thus occupying all the four sides of the room, which assumed the appearance of a sort of council-chamber. As, with the exception of the Japanese, the Druses are the politest and most courteous people I have ever met, a great part of our time is taken up in salutations and compliments. First we press our hands to our hearts and lips and foreheads, with great effusion. No sooner are we seated than we repeat this process as if we had not done it just before. Then, in flowery language, we ask each other repeatedly after our respective healths, and are profuse in our thanks to God that we are well, that they are well, that our families are well, and that we are permitted to enjoy the great privilege of meeting one another. Then coffee is brought in, and after drinking it we go through the same process of saluting each other all around. Then I request permission to light a cigarette, which is necessary, as the Druses never indulge in tobacco; indeed, the more rigid eschew coffee.

As I look around at the twenty or thirty sheiks, solemnly seated with their backs to the wall, I am much struck with the dignity of their bearing, the intelligence of their countenances, and their superior physique generally. As a rule, there is a religious and a secular sheik to each village, so that about half my entertainers exercise spiritual functions, and half temporal. There was nothing, however, in their dress to distinguish them. They all wore white turbans, black or striped *abbas*, or wide-sleeved cloaks reaching to the knee, beneath which was the usual flowing garment of the Oriental, and their feet were bare. Many of the Druses, both men and women, have brown hair and blue eyes, and complexions as light as our own, and some of both sexes are singularly handsome.

As all the sheiks had not yet assembled, we had not been long in conclave—indeed, had hardly exhausted our stock of compliments—before the singing of men and the firing of guns announced a distinguished arrival. Then we all went out to meet him, and I was interested in watching the method of greeting. I soon perceived that the forms of etiquette are most rigidly adhered to among them. When two of equal rank meet they clasp hands, and there appears a slight struggle — as they both bow their heads and lift their clasped hands towards their lips—as to who shall kiss the back of the other's hand first. This involves rather a curious twisting movement of the hands and heads, which produces a somewhat comical effect. Let any of my readers make the experiment, and, grasping each other's hands, try and kiss the respective backs of each without unclasping them, and the effort as to which shall succeed first makes quite a little game. My servant, who is a Moslem from Egypt, declared that they each kissed their own hands, and the argument waxed so hot between us that we had to refer the matter to a Druse to know which was right, so difficult was it to perceive exactly what really happened. If one felt himself inferior in rank to the other, he always succeeded in kissing the other's hand first, and snatching his own away before the other had time to kiss it. But if the dif-

ference in rank was still more marked, the superior made
no pretence of wanting to kiss the inferior's hand after his
own had been kissed.

Next came a great struggle as to who should take the
lowest place. The place of honour was a particular corner,
which, had I been better versed in their etiquette, I should
have insisted on declining; but I innocently accepted it, and
then the invariable struggle came as to who should be forced
to sit next to me. I observed that in most instances the re-
fusals were of that formal kind which young ladies indulge
in when they have made up their minds to sing, but decline
to do so until after they have been sufficiently pressed. I
suppose there were envyings, jealousies, pride, and other
base passions among my hosts as among other men, but if
so they certainly concealed their failings with marvellous
skill. One could not but be struck with the air of genuine
harmony and affectionate cordiality which seemed to prevail among them.

The respect they showed to the head sheik of all, and the
warm terms in which they spoke of him to me in private,
could not but have been sincere, and, indeed, he seemed to
deserve it. Though only a young man of about thirty-five,
he inherited his honours, coming as he did of one of the
most honourable Druse families; yet his distinguishing
characteristic was a marked humility and consideration for
others. His wife was certainly the most charming and lady-
like person I have yet seen among Druse women. She was
not more than three or four and twenty, with a fair complexion, magnificent eyes, and an elegant figure, a grace
natural to her characterizing all her movements. Indeed,
had she been dressed in the latest Parisian fashion, she
would have been a strikingly attractive person in any society,
nor would it have been possible by her features or complexion to distinguish her from any pretty American woman.
As it was, her dress was exceedingly becoming. On her
head was a long white veil; a loose, tunic-shaped jacket,
with full sleeves, covered an embroidered sort of chemisette,
and her short, flowing skirts partially concealed full trousers,
tight around the ankle. On her wrists were a pair of heavy
gold bracelets, and she was the only woman of the party

who indulged in the luxury of shoes and stockings. The
shoes, however, were always slipped off before entering a
room.

The Druse women of Galilee do not, like those of the
Lebanon, cover their faces; and, indeed, they are allowed
a freedom which contrasts strongly with the position of
their Moslem sisters. This wife of the head sheik enjoyed
a privilege denied to any of the other women who had accompanied their lords to the shrine, for she frequently sat
in the men's council, taking part in the conversation, though
modestly, and with great reserve. In talking to me, which
she did freely, I found that she was bright and intelligent,
and full of inquiries as to the manners and customs of the
females of civilization, in regard to whom she had an intense
curiosity. I do not know, however, whether, if it had been
fully gratified, it would have tended very much to her moral
and intellectual improvement. She had brought her baby
with her, and was generally surrounded by some of the
more prominent of the other ladies, who, however, treated
her with a marked deference. I watched her mode of greeting the different ladies as they arrived, with even more interest than I had that of the men. We read in the Bible of
people falling upon each other's necks; this was exactly
what the Druse women did, and very prettily and gracefully
they did it, while they recognized the men by a distant,
modest, and deferential salutation.

THE GREAT FESTIVAL OF THE DRUSES.

HAIFA, May 30.—Towards evening of the day on which I arrived at the great Druse shrine of Neby Schaib, near Hattin, most of the sheiks who were expected had arrived, with their retinues. It might have been a feudal gathering of olden time; the noisy welcome of the chiefs, the clansmen singing war-songs and firing guns, the women following on donkeys, all combined to make a scene which carried one back to the Middle Ages, and I never wearied looking at it.

My tent was pitched on the lowest terrace of the sacred building, for it is not allowed to the unbeliever to pass the night within those holy precincts. Indeed, it was an unprecedented privilege to be permitted even to camp on the terrace, where there was only just room for my tent, nor should I have been allowed to edge in so close to the mysteries of Druse worship had there been five square yards of level ground within a quarter of a mile. But the precipitous rocks frowned above us all around, and the comparatively open space below was crowded with camels, horses, and donkeys, compelled to chum together, whether they liked it or not, and where the incessant din added to the general uproar of the place. The constant and stentorian braying of donkeys, varied occasionally by a horse fight, mingled with the barking of dogs, the shrill scream of welcome or ululation of women, the loud singing and clapping of hands of the dancing circles, and the firing of guns, all augured badly for a night's rest.

However, there was no thought of going to bed yet; great piles of rice on which whole sheep had been skilfully dissected were now borne in on round platters, each carried by two men. There must have been from three to four hundred people now collected at the shrine, and the feeding of

10

such a multitude was no joke. Of these nearly half were
women, all in gala dress, the favourite colours being blue,
green, and red. I don't know that I ever remember in the
same number to have seen a larger proportion of pretty
women.

When I went up-stairs to the large vault which contains
the tomb of the prophet I came upon them unexpectedly,
all seated on the floor around the circular mats of parti-
coloured straw which they use as tablecloths. The room,
which was seventy feet long by forty wide, was crowded
with this laughing, chattering, feeding, feminine multitude,
with their glorious eyes, white, regular teeth, bewitching
smiles, and delicate fingers plunged up to the knuckles into
huge piles of greasy rice. Their invitation that I should
come and take pot-luck with them produced a mixed sentiment in my breast. However, it was only said as a joke,
for even had I desired I should not have been allowed to
accept it. The entertainment was exclusively feminine, and
I was surprised at so little reverence being shown to the
venerated shrine by the close proximity of all this festivity.

Taking off our shoes and picking our way between these
festive groups, we reached, at the other end of the hall, the
tomb of the prophet, enclosed in a wooden screen hung
with red cloth, while over the tomb itself was spread a sort
of green silk pall, embroidered with gold stars. Some of
the Druse sheiks who accompanied me reverently pressed
their lips to this. They then pointed out a square block of
limestone, in the centre of which was a piece of alabaster
containing the imprint of a human foot of natural size.
The toes are defined with more clearness than is usual in
sacred footprints of this nature, and the Druses stooped and
kissed the impression, assuring me that, if I would do so, I
should feel that the rock exuded moisture, and that its peculiarity was that it was never dry. I was constrained out
of politeness to appear to accede to their wishes, though I
refrained from testing the condition of the stone with my
lips, as I felt suspicious, considering how many lips had preceded mine, that any little dampness I might discover might
be easily accounted for otherwise than supernaturally.

The question of footprints in the rock suggests some interesting considerations. There are one or two others in different parts of Palestine, as in the mosque at Hebron, built over the Cave of Macpelah, and as they are artificial, it is probable that they are coronation stones. We know by tradition that in ancient times a custom of this sort existed in the British Isles, where footprints in rock exist, and there are Scriptural allusions which give colour to a similar hypothesis in Palestine. The pillar alluded to in the crowning of kings was probably nothing more nor less than a coronation stone; and the habit which existed in some countries of making the king stand with his foot in the impression of a print in the stone, as a sign that he would walk in the footsteps of his predecessor, may account for their occurrence in Palestine. Thus we read that Abimelech "was made king by the oak of the pillar that was in Shechem;" when Joash was anointed king by Jehoida, "he stood by the pillar as the manner was," and the same king "stood by a pillar to make a covenant, and all the people stood to the covenant." The place of the footprint at Neby Schaib, in its elevated position above the copious fountain which gushes from the base of the opposite cliff, and the remarkable cropping up of the alabaster through the rock, rendered it just such a spot as would be likely to be chosen for such a purpose, and I think we may fairly hazard the conjecture that the footprint at the Neby Schaib marks the coronation stone of the rulers in this part of the country in early Jewish, or perhaps even more ancient, times. It is far otherwise with the footprint of Buddha on Adam's Peak in Ceylon, and with that of Christ on the Mount of Olives, both of which I have seen, and both of which are natural, and bear only a fancied resemblance to the human foot, that of Buddha being a depression in the rock about five feet long. In the case of the print under consideration, there was a split in the rock across the centre, which the Druses accounted for by saying that when the prophet stepped here he split the rock.

Meanwhile the women, having finished their repast, now prepared for a dance on the terrace. The music consisted of singing, with a hand-clapping accompaniment, executed

principally by the spectators, while the dancers formed in
a circle, holding each other by the waistband, and rhyth-
mically swaying to and fro, as from time to time they
changed the character and the measure of their step. All
their movements were decorous, if not all actually graceful.
Sometimes one would separate herself from the ring, and,
advancing to the centre, perform a *pas seul*, while the others
danced around her, she the while flinging her hands aloft,
waving in each a light muslin veil, and making it float above
her head, while she kept time with her feet. But among
the Druses, as among most Orientals, the hands play as
prominent a part in their terpsichorean exercises as their
feet. The eminently good looks of the dancers were set off
by their becoming costumes. These consisted of outer
cloaks of a rich colour, linen or woollen, open all down the
front so as to display the whole underdress, with light sleeves
cut above the elbow, the whole trimmed either with wide
bands of reddish satin or with a rich cross-stitch embroidery
of silk. The unsightliness of the baggy trousers of dark
blue is lost under the long, semi-transparent chemise, which
falls over them as a white tunic, generally striped with
thicker white, and tastefully embroidered with silk around
the neck. The white sleeves of the chemise, widely pointed, and which flow about the forearm after escaping from
the short cloak sleeve, form a simple but very graceful
feature of this costume, whether they float freely or are
twisted, for convenience in work, about the elbow. Scarfs
of various bright colours are wound below the waist, and
the cloak is usually caught together below the bosom by
a cord or button, giving that double girdle often presented in ancient classical costume. The simple long, white
cloth, with the centre of one edge drawn low upon the
forehead, its two ends hanging down the back almost to
the heels, bound fast by a wide fillet of brilliant colour
tied around the head, completes very attractively, with its
ancient Egyptian appearance, this simple but highly characteristic dress, which is enhanced by necklaces and ban-
gles, according to the rank and position of the wearer.

Our attention was now distracted by some rival perform-
ances of the male part of the community in the courtyard

below. Here the singing and clapping of hands were louder and more vehement, and time was given by one gentleman who played a pipe and another who was a sort of bandmaster, and directed the changes of time and step. Here the central figure who danced in the circle, instead of waving veils or handkerchiefs, flourished a sword with great grace and dexterity, slashing it about in excellent time to the music, and within an inch sometimes of the noses, sometimes of the legs, of the performers. The dancers worked themselves up at last to a high pitch of excitement and perspiration, new ones perpetually dashing into the ring and taking the places of those who were exhausted.

At last the gayeties were put an end to by the sheiks, who took no part in them themselves, but looked on with solemn dignity. The "okâl," or initiated in the holy mysteries, despise all such frivolities, which are reserved for women and the uninitiated. Most of these had been sitting in a circle in a quiet part of the terrace by themselves, discussing either religion or the political questions affecting the interests of their nation, most probably the latter; but the hour had now arrived when the serious business of the night was to begin and festivity was to cease. The uproar died away, the elders wished us good-night, and silently trooped up the stone stairs to the great hall, whence issued the younger part of the female community, and I retired to the door of my tent to sit in the bright moonlight and contemplate the strange surroundings of my night quarters.

Soon there broke upon the stillness of the night the measured cadence of a sacred chant. Now it swelled, as numerous voices, male and female, took up the chorus; now it died away to a single voice. Never before, probably, had stranger been able to listen so closely to the prayers and invocations which characterize the mysterious and occult worship of the Druses. One thing surprised me, which I think is not generally known, and this is that women undoubtedly take part in some of their forms of worship, not, however, in all, for on the following night they were excluded, and the service was conducted by males alone. At last I went to bed, but not to sleep; the noises of the animals, to which I was in close proximity, for a long time banished repose, and when at last it came fitfully, I heard ever and anon the rhythm of the sacred chant. Throughout two entire nights, to my certain knowledge, did these Druses pray and sing, though, as I fell asleep on each occasion towards morning, I cannot precisely say at what hour their service was concluded.

There can be no doubt that, while these gatherings are essentially religious in their character, they are largely used for political purposes. In this respect a wonderful organization exists among the Druses. Although the nation may be said to be divided into three sections, of which one—by far the largest—occupies the mountains of the Hauran, known as the Jebel Druse, another the mountains of the Lebanon, and the third and smallest the hills of northern Galilee, they keep up a close contact with each other, and meetings such as these afford opportunities for them to hold counsel in regard to the political fortunes and condition of the nation. The Druses of the Jebel Druse, who form two thirds of the nation, have only this year made peace with the Turkish government, with whom they were at war last year. The impracticable nature of the country, combined with their own bravery, enables them to maintain a sort of quasi independence. They are free from the conscription, have a governor, or Caimakam, chosen from among themselves, and their taxes are little more than nominal. The Druses of the Lebanon come under the special statute relating to the government of that province, and as this is subject to the supervision of the six European treaty powers, their position is secured, and they have no cause of grievance, though they are in close contact with their neighbours, the Maronites, with whom they live on terms of considerable tension. The Druses of Galilee differ in position from the other two sections of the nation, in that they enjoy no privileges of any kind, but are, on the contrary, less fortunately placed in their relations to the government than either Moslems or Christians, the former being naturally, to a certain extent, favored by their government, and the latter being always able, in case of a grievance, to appeal to some Christian European power. These Druses are, however, absolutely without protection of any kind, and have many grievances unredressed, and many acts of hostility on the part of the peasantry of other religions, among whom they live, to struggle against. The only consolation they enjoy is the support and comfort they derive from the close tribal family connection which they keep up with the other two more fortunate branches of the nation. It is easy to perceive, therefore, why they should attach great value to these religious gatherings, and utilize them for secular purposes. There can be no doubt that the character of their religion, with the secrecy which surrounds it, enables them to organize in a special manner, and that the theocratic element which enters into their political constitution gives them a cohesion, a unity, and a power for combined action which the Christian sects, with their jealousies, bigotry, and internal dissensions, do not enjoy.

HAIFA, June 22.—While my two days' experiences at the Neby Schaib, described in my last two letters, were in the highest degree novel and picturesque, and enabled me to obtain an unusual insight into the manners and customs and religious observances of the Druse nation, my stay at this celebrated shrine of their pilgrimage was by no means destitute of archæological interest. The village of Hattin, which is in the immediate neighbourhood of the tomb of the prophet, forms the centre of many sacred and historical associations, while it is in itself a place of unusual beauty of situation.

In the overhanging rocks on the other side of the gorge, immediately opposite my tent, were several sepulchral chambers, all traditional burying-places of persons more or less historical. Some of these I examined. The largest was one entered by a doorway, which had recently been inhabited, for the framework of a wooden door to it still remained. It was supposed to be the burial-place of one of Jethro's daughters. We are told by Josephus that his family followed the Israelites out of Midian. Its last occupant was an Indian hermit, who had lived here in solitude for three years, when, getting tired of his seclusion, he had gone to Tiberias about a year ago, married there, and immediately disappeared with his wife, no one knew whither.

About a hundred yards from the Neby there issues from the mouth of the gorge a copious spring which, in fact, forms the source of a brook, that ultimately finds its way into the Sea of Galilee. It commences its beneficent course, however, by fertilizing a large area immediately surrounding the village, where flourishing gardens of oranges, lemons, figs, apricots, pomegranates, and other fruit-trees impart an air of luxuriant fertility to the landscape not common in

these parts. Among these gardens is one which was purchased a few years ago by Sir Moses Montefiore, and presented by him to the Jews of Tiberias. Here I went, at the
invitation of the overseer, and, seated on mats under the
spreading arms of a fig-tree, I listened, while I sipped his
coffee, to his tale of woe: how last year he had resisted what
he considered an exorbitant charge for taxes, how his garden had in consequence been invaded and despoiled by the
tax-gatherers; how, being a British-protected subject, and
the garden being the property of British subjects, he had
appealed to the British consul for redress; how he had
spent £50 in the effort to obtain it, and had found British
protection not only a broken, but an expensive reed to trust
to; and how he was driven, by the refusal of the British
government to protect its subjects, to try and protect himself by the plentiful expenditure of backsheesh. I explained
to him that it was not the habit of the British government
to protect its subjects, but rather to abandon them, even
though they might be of exalted rank, and their lives might
be at stake; and then I went in search of ruins.

I found some immediately adjoining the garden. What
had evidently once formed part of an old Byzantine church
was here turned into a mosque; and upon one of the stones
was a curious Cufic inscription. In some of the other gardens were traces of foundations, indicating that in old times
Hattin must have been the site of a considerable town. It
is about two miles from the ruins of Irbid (which is no
doubt the Arbela of Josephus), and is probably the Caphar
Hittia of the Talmud, but I find no mention of the Hattin
ruins in the memoirs of the Palestine Exploration Fund,
nor of the Cufic inscription which I found. The way to Irbid lies across the plain, on which a collection of seven
basalt stones in a ring are called the "Hajaret en Nusara,"
or "stones of the Christians," because tradition has it that
it was here that Christ performed the miracle of the seven
loaves and two fishes.

The plain was now waving with grain, nor would it be
possible to imagine a more fertile or luxuriant upland. On
its margin, where it breaks off abruptly into the marvellous
gorge of El-Hamam, with its precipitous sides rising twelve

hundred feet sheer up from the little stream which trickles at their base, are the ruins of Irbid, interesting as containing the remains of the oldest Jewish synagogue probably to be found in Palestine.

The steep hillside which slopes down to the edge of the cliff is very rocky, and numerous sarcophagi are carved on the surfaces of the natural slabs. The largest measure from six feet to six feet five inches long, and one foot ten inches deep, being round at the head and square at the foot, which is slightly deeper. There was a ledge cut round to receive the stone cover, and a channel made to keep the surface water from running in. They were of all sizes, some, evidently, for small children and babies. But the most remarkable tomb was one which opened out of a deep, rock-cut chamber, which appeared to have been in connection with a wine-press. The antechamber formed a sunk court, about twenty feet by ten, and contained a sarcophagus. It opened into a tomb containing six loculi. My guide was the Jew who had entertained me in the garden, and who was well versed in local traditions.

He informed me that here were supposed to be buried four of the sons of Jacob, he did not know which, and Jochabed and Dinah. He also pointed out to me the tomb of the Rabbi Nitai, who was supposed to have built the synagogue I had been examining, and who was a native of the place, and lived about two hundred years B.C.; also a mound of stones covering apparently a rock tomb, which he declared was the burial-place of Seth, the son of Adam; but, although from much habit I am accustomed to swallow a fair amount of traditional information, I was unable to push my credulity thus far. It is described, however, by the Rabbi Gerson, A.D. 1561, as being in a cave with a spring to which a flight of steps led down. The tombs of Zerah and Zephaniah were also pointed out. Indeed, there are few places in Palestine where in the same limited area such a number of distinguished personages of sacred history are buried as in the neighbourhood of Arbela, or Irbid. I do not now include the tombs of the numerous rabbis whom the Jews hold sacred. If it has a character for sanctity, it must at one time have had a reputation for strength. From its position it must always have been a military stronghold. Josephus tells us, in his "Life," that when he was Governor of Galilee he fortified it, and laid up stores of grain here; and it is without doubt the Casale Ardelle of the Teutonic knights (1250 A.D.), the *d* being an error for *b*, as it is mentioned in connection with Tiberias and Beisan, both places not very distant.

The only Biblical reference to this place is that made by Hosea, when he says, "Therefore shall a tumult arise among thy people; all thy fortresses shall be spoiled, as Shalman spoiled Beth-Arbel in the day of battle." As we stand here we can almost look into the caverns with which the face of the opposite cliff is perforated, while the one on the edge of which we stand is literally honeycombed with these subterranean abodes. They are of immense extent, and are placed over each other in different stories; some are walled up, leaving doors and windows. Some idea of the extent of this singular natural fastness may be formed from the fact that it is capable of containing six thousand men. The caves communicate with each other by subterranean galleries. These are the fortified caverns mentioned by Josephus in connection with Arbela. Bachides, the general of Demetrius, the third King of Syria, when he invaded Palestine, encamped at Arbela and subdued those who had taken refuge in the caves. This event is narrated in Maccabees, where the caves are called "stories." It was here, also, that Herod the Great had his famous fight with the robbers who had made their dens in the caves, letting down his soldiers in baskets, and fighting them in mid-air.

I was determined to push my explorations to the summits of the rocky crests which frowned above, and are called the Horns of Hattin. Scrambling up the steep, rocky hillsides, we found ourselves at last obliged to leave our horses and make our way on foot over the huge blocks of basalt which are thickly strewn around these singular peaks. On reaching the top we found that they had been artificially superimposed one on the top of another, so as to form a rocky rampart of immense solidity. Both crests had, at some period of remote antiquity, been thus fortified. Beneath one of them were the foundations and ruins of an ancient town which the inhabitants call "Medinet el-Inweileb," or "the ruins of the long tower." At the southeast of the hill is an oblong cavern cut in the rock and cased with cement, which may formerly have been a cistern; and not far from it are the foundations of a building which the natives say was a Christian church before the conquest of the country by the Mohammedans, who subsequently converted it into a mosque. Nothing could be more striking than the view from the summit of the highest horn. Immediately beneath us, some six or seven hundred feet below, I looked down into the gloomy gorge, with the white walls of the Neby Schaib contrasting with the black basalt rocks, its terraces covered with groups of brightly costumed Druses, their songs as they danced in circles reaching us on the still air of evening, and beyond, the modern village of Hattin, surrounded by orange-groves and fruit-gardens of the most brilliant green. Stretching away on all other sides were vast uplands of waving grain, till they either sunk away into valleys or terminated at the base of hills which rose abruptly above them. To the northeast the precipitous sides of the Wady Hamam, honeycombed with caves, formed a vista through which appeared in the distance a green strip of the plain of Genesareth; beyond it the waters of the Sea of Galilee, seventeen hundred feet below us, gleamed in the setting sun. From its eastern margin rose the steep cliffs above which is the vast plateau of Jaulan, once the grazing lands of the flocks and herds of Job, while a line of conical volcanic peaks, backed by snow-clad Hermon, closed the prospect.

THE JEWISH FEAST OF THE BURNING AT TIBERIAS.

HAIFA, July 8.—In the early days of May there is annually celebrated at Tiberias a festival in honour of the Rabbi Mâir, at the large shrine built above his tomb, within a few hundred yards from the sulphur baths. Thither, having terminated my visit to the Druses, I determined to repair to witness the nocturnal ceremonies.

I was escorted to the extremity of the village of Hattin by a band of young Druses, firing guns and singing complimentary odes, who thus sought to speed with honour the parting guest, and soon found myself crossing the plain and entering upon the steep descent that leads to the shores of the lake. It was a soft, balmy evening, about sunset, when I reached Tiberias, and found the whole population in movement.

The distance from the town to the tomb of the rabbi is about a mile and a half along the lake shore, and the road was crowded with merry groups of Jewish men, women, and children in gala dress, all flocking to the place of meeting. The two or three boats of which the lake can boast were even put into requisition, and were slowly drifting down, their large sails hardly filled with the gentle breeze, and packed to overflowing with women and children. Tiberias contains between three and four thousand Jews, and certainly more than half that number must have turned out, to say nothing of those attracted from Jerusalem, Safed, and other places. As those who inhabit Tiberias are nearly all Sephardim, or Spanish Jews, the men wear the Oriental dress, while the women indulge in a costume in which the Western fashions seem grafted on those of the East. The visitors, who were for the most part Ashkenazim, or German Jews, could easily be distinguished, as they always appear in the clothes to which they are accustomed in eastern Europe. It must be confessed that the flowing robe of Asia is preferable to the long coat or gabardine of Russia and Roumania.

The men usually walked, but a favourite method of locomotion among the women was donkeyback, and very comical they looked, sitting astride very wide pads, with their skirts well up to their knees, and their necks and wrists and foreheads bedizened with ornaments, while their wigs were often a perfect garden of flowers. However pretty some of the faces of the younger members of the female community might be—and they could not compare for good looks with the Druse girls—nothing can compensate for the abominable practice which prevails among them of shaving their heads and wearing wigs of black hair, which come low down upon the forehead, and the falseness of which no attempt is made to disguise.

It occurred to me upon this occasion, as I contrasted their chevelure with that of the Druses, to speculate on the custom of Druse hairdressing, which is nothing more nor less than that square cutting across the forehead of locks drawn over it which has been so much in vogue in England and America for the last fifteen years, popularly called "banging," and which was supposed at first to be copied from the well-known picture of Raphael as a child. I have since inquired of some fashionable young Syrian ladies, and the younger ones assured me at first that the Druses must have copied this from the Parisian fashions lately introduced at Beyrout—an obvious impossibility. On applying to older ladies, however, they confirm the curious fact that this banging has always been a custom with the Druse people. The fine ladies of the present generation have little guessed whom they were imitating in setting saucers upon their own heads and those of their little ones, and snipping their hair around them just above their eyes. Nothing could exceed in vulgarity the tinsel ornamentation of the Jewish headdresses, and, to increase the effect, various pigments were apparently used by many of the ladies to improve their complexions.

As this festival takes place in the height of the bathing

season, the shore of the lake at this point presented an appearance of unwonted animation. There were some thirty or forty tents pitched round the bath-house, which an enterprising Syrian has leased this year from the government, and whitewashed; he even went so far as to offer to build a carriage-road at his own expense for the mile and a half which it is distant from the town, so as to accommodate patients who had no tents of their own; but this was the thin edge of a wedge of civilization at which the authorities took alarm, and he was sternly forbidden to spend any of his own money for the public convenience in the manner proposed. The result is that the bathers are all obliged to live in tents or mat huts, which are unbearably hot during the day, or ride from the town and back again for every bath.

Patients from all the neighbouring parts of Syria now mingled with the Jewish crowd, and streamed up the short ascent which leads to the tomb, the terrace of which was already thronged. Passing through an archway, I entered a courtyard where the usual circular dance was in progress, the performers being exclusively male. The bedizened females sat in groups, feasting on good things they had brought with them, and smoking narghiles. Their small children were tricked out gaudily, and by the light of numerous flaring lamps the general effect was quaint and gay enough.

Ascending from this scene of revelry up a massive stone stair, I entered a chamber where the tomb of the rabbi was surrounded by a wooden enclosure, inside of which were sundry rabbis and their neophytes praying, with the swaying motion of the body peculiar to that act of worship, the whole brilliantly lighted with lamps. There was in the centre of this chamber, which was crowded, an immense chandelier, of which only a few lamps were lighted, and beyond it I was ushered by a Jew, who volunteered to be my guide, into another room, stifling hot, in which sat the chief rabbi himself. Here a man was perpetually shouting in a stentorian voice something which I failed to understand. The chief rabbi, however, to whom I was introduced, explained to me that he was at that moment selling by auction the privilege of lighting the bonfires which were soon

to blaze in honour of the deceased rabbi and Simon Ben
Jochai, who, however, seems to be buried elsewhere. This
privilege was put up at two napoleons each, and the first
finally went for three, a fact which the rabbi announced to
the audience in a sonorous Hebrew chant. Then the other
lighting privilege was bought for a little less, the money,
according to my informant, being given to the poor. After that a dozen more sales were made, simply for lamp-
lighting, the amounts bid averaging half a napoleon.

Then a sort of procession was formed, and the crowd
surged out down the steps to the courtyard, in the centre of
which were two columns, each surmounted by a sort of
large saucer. The excitement now became great, the dancing stopped, and men and women joined in noisy acclama-
tions. A man bearing aloft an iron cradle full of flaming
rags, which had been lighted by the highest bidder, placed
them in the saucer at the top of the column and poured a
bottle of kerosene oil upon it. People now came forward
with offerings to be burned. These consisted, for the most
part, so far as I could judge, of old handkerchiefs and scarfs.
The theory is that they should be articles of value, covered
with gold and silver embroidery, and that, after they have
been committed to the flames, the residue of gold and silver
which remains should be scraped up and given to the poor;
but I doubt whether the residue of the rags which I saw
would amount in value to ten cents. Then the second bonfire was lighted, and as both piles blazed up and shed their
lurid glow over the eager faces of swarthy men, with their
long ear-curls, and bedizened women, the scene was in the
highest degree novel and picturesque. The proceedings
were not, however, characterized by the gravity and harmony befitting the occasion.

As I looked down upon the crowd from the steps upon
which I was standing, I observed suddenly a violent commo-
tion, which soon culminated in blows and sharp cries, and
the crowd began to surge violently to and fro. I failed to
discover the cause of the disturbance, but it was speedily
interrupted by a strong body of Turkish police, who rushed
in brandishing their muskets and laying about them with
the butt ends. The riot speedily subsided under this op-

portune display of energy, and the ringleaders were hustled off with commendable promptness.

Meantime a somewhat similar ceremony was taking place in the adjoining courtyard, where some wicker lamps were being lighted. The pilgrims who filled this court were Ashkenazim, and in their more European clothes they were by no means so picturesque a crowd. It is a singular fact that the Sephardim should be confined to one court and the Ashkenazim to another. There is, indeed, very little sympathy between the two great branches of the Jewish race in Palestine. They live for the most part in different cities, and have but little intercourse with each other. Thus, nearly all the Jews in Tiberias are Sephardim, while those at Safed are Ashkenazim.

The ceremonies which I have just described are a mild edition of what was to take place on a far larger and more important scale at Meron a week later, but as these latter differ in no important respect from those which I witnessed, I did not think it worth while to stay for them. Jews come from great distances to take part in the burnings at Meron, where a great number of bonfires are made in honour of the numerous celebrated rabbis who are buried in the neighbourhood; and here I was assured that articles of great value are consumed, and the festivities are of a much more noisy character, and last through the whole night instead of winding up before midnight, as was the case at Tiberias. I did not even prolong my stay till this hour, satisfied with having assisted at ceremonies which prove that the Jewish is not exempt from that tendency which characterizes all other religions, of pandering to the grosser tastes of the masses.

11

HOUSE-BUILDING ON CARMEL.

DALIET-EL-CARMEL, July 12. — Those readers who may have read my letters from Palestine, may remember that last year I took refuge from the summer heats at the village of Esfia, on the highest point of Mount Carmel, where I established a temporary camp. The disadvantage of living under canvas is that, though it may secure you cool nights, it affords but insufficient shelter from the noonday sun. I therefore determined to build myself something more substantial. My experiences of house-building on Carmel have been both characteristic and instructive.

When I announced my intention to the villagers of Esfia, they professed the greatest enthusiasm, and the owners of the land which I had chosen for a site expressed their desire to make me a present of it, so anxious did they pretend to be that I should settle among them. I absolutely refused, however, to receive anything as a gift, and told them to name their price. This they modestly put at $650. As the most trustworthy estimate I could obtain put its value at $50, I said I would reconsider my original decision and accept it as a gift. This seemed to afford them intense amusement. Offers of this sort were merely complimentary, they said, and meant nothing. I replied that the joke of offering me the land for nothing was only equalled by their asking me twelve times its value, which I should also consider meant nothing. They came down at a bound to $250, provided I would pay the costs of the transfer. This I found to mean procuring them a valid title to the land, which they admitted they had not got, and which it would cost $50, expended in bribes to the government, to obtain. I suggested that I might in that case expend the $50 in procuring a valid title from the government in my own name, and pay them nothing, seeing that, though theoretically, they were not practically, the owners of the land. This, though it might possibly have been accomplished, would have placed me in open warfare with the village. Rather than live there under such conditions, I declined to have anything more to do with people who had shown such dishonest and grasping propensities. I will say, however, that these were confined exclusively to the Christian section of the population, who claimed the ownership of the site, and that the Druses held themselves aloof and repudiated all participation in the negotiations, expressing great indignation at the conduct of the Christians, and offering me sites elsewhere.

I was too disgusted with these latter, however, to be tempted to live near them, and was casting about in despair for an alternative, when one day I received a visit from the Druse sheik of Dalieh, the only other village on Carmel, and distant about thirteen miles from Haifa, who arrived in great distress to tell me that his only son had just been drawn as a conscript for the army, and that the whole family, including his son's wife, whom I had remarked on the occasion of a former visit as one of the most beautiful girls I have ever seen, were thrown into the greatest grief, as they were unable to pay the $250 which was required to buy a substitute. I rode up to the village to inquire into the matter, and, in return for the required sum, which I paid, received a vineyard and garden of fruit-trees, with a good title, and a site far surpassing in loveliness of situation that which I had failed to secure at Esfia. The whole village turned out *en masse* to express their gratitude and make professions of service. As the village is exclusively Druse, and does not contain a single Christian inhabitant, I felt that these were to be relied upon; nor, so far, has this confidence turned out misplaced. The sheik to whom I had thus been able opportunely to render assistance, was the spiritual head of the village. Its temporal affairs are managed by another sheik. The site for my house was only divided by a terrace from the little Druse place of worship, where, however, the services are conducted under the strictest secrecy. The whole hillside here is terraced with vines, pomegranates, and wide-spreading fig-trees, at an altitude

of thirteen hundred feet above the sea, which is distant as
the crow flies about five miles. It commands a magnificent
view of it and of the picturesque ruin of Athlit on its projecting promontory, while a smiling valley, the sloping hills
of which are partially cultivated and partially covered with
copse-wood, winds down to a wild gorge between whose precipitous cliffs one enters the plain of Sharon.

The difficulty in placing the house was to do so without
having to cut down any of the fig-trees that formed a sort
of bower in which we had to nestle, and which secures us
abundant thick shade. No sooner did we begin to excavate
for the foundations than we came upon huge, massive cut
blocks of stone, which evidenced the existence of some previous building of great antiquity. Soon there turned up a
beautifully carved cornice, then a coin of one of the Con-
stantines of the period of the Byzantine Empire, then about
a dozen iron rings about two and a half inches in diameter,
attached to iron staples, and a quantity of nails about four
inches long, all heavily encrusted with rust. These were
dug up about two feet beneath the surface. Then came
handles of jars and fragments of pottery, some pieces of old
glass, one apparently the stem of a vase, and quantities of
tesseræ, showing the existence of a tessellated pavement
somewhere beneath. I was sorely tempted to diverge from
building into excavating, but I should have destroyed my
site, indefinitely postponed the erection of the house when
time was of the utmost value, and forfeited my contract
with the builder. So I have had to do the barbarous thing
of building on the top of what may be a most interesting
ruin, and of actually using the old foundations and some of
the stone which composed this house of the ancients.

The most of the stones of which the house is built come,
however, from the ruins of Dubil, the extensive remains of
which are about a mile distant. Here is the finest collection
of rock-cut tombs on Carmel; while the number and size of
the cisterns, the huge circular stones of the old olive-presses, the basins carved in the solid rock as wine vats, the
fragments of columns, and the area over which the solid
foundations of the former town extend, prove that it contained, in the most ancient times, a larger population than

any other spot on the mountain. I am able to say this with the more confidence as I have visited over twenty other sites of ancient towns on Carmel. From this almost inexhaustible quarry of old dwellings is my new one mainly constructed, and thus do I live and move and have my being amid the relics of a most remote past.

One of the most puzzling of these is an immense roller, which I came upon in making a terrace for the veranda, from which it now projects as a conspicuous ornament. It is eight feet long, but one end has been a good deal broken, and it may have been longer. It tapers very slightly at both extremities, and is nine feet in circumference around the centre, the ends being about two feet six in diameter. It has four parallel lines of slots a little over two feet apart, each slot about eight inches long and three deep, and two wide at the top. There are four of these slots in each line, and they are about eight inches apart. The whole mass weighs probably from three to four tons. We had quite a force of men to move it into its present position. I leave it to the wise in such matters to conjecture what its possible use may have been. I have seen others scattered about in some of the ruins on the mountain, generally near olive-presses. I think they had some reference to the crushing apparatus.

But by far the most important find—and this was not made until after the house was finished and we were clearing up the débris—was an ancient cistern; and, as luck would have it, it was just in the position in which I would have put a cistern had this not appeared ready to hand, thus saving me an expenditure of about $200. The aperture, cut in the solid rock, is two feet three inches square. It is then hollowed, demijohn shape, out of the rock to a depth of fourteen feet, with an average breadth at the bottom of twelve feet. In the bottom is a circular hole five feet in diameter by three deep. This is evidently for cleaning out the cistern, and is a good idea, which I should suggest be adopted by us moderns. It is plain that if, instead of having a flat bottom to a cistern, you have a hole in the bottom into which you can sweep all the dirt, the process of cleaning is simplified. It took four men several days to clean out this old cistern. It contained a great quantity of fine mould, some broken earthenware jars, a good many large stones, and a rather good fragment of a glass cup. The old cement is still visible, about half an inch thick.

Besides the cistern, I have found a cave, formerly a tomb, close to the house, which I shall use as a cellar, and store away my wine in the stone coffins, or loculi, in which the bones of some ancient characters have reposed. From all which it will appear that house-building in Palestine, if it is attended with the inconveniences arising from the backward state of civilization, may nevertheless possess a charm of its own.

If some of our appliances are rough-and-ready, they often possess the merit of cheapness. Plastering, for instance, is an expensive luxury; but the natives have a way of plastering the walls which is nearly as good, and by no means costly. This is entirely done by the women, who come and sift soil, which they mix with cut straw and water, and knead into a paste. When they have plastered the walls and floor with this, they make another with a peculiar, fine white clay, which they dig from certain places in the hillsides, and, mixing this also with finely chopped straw, lay it on as an outer covering. It makes a very pale yellow coating for the walls, which is by no means unsightly. It is not so good, however, for the floors, as it is said to give a better harbour for fleas than another and more expensive cement which is made with lime, and is called barbarica. This is better also for the flat roofs, as it is more impervious to water in the rainy season.

These roofs enable us to double our accommodations in a most economical fashion. For instance, we have a guest coming, and if the house is full, we build him a leaf hut on the roof at the extravagant rate of 75 cents. These charming little leaf huts, which can be made most snug and comfortable when lined with mats, can be multiplied at will over the whole roof, and the occupants have a cooler time and a more extensive view than the dwellers in the stone chambers beneath. As, however, in these climates air and room add materially to comfort, our principal living-room is thirty feet by twenty, and fifteen feet high, though I have not aspired to anything but a summer cottage, and the whole cost has not exceeded $800.

In the eyes of the natives, this modest erection has seemed something palatial. The people of Esfia have come over, green with envy of their Dalieh rivals, and bitterly reproaching themselves with the short-sighted cupidity which has deprived them of the prestige which now attaches to Dalieh, and filled with regret at the loss of the money which would otherwise have been spent among them, while to the Dalieh villagers it is a source of pride and delight. Whenever any Druse sheik comes from a neighbouring village, he is at once brought to see the sight. The consequence is that I have no lack of visitors, and, foreseeing this, took care to have a special apartment called a "liwan," exclusively devoted to their reception. They are thus barricaded from the rest of the house. Otherwise, with the prying curiosity which characterizes the race, privacy would be impossible. As it is, from morning to night there is always a group round the kitchen, much to the detriment of culinary operations and the annoyance of the servants engaged in them. Still, in order to keep on good terms, we have to make concessions, to waste time over much drinking of coffee out of minute cups, to hear their gossip on local politics, and, what is still more difficult, to try and give them some larger ideas than the very narrow ones which they have acquired upon these wild hillsides.

Altogether, although their defects are of a somewhat trying kind, and their essential insincerity makes them arrant humbugs, they are rather pleasant humbugs, and, provided they do not test one's affection by too many invitations to dinner, which involves squatting on your heels and eating with your fingers, the Druses are, taking them altogether, by far the most agreeable class of people to live among in Palestine.

DOMESTIC LIFE AMONG THE DRUSES.

DALIET-EL-CARMEL, Aug. 1.—A residence in a Druse village upon the familiar terms which I have now established with the inhabitants of this one, opens up a phase of existence so utterly foreign to all Western notions of domestic life, and involves experiences so novel and characteristic, that I am constantly receiving illustrations of the truth of the saying that one half of the world has no idea how the other half lives.

Early the other morning, for instance, my native servant appeared in a state of no little excitement to tell me that there had been a row in the night in the village, from which my house is distant only a few hundred yards, and that a young man was being killed. This was modified a few minutes after by the arrival of some weeping females, who said that if the young man could not find a place of refuge somewhere he would be killed; and, as if to emphasize this statement, no great interval elapsed before, on going out into the kitchen, I found the young man in question clinging to the legs of the kitchen table as though they were the horns of the altar. He was a not very prepossessing-looking young man of two or three and twenty, and on my appearance he abandoned the legs of the table and rushed at my hand, which he seized and kissed effusively. It is astonishing how affectionate a man can become under the influence of panic. I told him to go back to the table-legs and hold on there, and consider himself perfectly safe. I felt I could say this with a feeling of proud satisfaction, for had I not the British government at my back, and is not the British government celebrated for the chivalrous promptitude with which it rushes to the rescue of those in bodily peril?

Meantime I sent for the spiritual sheik of the village, as

the secular one, who is the real supreme authority in such matters, happened to be absent. Now, so far as I have been able to ascertain, the whole village, consisting of some five hundred souls, is related to the two sheiks, for the population has gone on marrying and intermarrying till the relationships are unfathomable. The young man in question was the youngest of four brothers, and he had one sister who had married the spiritual sheik's son. His mother, after having this numerous family, had married the secular sheik, who had himself had two sons by a former wife and who has one daughter by his present one. You will observe that the affair was already becoming mixed, and a strong suspicion was gradually stealing over me that there was a woman at the bottom of it. Such, indeed, proved to be the case; in fact, there turned out to be two.

Now it happened, and this is not peculiar to the domestic relations of the Druses, that the secular sheik's sons by his first wife were very jealous of the children of their stepmother, and hated that elderly lady herself with the cordial hatred not unknown to stepchildren. They had contrived so to embitter the family circle, that the secular sheik, partly for the sake of peace, and partly, as I afterwards discovered, for another reason, had banished her for two years past from the marital roof; indeed, it had often been a matter of surprise to me when calling on this sheik, or dining with him, that I was always waited on by his daughter and not by his wife.

Now the mystery was solved; but the sheik did not extend this inhospitality to his stepsons, and the young man now holding on to the kitchen table was especially favoured, and, although not an inmate of his stepfather's house, made himself too much at home there to suit his half-brothers. They determined, therefore, to drive him forth. Now, the sheik had another brother, who had a wife much younger than himself, and who, it was whispered, was much admired by the obnoxious young man. And it being the end of Ramadan, and the village being in a state of nocturnal festivity, people were in a mood for mischief all around, and, rightly or wrongly, the young man being found in the sheik's brother's house in the middle of the night, fell un-

der grave suspicion, and a tremendous tumult took place,
in the course of which the sheik's son belaboured his stepmother, being assisted thereto by his uncle; and here I may
incidentally remark that Druse men appear to think nothing
of beating their friends' wives, whose husbands seem to
think it quite natural they should do so. Perhaps it saves
them the trouble; anyhow, on this occasion the women gave
vent to their tongues, and the men retaliated with blows.
Of course, the women took the part of the gay but indis-
creet youth, who declared that he was in search of a missing
cow, though it was suggested with some force that to go
and look for her on the roof of the sheik's brother's house
after midnight showed an unpardonable ignorance of the
usual haunts of cows. The whole of the secular sheik's
first family, therefore, and their relations to the fifth degree,
who form the majority of the male population, refusing to
admit any such excuse, and considering the young man's
guilt proved, vowed to have his life, death being the not
uncommon penalty among them for a crime of this sort;
but the whole of the spiritual sheik's family, which seems
to me to consist principally of all the women in the village,
accepted the young man's version of the affair, and maintained his innocence; and, with that knowledge of human
nature which characterizes the sex, they instinctively turned
to me as their natural ally, and hence I was saddled with the
protection of this too-susceptible and much-menaced youth.

The position was delicate, for though I am not insensible
to the advantage of possessing the suffrages of the female
part of the community, I desired also to stand well with the
males, and I felt that to interpose between them and the
object of their vengeance was likely to prejudice me in
their eyes. At the same time one could not turn a youth
out of one's kitchen to go like a sheep to the slaughter,
even though he may have been an erring lamb. Moreover,
when I came to hear the spiritual sheik's version of the
story, though it was undoubtedly one-sided, the question of
guilt did not appear to be satisfactorily established. So I
sent for the injured husband, and the sheik's son, who had
beaten his stepmother, to hear their version of the matter,
but they refused to answer my summons.

Under these circumstances I determined to wait for the return of the secular sheik, which took place the same evening. After sympathizing with him on the distracted condition of his household, I asked him if he could suggest the best course of action for me to pursue, as it was evidently impossible for me to board and lodge his stepson for an indefinite time on the kitchen table. This, he admitted, was an undue tax on my hospitality. I asked him if he could not exercise sufficient authority over the members of his own family to protect the life of his stepson. This, he said, he could do while he remained in the village, but as he was constantly being called away on business, he could not answer for what might happen in his absence.

I then asked whether it might not be best to send the young man away from the village until the storm had blown over. I had suggested this to the spiritual sheik, but he said that in that case the youth's mother would follow him; and, as I remarked to the secular sheik, I was loath to propose this to him, as it would separate him from his wife. The sheik, with apparent distress, observed that his wife did not see much of him. I asked whether I could not be the means of healing this breach, and whether he would allow me to send for his wife; this he at once assented to, but the old lady refused to come. This refusal on her part seemed to afford the sheik immense relief, seeing which, I remarked, "Perhaps, if your wife did go away with your stepson, you would not mind it very much." "No," he said, "I should not mind it very much."

I have since discovered that he is very anxious to get rid of her, in order to marry some one else. So I packed the young man off to a Christian of my acquaintance at Esfia, two miles off, thinking his mother would follow him; but not a bit. She has now taken up her abode with the spiritual sheik, and I am at this moment employing her to make a mud floor under a fig-tree, on which I intend to put beehives. I rode over a few days ago to Esfia, and found the young man comfortably installed with his Christian host, who, with true Arab hospitality, charges him nothing for his entertainment, but who will probably be indemnified for it by a present from the spiritual sheik. Meantime, influences are at work to prepare the way for his safe return, and I trust that I have so managed these delicate negotiations as to secure me the good-will of both factions, though I am afraid that the breach between them will never be healed until the secular sheik divorces his present wife and takes a fresh departure by uniting himself to the lady of his affections.

CIRCASSIAN HIGHWAYMEN.—A DRUSE FESTIVAL AT ELIJAH'S ALTAR.

DALIET-EL-CARMEL, Aug. 15.—About this time last year, when I was at Esfia, we were suddenly disturbed by the intelligence that a German teamster, whom I have been in the habit of employing, had been attacked in the night at the bridge over the Kishon, distant about three miles from my camp, while on his way from Haifa to Nazareth, by four Circassians, who, suddenly surrounding him, pointed their guns at his head, thus preventing him from using his revolver, which they stole from him, at the same time cutting the traces of his team and carrying off a valuable pair of horses, leaving the poor man helpless with his wagon at about one o'clock in the morning, far from any help, but thankful to have escaped with his life.

The whole machinery of the local police was put in motion, and the authorities professed to take up the matter in earnest. Some of the German colonists scoured the country in pursuit of the robbers, who appear to have fled to some Circassian colonies which were established about five years ago on the plains of Iturea, near the foot of Hermon, beyond the Jordan, and there all trace of them was lost. They had got among friends, who covered their tracks, and the horses were never recovered.*

Since this time the colonists, who are constantly travelling in their wagons between Haifa and Nazareth, and in the hottest weather generally make the journey by night, always go two or three together, and had not been molested until a few nights ago, when two of them started for Nazareth, one of them the victim of last year. His companion, who had left Haifa a little before him, expecting to be shortly overtaken, was jogging along at about 8 P.M., and

---

* A year later the thieves were found, and the Circassian colony to which they belonged was compelled by the government to refund the Germans the value of the horses.

was not above four miles distant from Haifa, when a Circassian rode past him, wishing him good-evening. The German returned the salute, but his suspicions were roused by the man's manner, and he got his revolver ready. Almost immediately after he heard a whistle, the man who had passed him turned sharply back, and two others sprang upon him from an ambush, where they had been concealed, by the roadside. One of them seized his horses' heads, while the others began cutting the traces. The teamster instantly jumped from the box, and, unwilling to shoot before it was absolutely necessary, closed with one of the robbers, striking at him with the butt of his pistol. He was, however, nearly overpowered, and had just time, as he saw his adversary draw a knife, to send a bullet through him. At this moment he received a severe blow on the back from one of the other men, who rushed to the assistance of his comrade, but the German, who was an old soldier and had been through the Franco-German campaign, was a quick shot, and knocked this man over with a second barrel. At this moment a fourth Circassian appeared upon the scene. Fortunately, the attacking party were only armed with knives. The two remaining Circassians now, seeing that two of their number had been disposed of, began to draw off their bodies, it being a first principle of their warfare to carry away their dead. This gave the German, who was scarcely able to raise himself from the ground, a chance to fire two more shots, but, as it seemed at the time, without effect, and the two Circassians, throwing the bodies of their companions over their horses, made off.

By this time the other German teamster, who had been a quarter of a mile behind, but had pushed on on hearing the shots, came up and helped his wounded friend. He, however, was able to continue his journey to Nazareth, and in a few days recovered from the effects of his bruises. Meantime information has been received from a peasant where the Circassians passed the night, that one of them had been killed on the spot, that another died of his wound shortly after he was brought to his cottage, and that the third had a ball through his leg, but that his wound had not been sufficiently serious to prevent his continuing his journey the following night with the corpses of his companions. One would think, under these circumstances, that if the authorities chose there could be no great difficulty in tracing the miscreants; but no steps whatever have been taken in the matter, which is, perhaps, the best solution of it, for whenever a foreigner is unhappily obliged to kill a native in self-defence in this country the chance is that he has to stand his trial on a counter charge of murder. Now, thanks to the precautions taken by the Circassians, and the apathy of the government, there is no proof of any one having been killed, and the Circassians have received a much severer punishment than any that would have been inflicted upon them for horse-stealing by the authorities, and they are likely to be careful how they meddle again with the Germans.

Opinions are divided as to whether they will seek their revenge or not. The Germans still continue to team by night to Nazareth, but they go in parties of never less than three wagons together, and well armed. Had the robbers been Bedouins or native Arabs, this encounter would mean a blood feud, and sooner or later revenge would be taken; but I once spent some weeks with the Circassians in their own country, and I do not think that they have the same custom of vendetta. Indeed, notwithstanding the fact that they are a most lawless and thieving set as colonists, I found them a very safe and pleasant people to travel among in their own mountains, where they have their code of honour and hospitality, and I have spent a day with them in one of their colonies beyond Jordan, and received nothing but civility. It would, however, be better to keep them in those wild and half-savage regions than bring them within range of the temptations which civilization offers to them.

I have just seen a man who has been paying them a visit at the old city of Jerash, which, with the exception of Palmyra, is the most perfect Greco-Roman ruin which exists to the east of Baalbec. My informant tells me that in the course of their excavations for stone for their habitations they are making great discoveries. They have unearthed a heretofore undiscovered and unsuspected temple, with a subterranean conduit of flowing water, and many fragments of statues and coins. One large jar of gold coins, worth $50 each, was an immense prize, which they only succeeded in keeping by paying a bribe to the government official of $2500. My informant saw one of these coins, but, as he was a native, and ignorant of such matters, his description was too vague to convey any definite idea of their date. I should feel much tempted to pay these ruins, which I have already examined once, another visit, but of late years the government throws so many obstacles in the way of travellers to the east of the Jordan that such a journey now may expose one to annoyances.

Meantime, there are many objects of interest in this immediate neighbourhood; within a distance of three miles I have found the extensive remains of what have been undoubtedly iron and copper mines. The former ore was present in large quantities, and the day may come when this discovery may prove of considerable value to this part of the country, though it would be useless, under existing conditions, to take any steps towards its exploration now. It is probable that the old iron rings which I found in digging the foundations of my house were made from this ore.

I have also found a curious square structure, fourteen feet in height, twelve feet square, composed of stones averaging three feet by two, by about one in thickness, all carefully squared, and laid one upon another without cement, the whole forming a perfectly solid erection of great antiquity. It may possibly have been a vineyard watch-tower. It is on the way from here to the "Place of Burning," or Elijah's sacrifice, and is the second I have found in that neighbourhood, the other being considerably smaller. I came upon it accidentally on the occasion of a Druse picnic to which I was invited, and which took place at the "Place of Burning," in celebration of the last day of the feast of Ramadan, which the Druses seem to observe as well as the Moslems, though on a different day.

The female population of the village, in their gayest dresses, had preceded us on donkeys. I accompanied the sheik, who had drawn up on a little plain outside the town about a dozen horsemen as an escort, and thus, after a little of the usual imitation of the equestrian game of the djerrid,

at which, in default of the real thing, the horsemen delight
to exercise their horses by a mock encounter, we formed in
a sort of procession, the young men of the village on foot,
armed with great clubs, chanting songs of love and war,
as they marched in front. There were from two to three
hundred persons collected on the flat space in front of the
church which the Carmelite monks have recently erected on
the supposed site of Elijah's altar. And here the usual
dancing-circles were formed, and the fun of the day commenced. But it was melancholy fun. How could it be
otherwise, when the young men and women are not allowed
to dance together, scarcely even to speak to one another?
It was quite pitiful to see half a dozen of the prettiest girls
that could be found in Syria sitting under the shade of a
tree, gossiping, and looking at half a dozen fine, stalwart,
handsome young fellows prancing about on their horses, or
singing and dancing, without there being the ghost of a
chance of a flirtation. The girls cooked together and ate
together and danced together and sang together, and the
young men amused themselves apart as best they could.
As the delights of flirting are unknown to them, I suppose
they did not miss them; but as I looked at the young people of both sexes thus divided, I wondered what would be
the result of a similar experiment if it were tried at an
American picnic.

It was a curious sight to see a bevy of at least fifty wom-
en and girls rush into the Carmelite chapel, which during
the week is left in charge of a Druse, who on this occasion
did the honours of it to his coreligionists, who scampered
all over the premises, gazing wonderingly at the altar ornaments, and forming large dancing-circles on the flat
roof. I could not exactly find out why the Druses chose
the place of Elijah's sacrifice as the scene of their festivity,
but there is no doubt that the traditions of a special sanctity are attached to it in their religion as well as in that of
the Roman Catholics, and that the slaughter of the eight
hundred false prophets by the holy man whose prayers for
rain were heard on this spot, and upon whom the divine vengeance was invoked, appeals to a sentiment which is common to the Christian, the Moslem, and the Druse religions.

12

ARMAGEDDON.—THE BOSNIAN COLONY AT CÆSAREA.

DALIET - EL - CARMEL, Sept. 11. —There is no fact at first more puzzling to the traveller in Palestine than the contrast between the misery and poverty of the fellahin and the extent and fertility of land owned by each village. This is, however, the inevitable result of the various fiscal devices to which the government has been compelled to resort, in order to provide a revenue which shall meet the needs of its internal administration, and the claims of its foreign bondholders. These press more severely on the peasant class than on any other in the community, and as the financial necessities of the empire increase, new methods are being constantly devised to meet them. Thus the latest arrangement requires the taxes to be paid in money instead of in kind, as heretofore, the amount being assessed on an average of the crops extending over a period of five years. This has produced the greatest consternation among the peasantry throughout the country, who find themselves quite unable to meet this new demand, and who are compelled, in consequence, to resort to extortionate money-lenders, who charge from thirty to forty per cent. for their advances, thus ruining the fellahin, whose villages are all destined by this process to fall into the hands of these grasping usurers, while the peasants remain upon them as serfs, merely receiving so much of the crop as will keep them from starving. Thus it happened that, in the belief that I had more bowels of compassion than their own countrymen, I was applied to by the villagers in all directions; among others, by those who owned the lands of Lejjun, or the biblical Megiddo. This is generally supposed to be identical with Armageddon, and the notion of becoming the proprietor of a battle-field which possesses such interesting historical associations in the past, to say nothing of the future, which may be mythical or not, according to theological fancy, induced me to pay a visit to that celebrated locality. Its position was as tempting as its sentimental considerations were remarkable. Here, jutting out into the plain of Esdraelon, of which it commands an extensive view, stands the Tell et Mutsellim, or governor's hill, upon which the traces of what may have been a palace are distinctly visible. Right opposite to us across the plain, about twelve miles distant, the houses of Nazareth gleam upon the lofty hillside; to the right are Tabor, Little Hermon, and Mount Gilboa, with the mountains of Gilead in the rear. Beneath, circling round the base of the mound, are "the waters of Megiddo," a copious stream, turning two water-mills and irrigating an extensive tract of plain. Behind us is an undulating plateau covered with the ruins of the ancient city. Here are fragments of columns, carved capitals and cornices, and I found some subterranean chambers into which I crawled, and which, as they connected with the stream by stone conduits, I assume must, in old times, have been baths. The peasants have found antiques of various kinds, and I was shown the hand and forearm of a female figure, life-size, and beautifully carved in marble, which they had dug up. There is no saying what treasures the fortunate proprietor of this place may not unearth, and with the wealth of water at his command, of which but little advantage is now taken, he might have extensive gardens and orange groves. From this point a great military road passed, in the most ancient times, connecting Galilee with the coast road. Along it, before the conquest of Canaan by the Israelites, Thothmes, the King of Egypt, led his invading hosts into Syria. Here, by "the waters of Megiddo," was fought the great battle between Barak and Sisera, when the stars in their courses fought against Sisera; and on the same ground, six centuries later, the hosts of Pharaoh Necho met the army of Josiah, King of Judah, and vanquished it, while the king himself, being "sore wounded" as he rode in his chariot, was carried away to Jerusalem to die.

On making inquiries of a practical kind in regard to the

present financial position of this property and its peasant owners, I began to suspect that any foreigner who desired to become its possessor would find himself involved in a struggle of a different kind from that of which in past times it has been the scene, and one more consonant with the spirit of the age in which we live. The invasion of Palestine of late years by foreigners of all religions and nationalities, the constant influx of Jews, and the increasing attention which the Holy Land is concentrating upon itself, has so far alarmed the Porte that foreigners are practically prohibited from purchasing any more land in the country; and the peasantry of the villages who applied to me for assistance were informed that, even if I were prepared to lend them money, they were not to be allowed to borrow. I was thus relieved of the great annoyance of having constantly to refuse applications, which, under any circumstances, I could not have satisfied.

From Megiddo I followed the historical highway through the mountain, which, in the days of Christ, when Cæsarea was rising into its grandeur, must have been one of the most frequented routes in the country. The road led through charmingly diversified scenery. I turned off from it to ascend to the town of Umm-el-Fahm, an important place, containing about two thousand inhabitants, situated on copse-clothed hills, at an elevation of fifteen hundred feet above the level of the sea, and commanding extensive views. Here I was the guest of a local millionaire, noted for his penurious habits and his grasping nature. His ragged appearance and humble establishment did not belie his reputation. I had, however, no reason to complain, for, if the accommodation was rough, his intentions were certainly hospitable.

The romantic valleys by which the village is surrounded are thickly planted with olive groves, which contain over a hundred thousand trees, and are a great source of revenue. While, when they are too far from the village for the protection of any crop, the hillsides and summits are clothed with a dense undergrowth of scrub oak, terebinth, and other shrubs, which are only prevented from becoming forest trees by the charcoal-burners; but their quick growth testifies to the richness of the soil. To the north the range extends for fifteen miles, to the base of Carmel. The woodland disappears, and is succeeded by rolling chalk downs, affording magnificent pasturage and good arable land, for it is well watered, and from its temperate and healthy climate is called the "breezy land."

The villages here are small, few, and far between, and there is room for a large population; but the most tempting land of all is the tract between Umm-el-Fahm and the sea, where the oak-trees which are scattered over the pastures and cornfields attain a large growth, and the country presents the appearance of an immense park. From an artistic point of view the woods and the farm lands are so combined as to form the most perfectly diversified scenery, just where the rolling hills slope gently down into the plain of Sharon. It was across this country that our road lay to Cæsarea, which was our objective point, first, through the thick copse of the upper valleys, and so out upon the park-like uplands, where the whole population was out in the fields gathering the crops, which strings of camels were conveying to the village threshing-floors. Here and there was a money-lender from Acre or Beyrout, squatting under an umbrella, to see that the peasantry did not rob him of his share. This is a busy time with these gentry, who are the bloodsuckers of the fellahin, to whom they advance money at exorbitant rates of interest, while the latter, in revenge, resort to every conceivable device to conceal from them the real extent of the crop, and to make the proportion coming to them as small as possible.

At one village called Ararch I found three old Roman arches, a fine fragment of a column, and some rock-cut tombs, which seem hitherto to have escaped observation. The remains indicate that it must have been a place of considerable importance, but I have not yet been able to identify it. The plain of Sharon, where we struck it, is being by degrees brought into cultivation, partly by colonists, Circassian and Bosnian, and partly by native capitalists. The peasantry themselves are rapidly losing all proprietorship in the soil, unable to contend against the exactions of the government tax-gatherer, on the one hand, and of the

usurious money-lender, on the other; but while they are
yearly becoming more impoverished and dependent, the
wealth of the country is steadily increasing, and its development must follow as a matter of course, though, in accordance with the tendencies of modern civilization, it will be
at the expense of the masses.

I went to lunch with the largest of these local magnates.
He was a Turk, and spoke Turkish in preference to Arabic.
He had, as may be supposed, little sympathy with the Arab
peasantry, who were practically his serfs, and their condition was by no means improved by their lands having fall-
en into his hands. On the other hand, they never would
have introduced the civilized iron ploughs with which he
was bringing land into cultivation. His farm-house was a
large, straggling, isolated building, which stood on a hillock
in the plain, with extensive outhouses and dependencies,
not unlike the residence of a Southern planter, while, curiously enough, a large proportion of his farm hands consisted of African negroes located in a village hard by—but
he had none of the lavish hospitality which characterized
the landed proprietors of the South.

A ride of an hour over a part of the plain which, from
the peculiar quality of its soil, is exclusively devoted to the
growth of water-melons, hitherto the sole export of the little haven of Cæsarea, brought me to that spot. Although
the remains of the old port have been used as a harbour for
coasting craft, these ruins have not been inhabited since
they were evacuated by the crusaders at the end of the
thirteenth century. Indeed, there is a curious prediction
connected with them, to the effect that the rebuilding of
a town here would immediately precede a great disaster
to Islam. It has been in consequence of this, as I have
understood, that while villages have sprung up on all the
other crusading ruins on the coast, this one alone has remained untenanted. However this may be, the spell is
broken now, for about six months ago the first instal-
ment of a band of refugees from Bosnia and Herzegovina
arrived here, having been allotted this ruin and the lands
surrounding it by the government, as the nucleus of a new
colony.

Apart from the great interest which these extensive ruins must ever have from an antiquarian point of view, I was anxious to visit Cæsarea to judge for myself of the prospects of this embryo colony, and make personal acquaintance with this new and interesting class of immigrants. Moreover, as the new town is to be built upon the ruins of the old, it was evident that I should never have another chance of seeing what these were like. They have already during the last twenty years served as a quarry from whence the magnificent building-stones, cut originally by Herod the Great when he built the town, have been transported in thousands of boat-loads to Acre and Jaffa. The ruins have therefore lost much of the pristine grandeur which is described in the records of travellers in the early part of the present century. In a few years more they will probably have disappeared altogether. The subterranean treasures, whatever they may be, will, however, remain untouched, and the Schliemann of a future age will find here the traces of five successive epochs of civilization. On the top he will find the ruins of the stone houses of the Bosnians and Herzegovinians, now in process of erection; below them the foundations of the great Crusading fortress, and below them again the remains of the first Mohammedan period; beneath them, traces of the Byzantine period, and, at the bottom, the tessellated pavements, the fragments of carved marble, the statuary, and the coins of the Roman period.

Meantime it is a singular fact that the strip of coast from Haifa to Cæsarea seems to have become a centre of influx of colonists and strangers of the most diverse races. The new immigrants to Cæsarea are Slavs. Some of them speak a little Turkish. Arabic is an unknown tongue to them, which they are learning. Their own language is a Slav dialect. When the troubles in the provinces of Bosnia and Herzegovina first broke out, which led to the Russo-Turkish war, a howl of indignation went up from the philanthropists on both sides of the Atlantic, but especially from the Radical party in England, against the Turkish government, for its persecution of the Slav population of the Danubian provinces. Nor do I think that the general

public have yet realized the fact that of these Slavs more
than half were Moslem, and that the Turkish government
was not persecuting them more than it was persecuting
any other of its subjects, but that the persecutors of the
Slav peasantry, who were Christian, were the Slav aristocracy, who were Moslem. It was, in fact, not a question
of an oppressed nationality, but a strictly agrarian question
between people of the same race. When it was settled by
handing over the provinces to Austria, the Slav-Moslem
aristocracy, finding themselves in their turn persecuted by
their former peasants and the Christian power which protected them, migrated to the more congenial rule of the
sultan. So the curious spectacle is presented of a Slav population migrating from Austrian rule to Asia, in order to be
under a Moslem government.

Close beside the new Bosnian colony there are planted in
the plain of Sharon two or three colonies of Circassians.
These are the people who committed the Bulgarian atroci-
ties. The irony of fate has now placed them within three
or four miles of colonists belonging to the very race they
massacred. They, too, fleeing from government by Christians, have sought refuge under the sheltering wing of the
sultan, where, I regret to say, as I described in a former letter, they still indulge in their predatory propensities. In
immediate proximity to them are the black tents of a tribe
of Turcomans. They belong to the old Seljuk stock, and
the cradle of their tribe gave birth to the present rulers of
the Turkish Empire. They have been here for about three
hundred years, and have forgotten the Turkish language,
but a few months ago a new migration arrived from the
mountains of Mesopotamia. These nomads spoke nothing
but Turkish, and hoped to find a warm welcome from their
old tribesmen on the plain of Sharon. In this they were
disappointed, and they have now, to my disgust, pitched
their tents on some of the spurs of Carmel, where their
great hairy camels and their own baggy breeches contrast
curiously with the camels and costumes of the Bedouins
with whom we are familiar.

Besides the Slavs, the Circassians, and the Turcomans,
we have the Jewish colony of Zimmarin, distant about

ten miles from Cæsarea; the German colony at Haifa, and the Druse villages on Carmel, making, with the Bedouins, the negroes, and the native fellahin, no fewer than nine different races engaged in the cultivation of the soil in this neighbourhood.

CÆSAREA.

DALIET-EL-CARMEL, Oct. 2.—The habit of tourists of visiting only those spots in Palestine called holy places, or to which some striking Biblical association is attached, causes them to neglect ruins of the highest historical interest, and which are often as well worth seeing from a picturesque as from an archæological point of view. They make an effort to go to Nazareth, which differs in no respect from an ordinary Syrian town, and which does not boast a single object of antiquarian interest, while they omit from their programme, because it is not included in the books, a ruin like Cæsarea, a city unsurpassed for grandeur and magnificence by anything in Palestine when Herod raised it to the dignity of a metropolis, and the scene of many important events, both Biblical and historical. Here Peter baptized the first Gentile convert to Christianity; here Philip lived with his four daughters, engaged in missionary work; here Paul preached before Felix, and "almost persuaded" Agrippa to become a Christian. It was in the theatre, the remains of which are still to be seen, that Herod made his oration to the multitude when "the angel of the Lord smote him, and he was eaten of worms and gave up the ghost." It was in the streets of Cæsarea that, on the occasion of a quarrel between the Greek and Jewish population, twenty thousand Jews were massacred. Here the celebrated historians Eusebius and Procopius were born, and here was found, when the city was taken by the crusaders, the hexagonal vase of green crystal which was supposed to contain the Holy Grail.

The old Roman wall can be traced for a mile and a half, enclosing an area strewn with the remains of a theatre, hippodrome, temple, aqueducts, and mole; while a second line of fortification, still in admirable preservation, and over half a mile in extent, marks the *enceinte* of the old Crusading fortress, with its castle and donjon keep, its cathedral, its Northern church, and harbour. This tendency on the part of travellers is the more to be regretted as the opportunity of examining these extensive ruins is now about to pass away, never again to return.

The Slav colonists, whose immigration I described in my last letter, are laying out broad streets right across the most interesting ruins, using the old foundations, appropriating the beautiful masonry, the white stones which formed the temple built by Herod, and the brown limestone blocks of the cathedral of the crusaders, quarrying into ancient buildings beneath the surface of the ground, levelling down the ruins at one place, levelling them up in another, and so utterly transforming the whole picturesque area that it will soon be no longer recognizable. Within five months over twenty good stone houses have been built, some of three stories high, others with vaults for merchandise and storing grain; in some cases the old Crusading vaults, evidently used for the same purpose, have been made available. The dwellings are being built on the plan which renders the towns of the Moslem Slavs of European Turkey so dull and uninteresting; they are all enclosed with courtyards, the high stone walls of which jealously guard the harems of the proprietors. In this respect these western Mohammedans are far more particular than the Arabs, who allow their women comparative freedom; but during the period of my stay in Cæsarea I did not see one of the female colonists.

Their male belongings, however, were most hospitable, especially when they found that I knew their country and was familiar with Mostar and Cognitza, in the neighbourhood of which towns had been their former homes. They were the landed aristocracy of their own country, and have, therefore, brought a considerable amount of wealth with them. A large tract of the most fertile land of the plain of Sharon has been donated to them by the Turkish government, and there can be no doubt that the country will gain by their settlement in it. In manners and costume they form a marked contrast to the natives, who are evidently much impressed by their wealth and dignity.

The lower or peasant class of Bosnia and Herzegovina were not obliged, when the country was conquered by the Moslems, to change their religion, and they have continued Christians; while the descendants of their masters, who remained the proprietors of the soil, became bigoted Mussulmans. The consequence has been that now that the country has been handed over to the Austrians, the Christian peasantry have naturally found protection from the authorities against the oppression of their former masters, who, unable to endure the humiliation of seeing the tables turned, and their old servants enabled to defy them with impunity, have sold all their possessions and migrated to the dominions of the sultan, rather than endure the indignities to which they declare they were exposed from their new Christian rulers and their old Christian serfs—very much on the same principle that the Southern States became intolerable to some of the landed proprietors after the emancipation of their slaves. Whether they will agree with their Circassian neighbours remains yet to be seen. They form the *avant garde* of a much larger migration which is to follow as soon as arrangements can be made to receive them. One of the leading men, who has opened a store, assigned me an unfinished house as a lodging, and said that he intended to enlarge it into a hotel for travellers.

It is worthy of the notice of intending travellers in Palestine next season that they can now drive the whole way, if they wish, in wagons belonging to the German colonists, from Jerusalem to Nazareth, in four easy days, instead of having to ride, and camp in tents as heretofore. There are excellent hotels at Jaffa. The next stopping-place would, now that accommodation is promised there, be Cæsarea, the next day to Haifa, where the hotel is being enlarged and put on a thoroughly comfortable and European basis, and the next day to Nazareth, where good quarters can be obtained at the convent, but where, if this route comes to be adopted, a hotel will doubtless shortly be built. As soon as travellers give up their present expensive habit of travelling through Palestine with tents, the hotel accommodation will be increased, and the existing carriage roads, as well as the vehicles which traverse them, be improved. The government has recently determined to construct a carriage road along the coast from Acre to Beyrout and Tripoli, which, if it is carried out, will alter all the existing conditions of travel.

The most striking features of the ruins of Cæsarea are the Crusading castle and the old Roman mole. The former is built upon a long, narrow reef or breakwater, partly artificial, which runs out into the sea for one hundred and sixty yards, forming the southern side of the harbour, while the northern side is formed by a sort of mole or jetty more than two hundred feet long, which is composed of some sixty or seventy prostrate columns lying side by side in the water like rows of stranded logs. They are from five to twenty feet in length, and average about eighteen inches in diameter. I never in my life before saw such an array of granite pillars so closely piled together or used for such a purpose. Indeed, to judge by those which remain, Cæsarea must have been a city of columns. The crusaders used them to thorough-bind their walls, from which the butts project like rows of cannon from the side of a man-of-war. They must have built many hundreds of old Roman columns thus into their fortification.

The Crusading wall enclosing the town rises from a moat which is about forty feet wide, but, being much filled in with rubbish, is not more than five or six feet deep. The wall itself is about nine feet thick, with buttresses at intervals which are from thirty to fifty feet long and project from twenty to twenty-six feet; but it is especially in the castle and donjon, which is built out into the sea on the projecting reef, that the columns are used as thorough-bonds. Some of these are of red granite, others of gray. The Bosnian colonists are perching a *café* on the ruins of the old donjon, immediately above two magnificent prostrate columns of red granite, nine feet long and four in diameter. I observed here also a finely polished block of red granite over six feet square and three feet six inches thick. There is also a curious double tessellated pavement, evidently of two periods, as the upper tesseræ are at least six inches above the lower ones. I am afraid, as the masons are working immediately above them, they will soon disappear, as

will also a beautiful carved capital in white marble. I
scrambled up to the top of this picturesque ruin, where the
rib of the groined roof of the upper chamber still remains
supported on a corbel in the form of a human head, and
looked out of the pointed, arched window sheer down seventy feet on the sea, beating against the base of the sea
wall. The mouth of the small artificial harbour is about
two hundred yards across, but the latter is too much exposed and too small ever to be of much value.

Among the Roman remains, the hippodrome, the theatre,
and the aqueduct are the most interesting. The first is a
sunken level space about three hundred yards long by one
hundred wide, surrounded by a mound, and in the middle
are three truncated blocks of red granite, which, when standing on each other, must have formed a conical pillar about
nine feet high and seven feet diameter at the base. There
is also another fine block of red granite nearly forty feet
long and four feet in diameter, which has been broken.
The theatre is a semicircular building of masonry in an immense artificial mound, surrounded by a trench near the sea.
It is mentioned by Josephus as capable of containing a large
number of persons. Indeed, the account by this historian
of the building of this city by Herod the Great, which I
have just been reading, is most interesting. It occupied
twelve years, and was finished thirteen years before Christ.
He says that the stones of which the sea wall was built were
fifty feet in length, eighteen in breadth, and nine in depth.

For nearly six hundred years it was a Christian city and
the seat of an archbishop, then for five hundred years it fell
under Moslem rule, and an Arab traveller in A.D. 1035 describes it as "an agreeable city, irrigated with running water and planted with date palms and oranges, surrounded
by a strong wall pierced by an iron gate, and containing a
fine mosque." Then for one hundred and fifty years it remained a Crusading stronghold, while its final and complete
destruction by the Sultan Bibars took place in 1265 A.D.,
since which time it has remained a howling wilderness. I
have dwelt somewhat fully on the present aspect of the
ruins, as the transformation they are undergoing will soon
be complete.

From Cæsarea I followed the coast northward with the high-level aqueduct, which in places is still in tolerably good preservation, on my right. This aqueduct was the chief source of the water supply for the inhabitants. It was eight miles long, and at one point tunnels the rock for a quarter of a mile, thirty feet below its surface. There was also a low-level aqueduct, three miles long, which drew its water supply from the Crocodile River. At some seasons this is a dangerous stream to ford, though I experienced no difficulty. That it is not misnamed I possess indisputable proof, for a few weeks ago an Arab acquaintance presented me with a piece of crocodile skin about a foot square, cut from the hide of a crocodile which he himself helped to kill in this river. Passing Tantura, which also contains some Crusading ruins and rock-cut tombs, I reached the Jewish colony of Zimmarin, which I had not visited for eighteen months, and where I was pleased to find the colony in a thriving condition, the colonists hopeful, industrious, and contented, the crops promising fairly, and their progress only checked by the refusal of the government to allow them to build permanent dwellings, a difficulty which it is hoped may be overcome by a judicious display of firmness and patience.

DALIET-EL-CARMEL, Oct. 15.—In order to really understand this country, to become acquainted with the inner
life of its inhabitants, to familiarize one's self with their
manners and customs, their necessities, and their aspirations,
such as they are, and to arrive at a true estimate of the national character, it is needful to remove one's self from any
centre of so-called civilization, however crude, and to live
among them, as I have been doing for the last three months
and a half, not as a stranger, but as a villager owning property, identified with their local interests, and with a will
to afford them such practical counsel and aid as may lie in
one's power. People wonder what I can find to do in a remote Druse village in the back parts of Carmel; but in
practice the days are not long enough to deal with the
varied interests that crowd into them.

Scarcely a day passes that visitors do not arrive from
some of the surrounding villages—sheiks of high or low degree, as the case may be—generally with polite invitations
that I should return their visits, which I know from experience means a financial proposition of some sort in reserve,
for all the villages are more or less embarrassed in their pecuniary circumstances, and have been so victimized by the
native money-lenders of Haifa that they eagerly turn towards any one who they think possesses bowels of compassion.

The return visits which these invitations involve are often
highly characteristic in their attendant circumstances, and
in the varied incidents which accompany them; and, besides,
they give one an opportunity of becoming minutely acquainted with the neighbourhood, and afford one an insight
into the motives by which Oriental human nature is actuated.
There is, for instance, a village about four miles from here,

so beautifully situated among its olive groves, as seen from
a distance, that I had long intended paying it a visit, and
wondered why its sheik had never come to make my acquaintance. The mystery was explained one day by an old
woman whose extreme poverty had induced me to employ
her as a water-carrier. On asking how she had become so
destitute, she said that she was a widow, and that her only
son and support had been waylaid and murdered some
months previously by some of the young men of the village
in question. All her efforts to obtain justice had been unavailing, and since then the two villages had not been on
visiting terms.

As none of the inhabitants of Dalieh would accompany
me, I found my own way one day to the village, to try and
discover the rights of the story. I was received with great
politeness by a tall, gentlemanlike man, whom I supposed
to be the sheik, but who turned out to be the very individual who had been accused of the murder. Soon the sheik
and a number of village notables arrived, and, seated around
the neatly-matted guest-chamber, we exchanged compliments and discussed the topics of the day. These all turn
upon the payment of the new government taxes; and the
price of wheat this year has been so low that the unhappy
peasantry are driven to their wits' end, and finally to usurious money-lenders, to obtain the necessary cash. In this
emergency I am appealed to in every direction for assistance, and I was well aware that our interview on this occasion would not terminate without the usual demand.

When it came, I saw my chance for alluding to the delicate subject of the murder, and the objections I entertained
to lending money to people who were in the habit of mur-
dering their neighbours. They admitted the murder, which
had been attended with robbery, but my host denied that
he had been in any way implicated, though he had unjustly
suffered several months' imprisonment on suspicion, and had
only been finally released on payment of a heavy sum as
backsheesh. It seems that the evidence as to who the culprit really was rested on the dying deposition of the victim,
who had been attacked by four men, all of whom he named
on his deathbed. On the other hand, my host had succeeded

13

in proving an alibi. The real culprit had, he said, escaped,
and had never ventured back to the village.

Under these circumstances I refused any loan of money,
unless the notables of the village would come to Dalich,
tender their humble apologies, offer a money indemnity to
the mother of the murdered man, and effect a complete
reconciliation. This, according to Arab custom, is a solemn
ceremony, which must be performed in the presence of the
notables of neighbouring villages; but it yet remained to
be seen whether the indemnity question could be arranged
at Dalich, as the man who said he had been unjustly accused declared that he had already suffered so much, in
person and in purse, that he was indisposed to do much in
that line. The poor widow, in spite of her destitution, was
still more intractable; she thirsted for vengeance, for which
she said no money could compensate. However, I have
hopes of bringing them both to reason, and so healing the
feud which extends to all the population of both villages.
Meantime the loan stands in abeyance.

There would, indeed, be a good opening for a professional
peacemaker in these villages, where feuds are bitter and
prevalent, not merely between different villages, but between rival sheiks in the same locality. There are almost
always two, and sometimes three, of these in each village who are not on speaking terms, and who each have
their partisans, so that the opposing factions keep themselves entirely aloof from each other. More than once I
have had occasion to call on the same day on two rival
sheiks. In that case one escorts me until he sees his enemy
in the distance. He then takes leave of me, and I stand
still until the other comes up to take me in charge. These
sheiks, I am sorry to say, often combine with the money-
lenders against the interests of their own fellow-villagers.
The mode by which a money-lender obtains possession of a
village is simple; he goes to the sheik, and says: "You and
your village are unable to meet the government demands;
if you will persuade your village to borrow from me at
forty per cent., I will give you so much commission, and if
at the end of three years you can manage irretrievably to
ruin your villagers, so that I can come down upon them and

obtain possession of the village in satisfaction of my debt
for half its value, your profit shall be so much, and you
shall retain such a share of the village lands." As the
sheiks wield an unbounded influence over their own fac-
tion, this would be an easy operation were it not for the
rival sheik, who is in negotiation with a rival money-
lender. When two money-lenders take to fighting over
a village there is some chance for the villagers, and from
this point of view the feuds of their sheiks are not an un-
mixed evil.

Where a sheik is supreme, as at Dalieh, he has practically
the fortunes of the villagers in his hands, and he must be
watched to see that he uses his influence and authority just-
ly. The only man in a position to watch him is the person
upon whom he depends for assistance to meet the government demands. If this individual happens to be content
with a moderate rate of interest, and to have no ulterior designs upon the village itself, it is evident that he may have
it in his power to do a great deal of good. The villagers
are quite astonished if one comes to them and says, "I do
not want your village, I only want your good-will. I desire
to help you out of your financial scrape, and I am willing to
lend you money at the legal rate of interest if you will furnish me with the necessary security." Any one saying this
finds at once that he has arrayed against him the money-
lenders, who take three times the legal rate of interest; the
government officials, who go shares with the money-lenders;
and, in many instances, the village sheiks themselves, who,
of course, find their interest lies rather with these two
classes than with the unhappy villagers. These latter, accustomed to be plundered all around, naturally do not know
whom to trust, and are apt to look with suspicion on a new
proposal, however favourable and disinterested it may seem.
The obstacles, therefore, to the working-out of improved
conditions by any single man, even in the case of one village, seem almost insuperable, and can only be overcome
by much personal intercourse with the villagers themselves.

The Druses are sensitive to kindness, and grateful for it,
and as there are generally some sick in the village, and

quack doctoring, provided one treads cautiously, is better
than none, we do a good deal of empirical practice, and our
efforts have met with such success that we are obtaining a
somewhat alarming reputation. Of course, we come across
difficult cases, as, for instance, the sheik's daughter. She is
rather a nice-looking girl of eighteen, with a crick in her
neck and an asthmatic affection. On asking how long she
had been ill, we were informed that her mother, on the occasion of her birth, was so angry at finding the child was a
girl and not a boy, that she threw her out of the window,
and she had never been well since. Cases of this sort we
don't attempt to grapple with, but I have ceased to wonder
at the sheik having taken a dislike to the old lady. Indeed,
my own feelings towards her have entirely changed since
hearing of this episode, and, although it happened eighteen
years ago, I treat her with comparative coolness.

Why the sheik hesitates so long about divorcing her I
fail to understand, more especially as he is anxious to marry
a young and handsome girl. I have discovered, by the
way, that divorced people are never allowed to meet again,
even in the street, after the separation has finally taken
place. I saw a young friend of mine, in a fit of passion, divorce his wife last year. She was young and pretty. He
married again, but has already repented, and wants to divorce his present and remarry his first wife, whom he has
never seen since; but Druse law is inexorable on this point.
There was a meeting of elders on the subject, but they decided that it was impossible. So now, when this rash
young man sees the former partner of his life at the other
end of the street, he is obliged hurriedly to turn around and
walk the other way, with a sadly beating heart and repent-
ant spirit.

Some weeks ago we opened a boys' school at Dalieh,
where English and Arabic were taught. In a few days we
had an average attendance of over fifty children, while we
received applications from more than twenty girls, which
we were making arrangements to satisfy, as the desire
which the parents manifested to have their children edu-
cated was so strong that we felt it should be encouraged
in every possible way. One day, however, a summons ar-

rived for the sheik to appear before the authorities, when he was informed that a fine of $250 would be levied on every child who ventured to go to school; a threat which, to my great regret, most effectually extinguished that humble institution.

THE ARISTOCRACY OF MOUNT CARMEL.

DALIET-EL-CARMEL, Oct. 30. — I have been making acquaintance with some of my neighbours, and will take you with me to call upon what in England would be called the leading members of the county aristocracy. They are the blue blood of this region of country, the families which in the early part of the present century exercised power of life and death, and supreme control, over the inhabitants for many miles around; who thought nothing of calling out their retainers and resisting the constituted authority, whether it was that exercised by the various pachas of Acre, who, though nominally Turkish governors, were themselves quasi-independent, or the more iron rule of the Egyptian conqueror, Ibrahim Pacha, to which, however, they were eventually forced to succumb.

One of these families lives at a village about two hours' ride from here. In response to a letter couched in the most flowery Oriental hyperbole, in which my rank is exalted, my virtues are exaggerated, and the beneficent warmth which my presence is supposed to radiate is dwelt upon, I determine to shed it upon the writer of the letter; in other words, to pay him a visit in the gardens to which he has invited me. Our way lies down a wild, romantic gorge which leads to a valley situated among the lower spurs of Carmel, beyond the confines of the mountain proper, where the country is broken up by volcanic action into chasms and precipices, well adapted for defensive purposes, and admirably calculated to be the stronghold of a not over-scrupulous tribal chief. The village itself is situated upon a high conical mound, rising some three hundred feet above the plain; and towering above the surrounding houses is the high, two-storied, half-castellated mansion. It is not thither that I am at present bound, but to a narrow valley about a mile distant from it, which is wedged in between frowning precipices, and is a bright green strip, in delightful contrast to the gray, overhanging crags, for it is a dense mass of orange, lemon, fig, pomegranate, olive, quince, and other fruit-trees, the result of a crystal fountain which gushes from the rock and fertilizes this fairy-like scene.

These are the summer gardens of my host, and from them, as he sees me approach, he issues, with several of his retainers, and leads me to an arbour of overhanging trees, whose dense foliage forms an impenetrable shade against the noon-day sun. Here carpets have been spread, cushions arranged, narghiles and coffee have been prepared, and the circle is formed and the compliments interchanged which are the invariable prelude to an Eastern entertainment. Soon appear, on prancing horses, a picturesque group of men in white flowing _abbayes_, or transparent summer robes, which flutter gracefully in the wind. They are richly embroidered, and the horses are gayly comparisoned; these are the brothers, nephews, and other members of my host's family. One of them is a holy man, who has studied theology in the celebrated seat of Moslem learning, the College of El-Ahzar, in Cairo, and he is much respected and looked up to in consequence.

Knowing that I cannot introduce a more grateful topic, and anxious to stave off as long as possible the financial one, which I suspect is in the background, I ask the dignified group of narghile smokers by which I am surrounded to tell me something of their family history. About four hundred years ago, they say, their ancestors came from the Hedjaz, being a branch of the tribe of Beni Ab Arabs, whose home were the deserts near Mecca, and who were closely related to the family of Mohammed. It is this ancestral connection with the Prophet which has always given the family the great prestige and consideration which it has enjoyed. In those days they came into the country as conquerors, and, settling themselves in their present village, soon reduced the surrounding district to subjection, and continued to rule it, nominally subject to the Pacha of Acre, but really independently, until the invasion of Palestine by Ibrahim Pacha, when, after a sturdy resistance, they were overcome, and the grandfather of my host was executed and the greater part of their lands taken from them. From that time the fortunes of the family began to decline. On the restoration of the country to the sultan, by means of the intervention of England, they derived no benefit. The Turkish government took care not to re-establish an influence which in former times had proved so formidable, and, indeed, one of my hosts had spent two years in prison. Some say it was because he had manifested a spirit of too great independence, but others allege that it was for the more prosaic reason of an inability or refusal to pay his debts.

At all events, when the money-lending question came up, not then, but on the occasion of a return visit which they afterwards paid me, I was assured by those who ought to know that my picturesque, hospitable, dignified, and aristocratic hosts were—well, I won't exactly repeat what it was said they were, but they were not just the kind of people that one would select to lend money to. This grieved me exceedingly, not because I wanted to lend them any, but because they were such gentlemen; in fact, I have been there since, and been very royally entertained in the old castle—where the guests' room is gorgeously furnished, for this part of the world—in order to make my peace for not lending them money; for it is considered an insult, after you have been a man's guest and he asks you to accommodate him financially, if you refuse—which is perplexing when he has no satisfactory security to offer. Now, I want to keep on good terms with this powerful and fascinating and somewhat scampish family without losing my money to them, and the problem I am engaged in solving is how to do it. I have a horrible suspicion that it will yet be solved rather to their satisfaction than to mine.

Under these circumstances, paying aristocratic visits does not seem likely to be an altogether profitable occupation; but they are not always attended with embarrassments of this nature. I have other aristocratic friends, who live about five hours distant from here. They are also originally from the Hedjaz; they also claim kinship with the Prophet, and they also once ruled a large tract of country. In fact, the two families divided the whole of this country between them, and their history has been almost identical.

My visit to this family was in some respects highly characteristic. My way led across the Ruhah, or "Breezy-land," across open, rolling downs, fairly watered, and covered with the remains of what was once a magnificent oak forest. The trees are now dotted singly over it, in park-like fashion. The village itself was beautifully situated at an elevation of about seven hundred feet above the sea, on the side of a thickly wooded mountain, twelve hundred feet high. On this occasion my host, who came out to meet me, led me to an elevated platform in front of the village mosque, an unusually imposing edifice. Here, under the shade of a spreading mulberry-tree, were collected seven brothers, who represented the family, and about fifty other members of it. They were in the act of prayer when I arrived—indeed, they are renowned for their piety. Along the front of the terrace was a row of water-bottles for ablutions, behind them mats on which the praying was going forward, and behind the worshippers a confused mass of slippers. When they had done praying, they all got into their slippers. It was a marvel to me how each knew his own.

They led me to what I supposed was a place of honour, where soft coverlets had been spread near the door of the mosque. We formed the usual squatting circle, and were sipping coffee, when suddenly every one started to his feet; a dark, active little man seemed to dart into the midst of us. Everybody struggled frantically to kiss his hand, and he passed through us like a flash to the other end of the platform, followed by a tall negro, whose hand everybody, including my aristocratic host, seemed also anxious to kiss. I had not recovered from my astonishment at this proceeding, when I received a message from the new-comer to take a place by his side. I now found that he was on the seat of honour, and it became a question, until I knew who he was, whether I should admit his right to invite me to it, thus acknowledging his superiority in rank—etiquette in these matters being a point which has to be attended to in the East, however absurd it may seem among ourselves. I therefore for the moment ignored his invitation, and asked my host, in an off-hand way, who he was. He informed me that he was a mollah, held in the highest consideration for his learning and piety all through the country, upon which he, in fact, levied a sort of religious tax; that he was here on a visit, and that in his own home he was in the habit of entertaining two hundred guests a night, no one being refused hospitality. His father was a dervish, celebrated for his miraculous powers, and the mantle thereof had fallen upon the negro, who had been his servant, and who also was much venerated, because it was his habit to go to sleep in the mosque, and be spirited away, no one knew whither, in the night; in fact, he could become invisible almost at will.

Under these circumstances, and seeing that I should seriously embarrass my host if I stood any longer on my dignity, I determined to waive it, and joined the saint. He received me with supercilious condescension, and we exchanged compliments till dinner was announced, when my host asked whether I wished to dine alone or with the world at large. As the saint had been too patronizing to be strictly polite, I thought I would assert my right to be exclusive, and said I would dine alone, on which he, with a polite sneer, remarked that it would be better so, as he had an objection to eating with any one who drank wine, to which I retorted that I had an equal objection to dining with those who ate with their fingers. From this it will appear that my relations with the holy man were getting somewhat strained.

I was, therefore, supplied with a pyramid of rice and six or seven elaborately cooked dishes all to myself, and squatted on one mat, while a few yards off the saint, my host, and all his brothers squatted on another. When they had finished their repast their places were occupied by others, and I counted altogether more than fifty persons feeding on the mosque terrace at my host's expense. Dinner over, they all trooped in to pray, and I listened to the monotonous chanting of the Koran till it was time to go to bed. My host offered me a mat in the mosque, where I should have a chance of seeing the miraculous disappearance of the negro; but as I had no faith in this, and a great deal in the snoring by which I should be disturbed, I slept in a room apart, as exclusively as I had dined.

I was surprised next morning to observe a total change in the saint's demeanour. All the supercilious pride of the previous evening had vanished, and we soon became most amiable to each other. That he was a fanatic hater of the Giaour I felt no doubt, but for some reason he had deemed it politic to adopt an entirely altered demeanour. It was another illustration of the somewhat painful lesson which one has to learn in one's intercourse with Orientals. They must never be allowed to outswagger you.

THE JORDAN VALLEY CANAL.

HAIFA, Nov. 10.—In one of my former letters I described the nature of the concession which had been obtained by some capitalists at Beyrout for the construction of a railway from Haifa to Damascus, and of the survey of the line, which had already been completed half-way to the latter city. The matter has been the subject of a good deal of financial intrigue, and the capital which was sought for in London has not been forthcoming in consequence. A new element of uncertainty has just been imported into the project by the agitation created by the proposal to connect the Red Sea with the Mediterranean by means of a ship canal, which, commencing at Haifa, should be cut through the plain of Esdraelon to the valley of the Jordan, letting the waters of the Mediterranean into the Ghor, as that valley is called, and connecting the lower end of the Dead Sea with the Red Sea by a canal which should debouch at Akaba.

This project originated principally among British ship-owners and capitalists, who have hoped in this way to destroy the monopoly which M. de Lesseps claims to possess of water communication between the Mediterranean and the Red Sea across the Isthmus of Suez. As the proposed canal does not touch the isthmus, the French company would have no ground of complaint. As, however, great uncertainty still exists as to the practicability of the scheme, a sum of £10,000 has been subscribed by the promoters of the proposed company to make the preliminary surveys, and to obtain the necessary permission from the sultan to do so. According to the first accounts, his majesty set his face against any survey of the kind proposed, but the latest advices would go to show that he has changed his mind, and it would seem not only that the requisite permission has

been granted, but that the surveying party are actually on
their way to Port Said.

It will now be interesting to consider, by the light of our
present information, what are the chances of success, what
is the nature of the obstacles the scheme will have to encounter, and how it proposes to overcome them, so far as
they are known. In the first place, it does not follow, because the sultan has granted permission for the survey, that
he will afterwards, supposing it to be found practicable,
grant a firman for the accomplishment of the work. The
advantages he will derive from it are: Easy access to his
dominions in Arabia, which extend as far south as Aden;
an enormous sum of money, which will be paid to him in
compensation for about fifteen hundred square miles of land
submerged, chiefly government property, and a large annual
income to be derived from tolls on the canal, and the development of extensive tracts of fertile country, especially
to the east of the Jordan, which are now inaccessible and
unproductive. That such a canal would add immensely to
the resources of the empire, and be a source of great profit,
there can be no doubt. On the other hand, it would almost
amount to the virtual annexation of Palestine by England,
whose influence in that country, backed by the enormous
expenditure of capital which would be involved, would be
supreme. It is a question, therefore, whether the sultan
would consider that the pecuniary advantage which he
would gain would be compensated by the political sacrifice
which would have to be incurred.

In regard to the engineering difficulties, so far as they
are known, the only records of levels which we have of the
elevation of the land between the Red Sea and the Dead
Sea are those made at different times by three Frenchmen
—Mons. Lartet, Mons. Vigne, and Mons. Luynes. These
only differ nineteen feet—the lowest being seven hundred
and eighty-one feet, the highest eight hundred; but it must
be remembered that these are not the result of actual survey, but of rough estimates, and there may be depressions
in the dividing ridge which may have escaped these gentlemen's observation.* The dividing ridge is said to be cal-

* Since the above was written the dividing range has been carefully sur-

careous rock—the summit level distant fifty-two miles from
the Red Sea and fifty-eight from the Dead Sea, which is
nearly thirteen hundred feet lower than the level of the
ocean—and it is assumed that the engineering work would
be facilitated by the scour which would be caused by the
sea rushing down such a steep incline in a distance of one
hundred miles. It is not, however, proposed to let the full
force of the ocean in from this end. The operation of
flooding the Jordan valley would be commenced at Haifa;
from this point to the sea-level in the Ghor is only twenty-
five miles. The highest point in the plain of Esdraelon is
one hundred and fifty-seven feet above the sea. Through
this it is proposed to cut a canal two hundred feet wide and
forty feet deep. The volume of water thus let in, it is calculated, would be regulated to an inflow which would equal
about twenty Jordans, and, allowing for evaporation, it is
estimated that in five years the Dead Sea and the whole
valley of the Jordan would be submerged to the sea-level.

The effect of this submergence would be, of course, to
bury the Dead Sea under twelve hundred feet of ocean, and
to create an inland sea about ninety miles long and from
four to six wide. Jericho, Beisan (the ancient Bethshean),
and Tiberias would be the principal places submerged, besides a few small villages. With the exception of Tiberias,
none of these are, however, of any importance. Tiberias
contains a population of over three thousand, chiefly Jews,
and a Latin and Greek monastery. Apart from the question of compensating this population, and paying for the
fertile lands which they occupy, a very important political
question enters into consideration. The French have been
the protectors of the Latin monastery at Tiberias from
time immemorial, and the Russians occupy the same position with regard to the Greek monastery. Are these two
powers, whose interests would be in different ways vitally
affected by the success of the scheme, likely to be induced
to consent to it by any proposal of pecuniary indemnifica-
tion? Its success would utterly ruin the Suez Canal and
almost extinguish French influence in Syria, while Russia,

---

veyed, and the lowest part found to be between six and seven hundred feet
above the level of the Red Sea.

which now aims at the annexation of Palestine and the occupation of Jerusalem, where her influence is at this moment
greater than that of any other European nation, would find
herself practically cut off from it by an inland sea, the private property of her traditional enemy. In both countries
the governments could appeal to the religious sentiment of
the people to support them in resisting, even to a war if
necessary, the flooding of the holy places at Tiberias which
they have guarded for so many centuries.

Nor would this sentimental feeling be confined to France
and Russia. Even in England and America there would be
a strong objection to the Lake of Tiberias, with the historic
sites of Capernaum and the other cities on its margin, which
were the scenes of some of the most remarkable ministrations of our Lord, being buried five hundred feet deep beneath the sea. Curiously enough, the project is no less
keenly supported by one set of religionists than it is condemned by the other. The former pin their faith to the
prophecy contained in the forty-seventh chapter of Ezekiel,
eighth to tenth verses, where it is predicted that "fishers
shall stand upon the sea from En-gedi even unto En-eglaim,"
but even this would not be the case if the scheme were carried out, for then En-gedi would be several hundred feet
below the surface of the sea.

The sanguine supporters of the scheme maintain that it
can be accomplished for eight millions sterling, while its op-
ponents have entered upon an elaborate calculation to prove
that the lowest figure is £225,573,648 and some odd shillings.
Supposing, as seems not impossible, that the one set prove
too little, and the other too much, if it could be done for
fifty millions sterling it would pay a fair interest. The
last year's receipts of the Suez Canal, which cost twenty
millions, were £4,800,000. The whole length of the canal
would be two hundred and fifty miles, of which, however,
only about one hundred and twenty would be actual cutting,
but cutting of a nature unparalleled in the history of engineering. My own impression is that, both from a political
and an engineering point of view, it will be found to be
impracticable; but who can say in these days what science
may not accomplish or what combinations of the Eastern
question may not arise to remove political difficulties?

LOCAL POLITICS AND PROGRESS.

Haifa, Nov. 27.—The native population here is in a high state of excitement at news which has just reached us. The government, it is reported, intends transferring the seat of the provincial government from Acre to this place. This change has been recommended on the grounds of the superior excellence of the harbour of Haifa, of its increasing export trade and rapidly growing population, and, above all, of the constantly augmenting influence of foreigners, which is the natural result of the inflow of their capital and of their industry and enterprise.

The old fortress of Acre, at present the residence of the governor, or mutessarif, contains a population of about nine thousand, pent up within the walls of the fort and crowded into an area of little more than fifty acres. They are for the most part fanatic Moslems, which means a state of stagnation in industry and commercial pursuits; and in consequence of the military rule which prohibits any extension of the town outside of the walls of the fortress within range of the guns, no expansion is possible to the inhabitants. The population of Haifa, on the other hand, is increasing with great rapidity, and the place seems to resound from one end to the other with the clink of the stone-mason's chisel, as new houses spring up in all directions. These considerations would not alone, however, account for the resolution at which the government seems to have arrived.

Three fourths of the population of Haifa are either Roman or Greek Catholics; in other words, they are under the protection of the French Consul when religious questions are concerned; and the policy of the French government in Syria has been to extend its religious protectorate into political and secular matters, to a degree which is constantly giving rise to awkward questions and complications not devoid of danger.

A great part of the house property in the town of Haifa is owned by the monks of Mount Carmel, who consider the whole of Carmel, from the monastery at the western extremity of the mountain, to their chapel at the Place of Elijah's Sacrifice at the other end, as a sort of private preserve, and push their religious pretensions to such an extreme that they look with the utmost jealousy upon any foreigner who attempts to buy land in the mountain, and oppose any such proceeding with all their energy.

The policy of the Turkish government, on the other hand, is to prevent any foreigners buying land there, or, indeed, anywhere else in Palestine, although they are entitled to do so by treaty; and in pursuit of this policy the local authorities are instructed to throw every obstacle in the way of foreign enterprise of all descriptions, but especially to render it impossible for persons not subjects of Turkey to acquire landed property. They have, on these grounds, used their utmost endeavors to ruin the Jewish colony of Zimmarin, which is also in the neighborhood of Haifa, by prohibiting the colonists from building houses for themselves, on the ground that they have no right to the land. They have based this claim on the allegation that the proprietor of the property, who was an Austrian Jew, in whose name it was bought for the colonists, died childless, and, according to Turkish law, landed property reverts to the Turkish government under these circumstances; and the government therefore claimed the property. It so happened, however, that the owner did not die childless. Indeed, I know his son myself, but the government refused to admit the evidence of any but Moslems as to whether he had a son or not, a demand which, as the deceased proprietor did not live in Turkey, it was naturally impossible to comply with. The question has therefore been pending between Baron Rothschild, who took over the property on the death of its nominal proprietor, and the Turkish government for nearly two years; but I understand that permission has at last been obtained for the erection of houses by the colonists, and the affair has been arranged.

The fact, however, that foreign questions are constantly arising at Haifa, either out of French pretensions or the

14

claims of the German or Jewish colonists, and that no such
questions are possible at Acre, where there is but a limited
Christian or foreign population, has rendered it desirable in
the eyes of the Governor-general of Syria to suggest the
removal of the governor of the district to this place. The
change has not yet been sanctioned at Constantinople, and
the inhabitants of Acre, where property will suffer an immediate depreciation, have been pouring petitions into Constantinople to protest against the change, urging as a reason
that they, who were loyal and devoted subjects of his majesty, will suffer; while the population of Haifa, composed
principally of Christians and foreigners, will benefit. It is
just possible, however, that the government may consider
that the loyalty and devotion of the petitioners form the
best reasons why the governor should be moved to a place
where the loyalty and devotion of the people are not so
assured, and should therefore be watched. At all events,
there can be no doubt that the change, should it take place,
will cause an immediate rise in the value of property here,
and that there will be a considerable influx of people from
Acre to this town, which has the advantage in summer of
being a much cooler and more agreeable place of residence.

Meantime, advantage has been taken of this opportunity
to remove the present governor and replace him by a more
intelligent and active functionary, a change which has caused
great satisfaction, both to Moslems and Christians, as, in
spite of his fanaticism, he had contrived to make himself
very unpopular with the former, while he altogether failed
to keep the peace at Acre between the rival sects of the latter, who, though very limited in number, were constantly
engaged in broils. Moreover, it is not the habit of the
Turkish government to retain its functionaries, under any
circumstances, long at the same post.

The only drawback to Haifa as the new seat of government is its limited water supply. At present the town depends entirely upon its wells, and although an abundance of
water can be found at a trifling depth, it is usually a little
too brackish to be altogether palatable. Under these circumstances it became of the utmost importance, in view of the
proposed change, to try and find a spring, sufficiently copi-

ous and near the town to be utilized, and it occurred to a
friend and myself that such a one might exist at Rushmea,
where are the ruins of an old Crusading fort, which I have
described in a former letter, distant about an hour's ride
from the town, at an elevation of about seven hundred feet
above the level of the sea. There is a well here called the
Well of Elias, into which I once descended, and found that
it was supplied with water which entered through a tunnel
in the rock, but had no outlet; and the shepherds told me
that, however much they watered their flocks, the water
always remained at the same height, while in winter, although
the well was eight feet deep, the water rose in it so high as
to overflow the mouth. Under these circumstances it was
evident that the well was, in fact, a sort of back-water of
some underground stream or rivulet, which found a subterranean channel for itself. This we determined, by excavation, to try and discover.

We therefore commenced digging near the well, and about
two feet from the surface struck the roof of a subterranean
aqueduct. Uncovering this, we found that the channel had
become silted up with mud, which required to be removed.
We then found that we were in an arched tunnel, the sides
of which were roughly built with stone, while the floor was
paved with the same material, in which a channel had been
cut, but it was four inches higher than the water in the well.
We were therefore obliged to take it up, cutting, altogether,
a trench thirty yards long and eight feet deep. On drawing
the water off by means of this channel, we uncovered the
mouth of the tunnel, by which it entered, sufficiently to send
in a man with a light. After wading through the mud for
a few paces, he came upon a vault beautifully cemented,
thus proving that in ancient times the stream had been
utilized. It would have involved a greater expense, however, to clear out than I was prepared to incur, unaided by
the community for whose benefit it would have inured. As
it was, the stream thus discovered was almost sufficient in
volume to be worth conveying to Haifa, a distance of three
miles, and could doubtless be much increased. In the course
of our excavations we came upon several large blocks of
square stone, which had formed part of the ancient tunnel.

The project of the railway from Haifa to Damascus, the concession for which had lapsed in consequence of the combined greed and apathy of the first grantees, is now revived under more favorable auspices, and I have little doubt that the change of the seat of the government to this place will give it a renewed impetus, so that before long it will be carried out.

Meantime, unwonted energy is displayed by the government in improving our communications. Having occasion a few weeks ago to ride to Beyrout, I saw the surveyors at work tracing out a line for a carriage road to connect that important city with Haifa. The distance is about eighty miles, and there are no serious engineering difficulties in the way. This road is sadly needed, especially now, when, owing to the cholera in Europe, no steamer touches here on its way to Beyrout, although we are visited once a fortnight by one coming from that place after it has performed there a quarantine of five days. The habit, unfortunately, of the government of making the road, and postponing to an indefinite period the construction of the bridges, goes far to neutralize its good intentions. The towns through which the road passes are heavily taxed, and then, owing to the want of bridges, it is useless for a great part of the year. Should this road be completed, Beyrout, Damascus, Jaffa, Jerusalem, Nazareth, Haifa, Tyre, and Sidon will all be connected by roads over which stages could run; and this would go far to facilitate travel in Palestine, and enable tourists to dispense with that system of tenting which now renders it so slow and expensive.

THE IDENTIFICATION OF ANCIENT SITES.

HAIFA, Dec. 13.—The researches which I have been making into the oldest authorities, with the view of identifying the sites of the numerous ancient towns that once formed the homes of the extensive population which in ages long gone by inhabited this coast, have only served to reveal to me the enormous difficulty of the task. This difficulty is created partly by the confusion introduced by the crusading nomenclature and traditions, partly by the inaccuracy of the itineraries of early pilgrims and travellers, and to the discrepancies existing in the most primitive maps, and the contradictions in historical records. Thus between this place and Tantura, a distance of fifteen miles, I have visited the ruins of no fewer than nine ancient towns or villages, some of them of considerable size, not one of which, with the exception of Tantura, which is the Biblical Dor, has been positively identified. I do not include in these the ruins of towns a mile or more inland, which would double the number and convey some idea of the denseness of the population which once inhabited this section of the country. At the same time it is possible, from the varied character of these ruins, that some were far more ancient than the others, and that they may have existed as traces of a still more early people, when other cities, also now in ruin, were rich and flourishing. Thus we have on this coast remains of the early Phœnician period, of the Greek period, of the Roman or Byzantine period, and, lastly, of the crusading period —the latter too modern to be of any archæological interest. They consist merely of constructions built from the materials of the civilizations which had preceded it. Not content with using up these materials, the crusaders gave the towns and forts which they built wrong names, refusing to adopt the Saracen nomenclature, which was generally a corruption of the original Canaanitish or Hebrew, and attempting to identify them according to their own ideas of Biblical topography, or reading of Roman history, thereby introducing inextricable confusion. Thus we have William of Tyre, one of the crusading historiographers, gravely informing us that "Duke Godfrey de Bouillon awarded, with his usual magnanimity, to the generous and noble Tancred the city of Tiberias, on the Lake of Genasereth, as well as of the whole of Galilee and the sea-town of Kaypha (or Haifa), which is otherwise called Porphyria."

The Carmelite monks still cling to this tradition, although modern research has proved beyond a doubt that the site, at all events of one Roman city of Porphyrion, was at Khan-Yunis, a ruin, eight miles north of Sidon, and at least seventy miles from Haifa. To escape this difficulty some have supposed there were two Porphyrions, and that one was here, basing their argument on the fact that in the Onomasticon of Eusebius and Jerome there is a city marked at the point of Carmel, called Chilzon, and that Chilzon is the Hebrew for the murex, or shellfish which produced the purple dye found there in great quantities; hence Porphyrion, or the purple city.

In carefully examining these ruins, and remarking the great quantity of carved porphyry which is peculiar to them, I have thought it furnished a stronger argument in favor of what would seem an appropriate appellation. The crusaders even confounded the Sea of Galilee with the Mediterranean; thus they supposed a connection to exist between the town of Caiapha, or Caiaphas (the modern Haifa), which Benjamin of Tudela asserts to have been founded by Caiaphas, the high-priest, and Cephas, the Greek name of Simon Peter. Hence near Haifa the crusading clergy showed the rock where Simon Peter fished, called to this day Tell el-Samak, or the Mound of the Fish. Laboring under a similar confusion of idea, they built a fort out of the ruins of a place called at the present day Kefr Lam, a name which, no doubt, dates back before the times of the crusaders, and which they twisted into Capernaum, that place being, as we all know, on the Sea of Galilee. The Capernaum of the crusaders, however, is a village on the Mediterranean shore, thirteen miles down the coast from here.

The itineraries of the pilgrims and early travellers are scarcely less perplexing. They are generally careful to record the distances between the various places they visit, but rarely with accuracy. Their remarks, however, are naïve and amusing. I have just been reading the journal of a certain Antoninus, the Martyr, who travelled in Palestine about the year A.D. 530. Writing of Tyre, he says:

"The city of Tyre contains influential men; the life there is very wicked; the luxury such as cannot be described. There are public brothels, and silk and other kinds of clothing are woven."

We do not altogether see the connection in this last sentence. Going on, he remarks:

"Thence we came to Ptolemais (the modern Acre), a respectable city, where we found good monasteries. Opposite Ptolemais, six miles off, is a city which is named Sycaminus, under Mount Carmel. A mile from Sycaminus are the hamlets of the Samaritans, and above the hamlets, a mile and a half away, is the Monastery of Heliseus (or Elijah), the prophet, at the place where the woman met him whose child he raised from the dead. On Mount Carmel is found a stone, of small size and round, which, when struck, rings because it is solid. This is the virtue of the stone—if it be hung on to a woman, or to any animal, they will never miscarry. About six or seven miles off is the city of Porphyrion."

Now there are as many mistakes as there are sentences in this quaint account by the holy man. It is a matter of dispute which are the ruins of Sycaminus. Two ruins claim that honor, and one of these it undoubtedly is. They are only two miles apart, but the nearest is thirteen miles from Acre, instead of six, and the other fifteen. A mile from Sycaminus, he says, are the hamlets of the Samaritans. These have been identified beyond all doubt as a ruin called Kefr es Samir, two miles and a half beyond one of the above-mentioned ruins, and four miles and a half beyond the other. The Monastery of Heliseus, the prophet, "a mile and a half away," I have described in a former letter. It is the picturesque gorge and ruin called Ain Siah, but the place where Elijah met the woman of Sarepta was, if we are to believe the Bible, "at the gate of that city," at least fifty miles distant from Carmel. There is no doubt as to its site, between Tyre and Sidon. As to "the stone of small size, which, when struck, rings because it is solid," it happens to

ring because it is hollow. I have an interesting collection
of these geodes, found near Ain Siah, their peculiar shapes
having given rise to the legend that they were melons and
other fruits which the proprietor refused the prophet when
he was hungry, and which the latter therefore blasted with
petrifaction. And then comes the final statement about
the unhappy Porphyrion, which he puts six miles off, thus
probably identifying it with Athlit, and making confusion
worse confounded. First we have the Jerusalem Itinerary,
distinctly placing it to the north of Sidon, a position confirmed by other authorities; then we have William of Tyre
identifying it with Haifa, and now we have Antoninus putting it six miles off.

I will not inflict upon you all my reasons for coming to
the conclusion that the ruin at Tell el-Samak, the Mound of
the Fish already alluded to, is the site of Sycaminum, though
I doubt whether a larger population did not inhabit the city
two miles nearer Haifa, where the porphyry fragments
abound. To judge by the fine carvings at both places, they
must have been wealthy as well as populous, and their most
prosperous period was in all probability during the first
three or four centuries of our era. The coins which I have
found so far are of that epoch. Exploring the ruins of
what must have been the upper tower of Sycaminus, distant about four hundred yards from the Fish Mound, and
two hundred feet above it, a few days ago, I came upon a
cistern with four circular apertures. Upon being let down
into it I found it was seventy feet long, hewn out of the
solid rock, twenty feet broad, and twelve feet high from the
débris at the bottom, but in reality much deeper. The roof
was supported by three columns, four feet square, also hewn
from the living rock. The cement was still in some places
perfect, and the cistern must have been capable of containing a vast supply of water. It was about fifteen yards from
an angle of a wall composed of rubble, from which the ash-
lar had been removed, about four feet thick, and still standing in places to a height of four feet. In others the foundations of this wall were easily traceable. As the whole ruin
seems to have escaped the observation of the Palestine Exploration Survey, I measured it, and found the east wall to

be one hundred and twelve yards long, the south wall sixty-five, the west wall seventy, and an intersecting wall forty. I could find no traces of a north wall. It was probably a fortress, which was supplied by the cistern already mentioned. In the neighborhood were some fine rock-cut tombs, two with six loculi, each in a good state of preservation. I also picked up a piece of white marble on which was an inscription in early Arabic characters, but only the word "Allah" and two or three more letters remained on the fragment.

At Kefr Lam, the crusaders' Capernaum, which I had occasion recently to visit, I discovered two very remarkable vaults, each forty feet long by twelve broad and seven high. The roof was supported by five arches, each arch composed of a single stone four feet broad, on the top of which huge flat stones had been laid. I have never seen any constructions like these vaults, and think they probably dated from a very ancient period. In the immediate neighborhood the peasantry had recently opened an ancient well, thirty-five feet deep, the water being approached by a flight of steps round two sides of the well, the shaft of which was about thirty feet square. There were no fewer than seventeen handsome rock-cut tombs in the neighborhood of the village, and I regretted that I had not time to prolong my investigations, as I feel convinced that the vicinity would repay examination. As it is, I have obtained from the villagers several good specimens of terra-cotta lamps, two curious alabaster saucers, some coins, and other antiquities.

THE SEA OF GALILEE IN THE TIME OF CHRIST.

HAIFA, Dec. 26.—In reading the works of Dr. Kitto and other writers who have endeavoured to present a picture of the manners and customs of the population which inhabited Palestine in ancient times, I have been much struck by the erroneous impressions which the descriptions of those writers are calculated to convey in many important respects. This has arisen from the fact that while they have portrayed, with tolerable accuracy, the rude civilization of the original inhabitants and the subsequent civilization grafted upon it by their Jewish conquerors, they have left out of consideration the changes worked upon, and the modifications introduced into, the social conditions thus produced by that still higher and later civilization which resulted from Greek and Roman invasions. Thus while they carefully trace back the habits of the modern fellahin, and show that they differ slightly from those of the peasantry of the country in the time of Christ, and invoke the testimony of modern Bedouins as evidence of a mode of life which has undergone no perceptible alteration since the days of Abraham, they leave out of account altogether that magnificent Roman and Byzantine civilization, traces of which still exist in such abundance as to astound the traveller with its splendor and its richness, but which has passed away like a dream, leaving nothing behind but the coarse barbarism which has succeeded it, and which is almost identical in character with what it supplanted. Hence it is that these writers have found those resemblances between the modern and ancient manners and customs of the inhabitants of this country by which they were so much struck, and which they have given to the public as furnishing an accurate picture of what ancient Palestine was like.

We are so much in the habit of confining our interest in

this country to its history before the time of Christ that it
will probably strike many with surprise to learn that the
most flourishing epoch of its history was subsequent to that
time; that never before had the arts and sciences reached
so high a pitch; that never before had its population been
so wealthy and luxurious, its architecture so grand, its commerce so flourishing, and its civilization generally so advanced. It is true it had lost its independence, and was
only a Roman province, but it is just because it was one,
and not a Jewish kingdom, that our impression of its actual condition at the time of Christ is apt to be so erroneous.

This fact has been very forcibly brought to my notice in
a recent trip which I have made along the shores of the Sea
of Galilee, more especially along its little-explored northern
and eastern coasts, where the evidences of the wealth and
luxury of the former inhabitants still remain in unexampled
profusion. In reading in the Gospels the narrative of the
works and life of Christ, so much of which was spent upon
the shores of the lake, in one of the cities of which he for
some time took up his abode, most of us have endeavoured,
probably, to picture him to ourselves amid purely Jewish
surroundings and conditions closely resembling those which
we have been in the habit of associating with that previous
period of Jewish history with which we are familiar in the
books of the Old Testament. So far from that being the
case, the part of the country in which his ministrations were
principally exercised, was beyond all others a centre of Roman life, with all its luxurious accompaniments. Nowhere
else in Palestine was there such a congeries of rich and
populous cities as were crowded round the shores of this
small lake. Nowhere else could the Jewish reformer come
into closer contact with the rites of a worship alien to his
own.

On the shores of this lake might be seen temple after
temple rearing their vast colonnades of graceful columns,
their courts ornamented with faultlessly carved statues to
the deities of a heathen cult. Here were the palaces of
the Roman high functionaries, the tastefully decorated
villas of rich citizens, with semi-tropical gardens irrigated
by the copious streams which have their sources in the

plain of Genesareth and the neighbouring hills. Here were broad avenues and populous thoroughfares, thronged with the motley concourse which so much wealth and magnificence had attracted—rich merchants from Antioch, then the most gorgeous city of the East, and from the Greek islands, traders and visitors from Damascus, Palmyra, and the rich cities of the Decapolis; caravans from Egypt and Persia, Jewish rabbis jostling priests of the worship of the sun, and Roman soldiers swaggering across the market-places, where the peasantry were exposing the produce of their fields and gardens for sale, and where fish was displayed by the hardy toilers of the lake, among whom were those whom the Great Teacher selected to be the first recipients of his message and the channels for its communication to after ages.

Thus it was, as I rode along the margin of the sea the other day, that I was enabled to repeople its shores in imagination by the light of the remains with which they are still strewn, and, overtaken in its desolation by the shades of night, to fancy its now gloomy shores ablaze with the scintillations proceeding from the lamps of at least a dozen large cities, and the almost continuous street of habitations which connected them, and to illuminate its now dark and silent waters with countless brilliantly-lighted boats, skimming over its smooth surface, containing noble ladies and gallants on their way to or from scenes of nocturnal festivity, or indulging in moonlight picnics, with the accompaniments of wine and song and music. That life in these cities was profligate and dissipated in a high degree we may gather from Christ's denunciation of Bethsaida, Chorazin, and Capernaum, which he declared to be so much more wicked than Tyre or Sidon, or even Sodom, that it would be more tolerable in the day of judgment for those cities than for the three he was denouncing. That among these Capernaum was the one of the greatest splendor, and was puffed up therefore with the pride of its own pomp and magnificence, we may gather from the indignant apostrophe: "And thou, Capernaum, which art exalted unto heaven." It may have been because he considered this city the wickedest, as it appears to have been the largest on the lake, and therefore

the most in need of his ministrations, that he chose it for
some time as his residence. Hence it came to be called
" his own city." This circumstance invests it with a special
interest in our eyes.

Unfortunately, a violent contest rages between Palestin-
ologists, if I may be allowed to coin the word, as to the
exact site of Capernaum. The two places which claim this
honor are now called Khan Minieh and Tell Hum respectively. Until lately the weight of opinion was in favor of
the former site; latterly the researches of Sir Charles Wilson, on behalf of the Palestine Exploration Fund, have convinced that accomplished archæologist and careful explorer
that the true site of this celebrated city is to be found at
Tell Hum. It would weary my readers if I were to quote
all the texts relied upon by the disputants to maintain each
hypothesis, supported by calculations of distance, the accounts of Josephus, and of early pilgrim or Arab travellers.
The subject has been pretty well thrashed out, but I doubt
whether it is even yet exhausted. I incline strongly to the
Tell Hum theory, but as Khan Minieh comes first on our
way as we glide from Tiberias to the head of the lake, as it
is unquestionably the site of what was once a city, and as it
is a highly picturesque spot, and one, moreover, full of Biblical interest as being, if not Capernaum itself, within three
miles of that city, and therefore a spot which must have
been the scene of some of Christ's labours, I will begin by
describing it.

The plain of Genesareth, the unrivalled fertility and luxu-
riance of which, though it is now uncultivated, I described
in a former letter, when I crossed it eighteen months ago
on my way to Safed, is terminated at its northern extremity by a mountain range, which projects in a lofty and
precipitous crag into the lake, and renders any passage
round it by land extremely difficult. This projection forms
a little bay, or rather rush-grown lagoon, running back into
the head of the plain. Into it falls a small stream, powerful
enough, however, to turn a mill. It is this building and the
ruins of an ancient khan near it, which was itself constructed from the remains of an ancient city about three hundred
yards distant, which is now called Khan Minieh. The true

site of the old city is not, however, where the khan now
stands, but not far from a fountain, shaded by an old fig-
tree, from which the fountain takes its name—Ain el-Tin,
or the Fountain of the Fig-tree, which suggests the idea
that either the name is very new or the fig-tree very old.
A plentiful supply of water flows from it, slightly brackish,
with a temperature of 82° Fahrenheit. The water is crowded with fish and surrounded with green turf. It appears to
be one of the seven fountains mentioned by Theodorus,
A.D. 530, as being two miles from Magdala, the city of Mary
Magdalene, in the direction of Capernaum.

Near this fountain are some old foundations and traces of
ruins, but these for the most part cover a series of mounds
where a few walls are visible, but no traces of columns,
capitals, or handsome blocks of stone, and much smaller in
extent than those of Tell Hum. Indeed, the whole area is
not more than two hundred yards long by one hundred
broad, and this is one reason for supposing that it cannot be
the site of that important city. The khan itself is at least
as old as the twelfth century, being mentioned by Bohaed-
din in his life of Saladin. A road from here leads up the
steep hillside to Safed. The view from it, as we ascend to
some elevation above the plain, is very beautiful. That fertile expanse which Josephus calls "the ambition of nature,"
lies stretched at our feet, with the waters of the lake rip-
pling upon its pebbly beach, while we look right up the
gorge of Hammam, its beetling cliffs on both sides towering
in rugged cave-perforated precipices to a height of twelve
hundred feet above the tiny stream which, compressed between these lofty walls of limestone and basalt, winds its
way to the lake.

But it is not up the wild mountain-side that our present
way lies; so, taking our last look at the crumbling walls of
the old khan, at the picturesque water-mill, the ruin-strewn
mounds, and the grassy lagoon, we prepare to skirt the rocky
flank of the ledge which here dips into the waters of the
Sea of Genesareth, and by which we hope to reach the
ruins of Bethsaida.

THE SCENE OF THE MIRACLE OF THE FIVE LOAVES AND TWO SMALL FISHES.

HAIFA, Jan. 6, 1885.—If, as I stated in my last letter, students of Biblical topography have been much exercised in their minds as to the identification of the ruins on the northwest shore of the Sea of Galilee, which indicate the site of the once famous city of Capernaum, and have applied not only a great amount of antiquarian research and of time in the way of minute local examination and literary labor in the hope of definitely settling this knotty point, there is another upon which they have no less anxiously expended their ingenuity. This is to solve the vexed question as to whether there were, in the time of Christ, two Bethsaidas or one. This question would never have arisen but for the confusion introduced into the scriptural narrative by the puzzling accounts given in all the four gospels of the miracle of the feeding of the multitude with five loaves and two fishes, the scene of which the four evangelists are unanimous in describing as having been in a desert spot which must have been on the eastern side of the lake, for immediately afterwards "they crossed over to the other side," arriving at Capernaum, which was on the western side. But according to one (Luke) this desert place (on the eastern side) belonged to a city called Bethsaida; and according to another (Mark) Christ, after the miracle, "constrained his disciples to get into the ship and go to the other (or western) side before, unto Bethsaida, while he sent away the people." Hence the confusion; starting from the western side, they take ship, cross over to a desert place belonging to Bethsaida; the miracle is performed there, and the disciples are constrained by their Master to take ship and cross the lake back again to what must be another Bethsaida. Then the storm arises, he comes to them on the waters, and they finally reach Capernaum in safety.

Reland, the learned geographer of the last century, was the first to invent the second Bethsaida on the western side, which is not mentioned by either Josephus or Pliny, the latter of whom distinctly puts it on the eastern side; and I have not been able exactly to discover upon what authority Reland hit upon this easy solution of the problem. The only historical Bethsaida of which we have any certain record was a place at the northeastern extremity, originally a village, but rebuilt and adorned by Philip the Tetrarch, and raised to the dignity of a town under the name of Julias, after the daughter of the emperor. Here, in a magnificent tomb, Philip was himself buried. On the other hand, we have indications of the existence of another Bethsaida in the mention of a Bethsaida which was the birthplace of Peter and Andrew and Philip, which Mark tells us was " in the land of Genesareth," and therefore on the west shore of the lake. Supposing Tell Hum to be Capernaum, and the western Bethsaida to be on the site usually assigned to it, this hypothesis would give us two Bethsaidas only six miles apart, not a very probable supposition; or else we have to suppose that the land of Genesareth extended across the Jordan to the east side, which we know to have had another name, and to have been in another province; or to suppose, as Dr. Thomson—who resolutely refuses to have two Bethsaidas—does, that half the town was on one side of the Jordan and half on the other, and that the half on the west side was called Bethsaida in the land of Genesareth, though the plain of that name is five miles distant. Moreover, there are no ruins conveniently placed to support the presumption, which is very strained. Altogether the subject is one which has puzzled every Biblical geographer hitherto, and, after a careful examination of all their arguments, I find myself just as much in the dark about it as when I entered upon the investigation. As, therefore, after visiting all the disputed localities, I do not feel any the more competent to enlighten your readers, I will confine myself to describing the different places which have been suggested as the sites of these cities, as well as of others which I visited in the section of country to the east of the Jordan, some of which I was the first to discover, and none of which have been positively identified.

Meantime, the scene, which the tradition of many centuries located erroneously as the spot upon which the miracle took place, is exactly above us as we wind along a rocky path cut in the precipice which overhangs the Sea of Galilee. This huge impending crag is crowned by an artificial plateau, which is two hundred feet long by one hundred broad, and in the northwest angle are the remains of a wall and the ruins of a building, probably a fortress of some sort. This spot was known in the middle ages as the Mensa Christi, or Table of Christ. In olden time the great Damascus high-road ran just below, and the fort above doubtless commanded this pass; but it has become impassable, and the path now follows the channel of an aqueduct hewn out of the living rock. For about two hundred yards we find ourselves riding along the narrow floor of this ancient watercourse. On our left the smooth rock rises precipitously, and on our right it forms a wall from three to four feet high, over-which we could drop a stone perpendicularly into the waters of the lake. The aqueduct which thus forms our singular roadway is about three feet wide; emerging from it, after we turn the angle of the rock, we find ourselves overlooking a little bay, into which rushes a brawling torrent, the largest which enters the lake excepting the Jordan, and which here turns a mill. It is, however, only a few yards long, as it bursts from the ground in great force, in what is by far the most powerful spring in Galilee, and is, without doubt, the celebrated Fountain of Capernaum mentioned by Josephus as watering the plain of Genesareth. This it did by means of the aqueduct which we had already traversed, the distance from the fountain to the plain not being above a mile. Besides the principal fountain, which is estimated as being more than half the size of the celebrated source of the Jordan at Banias, there are four smaller fountains, all more or less brackish, and varying in temperature from 73° to 86°.

One of the special subjects of interest connected with these fountains is the presence in them of the remarkable fish called the coracinus. The only known habitats of this fish in the world are in the Nile, in a fountain which I have also visited in the plain of Genesareth, called Mudawara, and in

15

this spring. Josephus accounts for its existence here, as
well as in the Nile, by a hypothetical subterranean water
communication with the great river of Egypt. Modern
geologists point to it as an evidence of the fact that in some
long bygone period Palestine might have been included in a
great Ethiopian basin. However the circumstance is to be
accounted for, it is most remarkable, and was doubted until
Canon Tristram verified it twenty years ago by a somewhat
singular experience. Crossing the little stream which issues
from the fountain of Mudawara and flows into the lake, and
which happened to be very low at the time, he was surprised
to observe a quantity of fish wriggling along in single file,
and so close together that the mouth of one touched the tail
of the one before it. In places there was so little water
that they had to flop across intervals of almost dry land;
here he caught them easily with his hand, and, as many
averaged three feet in length, he was not long in making a
good bag. What surprised him most, however, was to find
that as soon as he laid hold of one it began hissing and
screaming like a cat. Making a bag of his cloak, he carried them off in triumph to his camp, which was three
hours distant, and could hear them hissing and caterwaul-
ing in it all the way. He describes them as being a most
delicious fish to eat, something like an eel in flavor, and
possessed of extraordinary vitality, as some of them were
still living after they had been two days out of the water.
The last volume just issued by the Palestine Exploration
Fund contains a print of this extraordinary creature, which
has a long, slender body, apparently not much thicker than
that of a good-sized eel, with two long fins, one on the back
and one on the belly. The mouth, with its long, cartilagi-
nous streamers (I do not know the ichthyological term for
them), somewhat resembles that of a catfish. I unfortunately
had no means of fishing for them on the occasion of my visit,
and they did not happen to be migrating to their spawning
grounds, which they were evidently doing when Tristram
caught them; but my late experiences on the shores of the
lake have been so full of interest that I propose to make
another visit in the spring, when I hope to go supplied with
tackle, and to give you my own piscatory experiences.

There is a small tract of fertile land in the rear of the mill, but no ruins except those connected with mills or water-works. Nevertheless, it is impossible almost to conceive that a position so favored by nature should not have been the site of a town, and it is on this spot that many geographers place the western Bethsaida. There are no apparent grounds for their doing so beyond the necessity of finding a spot somewhere which should support their hypothesis. If, however, they must have a second Bethsaida, I should rather put it a mile farther off, at Khan Minich, instead of so very close to Capernaum as this would be, always supposing Tell Hum to be Capernaum, which is only two miles distant from this spot. Dr. Thomson's theory that El-Tabghah, the modern name of this place, was the grand manufacturing suburb of that large city, from which its fountain took its name, seems to me rational. Here were the mills, not only for it, but for all the neighbourhood; so also the potteries, tanneries, and other operations of this sort would be clustered around these great fountains, a theory somewhat borne out by the name, Tabghah, which resembles the Arabic word Dabbaga, meaning tannery.

There is no doubt that in this neighbourhood somewhere, probably on the plain of Genesareth, was the location of a town far older than any of those whose sites we are now discussing, and this is the Chinneroth mentioned in the Old Testament, from which the lake, in days long anterior to those of Christ, took its name, and which the Talmud renders Ginizer, which is therefore doubtless identical with Genesareth. Indeed, it may be noted as a curious fact, which has been forced upon me by these investigations, that the towns noticed in the Gospels, excluding the large cities, such as Jerusalem, Tyre, and Sidon, are almost all places not mentioned in the Old Testament. Nazareth and Capernaum, Bethsaida, and Chorazin and Tiberias are names never occurring in the Hebrew Scriptures; and the scenery of the life of Christ lies, as a rule, apart from the centres, religious or political, which reappear again and again in the earlier episodes of Jewish history.

CAPERNAUM AND CHORAZIN.

HAIFA, Jan. 20.—Perhaps the most interesting spot in the world to those deeply under the influence of that charm which association lends to places hallowed by the ministrations of the Founder of Christianity is to be found in a desert, rock-strewn promontory on the northwest shore of the Lake of Tiberias; for among these piles of hewn blocks of black basalt still remain the ruins of a great synagogue, within whose walls, the foundations of which may still be distinctly traced, were collected the multitudes who flocked to hear the teaching of Christ. While modern tourists resort in crowds to Jerusalem to visit the mythical sites which are supposed, upon the vague basis of ecclesiastical tradition, to be identified with episodes in the life of the great Teacher, scarcely one ever finds his way to this remote locality lying just out of the beaten track along which Cook leads his herds of sightseers; and yet it is probable that the greater part of that period in the life of Christ, the record of which is contained in the four Gospels, was spent at Capernaum, which the most careful investigation, by the highest authorities in such matters, has identified with these ruins of Tell Hum, amid which I was just now standing. Here it was that Christ cured Peter's mother-in-law, restored the paralytic, called Matthew, cured the centurion's servant, raised Jairus's daughter from the dead, and obtained the tribute of money from the mouth of a fish. It was here that he spoke the parables of the sower, the tares, the treasure hid in the field, the merchant seeking goodly pearls, and the net cast into the sea. Sir Charles Wilson, whose researches on this spot led him to identify it as being the site of the city of Capernaum, believes this synagogue was, "without doubt, the one built by the Roman centurion (Luke vii. 51), and, therefore, one of the most sacred spots on earth." It was in this building, if that be the case, that the well-known discourse contained in the sixth chapter of John was delivered; and it was not without a strange feeling, says the same explorer, "that, on turning over a large block, we found the pot of manna engraved on its face, and remembered the words: "I am that bread of life. Your fathers did eat manna in the wilderness and are dead."

This very synagogue was probably the scene of the healing of the demoniac and of the delivery of many of those divine lectures on faith, humility, brotherly love, and formality in worship, as we read at the end of one of them: "These things said he in the synagogue as he taught in Capernaum." Perhaps it was in the little creek, where a boat was now riding at anchor only a few feet from the shore, that Christ taught the people from the boat so as to avoid the crush of the multitude. It was doubtless in one of these inlets that James, the son of Zebedee, and John, his brother, were mending their nets when, being called, they left their ship and followed him; and it was on this coast that Andrew and Peter were casting their nets when they were summoned to become fishers of men. It has a higher claim to be called the birthplace of the religion which has since revolutionized the world than any other spot upon it; and it is a matter of some surprise to me that neither the Greek nor the Roman Catholic churches, in their zeal to discover holy places, which may serve as levers for political intrigue, have yet thought of occupying this one, which would seem the holiest of all. Perhaps it would lead to a comparison between their practice and the teaching of which it was the scene, which might give rise to some inconvenient reflections.

Apart from their associations the ruins themselves are not particularly striking. They cover an area of about half a mile in length by a quarter in breadth, and consist chiefly of the black blocks of basaltic stone which formed the walls of the houses. The traces of the synagogue, however, remain sufficiently for the building to be planned. Built of white limestone blocks, it must have formed a conspicuous object amid the black basalt by which it was surrounded. It was seventy-five feet by fifty-seven, built north and south, and at the southern end had three entrances. Many of the columns and capitals have been carried away, but enough still remain to convey some idea of the general plan and aspect of the building. The capitals are of the Corinthian order, and there were epistylia that rested upon the columns and probably supported wooden rafters. There are also remains of a heavy cornice and frieze. The exterior was probably decorated with attached pilasters.

Two miles north of Capernaum are the ruins of Chorazin. There is no difficulty in identifying the site, which may be determined partly by the itineraries of early travellers, and partly by the similarity of the modern name, Kirazeh. The path to them leads up the sloping, rocky hillside, but, owing to the peculiar character of the masonry, which is barely to be distinguished at one hundred yards from the rocks which surround it, the extent and importance of these ruins have been overlooked until quite recently. They cover an area as large as, if not larger than, those of Capernaum, and are situated partly in a shallow valley, partly on a rocky spur formed by a sharp bend in the Wady Kirazeh, here a wild gorge eighty feet deep. From this spot there is a beautiful view of the Lake of Tiberias to its southern end; and here, too, are gathered the most interesting ruins—a synagogue with Corinthian capitals and niche-heads cut, not, as at Capernaum, in limestone, but in hard black basalt. The dimensions of this building are about the same as those of the one at Capernaum, but the interior is a mass of ruins. Two pedestals still remain *in situ*, and a portion of the wall. The characteristic of this synagogue is an excess of ornamentation of rather a debased kind. The niches are most elaborate, and remain as sharp as when they were cut in the hard material used. The mouldings of the door-posts are similar to those used in other synagogues, and there are many stones cut with deep mouldings and pieces of classical cornices strewn among the ruins.

Many of the dwelling-houses were until recently in a tolerably perfect state, the walls being in some cases six feet high; and, as they are probably of the same class of houses as that in which Christ dwelt, a description of them may be interesting. They are generally square, of different sizes, the largest, however, not over thirty feet square, and have one or two columns down the centre to support the roof, which appears to have been flat, as in the modern Arab houses. The walls are about two feet thick, built of masonry or of loose blocks of basalt. There is a low doorway in the centre of one of the walls, and each house has windows twelve inches high and six wide. In one or two cases the house was divided into four chambers.

We now pushed on to the point where the Jordan enters the lake, distant about three miles, for it was only on the other side of that river that my exploration of new ground might be said to commence. I had been attracted hither by rumours which had reached me of a remarkable stone which was said to be in the possession of an Arab, on which were pictorial representations and inscriptions. As my information on the point was somewhat vague, I rode up to a Bedouin encampment, near which was also a collection of mud hovels occupied by fellaheen, which were situated on the west bank of the river. They were naturally so suspicious that I pretended at first to be merely anxious to have a guide to show me the ford, but it was not until the old sheik himself appeared that I could find any one willing to offer me the slightest assistance. They gazed at me with open-mouthed stupidity, real or assumed, and the sight of silver scarcely moved their stolidity. Far different was it with the eagle-eyed old gentleman who, having seen the group assembled round us, strode up from the Bedouin encampment, and at once entered into the spirit of the thing. Not only was he prepared to show me the ford, but, for adequate consideration, would take me to all the ruins in the neighbourhood, with the positions of which he professed an accurate acquaintance, if I would only wait until he went for his horse. This I was only too happy to do, and in a few minutes he galloped up with his *kufiha* and *abbaye* fluttering in the wind, a genuine son of the desert. We forded the Jordan by following the little bar which it makes on entering the lake, the water reaching to our saddle-flaps, and, following the shore, here a grassy plain for half a mile, reached a large square building, charmingly situated near some trees on the margin of the water. This was the granary and storehouse of the great Arab proprietor of the neighbourhood, the only building with any pretensions for miles round; and it was the local agent of this man, himself a resident in Damascus, whom I now found to be in possession of the relic I had travelled so far to see. My disappointment may be easily conceived when I was told that he had gone to Damascus, and would not return for a week. My disgust, as I squatted beneath the walls of this detestable building, making a lunch off hard-boiled eggs, and revolving burglarious schemes of entry, all of which came to naught, may easily be imagined. The fact that the building itself was surrounded by ruins was small consolation, for these consisted only of large hewn blocks of black basalt, and the foundations of houses which were clearly to be traced, but the area they covered was not extensive, and I could not find any indications of any public building. The name of the spot is El-Araj, which signifies The Lame, but I was unable to identify it with any Biblical locality.

DISCOVERY OF AN ANCIENT SYNAGOGUE.

Haifa, Feb. 2.—I narrated in my last letter the disappointment I experienced when, after making a pilgrimage to the
north end of the Lake of Tiberias for the express purpose
of seeing some stones covered with inscriptions and pictorial
representations, said to be in the possession of the agent of
a rich Arab proprietor, I found their owner gone and the
relics locked up in a building of which he had taken the key,
and all ingress to which was impossible. The Bedouin sheik
whom I had picked up as a guide at a neighboring encampment, seeing my chagrin, comforted me by the assurance
that if I would only follow him he would take me to a place
where I could find others which were quite as good. I
mounted my horse, therefore, in somewhat better spirits, as
from his description of the locality I knew it must have
escaped the attention of all former travellers, and consoled
myself by the reflection that a discovery of some importance
might still be in store for me.

Our way took us due north across the fertile plain of
the Butéha, an alluvial expanse about two miles in length
by one in breadth, formed by the detritus which, in the
course of ages, has been washed down the Jordan, and the
winter torrents which rush into the plain down the wadys
that descend from the elevated plateau of Jaulan.

The Butéha is not unlike the plain of Genesareth. Both
are well watered and extremely fertile. Butéha has the
largest and most prominent brooks, Genesareth the most
numerous and abundant springs. The old traveller, Burck-
hardt, says that the Arabs of the Butéha have the earliest
cucumbers and melons in all this region. It was on this
plain, at the foot of the hill or " tell " we were now approaching, that Josephus fought the Romans under Sylla, concerning which battle he says: " I would have performed great

things that day if a certain fate had not been my hinderance, for the horse on which I rode and upon whose back I fought fell into a quagmire and threw me to the ground, and I was bruised on my wrist and was carried into a certain village called Cuphernome or Capernaum."

The tell which rises from this plain, about a mile and a half from the lake, is thickly strewn with ruins, consisting of hewn blocks of black basalt, with which, in the ancient times, all the houses in this region were constructed; but as yet no traces of any large building have been discovered. It has, indeed, been very rarely visited, but it is considered by many to be the site of Bethsaida-Julias and the scene of the miracle of the loaves and fishes. At present all we know for certain is that one of the Bethsaidas was somewhere in the Butéha; that Josephus in his descriptions advanced it to the dignity of a city, both by reason of the number of inhabitants it contained and its other grandeur; and that inasmuch as the plain of the Butéha contains many heaps of ruins, none of any very great extent, any of them may be Bethsaida, while if it were a large city in our modern acceptation of the term, the whole plain would not be large enough to contain it.

Indeed, one is much struck in exploring the ruins of the country by the limited areas which they cover. I am afraid to say how many sites of ruined towns I have visited in Palestine, certainly not less than forty; and I think one could crowd them all into the area occupied by the ruins of one large ancient Egyptian city—Arsinoë in the Fayoum, for instance; but then the ruins of an Egyptian city are composed mainly of mounds of potsherds, while these consist of large blocks of building stone, either limestone or basalt, measuring generally two feet or two feet six one way, and a foot or eighteen inches the other. Then they are usually comparatively near together; all around the Lake of Tiberias, and in the country in its vicinity, they are generally not more than from one to three miles apart; so that this section of country must have been very thickly peopled. The ruins of Et-Tell are now built over by the Arabs, who live in a squalid village among the basalt blocks which formed the mansions inhabited by the more highly civilized race which occupied the country in the days when all this region was the favourite haunt of Christ and his disciples.

Leaving Et-Tell on our left, we followed the east bank of the Jordan for more than a mile. This river is here very rapid, and, splitting into numerous streams, whirls past the small islets they form. It is the very ideal of a trout stream, on which on some more propitious occasion I propose to cast a fly. Meantime, even had I been provided with the requisite tackle, I should have been obliged to forego the temptation. It was on the steep rise of a hill, about a hundred yards from the river, that my guide suddenly stopped. Here was a small collection of Arab hovels, recently constructed, and it was in their search for stone, last summer, that the natives had for the first time uncovered the ruin which now met my delighted gaze.

I found myself in the presence of a building the character of which I had yet to determine, the walls of which were still standing to a height of eight feet. The area they enclosed was thickly strewn with building-stones, fragments of columns, pedestals, capitals, and cornices. Two at least of the columns were *in situ*, while the bases of others were too much concealed by piles of stone to enable me to determine their original positions. My first impression, from the character of the architecture which was strewn about, was that this was formerly a Roman temple; but a further and more careful examination convinced me that it had originally been a Jewish synagogue, which at a later period had been converted to another use; probably it had been appropriated by the Byzantines as a basilica, or Christian church. This was the more probable, as the existing walls had evidently been built upon the foundations of a former structure. The massive stones were set in mortar, which is not the case with the synagogues hitherto discovered; and I should doubtless have been completely at fault in classing this building had my attention not been already directed to the remains of the synagogues brought to light recently by the exertions of the Palestine Exploration Fund.

I was now fortunately in a position to compare the dimen-

sions, ground-plan, and architectural fragments which were
strewn about, with those which distinguish the synagogues
already discovered, in regard to whose original character
there can be no doubt, as the Hebrew inscriptions and sacred
Jewish symbols carved on the lintels prove it. The building measured forty-five feet by thirty-three, which is exactly
the measurement of the small synagogue at Kefr-Birim.
The columns were exactly of the same diameter. The floor
was depressed, and reached by a descent of two steps, which
were carried around the building in benches or seats each a
foot high, the face of the upper one ornamented by a thin
scroll of floral tracery. These features occur in the synagogue at Irbid. There was a single large stone cut into the
shape of an arch, which had evidently been placed on the
lintel of the principal entrance, like the one which stands to
this day over the doorway of the great synagogue at Kefr-
Birim. The niches, with the great scallop-shell pattern
which distinguishes them, almost exactly resemble those of
the synagogue of Kerazeh or Chorazin; while the cornice,
which was extremely florid, and not unlike what in modern
parlance is called " the egg-and-dart pattern," though differing in some respects from the cornices hitherto observed,
was evidently of the same school of design. The capitals
were two feet three inches high, and Corinthian, in the same
style and of the same dimensions as those of the small synagogue of Kefr-Birim, and there was the upper fragment of
two semi-attached fluted columns, with Doric capitals, the
ditto of which is to be found at Irbid. The two columns *in
situ* exactly answer in position those of several of the synagogues, and though the position of the door, which was in
the centre of the western wall, was somewhat unusual, this
was accounted for by the fact that the building had been
excavated from the hillside, so that the top of the east wall,
nine feet of which was still standing, was level with the surface of the slope of the hill.

The only convenient entrance was in the wall of the side
immediately opposite to it. The name of this most interesting locality was ed-Dikkeh, a spot hitherto unvisited by any
traveller. Indeed, if it had been visited, it would have been
passed unnoticed, for its antiquarian treasures have only

been revealed for the first time a few months ago. The word ed-Dikkeh means "platform," a name, considering its position, not inappropriate; but I have not been able to identify it with any Biblical site.

The area of ruins apart from those of the synagogue itself was not very large, but the situation was highly picturesque. Half a mile to the north of where we stood the Jordan forces its way through a gorge which I hope some day to explore, while immediately below us it rushed between numerous small islets. Opposite the hills swelled gently back from its western bank, behind us they rose more abruptly to the high table-land of Jaulan, while to the southward stretched the plain of Butêha, with the Lake of Tiberias in the distance.

Meantime the few wild-looking natives who inhabit this remote locality clustered around me, as they watched me measuring and sketching, with no little suspicion and alarm. "See," said one to another, "our country is being taken from us." My request for old coins only frightened them the more. They vehemently protested that not one had been found, an assertion which, under the circumstances, I felt sure was untrue; nor did the most gentle and reassuring language, with tenders of backshish—which was nevertheless greedily accepted—tend to allay their fears. I have forgotten to mention what was perhaps the most interesting object of all, and this was the carved figure of a winged female waving what seemed to be a sheaf in one hand, while her legs were doubled backward in a most uncomfortable and ungraceful position. It was on an isolated slab about six inches thick, and two feet one way by eighteen inches the other.

The area of the hillside all around was strewn with the blocks of building-stone of which the town had been built. It had apparently not been a very large place, but as the villagers will probably continue their excavations for their own purposes next summer, it is not at all unlikely that they may bring some more interesting remains to light. I earnestly impressed upon them the necessity of preserving these, promising another visit next year, when I would reward them in proportion to the carvings, coins, or other antiqui-

ties they could provide for me; but they listened to my ex-
hortation with such a stupid and suspicious expression of
countenance that I did not derive much encouragement from
their reluctant consent.

CHARACTERISTICS OF THE RUINS OF SYNAGOGUES.

Haifa, Feb. 16.—I described in my last letter the discovery of the ruins of an ancient Jewish synagogue at a spot on the east bank of the Jordan, about three miles north of the upper end of the Lake of Tiberias. As the question of ancient Jewish synagogues is one of great interest, in regard to which considerable misapprehension prevails even among archæologists, I may be excused for entering upon a short disquisition upon the subject, as I am not aware that the great light which has been thrown upon it by recent Palestinian research has yet been distributed in a popular form to the general public, and the old and recognized authorities are often misleading. For example, "Smith's Dictionary of the Bible" contains a long article on Jewish synagogues which has hitherto been considered the great authority on the subject, in which I observe that it states under the sub-head "Structure:"

"Its position, however, was determined. It stood, if possible, on the highest ground in or near the city to which it belonged. Its direction, too, was fixed. Jerusalem was the Kibleh of Jewish devotion. The synagogue was so constructed that the worshippers, as they entered and as they prayed, looked towards it."

This may have been the case in respect of the earlier synagogues, long anterior to the time of Christ, the traces of which have been lost, but in the case of eleven which have been discovered by the officers of the Palestine Exploration Fund, since the above was written, no such rules have been adhered to. These all date either from the time of Christ, or shortly before it, to three centuries after it. We know they were synagogues, and can approximately calculate their dates, from the Hebrew inscriptions found on some of them, and from the emblems with which they were ornamented, such as the pot of manna, the seven-branched candlestick, and other purely Jewish devices. In the cases of these synagogues, many of which I have seen, the builders have by no means selected the most prominent positions; the existing remains have, with two exceptions—at Irbid and at ed-Dikkeh, where the ground would not admit of such an arrangement—their doors on the southern side, so that every Jew entering would have to turn his back on Jerusalem. The ark, if there was one in these synagogues, would necessarily, in that case, be placed at the northern end, and the worshippers would therefore have to pray with their backs to Jerusalem.

We know, besides, how abhorrent to the Jews were the figures of animals, and the popular impression has been that none such were permitted to decorate their synagogues; yet in these synagogues we find them prominently carved in stone in six out of the eleven. The carved figure I found at ed-Dikkeh makes a seventh, and they probably existed in the others and in greater quantities than those already noted, but have been destroyed by the Mohammedans as contrary to their religion. As may be supposed, as they were all built at nearly the same period, there is a great similarity in the architecture of the synagogues recently discovered. It is of an extremely florid and somewhat debased Roman type. In all of them the same class of mouldings is observable. There is a great resemblance in the niches and cornices, while the capitals show some variation, being Corinthian, Doric, and Ionic. There is also a great similarity in the ground plan and in the position of the columns. In the case of a Roman temple these are all in colonnades outside the building, in cases of synagogues they are all within it. There should be no possibility, therefore, of confusing a synagogue with a Roman temple, even though it abounds with Roman architecture; but it is not always so easy to distinguish it from an early Christian church, or basilica, where the columns were also inside. The reason that the architecture of these latter synagogues was so purely Roman in character is to be found in the conditions under which they were built. Shortly after the destruction of Jerusalem by the Romans, the Jewish Sanhedrim was established at Tiberias, under a patriarchate whose authority was recognized by the foreign communities at Rome and in Asia Minor, and large numbers of these came to live in the district, while alms poured into the treasury at Tiberias from all directions. It thus became very wealthy, and the centre of a great Jewish population. It was recognized by the Romans, and by them granted many indulgences, and, during the reign of Antoninus Pius, A.D. 138–161, increased in power and influence.

At the beginning of the third century the Jews were in high favor with the Emperor Alexander Severus, who was even called the Father of the Synagogue, and this name may have been given him from his influence over the erection and architecture of these buildings. It seems, therefore, almost a certainty that the Roman emperors aided and inspired the erection of these synagogues. They were built by Roman labor, for the Jews, being immersed in commercial pursuits, by using Roman workmen, obtained much finer results than we are led to think they would themselves have been capable of. No synagogues of the kind have been found in other countries, though there were many in Babylon and in the colonies of the Jews, and this type has never been perpetuated in later works, while we have seen how many points in their religion were disregarded in their design and ornamentation. We may therefore suppose that they were forced upon the people by their Roman rulers at a time when they were completely submissive to their power, and directly they were able they deserted such pagan buildings as a disloyalty to their religion. It is stated that Rabbi Simon, son of Jochai, is the founder of many of these buildings. Indeed, it is related that he built with his own money twenty-four synagogues in this part of the country. As he was a most fanatical teacher of the law, it is evident that if he erected so many buildings in such violent contradiction to many points of his own religion, he must have done it under great pressure. These synagogues built under Roman auspices were probably only an alternative evil; they had to choose between having them or none at all. With the exception of one on Carmel, and a problematical one at Shefr-Amr, about six miles from Haifa, all the syna-

16

gogues hitherto found have been within the immediate limits of what was formerly the patriarchate of Tiberias. The fact that the building at ed-Dikkeh would be included in this district is an additional reason for assuming it to have been one of this class of synagogues, and, if so, we should probably be accurate in fixing its date at somewhere in the first or second century after Christ.

From ed-Dikkeh I proceeded under the guidance of the old sheik, who was much pleased at the satisfaction which I evinced at his successful leadership thus far, in an easterly direction to another place, where he assured me that the villagers had also been at work getting out stone during the summer, and had unearthed some more old ruins. Our way led us along the flank of the Jaulan hills, with the plain of the Butêha on our right, and, after a ride of about an hour, we reached a village of huts, in the midst of which was the anticipated excavation. I could not quite expect such another stroke of luck as that which had befallen me at ed-Dikkeh, but yet I had no reason to be dissatisfied. Here, upon a terrace built of large blocks of basalt about five inches in height, I found a curious condition of things. The villagers had laid bare, eighteen inches below the surface of the earth, the cement floor of an old chamber about twenty feet in one direction. I could not tell how far it went in the other, as it was still covered with earth, but where it abruptly terminated it revealed, about eighteen inches beneath, another floor of some building of much older date, across which it had been built diagonally. This floor was of stone. It, too, had been cleared for some distance by the natives, and upon it was standing, at intervals of six feet apart, five solid cubes of stone, measuring two feet each way, which had probably been the foundations or lower stones on which had been placed the pedestals of columns. As this lowest floor was three feet below the present surface of the ground, the top of these stones was one foot below it, and the line of them may have continued, though only five had been uncovered. I have no means of conjecturing what the building may have been. I found many fragments of columns and capitals strewn around among the ruins, which covered a larger area than those at ed-Dikkeh, and which, like them, are a new

discovery, though what its results may be must depend very
much upon further excavation. I impressed upon the villagers here, as I had already done at ed-Dikkeh, if, in the
course of their excavating for stone, they came upon any
with inscriptions or pictorial representations, to preserve
them; but I felt, as I did so, that my words fell upon deaf
or rather unwilling ears. They gazed at me with alarmed
stolidity, either not understanding or not caring to understand, and evidently dominated by the fixed impression that
my proceedings implied in some way the future ownership
of the soil. I looked from here wistfully up a valley, at the
mouth of which this ruin was situated, and at the head of
which others were reported to exist, but circumstances prevented me at the time from pushing my explorations in this
direction. Indeed, travel in this part of the country is attended with many difficulties, some political and some material, among the latter the chief one being, if one is unpro-
vided with a tent, the question of where one is to spend the
night. If, on the other hand, one is provided with a tent,
it involves a much larger retinue, increased expense, excites
even more distrust among the natives, and becomes sometimes dangerous from arousing their cupidity, and this ne-
cessitates having guards and escorts, which are the cause of
endless quarrels and annoyance, as the more people you have
with you the less are you your own master to go where you
like, and the more difficult it is to provide for man and beast.
It is a choice of evils at best of times, and the worry and discomfort can only be compensated for by good luck in obtaining results, and this is by no means always to be secured,
though thus far on this particular journey I had had no reason to complain. I now propose to tempt fate on the highlands to the east of Lake Tiberias, with what success remains
to be seen.

A NIGHT ADVENTURE NEAR THE LAKE OF TIBERIAS.

HAIFA, February 28.—The tourist who follows the ordinary track of Palestine travel from Jerusalem to Damascus inevitably passes Tiberias. Standing on the flat roof of the convent, where, if he is not one of a Cook's party, he is compelled to lodge, he has a splendid view of the lake and of the precipitous cliffs opposite, which descend abruptly to its margin from the elevated plateau behind, that averages two thousand feet above the level of the lake. That sheet of water being nearly eight hundred feet below the sea-level, the only engineering problem which presents itself to the consideration of the surveyors who have been engaged in tracing a railroad line between Haifa and Damascus is how to ascend from this depression to the highlands above.

The solution of the problem is to be found in a large wide valley called the Wady Samak, which is exactly opposite Tiberias, and up the unknown recesses of which our tourist looks with longing eyes. Practically this wady is a sealed book to the Palestine traveller. To explore it he would have to obtain special permission from the government, with a guard, and be exposed to all manner of extortion from his dragoman, who would take advantage of his ignorance to magnify the dangers and add to the already existing obstacles. Indeed, one of the most singular characteristics of Palestine travel is the close proximity of unknown and unexplored districts to beaten tracks. Just as it often happens in a large city, that in the immediate neighborhood of one of the most frequented thoroughfares there are back slums inhabited by thieves and criminals, into which no respectable person penetrates, so, in Palestine, within ten miles of a place like Tiberias, there are spots as yet untrodden by the foot of the explorer; but these are all to the east of the lake and of the Jordan. Almost every inch of western Palestine has succumbed to the exhaustive researches of the Palestine Exploration Fund.

It was on a gloomy winter afternoon that I found myself skirting the eastern shore of the lake with the view of attacking the mysteries of this interesting valley—interesting from a practical point of view, because I wanted to look at the possible gradients which it might offer for a railway, and still more interesting from an archæological point of view, because I felt sure that in searching for gradients I should find ruins. But the search was undertaken under difficulties. I was without a tent, because my journey partook of the nature of an exploratory dash, and a tent would have been an encumbrance. I was without a guide, because my guide had deserted me in consequence of one of those misunderstandings which are not uncommon between travellers and their guides; but I had two companions, baggage animal and servant, and an amiable soldier, upon whom, in case of trouble, it was supposed we should be able to rely for protection and aid.

Owing to a variety of causes, principally arising from a desire to find ruins where there were none, and to map certain wadys which are incorrectly laid down in the maps, we were about two hours later than we should have been when we reached the mouth of the wady. The clouds were lowering ominously, there had been no sun all day, and now that luminary seemed to have given up the attempt to shine upon us in despair, and to have made up his mind, in a fit of disgust, to retire permanently to rest. I felt, considering the journey up the unknown wady, which we still had to perform without a guide before I could hope to reach a resting-place (I did not look forward to its being much of a sleeping-place), that it had no business to get dark so early. However, it was still broad daylight, and we took our bearings by compass as carefully as was possible, and were encouraged by observing that the track we were on was a broad and well-beaten one, and which, as the formation was white limestone, would show plainly even when it got dark. The valley I knew to be about seven miles long. The village we were bound for, the only village in it or near it, was at its

head. We had only to keep going straight up, and the path
we were on would surely lead us to it.

This fond delusion I hugged to my soul as we pushed on
as rapidly as our wearied steeds, which had been travelling
since daybreak, would allow us. The breadth of the valley
in a bee-line from one edge of the plateau above us to the
other was not less than two miles. It was a broad valley,
with many shoulders running into it from both sides, and
terraces here and there of cultivated land, the crops the
property of wandering Bedouins, who come here in winter
to sow them, and come back in spring to gather them.
Down the centre of the valley brawled, over a rocky bed, a
mountain brook, even in the dryest season a respectable
trout stream, and often after heavy rains an impassable torrent. On the present occasion, however, it was behaving
itself respectably, and gave us no trouble. It was fringed
with oleanders, and here and there received tiny tributaries,
which all helped to produce more vegetation than is usual in
Palestine valleys, and to enhance the beauty of scenery the
natural features of which were strikingly picturesque. As
long as it was light I could see natural terraces on the flanks
of the valley, up which it would be easy to take the line.
Then I saw where long curves must be taken, winding up
lateral hollows, through which we could twist the line up
the two thousand feet it had to ascend, and lengthen out the
seven miles of the wady to a distance which would suffice
for the required gradient.

Assuredly when that long-looked-for and much-to-be-de-
sired line is made, the stretch up the Wady Samak will be
one of the most romantic and interesting sections upon it,
while its well-watered slopes will doubtless tempt the specu-
lative agriculturist or stock-farmer to intrude upon domains
now appropriated by a few wandering Arabs, whose scanty
flocks might be increased tenfold without consuming half its
pasture, and who do not cultivate a tithe of its fertile soil.

While thus indulging in airy imaginings of the future,
darkness gradually closed in, and I became suddenly aware,
as so often happens in this world, that all my calculations
would have been sound in regard to my finding my way if
they had not been based upon thoroughly delusive premises.

The cause of my error may be summed up in the one word, basalt. I had forgotten one of the most remarkable geological features of this part of the country, and this is, that only the lower stratum of the range which rises from the east shore of Lake Tiberias is of limestone. All the rest is basaltic, and this formation is of vast thickness. The whole of this district is, indeed, an immense volcanic field, consisting of irregular heaps of amorphous lava and disintegrating scoriæ, with mounds of globular basalt. So that when darkness came on everything below me, as well as all above, seemed suddenly to have become as black as night. The path had disappeared as if by magic, and I called a halt, and we found ourselves on a patch of black rock, with exactly similar patches of black rock all around us. The outlines of the hills had vanished, the path had led us up from the bed of the torrent, so we no longer had that to guide us. To attempt to descend to it would have been madness, as we might have fallen over a precipice in the darkness; indeed, we were afraid to move, except with extreme caution, in any direction. We had a compass and matches, and knew that by keeping due south we might, if no accident befell us, and the rocks permitted a passage, ultimately reach the plateau; but we also knew that the direction of our night-quarters was due east; but here we ran the greater risk of tumbling into unknown transverse gorges with precipitous cliffs. We cautiously worked south, but our progress soon became barred by thorny brushwood, and we had to face the alternative of a night out-of-doors without water or anything to drink, and a very limited supply of food.

We were just bracing ourselves to this unpleasant prospect, when, in a southwesterly direction, we suddenly saw a gleam of light; it lasted for a moment, then seemed to go out. But that one ray was one of hope, and we steered cautiously for it. We had been scrambling by compass in the dark for about half an hour, and were just beginning to despair, when the bark of a distant dog put new energy into us, and not long after, around the shoulder of a hill, we came upon an encampment, and were greeted by the furious yells of the mob of noisy curs which infest the tents of the Bedouins. It was a startling apparition to burst upon these

nomads in their remote retreat—horsemen of a type they had
never seen before, and an armed soldier. Such children as
were awake set up a dismal squalling, the women cowered
tremblingly over their camp-fires under the pent roof of black
camels' hair. All the side of the tent being open, its whole
internal economy was exposed to view, and enabled us to
judge of the slight protection in the way of bedding or
clothing or covering of any sort which was provided against
the inclemency of the season.

Meantime the men had gathered round us, half timidly,
half threateningly. The presence of the soldier suggested
fear and suspicion, while the smallness of our party encouraged the bolder ones to look defiant. As far as I could
make out in the darkness there were about a dozen tents
here in all—apparently the fag end of an insignificant tribe
whose name I forget. It was at first impossible to induce
any one at that late hour to act as guide. Even abundant
offers of backshish failed to shake their suspicion, which
was to the effect that we wished to decoy one into durance
to act as a hostage until some arrears of taxes which they
owed the government should be paid up.

The other alternative was that we should take up our
quarters in the sheik's tent, whether he liked it or not, which,
with a piercing wind blowing, accompanied by sleet, was
not a very pleasant prospect. He seemed to relish it as little
as we did, and finally consented to be our guide as we made
some silver gleam in the firelight. As he seized his eighteen-
foot lance and mounted his ragged steed he looked like some
Arab Don Quixote; and as the camp-fire threw its ruddy
glow upon a group of wild-looking women, with dishevelled
hair and tattooed chins, crooning over a pot like the witches
of "Macbeth," and upon barelegged men, as they flitted to
and fro between the black tents, I thought I had seldom
gazed upon a more weird and unreal-looking scene.

How our guide could find his way up the rocky hillside
and across the prairie remained a mystery during the long
two hours that we followed him. Of this I feel sure, that
we scrambled up places in the dark that we should never
have thought of facing by daylight. The very horses
seemed to have become desperate, and to have abandoned

themselves to their fate. At last we dismounted and scaled the rocks like goats, every one, man or beast, doing the best he could for himself on his own account, and so at last, wearied and half-starved, for we had fasted for about ten hours, we reached the goal of our endeavour, too tired to see what an utterly miserable hole it was.

I passed a wretched night in a room in the middle of which a fire had been built, which filled it with smoke, for it had no other exit but the door, which it was too cold to keep open. Around the fire were stretched fifteen Arabs, who quarrelled with a government official, whom they were compelled to entertain, about their taxes, until they exhausted themselves, and then they exchanged their discordant wrangling for no less discordant snoring. After replenishing exhausted nature with the eggs which was all that my host could provide me with, and a tin of canned meat, I vainly tried to follow their example, but was too busily occupied in scratching to think of anything but fleas, and so tossed and tumbled and longed for the morning, when I proposed to enter upon a new field of exploration, for this was the village of El-Al, where I had heard that ruins existed; and as I had every reason to believe that in ancient times this neighbourhood had been the centre of a large population, I felt sure that they had left interesting traces, which were yet to be discovered.

KHISFIN.

HAIFA, March 15.—There is no part of ancient Palestine which offers a more fertile field for antiquarian research than that portion lying to the east of the Jordan, which fell to the share of the half-tribe of Manasseh. In Biblical times a part of it was called Golan, and its modern name of Jaulan is almost identical with its ancient appellation. It is to this day the finest grazing land in all Palestine, as it was in the days of old, when Job fed his vast flocks and herds upon its more eastern pastures, but it is now very sparsely inhabited. The sedentary population has all been driven away by the wandering tribes of Bedouins who have appropriated the country; the very few villages that remain are squalid and miserable, and the inhabitants live in terror for their lives, for they never know what day, or rather night, the Arabs may not be down upon them, and carry off their stock. They surround their houses, therefore, with large yards enclosed by stone walls, and it was in one of these that I found a lodging on the night that I had so nearly been obliged to spend in the wilds of the Wady Samak. Attached to these yards are large stone vaults, capable of containing great herds of cattle, and some of them apparently of great antiquity. In the one in which I staked my horses I found, on examining it in the morning, part of a Corinthian column, still *in situ*, standing to a height of about six feet. I failed to discover any more, but the vault was so dark that my examination was carried on with difficulty, and I had no time to spend over it. The sheik's house in which I lodged, and to which this vault belonged, was evidently, however, built on the site of what had formerly been a building of some importance, for in the yard, to my surprise and delight, I came upon a prostrate statue of a woman, life size. The head was severed from the body, and the feet had been broken off at

the ankles, but it was a fine specimen of Greek statuary.
Both the features and the drapery were beautifully executed.
The feet I found *in situ*, the ankles just appearing on a level
with the ground. On clearing this away I laid bare the feet,
which were still firmly fixed on the original pedestal, which
it would have required a great deal of labour to disinter. It
is not improbable that the pedestal is covered with carving
in *basso relievo*, and I promise myself at some future time to
dig it up. In the meantime both feet and pedestal cannot
be safer than where they are, more especially as my companions secured the head. This the sheik was induced to
part with for $3. The body was too cumbersome to carry
away now, as a camel would have been needed for its transport, and, as it is not of much value without the head, it may
be considered secured by the possession of that portion.

The statue apparently represented Artemis, as the left arm
clasped what seemed to be a quiver for arrows. The right
arm was unfortunately broken away, otherwise the statue
would be perfect when put together. The pedestal, without
doubt, contains an inscription describing the statue and the
goddess represented upon it. I was sorely tempted to de-
vote a day to its examination, but, in that case, I should
have been compelled to give up visiting some other spots of
interest which had never before been investigated, and the
hardships and discomforts of these preliminary dashes into
the wilds, more especially in the depth of winter, are so
great that one is not tempted to prolong them—my present
object being rather to know where to go at some future time,
when the conditions, political and otherwise, may be more
favourable than they are now. I therefore did not linger
longer than was absolutely necessary at this place. I had
seen enough to prove to me that it would, in all probability,
amply repay a fuller investigation, and I determined without delay to push on to a village called Khisfin, which I was
extremely anxious to examine, as it has hitherto escaped the
careful attention of all former travellers. And yet, from
the records which I have been able to examine in regard to
it, it must have been a place of considerable importance in
mediæval history, though hitherto my efforts to trace it back
to an earlier date than the beginning of the tenth century

or to identify it with any Biblical site have been in vain. Yakubi, an Arab geographer, who lived about the year 900 A.D., mentions it as one of the chief towns of the province of the Jordan. In his day Syria was divided into three provinces, namely: The province of Damascus, the province of the Jordan, and the province of Palestine. Yakut, in the thirteenth century, mentions it as a town of the Hauran district, below Nawa on the Damascus road, between Nawa and the Jordan. Khisfin was also at one time a fortress of the Saracens, as it is further mentioned as the place to which Al Melek Al Adil, Saladin's son and successor, fled after having been routed at the battle of Beisan by the Crusaders, who advanced upon him from Acre. As it is mentioned as being one of the chief towns of the province, so long ago as 900 A.D., it is probable that its importance dates from a much older period, as indeed was indicated by some of the ornamentation which I found there.

Securing my host, the sheik, as a guide to a locality which promised to be so full of interest, we started at a brisk pace across the plateau, in the teeth of a bitterly cold east wind and driving sleet, and, after riding an hour, came to the ruins of Nab, situated on a small mound. They consist of blocks of basalt building-stone, some traces of foundations, some fragments of columns and capitals, and a tank, dry at the time of my visit, but which evidently held water at some time of the year. It had, apparently, been much deeper at a former period, only the two upper courses of masonry being now visible. It was oval in shape, and measured sixty yards by thirty. This place does not appear to have been previously visited or described. Shortly after leaving it I observed masses of black stone, which, on nearer approach, proved to be the walls of a fortress that, my guide told me, was Khisfin itself. It loomed strikingly up from the grassy plain, and gave rise to pleasing anticipations as I galloped impatiently up to the base of the walls, and, jumping off my horse without even waiting to tether him, in my excitement, scrambled up a breach to see what was inside. I looked down upon a ruin-strewn area, but, alas, no columns, nor capitals, nor signs of Roman remains. This had evidently been in turn a Saracen and a Crusading construction. The outer walls measured sixty-eight yards one way by fifty-four the other. They are nine feet in thickness, and are eight courses of stone in height, the stones being from one foot to one foot six inches square; but some are much larger. Within the fort are the traces of a second or inner wall, forming a sort of keep in the centre; but the whole area was too much encumbered with ruin for any accurate plan to be possible in the limited time at my disposal.

A little beyond the fort stood the village itself. All the intervening and surrounding fields were thickly strewn with the large hewn blocks of black basalt of which the houses of the former population had been constructed, and which, to judge from the area which they covered, quite justified the description of Yakubi, that in his day this was one of the chief towns of the province, and the centre of a very large population. The present squalid inhabitants, few in number, seemed to live in a perfect quarry of these old building-blocks. No difficulty had they in finding material wherewith to build their houses, their large cattle vaults, and enclosing yards. They simply piled the tumbled masses of stone in a little more regular order, one above another, to make walls of any height or thickness they chose, without mortar or cement, and had houses that would last forever. As all the stones were beautifully squared and shaped, they had far more symmetrical walls, thanks to the ancients, than if they had been left to themselves. These black, massive huts all jumbled together with their vaults and yards, without regular streets or lanes, formed one of the strangest looking villages I ever saw. In some cases the walls were formed of stones placed diagonally, in others horizontally, in others perpendicularly. The very roofs were of stone, with earth on the top of them to fill up the cracks. Where hewn stone is so abundant and wood almost impossible to obtain, it is astonishing what uses the former can be put to. And now came a search which I would willingly have protracted over days instead of over minutes, which were all I had to give to it. To "do" Khisfin thoroughly one ought to examine carefully every stone in every house, besides the acres of stones by which the present village is surrounded. As it was, I went into as many houses as I had time for, and made sketches of what ornamentation I found. The natives had evidently used as lintels for their doorways the stones which had served the ancients for the same purpose. These were usually four or even five feet long, and many of them were ornamented with curious devices. They were in part Crusading and in part Saracenic. There were the tablets with half-effaced escutcheons, rosettes, bosses, crosses, and other Crusading emblems, which left no doubt in my mind that this must have been at one time an important Crusading fortress, though in the only book relating to the crusades which I happen to have by me no mention is made of it. There were several of those curious carvings, difficult to describe, which characterize Saracenic architecture as an evidence that the Moslem conquerors of the crusaders had also had a hand in its adornment; but what was more interesting, there were floral wreaths and carved devices which are a feature in Byzantine art, which gave clear evidence that before the conquest of this province from the Byzantine empire in the seventh century it had been an important city of that civilization which immediately succeeded the Roman.

The important question which I could not determine was whether, in the old Roman times, it had been a place of note. There can be little doubt that a future examination, of a more minute character than I was able to give, would determine this point, and it is not at all impossible that upon the old stones might be found seven-branched candlesticks, pots of manna, or emblems of a still older date, which would carry it back to Jewish times. Meanwhile I looked anxiously, but in vain, for an inscription which might throw some light on the subject, and it is certain that amid such a mass of ruin such are to be found. All my inquiries for old coins only tended to alarm the villagers, who looked on my proceedings with their usual suspicion, and associated my visit and my desire for old money with their taxes, which is the only idea that the fellah of Palestine seems able to connect with the visit of a prying and inquisitive stranger. The whole of the country which surrounds Khisfin is susceptible of the highest degree of cultivation; the land is eminently fertile and almost a dead level, capable of producing abun-

dant crops, if there were any people to cultivate it. As it
is, it is allowed to run to waste. It affords pasture to their
flocks, but these are scanty, through fear of the Arabs, and
the people, unable to rely upon the government for protection, and, indeed, being only aware that there is a government through its tax-gatherers, are sullen and suspicious
and discouraged, and utterly without energy to do more
than provide themselves with the barest necessaries of life.

Haifa, March 31.—From Khisfin, the ruins of which I described in my last letter, I struck off in a westerly direction under the guidance of the sheik who had been my host the night before, and who, now that he was convinced that I had nothing to do with tax-gathering, and was only possessed by what must have seemed to him an insane desire to find old stones and make pictures of them, took an evident pleasure in ministering to such a harmless form of insanity; in fact he became quite a bore on the subject. As he was naturally unable to appreciate any distinction between one old stone and another, he was constantly making me ride out of my way to look at some weather-beaten piece of basalt which had a fancied resemblance to a wild animal; or to a mound, the ruins on which belonged to a village that had been deserted within the last twenty years. Still I never could afford to treat his assurances with indifference, as there was always the possibility, until I satisfied myself to the contrary, that the stones to which he was guiding me might possess interest; and indeed on one occasion they did, for they turned out to be the ruins of a Roman town, where a few fragments of columns and capitals still remained to bear testimony to the particular civilization to which they belonged, and which, although they did not present any striking architectural features—indeed, the remains were somewhat insignificant—it was always a satisfaction to have been the first to discover. The name of these ruins was Esfera.

Near them a very singular and unpleasant accident occurred to me. I rode my horse to drink at what seemed a muddy puddle, which was about ten or twelve feet in diameter. Instead of being content to drink at the margin, he took two steps into it, and suddenly disappeared head first;

that is, his head disappeared, his hind-quarters remained for
a moment poised above the water just long enough to enable me to throw myself off backward into about two feet
of puddle. We had walked into an overflowed well. When
his hind-quarters at last went down into it his head came
up, or, at all events, as much of it as was required for
breathing and snorting, which he did prodigiously, evidently
in a panic of terror, while I stood drenched and shivering on
the bank in the cold east wind and sleet, wondering how we
were ever to get him out. The poor beast was out of his
depth, but the dimensions of the well were too limited to
enable him to swim, or even to scramble freely. Fortunately I had sent on my saddlebags by my servant, or the
animal would have been hopelessly weighted down. As it
was, it was only by the united efforts of the party tugging
at the bridle and stirrup-leathers that, after many futile
efforts, at the end of each of which he fell back and for a
moment disappeared altogether, we ultimately succeeded in
extricating him. Meantime my own plight was in the last
degree unenviable, the more especially as I was not in very
good health at the time, a consideration which induced my
companion, with a truly commendable devotion, to take off
his nether garments and insist on my wearing them instead
of my own, while he performed the remainder of the day's
journey in the slight protection which he wore beneath
them.

It was in this guise, and while still discussing my strange
mishap, that our attention was suddenly arrested by finding
ourselves surrounded by what are perhaps the most interesting of antiquarian objects, a number of dolmens. In a very
limited area—none of them were over two hundred yards
apart—I counted twenty. The subject of these rude stone
monuments of a prehistoric age is so interesting that I will
venture on a few words in regard to them.

The most remarkable point about Syrian dolmens is, that
while they have been found in numbers to the east of the
Jordan, not one has been discovered in Judea or Samaria,
and only two or three in Galilee; and those are doubtful
specimens. Indeed, it is only of late years that they have
attracted the notice of explorers east of the Jordan ; but

17

since attention has been specially directed to the subject, we have constantly been having new discoveries. Six years ago I found one of the first at a spot not more than twenty miles from the hitherto unknown field I had now come upon. That dolmen stood alone, and being previously unaware of their existence in this part of the world, I examined it with the greatest interest. Since then Captain Conder, during his hurried survey in Moab, has found above seven hundred in that part of the country, and the result has been that the controversy as to the purpose for which they were designed has been reopened with renewed vigor.

The dolmen, which usually consists of three perpendicular stones forming three sides of a small chamber, with a single huge covering slab as its roof, is found in almost every part of the world except America, though I saw a notice in a paper the other day of one having been discovered in Missouri. There are stone monuments in Central America, I believe, somewhat resembling them, but I am not aware that the point has been satisfactorily determined, and it is of the highest interest that it should be, as it would establish the existence of general contact between the universal families of that ancient stock which preceded both the Aryan and Semitic races, and which belonged, therefore, to the illiterate and prehistoric age of the use of bronze and of flint.

Dolmens have been found in almost every country in Europe. They are numerous in the British Isles, France, Denmark, Sweden, Norway, Prussia, and the south of Russia. I have myself found them in the mountains of Circassia, and they exist in Italy, Spain, and Portugal, in great numbers in Algeria and the north coast of Africa, in Asia Minor and India, and we have recently heard of them in Japan! Wherever they exist are generally to be found menhirs, or single monolithic stones, and stone circles, such as Stonehenge in England, or long rows of standing stones, such as those to be found at Carnac in Brittany, or smaller stone circles, such as are common to the east of the Jordan. Those found in Syria are generally placed in a position commanding an extensive view and in close proximity to water. They are either " free standing," that is, quite alone and isolated, or they are covered by cairns of stones; or they are, as the majority were in this instance, perched upon piles of stones.

It has been hitherto supposed that in all these cases they were sepulchral monuments, but it has been recently suggested that those alone beneath the cairns may have served this purpose, and those which were free standing or on cairns may have been used as altars. The basis for this conjecture consists in the fact that the flat covering stones of the Syrian dolmens are very often provided with cups or hollows, which may have served to hold sacrificial oil; and, moreover, the free standing dolmens are often on smooth rock, so that it would not be possible to inter a body beneath them. I have seen the covering slab to be as large as eleven feet long by five wide, though those in the field I was now examining were much smaller, some of the covering stones not being above five feet by three or four; this was probably owing to their being of basalt, which is much heavier than ordinary stone. Nearly all were trilithons, the covering slab being sometimes held in position by pebbles inserted under it; and in many instances they appeared to have a slight slant which was not the result of accident.

The natives here call them "Jews' burial-grounds," showing that the local tradition is in favor of their being sepulchral monuments, though it is very certain they date from a period long anterior to the Jews. Indeed, the probability is that the disappearance of these monuments from western Palestine, where they no doubt existed, is due to the command to destroy heathen monuments. Thus, in Deuteronomy, we find again and again repeated injunctions to overthrow the Canaanite altars, and to break or smash their pillars. These exhortations we find carried into practice by Hezekiah and Josiah in Judea, and as the Book of Deuteronomy was held sacred by the ten tribes as well as by the two, we are justified in supposing that they carried out the order in Samaria and Galilee. But the land to the east of the Jordan always contained a mixed population, over which the kings of Israel and Judah exercised but little control. Baal worship was rife in Bashan, Gilead, and Moab in the days of Jeremiah, and the reforming zeal of Hezekiah did not affect the land where Chemosh and Ishtar, Baal, Peor, Nebo, and

Meni yet continued to be worshipped. This accounts for dolmens not having been found, except with a few doubtful specimens, in Galilee to the west of the Jordan.

With the exception of the roughly excavated hollows in the covering slab, these rude stone monuments of Syria have, so far as is known, neither ornamentation nor rune nor other mark of the engraver's tool. In comparatively few instances they are made of hewn stone, very roughly cut, but generally they are of natural blocks and slabs entirely unformed. Thus, if there be any comparative scale of antiquity on which we can rely connected with the finish of the monument, the Syrian dolmens may claim to be considered among the oldest of their kind.

The word "dolmen," usually rendered table-stone, should, according to Max Müller, be more properly translated "holed" stone, implying either a gateway, such as is formed by the trilithon, or else applying to menhirs and dolmens pierced with a hole, as in the case of the Ring stone, the Odin stone, and a peculiar class of holed dolmens. The one I saw in Circassia was of this latter category. Instead of three stones supporting the covering slab, as is almost invariably the case in Syria, there were four, and in the centre of the fourth was a circular hole, about eighteen inches in diameter, or just large enough to allow a thin man to squeeze through. Some have supposed these holes to be connected with some sacrificial rite, others to be due to the superstition that the dead could not rest in peace in tombs without an inlet for air. But the whole subject is encompassed with mystery, and affords material for endless conjecture.

So also do the sacred stone circles, of which I have seen several to the east of the Jordan. They are held in the greatest veneration by the Arabs, who can give no rational explanation of the sacred character they possess, except that they have been sacred from immemorial time. Here, again, these may either have originally had a sepulchral character, or they may have had reference to that peculiar and most ancient worship of which the menhir or monolith was the emblem, for in some instances menhirs are placed in certain fixed positions in regard to the circles, or they may have had an astronomical significance. It is singular that to this day the reverential attitude of the Arab is outside of the circle with his face to the rising sun, while in India the same circles are to be found among the Khonds in connection with the worship of the rising sun, the tallest member of the circle being towards the east.

The conclusions at which we may proximately arrive with reference to these interesting monuments are — according to Captain Conder, to whose researches I am indebted for many of the foregoing remarks—that the menhir is the emblem of the earliest religious idea suggested by the creative potency; that the circle may either have a sacred significance connected therewith, or be a sepulchral enclosure; that the dolmen, when free standing, is more likely to have been an altar than a tomb, but when buried beneath a cairn it may have been sepulchral; that the cairn is not always sepulchral, being sometimes a memorial heap; and that all are relics of a long-buried past.

THE DISCOVERY OF UMM EL-KANATAR.

HAIFA, March 20.—When we had sufficiently satisfied our curiosity with regard to the dolmens, which I described in my last letter, the sheik who was our guide disappeared suddenly over the edge of the plateau on which they stood, down what seemed to be a precipice of black basalt. His reply to our anxious inquiry as to whither he was leading us—"to very old stones, with writing on them"—was a talismanic utterance which at once overcame all hesitation. On such occasions there rises in the mind of the cold and weary and half-starving traveller (and I answered to this description at the moment) visions of possible Moabite stones, trilingual inscriptions, and all the other prizes which reward successful Palestine research. I felt, therefore, ready to make any plunge into unknown depths that he might choose to suggest, but certainly this was a bad one. Some two thousand feet below us, distant not more than seven miles, gleamed the still waters of the Sea of Galilee. We stood on the upper edge of one of the branches of the Wady Samak, which leads down to it. To our left, scarce a mile off, we could see the old crusading ruin of the Kasr Berdawil, or Baldwin's Castle, perched on a promontory the sides of which are sheer precipices, thus offering to the old warriors a position of magnificent strength. It is one of the least known of the Crusading strongholds, but I was assured by a friend, who, so far as I know, is the only traveller who has visited it, that beyond a few crumbling walls there was absolutely nothing to be seen, so, as I had better game in prospect, I did not turn aside to it, as I had originally intended, but resolutely prepared to risk my neck amid the basalt blocks of the cliff down which the sheik was now disappearing. Fortunately, though it was a bad descent, it was not a long one. I never could understand how my horse managed it, for I had left him to take care of himself, finding my own legs a safer method of descent; but in these lonely regions the instinct of not getting separated from the rest of the party is as strong with animals as with men, and they may generally be trusted to follow their companions.

After scrambling down about five hundred feet we came to a sort of bench or narrow plateau, on the flank of the ravine, and on turning round a huge rock of black basalt came suddenly upon one of the most delightful scenic surprises which it was possible to imagine. Here in this wild, inaccessible spot, in ages long gone by, the ancients had evidently contrived a secure and enchanting retreat, for it was provided with the first requisite of beauty and of pleasure—a copious fountain of water. It lay in crystal purity in a still, oblong pool, beneath the perpendicular black rock. Against the rock, and projecting from it, were two large arches which had been constructed of solid masonry, with blocks of stone of immense size. One of these arches was almost destroyed, but the other was still in perfect preservation. It measured twenty-three feet in breadth, sixteen feet in height, and six feet six inches in depth, this being therefore the width of the fountain, which was also twenty-three feet long and about two feet deep. To my astonishment it contained numbers of small fish, which was the more surprising as it possessed no apparent outlet; but it was too cold and fresh and sparkling to be anything but a living stream, and probably disappeared by a subterranean passage through a large crevice which I observed in the rock.

The wide-spreading branches of a venerable oak which grew directly in front of the arch threw a delightful shade over it, while delicate ferns clothed the sides of the grotto, which seemed to woo us to a repose and indolence which was, alas, under the circumstances, denied to us. On the keystone of the arch there was a partially effaced inscription. Though it was sixteen feet overhead, and therefore inaccessible, I should not have abandoned some attempt to decipher it had I not felt sure that, even if I were close to it, it was too much defaced by the storms of ages to be legible. I feel little doubt, however, about its having been in the

Greek character; while on a slab of stone at the side of the spring I found carved the figure of a lion, which was in good preservation, and of which I made a sketch.

The sheik was so impatient to take me somewhere else that he scarcely allowed me time to avail myself of this tempting spot to take the refreshment of which I stood much in need. He told me the name of the place was Umm el-Kanatar, or, being interpreted, "the place of arches," a name evidently derived from its most striking feature, and he said there was a ruin close by. This turned out to be not a hundred yards distant, and consisted of walls still standing to a height of about seven feet, composed of three courses of stone, the blocks averaging about two feet one way by two feet six the other, but being in some instances much larger. These walls enclosed an area of about fifty feet by thirty-five, which was covered by a mass of ruins which had been tossed about in the wildest confusion. It was quite evident that it had been the work of an earthquake. Six columns, varying from ten to twelve feet in height, rose from the tumbled masses of building-stone at every angle. It was impossible without moving the huge blocks which encumbered their bases and hid their pedestals, and balanced them in all sorts of positions, to tell whether they were *in situ* or not. The huge moulded stones which formed the sides of the entrance, though still one above the other, had been shaken out of position, but they bore all the character of carving which is peculiar to Jewish architecture, and at once led me to conclude that here, as at Eddikke, I had discovered the ruins of an ancient Jewish synagogue, dating probably from the first or second century A. D. This impression was confirmed as I came to examine the ruin more narrowly. Here was the large stone cut in the shape of an arch, which had probably stood upon the lintel of the principal entrance; and here was a fragment of a handsome cornice of the same peculiar pattern I had found at Eddikke, resembling the egg-and-dart pattern of modern ornamentation. Here were the columns inside the walls of the building instead of outside, which would have been the case had it been a Greek temple, and here were the massive stones, not set in mortar, which would have been the case if it had been an early Christian basilica or church. Here, too, was a stone on which was carved the representation of an eagle, in deference to the prejudices of the Roman conquerors under whose auspices these synagogues appertaining to the Jewish Patriarchate of Tiberias were built, the work having evidently been executed by Roman workmen.

I could find no inscription, but it would take days to examine all the stones thoroughly, and it is most probable that a careful investigation of them would reveal something which would throw a still more definite light on the character and period of the building, though I confess I entertain very little doubt in respect to either. Altogether I regard these ruins of Umm el-Kanatar as the most interesting discovery I have yet made, and as being well worthy another visit and a more minute examination than I was able to bestow upon them.

The sheik now appeared to think he had done his duty, and expressed his intention of returning to his village and of leaving me to find my way down the Wady Samak by myself. This I did not object to, as there was still plenty of daylight, and I could, in fact, make out from where I was now standing the position of the ruins of Kersa on the margin of the lake, whither I had despatched my servants and baggage animals direct from my last night's quarters, with orders to await my arrival there.

It was up the branch of the wady that I was descending that the projected railway from Haifa to Damascus would have to be led, and it was some satisfaction to see that it offered facilities for the ascent of the line. The scenery was in the highest degree picturesque, the sides of the valley sometimes sloping back for some distance to the foot of the basalt precipices which formed its upper wall; at others these approached and formed projecting and overhanging promontories, like that on which the Kasr Berdawil was situated. We scrambled down by a rugged path to the small stream at the bottom with the view of following it, if possible, to its outlet on the lake, but this we soon found to be impracticable, and were assured by a Bedouin, whose hut we finally reached on its margin, that we must cross it, and make an ascent on the opposite side. This led us by a roundabout, hilly, but picturesque route across numerous and intersecting wadys, and past one ruin, of which nothing remained but the black blocks of hewn basalt. I was fortunate enough, however, to meet a man who told me the name, which I added to my list of unknown ruins, and so, after much scrambling, we reached at last the white limestone strata, and the purling brook again with its fringe of oleanders, and could see in the distance the one large solitary tree which we had given as our rendezvous, and beneath which our servants were standing, that marks the site of the ruins of Kersa, or the Gergesa of the Bible, where Christ healed the two men possessed with devils, and suffered those malignant spirits to enter into the herd of swine.

There is a discrepancy in the accounts of the Evangelists in their narrative of the incident. Mark and Luke, in our version, locate it in the country of the Gadarenes, but Matthew states it to have taken place in the country of the Gergesenes. The Vulgate, Arabic, and others that follow the Vulgate read Gergesa in all the Evangelists, and there can be no doubt that this is the correct reading, for the simple reason that the miracles could not have taken place in the country of the Gadarenes, a district which lies south of the Yarmuk, and at a long distance from the lake, the principal town, Gadara, the modern Um Keis, about the identification of which there can be no doubt, being at least eight miles from it. Now the account says that "when he came out of the ship immediately there met him a man," also that the herd ran down a steep place violently into the sea. To do this, if the incident had taken place at Gadara, they must have descended twelve hundred feet to the Yarmuk, swam across that river, clambered up the opposite bank, and then raced for about six miles across the plain before they could reach the nearest margin of the lake. Scarcely any amount of insanity on the part of the devils would account for such a mad career, but in point of fact it does not tally with the Scripture record, according to which they rushed down a steep place into the sea. This is exactly what they could do at Kersa. The margin of the lake is here within a few rods of the base of the cliff, where there are ancient tombs, out of which may have issued the men who met Christ on the

plateau above; and it is easy to suppose that the swine, rushing down the sloping cliff, would have enough impetus
to carry them across the narrow slip of shore at its base.
The remains now only consist of long lines of wall, which
may easily be traced, and of a considerable area strewn with
building-stones, which show that it must in old time have
contained a considerable population. This is the more likely
to be the case as it was the chief town of a district which
was called after it. In fact, this picturesque and interesting
Wady Samak, with its evidences of a former civilization,
and its "place of arches" and handsome synagogue, was, in
fact, "the country of the Gergesenes;" and there can be
little doubt that to Christ and his disciples the remote corners of it, which I had been one of the first to explore, were
intimately known.*

The ruins of Kersa are a good deal overgrown, and in the
cover which is thus afforded I put up a wild boar. He
dashed away so suddenly, however, that a bullet from a revolver, which was sent after him, failed to produce any result. I have little doubt that the old Roman road turned
from the lake at this point up the Wady Samak, as there are
traces here and there indicating such a probability. It will
be a singular commentary on the progress of events if it
turns out that it has taken the best gradient, and if, upon
its ancient track, the scream of the locomotive may in the
near future be heard waking up the long-silent echoes of the
country of the Gergesenes.

---

* The greater part of the Wady Samak and the surrounding country had,
immediately prior to my visit, been most accurately surveyed by Mr. Gottlieb
Schumacher, the son of the American vice-consul at Haifa, whose admirable
and exhaustive surveys are embodied in the proceedings of the English and
German Palestine Exploration Societies, and who was my companion on the
occasion of our discovery of the ruins of Umm el-Kanatar.

Haifa, April 26.—The fact that I am laboring under a peculiar phase of insanity, which takes the form of descending with a light into the bowels of the earth with a measuring tape, and writing down cabalistic signs of what I find there, whether it be in a cistern or a tomb, or a natural cavern, has become pretty widely known among the inhabitants of the neighbouring villages, and the consequence is that from time to time I receive information which may minister to this harmless monomania. The other day, for instance, a stonecutter whom I had employed on some building operations came to me with the intelligence that while he and some villagers had been getting out stone for a house at a place about twenty miles distant they had unexpectedly come upon a series of subterranean chambers. His account was so tempting that, though prepared by experience for disappointment when acting upon purely native information, I nevertheless thought the possible results worth an effort, and proceeded therefore to the village in question, which was situated in the centre of the Plain of Esdraelon. The sheik was at first somewhat reluctant to show me the spot, as the fellahin have an inherent suspicion of all investigations of this nature, believing them to be mysteriously connected with the discovery of treasure, which, when found, they will be accused of having concealed, and punished for it. He finally consented, however, to lead the way, and brought me to an opening in the earth, from the surface of which a flight of nine stone steps led down to a small paved court, about six feet square, which had now been emptied of the soil which had previously concealed its existence. The sides of this court, which were about twelve feet high, were formed of massive masonry, the blocks of stone being each from eighteen inches to two feet square, set in mortar. A short vaulted passage, three feet long, two feet six wide, and five feet high, led from it into a subterranean chamber of fine workmanship, and in such a high state of preservation that it was difficult to realize that from fifteen hundred to two thousand years had elapsed since its stone floor had been trodden by the foot of man. It was fourteen feet long, eight broad, and eight feet six in height, with a vaulted roof, the walls consisting of plain chiselled stones set in mortar, in courses of from two feet to two feet six inches in height. On the left of this chamber was a single koka, or tunnel, hewn in the rock for the reception of a dead body. The roof was vaulted and of solid masonry. On the side opposite the entrance was another vaulted passage, which was seven feet six in length, and led into a chamber hewn out of the solid rock, twelve feet by ten feet six, and six feet six in height. This contained three kokim and a loculus under an arcosolium; but the side of the loculus, as well as those of the kokim, had been much injured. The villagers, who had opened these tombs for the first time only a few weeks before, told us they had only found human bones in them, but I strongly suspect they had found ornaments which they were afraid to exhibit, though I offered them money. One or two glass bottles and earthenware jars they also said they had found and broken.

Not far from these tombs was another smaller excavation, the entrance to which presented the appearance of an ordinary cave, but on entering it we found ourselves in a small, circular, rock-hewn chamber, the floor so covered with rubble that it was not possible to stand upright. In the centre of the roof was an aperture eighteen inches square, opening to the sky, carefully hewn, and from it led a passage of masonry, the stones also set in mortar, two feet six broad, and about five feet to the point where it was completely choked with earth. Had I had time to excavate I should no doubt have found that it led into a tomb. The entrance to this passage was almost completely blocked by the capital of a handsome Ionic column; the column itself was eighteen inches in diameter. How it ever came to be wedged down in this underground passage I cannot conceive. Among the stones in the vicinity which had been unearthed by the natives I found one on which was carved a seven-branched candlestick, another of Jewish moulding, a sarcophagus, several fragments of columns, and a monolith standing ten feet from the *débris* at its base, with grooves and slots similar to others which I have seen on Carmel, but taller. I can only imagine it to have formed part of some olive-pressing machinery. In the neighbouring rocks were hewn vats and wine-presses.

The discovery of this tomb, with the peculiar characteristics which marked its construction, and the objects which surrounded it, afforded a fertile subject of conjecture. In order that my readers may understand the considerations to which it gave rise, I must enter a little more fully than I have hitherto done into the subject of the ancient Jewish methods of sepulture. These consist of sundry varieties, and it has been attempted to fix their dates from the variations which have been observed, as well as to discriminate by them between Christian and Jewish tombs. So far as my own investigation goes, I have been unable to fix any positive rule in the matter, my experience being that one no sooner forms a theory based upon observation, than one makes some new discovery which upsets it. Roughly, the tombs which I have investigated may be divided into the following categories : 1. Rock-hewn tombs containing nothing but loculi; 2. Rock-hewn tombs containing nothing but kokim; 3. Rock-hewn tombs containing both; 4. Masonry tombs containing either loculi or kokim, or both together; 5. Sarcophagi; 6. Rock-sunk tombs. A rock-hewn tomb is an excavation made in the solid rock (advantage generally has been taken of a natural cavern), and round the sides of the chambers so formed, which vary in dimensions, are ranged the receptacles for the dead. In some cases these are more than one chamber. In Sheik Abreikh, for instance, I counted fifteen opening one into another. Sometimes these are one above another, and one has to enter them from below through a hole in the stone roof which forms the floor of the upper chamber. A koka is a rectangular sloping space cut into the rock, tunnel fashion, extending six feet horizontally, sufficiently wide and high to admit of a corpse being pushed into it. A loculus is a trough cut laterally into the rock, which is arched above so as to form what is called an arcosolium. This trough is generally about six feet long, two feet six broad, and two feet deep. It is thus separated from the chamber by a wall of rock two feet high. A large tomb will contain as many as twelve loculi ranged around it.

At first it was supposed that the kokim tombs were the oldest; then it was found that loculi and kokim were sometimes found in the same tomb; and, indeed, there seems now to be no reason to suppose that one kind is older than the other. That the Christians used both is certain from the fact that Greek inscriptions with Christian ornaments are to be found over the doors of tombs containing kokim as well as loculi. Masonry tombs are only found in Galilee, where they are very rare. Indeed, so far as I am aware, this is only the sixth that has been discovered; but what gave it a special interest in my eyes is the fact that the stones were set in mortar, which is not the case with any of the others, ancient Jewish synagogues, as well as their masonry tombs, being built without cement. I therefore had made up my mind that this was a Christian tomb, the early Christians having evidently continued the Jewish method of sepulture, more especially as it is oriented, which is not the case with Jewish tombs; and, indeed, the character of the masonry and the fragments of columns and capitals lying about induced me to place it in the Byzantine period, possibly as late even as the fourth or fifth century A.D. But then I stumbled upon the stone with the seven-branched candlestick, an unmistakably Jewish emblem, which threw the date back. It is true that this stone was not built into the tomb, and might have formed part of a building of a date long anterior to it. Indeed, we know that on this spot, which is now called Jebata, and which is undoubtedly the Biblical Gabatha, was formerly a Jewish town of some importance, and its remains have doubtless got mixed up with those of a later Byzantine period, to which I still think it probable that the tomb which I discovered belongs.

It differs from any I have yet seen in the imposing character of its entrance. Its flight of nine handsome stone steps, leading down the open court, and the vaulted passage,

with its massive masonry, give it quite a peculiar character.
The entrance to the rock-hewn tomb is usually through a
small doorway from three to four feet in height, just large
enough to permit a man to squeeze through without very
great inconvenience, and it is usually closed by a circular
stone like a millstone, which runs in a groove, and can be
rolled across it, though sometimes the door consists of a huge
curved slab. The sarcophagus is too well known to need
description. The most remarkable collection of them which
I have seen is at Umm Keis, the biblical Gadara, where there
are at least two hundred, many of them ranged in two rows
on either side of the way leading out of the city. They are
of black basalt, and are often beautifully carved and highly ornamented. I do not think they were so much used by
the Jews as by Christians, though sometimes sarcophagi are
found placed in loculi. At all events, they were not the original Jewish method of burial, and, if used by them at all,
the habit was one which they probably adopted from their
Roman conquerors.

The sunk tombs are common in various parts of Galilee
—especially in the rocky hillsides of the range upon which
Nazareth is situated. They consist of rectangular troughs,
sufficiently large to contain a human body, sunk into the
surface of the living rock, and covered with a huge lid of
stone, sometimes flat, but more often cut conically, so as to
have a high central ridge. I have more than once endeavoured to remove these from the tombs, which had never been
opened, where they were still *in situ*, but never happened
to be accompanied by a sufficient number of men or to have
adequate leverage appliances with me. As these stones are
generally about seven feet long, three broad, and from two
to three feet thick, they require the application of no little
force to remove them. They vary in size, however, and I
have seen sunk tombs for babies not above eighteen inches
long. Apart from the interest which attaches to the whole
question of rock sepulture in Palestine, the most interesting
relics of antiquity are generally found in the tombs, while
not uncommonly valuable inscriptions are met with. Many
of them are ornamented with pictorial representations,
which have been laid on with coloured pigment, and the

designs are often curious and interesting. Altogether, although the investigation of these mortuary chambers is often attended with great difficulty and discomfort, they frequently furnish results which compensate for the fatigue that they involve.

18

GENERAL GORDON'S LAST VISIT TO HAIFA.

HAIFA, May 10. — The interest which attaches to the memory of the late General Gordon must be my apology for devoting a letter to my personal reminiscences of one whose singularly pure and lofty character attracted me to him at a time when he was comparatively unknown. Nothing is in fact more remarkable than the suddenness of the notoriety into which he sprang, a notoriety from which he of all men would have the most shrunk, and of the knowledge of which, by the singular fatality which isolated him from the world in his beleaguered garrison, he was to the last unconscious. Owing to his own modesty and love of retirement, and to the fact that his life had been largely spent abroad and in the service of foreign governments, he was personally almost unknown in London society. His friends consisted chiefly of his brother officers and a few congenial spirits whose acquaintance he had made in various parts of the world. By the public at large he had only been heard of as "Chinese" Gordon, and few cared to inquire what manner of man he was.

It was just twenty-nine years ago since I first met him in the trenches before Sebastopol. He was quite a young and unknown officer at that time, and I should have forgotten the circumstance had we not again come across each other three years afterwards in China, and upon comparing notes found that we had already met in the Crimea. He had not then been appointed to the command of the "ever victorious army," and was still a junior Captain of Engineers. I left China before he entered the Chinese service, and almost immediately after his arrival, so that I saw very little of him. Still, I had seen enough to make me watch his subsequent career with great interest, but our paths had not again crossed until one day, about two years ago, I received a let-

ter from Jaffa signed C. G. Gordon, asking for information
in regard to Haifa as a residence, and expressing his intention of possibly paying me a visit. As I have many friends
of the name, I was puzzled for the moment. The writer did
not mention anything in the letter to give a clew to his
identity, though it was addressed as from one old friend to
another. It was only accidentally that the same afternoon
the vice-consul here asked me if I knew anything of a General Gordon, as some letters had arrived to his care for an
individual of that name. I at once perceived who my correspondent must be. I immediately addressed him a cordial
invitation to pay me a visit, which he promptly responded
to, and we spent a few very pleasant days together. The
Hicks disaster in the Soudan had not then occurred, so
that the affairs of that country and its Mahdi had not yet
acquired the notoriety they were destined so soon to attain ; but Gordon's intimate knowledge of the country induced him to express his opinion in regard to its condition.

He deprecated strongly the whole course adopted by the
British government in Egypt from the beginning, warned
me that they underrated the nature of the movement in the
Soudan, to which country he was then in favour of granting
independence under native rulers, was entirely opposed to
English officers at the head of Egyptian troops, thrusting
themselves into the mess, and maintained that the whole affair should be settled by a civil commissioner, who should
at once be sent by England to the Mahdi to arrange with
him the terms upon which the Soudan should be rendered
independent of Egypt. As at this time the English had not
come into violent hostile collision with the Mahdi, Gordon
declared his conviction that such a mission would be favour-
ably received, and that a state of affairs might be arranged
which, although not so favourable to the Soudanese as he
could have wished, would leave them better off than under
Egyptian rule. His idea was that if the Mahdi did not show
himself amenable to reason, he might be threatened with a
rebellion of the local Soudanese chiefs, who, he felt convinced, could easily be induced to combine against him. In
fact, before going to the Madhi he would have sounded the

feeling of these chiefs, with a view, if necessary, to organizing a revolt against him.

In a word, his view was that the Soudan question should be settled by the Soudanese alone, that no Egyptians should be mixed up in the affair; and I have no doubt that if the British government had thought of availing themselves of Gordon's services at this juncture, the question of the Soudan might have been arranged satisfactorily to all parties, except, perhaps, the Egyptian and Turkish governments. He was at that time particularly strong on the necessity of a railway from Suakim to Berber, the concession for which was being then applied for by English railway contractors, who were sanguine of success. He assured me that they were wasting their time; that it was a concession the Egyptian government would never grant, as they were afraid if they did that the whole trade of the Soudan would be diverted to Suakim instead of, as now, coming down to Cairo. "It is a short-sighted policy," he remarked, "for without that railway Egypt will one day not only lose the trade of the Soudan, but the Soudan itself.

Not long afterwards there was a report that the concession had been granted, and he wrote me a long letter of many pages, which began with warning me not to believe the report, as it was quite impossible that it could be true, his knowledge of the Egyptian government convincing him that they would make promises, but that nothing would ever induce them to consent to this railway being made, unless they were coerced into it by the British government. He felt equally convinced that the British government had no intention of using their authority in this direction, as, in his opinion, they should do, and that the report, therefore, was without foundation. This, in fact, turned out to be the case.

General Gordon, after spending a few days at Haifa, returned to Jerusalem, promising to bring his tents two months later and pitch them next to mine at Esfia on the summit of Carmel. I was eagerly looking forward to his companionship in the delightful wilderness of this mountain, and had even marked out in my own mind a spot for his camping-ground within fifty yards of my own, when, to my great disappointment, I received a letter from him saying that he was so deeply interested in biblical studies at the Holy City that he felt it his duty to change his mind, as he might never again have an opportunity of verifying the correctness of the views he entertained in regard to the typical nature of its configuration.

Not long afterwards I received another long letter from him on the subject of the Jordan valley canal scheme, in which he took a warm interest. This led to a correspondence, as I entirely differed from him as to its practicability. Towards the end of the year he wrote, saying that he was suddenly summoned to the Congo, and bidding me adieu. Curiously enough, in my reply I said that I did not say good-bye, as I felt sure I should see him again before he left the country. A few days afterwards he once more turned up at Haifa. He had embarked at Jaffa for Port Said in a country sailing craft, and he had been driven by stress of weather so far out of his course that his crew finally ran in here for shelter.

At this time affairs in the Soudan were in a very acute stage, and we again discussed them at great length. His views had naturally undergone a change, as the policy which had been possible seven or eight months previously was impracticable now. He felt great doubt whether, if he went to the Soudan, he could succeed in achieving now what he was convinced he could have accomplished then, or whether the policy he had sketched out was longer feasible. "If it were not for the Soudanese, whom I love," he said, "the easy way out of it for the English government would be to invite the Turks to go, but it is not probable that they have the sense to make the proposition, or that the Turks would be such fools as to accept it."

He refused altogether to anticipate the possibility of his being sent to the Soudan, partly because he felt bound in honour to go to the Congo for the King of the Belgians, and partly because he had already had too many differences with the heads of departments under which he had served, and was regarded with too little favour, on account of his refusal to look at every question through official spectacles, to be a *persona grata* to the English government. He was detained here a week, during which time we not only discussed fully the Egyptian and Soudanese questions, but talked over old times in China, when he gave me many graphic descriptions of incidents in his Chinese campaigns, which have probably never been heard of, and which I now regret I did not record. His modesty was such that I could only compel him to narrate his own adventures by a process of severe cross-examination.

One of his marked peculiarities in conversation was his employment of phrases which he had himself coined to represent certain ideas. Thus he would say of a man: "So-and-so is a very good fellow, but he would never break his medal," by which he meant that he was ambitious. Gordon himself, when the Emperor of China gave him, in return for his services, a very valuable gold medal, fearing that the sense of gratification he derived from it might prove a snare to him, broke it up and gave away the pieces. Hence the allusion.

Again, he would say, if asked if he knew so-and-so. "I only met him once and then he rent me." From which I understood that he had felt it his duty on that occasion to give the individual in question a word of good advice, and that the only thanks was that the man resented it, or, in Scripture phraseology, "turned again and rent him."

One day I observed him writing notes on a slip of paper. He asked me the Christian names of two friends who were staying with me. I told him, and feeling, I suppose, that my curiosity ought to be gratified, he said, "I am writing them down on my prayer list."

Another day, after using some very strong language in regard to a very high personage who shall be nameless, he added quickly, "but I pray for him regularly." All this without a vestige of cant. If there was a thing he detested it was hypocrisy, and I trust I may not be suspected of it when I say that the thought of Gordon at Khartoum, and the knowledge that I was on his prayer list, was calculated to produce a lump in my throat. He was full of fun and a most cheery companion with those he knew intimately. He never forced a conversation in a religious channel. He brought with him from Jerusalem a raised model which he had made, to carry out his theory that the hill upon which the greater part of the city was built was in the form of a woman. Taking the mound commonly identified as "the place of the skull" as the head, the lines of topographical configuration certainly bore out the resemblance in a very remarkable manner. He was far more full of this than either of the Soudan or the Congo, and was taking it with him to Brussels to show the King of the Belgians. "I suppose, as you are the king's guest, you will go and stay at the palace," I remarked. "No, certainly not," he replied; "I shall go to a hotel. I don't want the king's servants to see my old comb." He left here on the 18th or 19th of December, 1883, and walked to Acre, twelve miles, to meet the steamer that was to take him direct to Marseilles. He sent his luggage in a carriage.

His last words as we parted were that he felt sure we should never meet again. I said he had been wrong once when he told me that he should not see me again, and I hoped he was wrong now. He said no, he felt that he had no more work to do for God on this earth, and that he should never return from the Congo. Within a month he was in upper Egypt.

It was characteristic of the man that scarcely any one in Haifa knew who he was. Seeing a very handsome garden belonging to a rich Syrian, near Acre, he strolled into it, and was accosted by the proprietor, who asked him who he was. He replied, "Gordon Pasha," on which my Syrian friend, who told me the story, laughed incredulously, and politely showed him out. Gordon meekly departed without attempting to insist on his identity. The proprietor told me that he felt convinced that he was being imposed upon, because Gordon, when spoken to in English, would answer in bad Arabic, and because, when asked his name, he took his card-case half out of his pocket, as though to give his card, and then, on second thought, put it back again and answered verbally. So my friend lost his chance of entertaining an angel unawares, which he has never ceased to regret, the more especially as his friends take a pleasure in teasing him about it.

My last letter from Gordon is dated Khartoum, the 6th of March. Now that he is gone, and his name has become a household word in almost all countries, and among the professors of all religions, the few among the natives who knew him here treasure up every trait of his marked individuality, and are fond of narrating anecdotes, which grow by repetition. His instinct of retirement and extremely unassuming manner concealed him, so to speak, from general observation; but his simplicity, purity, and absolute singleness of aim made him a sort of moral magnet, irresistibly attractive to those who came directly beneath the sphere of his influence. The potency of his virtue in life has been proved by the imperishable moral legacy which in death he has bequeathed to humanity.

THE CONVENT OF CARMEL *versus* THE TOWN OF HAIFA.

HAIFA, May 25.—It was from Carmel that in times of old a small cloud was seen rising not bigger than a man's hand, which overcast the heavens, and it is not impossible that a political incident which has just occurred here may prove the diplomatic commencement of a storm of another kind pregnant with untold issues. If we look back through history at the origin of some of its greatest events, we often almost fail to discover them, on account of their insignificance. When the moral atmosphere is charged with electricity, it needs but a spark to produce the shock; and so it is just possible that the upsetting of a few stones, on a barren hillside, may open up a question which may assume proportions of very considerable magnitude, as it involves the most dangerous of all elements in a dispute, that of religious fanaticism. The Monastery of Carmel, as your readers are doubtless aware, is situated on the spur of the mountain which projects in a point at an elevation of about five hundred feet above the sea. From this point the mountain gradually rises until it attains a height of about nine hundred feet, immediately behind the town of Haifa and the German colony. The mountain here spreads into an elevated plateau of some extent, affording extensive pasture-ground and good arable and vineyard land. For some years past the claim of the convent over a large area of this plateau has been a matter of dispute, but it only reached an acute stage the other day, when the towns-people were called upon to pay taxes on it. They naturally objected that they ought not to pay taxes on land the use of which they did not enjoy, and access to which was forbidden to them by a wall which had been built by the convent as the boundary to its possessions. In order to bring the matter to an issue, some thirty of the

German colonists and as many of the Moslem inhabitants of
the town went up in a body and proceeded *vi et armis* to
tear down the wall. While thus engaged some of the monks
emerged, armed with spiritual weapons alone. One of them,
elevating his cross, pronounced a solemn curse, first in German and then in Arabic, upon the profaners of their sacred
soil. The convent being under the protection of the French
government, a formal complaint was lodged against the action of the Germans in the matter, and a deputation, consisting of the German and French vice-consuls, were sent
down from Beyrout to inquire into it. Meantime the Turkish government interfered, as it had a right to do, seeing
that many Ottoman subjects had participated in the act complained of, and decided that the right of the convent to
erect the wall was a matter for the local tribunals to decide
upon, as well as the question of the validity of their title to
the part of the mountain claimed by them. In the meantime instructions were given that, pending the decision of
the court, the wall should be replaced in exactly the same
position, and of the same dimensions, as before its removal.
Advantage was taken of this order to rebuild the wall much
more solidly, and to increase its height far beyond the limits
prescribed in the order, and the result was the removal of
the local governor for negligence in not seeing that the instructions were properly carried out. Meantime the town
instituted a lawsuit against the convent, calling upon them
to substantiate their legal title to the land.

Now, one third of the population of Haifa is Moslem and
Jews, and about two thirds are Christian. The Christians
are all under the direct influence of the convent, and the
spirit of religious fanaticism runs high on both sides. On
measurement being made of the land claimed by the convent
it was found to amount to an area of about twelve square
miles. According to Turkish law the whole of this would
originally belong to the inhabitants of the town for their
common use, unless the town council had at some time or
other legally parted with it for an adequate consideration.
This it was denied on the part of the municipality that they
had ever done, and search was consequently made in the
records for the act of sale, which would have been registered.

On the other hand, the monks had a duly-signed document under which they claimed, but which, on further investigation, was found to be practically a fraud, as none of the formalities had been complied with, and the seal had been affixed illegally by an officer who had been induced for a certain consideration to perform the act. It is not contended that the monks were a party to this irregularity. They seem, indeed, rather to have been the victims of their agent at the time, who perpetrated it, leaving them under the delusion that they possessed a valid title, but the discovery left the court no alternative but to pronounce judgment against them. Against this judgment they have appealed to Constantinople, and it would be difficult to see how it could be reversed, were it not that the interests involved are of such a peculiar character that the purely legal side of the question may be overlooked.

The prestige which the order of barefooted Carmelites enjoys in all Catholic countries is so great that the most powerful influences will be invoked, and possibly not invoked in vain, in their favor. Strong articles have already appeared on the subject in the Continental press of Europe. The Emperor of Austria has, I understand, been personally appealed to, while the pilgrims, who, to the number of about four hundred, have already visited the sacred shrine this year, are every one of them missionaries who will be so many Peter the Hermits, invoking once more the faith of the true believer to protect the sacred mountain from the grasp of the infidel. But there is an element in the affair which removes it from the simple category of Cross *versus* Crescent, and that is, that the interests of some three hundred Germans are involved. As forming part of the population of Haifa, they enjoy equal rights with the rest of the towns-people, and Prince Bismarck is not a man to see their rights tamely abandoned to the monks. It is true that the question is one which affects exclusively the Turkish government, and there can be no doubt that it would not willingly deprive an Ottoman population of twelve square miles of mountain if they are legally entitled to it, but the united pressure of Catholic Europe might be too powerful a force for the Porte to resist single-handed. It is a different matter when they have the

German government at their back, and this quarrel over a right of way and a patch of hillside may yet be pregnant with important consequences. Had the convent entered upon large agricultural operations, their rights over land thus brought into cultivation could not be disputed. The complaint of the population is that they neither cultivate it themselves, nor allow others to cultivate it, or even to graze their flocks upon it. The exclusive possession thus claimed has deprived the German colonists of one of the most important desiderata for the success of their colony.

A retreat from the heats of summer is almost essential to the health of the colonists. If they had the right of way claimed they could, with ease, construct a wagon-road to the top of the hill overhanging the colony, where, at an elevation of nine hundred feet, they would be in full enjoyment of the sea breezes, while only half an hour distant from their homes. The money necessary for the construction of such a sanitarium was provided under singular circumstances a few weeks ago. I was riding just outside the town, on the Nazareth road, when to my surprise I met a foreign lady riding by herself, accompanied only by an Arab, an unusual sight in this country. Following her was a covered litter. On returning to the colony an hour later I found that the litter contained the body of the husband of the lady I had met. He had died in it on the road from Nazareth a couple of hours before I met the poor widow, a perfect stranger and unable to speak a word of the language, forming the solitary attendant of her husband's corpse. These painful circumstances enlisted the warmest sympathy on the part of the colonists, whose kindness and consideration so overwhelmed the lady, who was herself a countrywoman, that before leaving she presented the colony with a check for $7500. These simple people had no idea when they were lavishing their kindness on the widow that she was a lady of large fortune, and this was their unexpected reward. And it is with this money they hope to build their sanitarium.

HAIFA, June 7.—I was glad to avail myself of an opportunity to revisit Jerusalem after an interval of six years, and by a journey through a part of Judea to see the changes within that period. The attention which has of recent years been directed towards Palestine has perhaps produced more marked results in this province than in Galilee, and in some respects its progress has been more rapid. This is partly owing to the fact that for the past eight years it has been under the administration of a more than usually enlightened pasha, who exercises his authority independently of the Governor-General of Syria, and partly because its holy places prove more attractive both to Jews and Gentiles than do those of Galilee. Hence there has been a larger inflow of capital and of immigration.

Three miles from Jaffa lies the German colony of Sarona, which, like the one at Haifa, was founded some years ago by the Temple Society. It resembles the one there in the character of its buildings and general plan. There is a wide central street with neat stone and tiled roofed houses, and two rows of shade trees, with a short cross street, church, and schoolhouse, and that general air of cleanliness and comfort which Germans understand so well how to impart to their settlements. It is far inferior to Haifa, however, both on the score of salubrity and beauty of position, being situated on a grassy, rolling country destitute of woods, some miles from the sea and the mountains. There is therefore something forlorn in the solitude of its position. The inhabitants suffer a good deal from fever, and many deaths took place last year, which was unusually unhealthy. On the other hand, the fertility of the soil and its proximity to so large and prosperous a town as Jaffa, which now numbers close upon twenty thousand inhabitants, enables the settlers to do

somewhat better financially than those at Haifa. They are
engaged in extending the area of their orange-groves and
vineyards; and as the general experience is that the climate
of this country improves under the influence of husbandry,
it is to be hoped that a few more years will work a change
in this respect, as they certainly must in the general attrac-
tiveness of the place. The Temple Society has also a small
colony actually in the suburbs of Jaffa, the members of which
are engaged in commercial pursuits in that town, and are
doing well.

Since I last visited this place emigrant Jews from Russia
and Roumania have established no fewer than four colonies
in its neighbourhood, which, however, are scattered in different directions at distances of several miles apart. The
circumstances under which my journey was made prevented
me, unfortunately, from inspecting them as thoroughly as I
could have desired. Two of these are under the protection
of Baron Rothschild, and enjoy such pecuniary support from
him as will secure their future, in spite of the obstacles
which, owing to government opposition and other local
difficulties, they have had to encounter. So far as energy,
industry, and aptitude for agricultural pursuits are concerned, the absence of which has always been alleged as the
reason why no Jewish colony could succeed, the experience
of more than two years has now proved that such apprehen-
sions are groundless, and that with a fair chance Jews make
very good colonists, and are likely, in fact, to succeed better
in this country as agriculturists than in America, where they
have the skilled industry and indomitable energy of the
American farmer to compete with, instead of the helpless
ignorance and ingrained indolence of the native fellahin,
who are their only rivals here.

Besides these two colonies there are two others, one of
which has been struggling on unaided for the last seven years,
and which has latterly almost succumbed to the methods which
have been resorted to by the government to extinguish it,
but which has within the last month derived fresh aid and
encouragement from the visit of Dr. Adler, the Grand Rabbi
of London, and Mr. Wissotsky, the delegate of a society
which has recently been formed in Poland, called "The

Lovers of Israel." The visit of these two gentlemen marks a new era in the fortunes of the Petach Tikveh colony, as it is called, as it resulted in the substantial donation of a sum of £300, and in bringing it to the knowledge of the public. One of the chief drawbacks of the colony has been the unhealthiness of its site, and the purchase of a healthy hill-top, about half an hour distant, has been attended with so much difficulty that it is only now that the colonists have at last secured their title to it sufficiently to warrant the building of houses upon it.

Besides these four Jewish and two German colonies there has been for fifteen years established in the neighbourhood of Jaffa a large Jewish agricultural college, which was founded by the Israelite Alliance, for the purpose of educating Jewish youths in agricultural pursuits. It is a handsome and extensive building, standing a little to the right of the road from Jaffa to Jerusalem, amid groves of trees and gardens, and surrounded by a fine tract of arable land. Here are avenues of eucalypti and of bamboos, both trees unknown in this country, and which, from their novelty, form a striking feature in the plantations near the house. For many years this establishment was a source of permanent expense to its founders, and it was feared that the results would never justify the original outlay. Their perseverance has, however, met with its reward. The increase of the annual income last year amounted to $5000. One of the principal sources of revenue are the ethrogim, or gigantic citrons, which are used by the Jews all over Europe at some of their religious festivals, and which, if they can be guaranteed as coming from the Holy Land, command a fictitious price. Besides these they export oranges and vegetables, and have engaged in the manufacture of wines and brandy, for which they find a good sale. It is to be hoped that as Jewish colonies in Palestine increase, and the demand for skilled Jewish agriculturists conversant with the local methods of cultivation and familiar with the language is augmented, a better opening will be found for the youths who have received their education in this establishment. Hitherto the young men, after receiving a good education, of which agricultural science only formed part, have generally seen their way on leaving the college to engage in some more profitable and congenial pursuits than tilling the land. As a rule, middle-aged men with a limited education and large families make better agriculturists than ambitious and well-educated youths.

There is a fifth colony in Judea, which is nearer to Jerusalem than Jaffa, formed of Jews who have apparently been hired to become Christians, by being provided for as colonists; but so far it has proved a failure. The government has refused all permission to build. They are at present living in a large wooden shanty, and are said to be reverting to their old faith, as they find that the new one does not pay.

I have also heard of a sixth colony which is in process of formation, so that adding to these three which are in Galilee, there are altogether nine Jewish colonies now in Palestine—all of which, with one exception, have been established within the last two years and a half, in spite of difficulties which would have discouraged people animated by no higher sentiment than that of merely finding a living. However slow and uncertain their progress may be now, these first settlers may console themselves by the reflection that their experience as pioneers will be of incalculable value to their successors, when altered conditions may arise, which shall offer increased inducement to emigration.

Meantime, it is as well that intending immigrants should not be misled by the delusive reports which are promulgated from time to time of a change in the policy of the government in this respect. Practically the opposition to Jewish colonization on the part of the authorities is as stringent as ever, and any action taken upon a contrary hypothesis will only lead to disappointment.

This increasing tendency to flock into the Holy Land is not confined, however, to Jews alone. There is an annual augmentation in the number of pilgrims who invade it, of nearly all the Christian sects, besides those who establish themselves here under the influence of various religious hobbies. Thus the foreign and Jewish population of this province is constantly increasing, and the effect of this influx is more strikingly marked at Jerusalem than elsewhere; but it is natural that Jaffa, as the port of Judea, should also largely have benefited by its influence, and I was much struck by the growth of the place and the signs of its increasing prosperity. This is, no doubt, due also in some measure to the excellent carriage-road which now connects it with Jerusalem. I saw several large gangs of men at work upon those sections which still remain of the old rough track, which in former days made the journey between these places upon wheels a positive torture. It is true that many excruciatingly rough places still remain, but another year will remove them, and it is the intention of the present governor to extend the road from Jerusalem by way of Bethlehem (it is now almost completed to the latter place) to Hebron, and also to connect the rich country east of the Jordan with Judea by a carriage-road which is in immediate contemplation from Jerusalem to Jericho.

The rapidly improving facilities for travelling in Palestine, the annual increase in the number of tourists who each year visit it, the numerous ecclesiastical and charitable establishments which have been already constructed and are yearly extended, the influx of foreign capital resulting therefrom, and the increase of the foreign population, both Jew and Christian, all tend to give Palestine an exceptional position as a province in the Turkish empire. It is the only one, indeed, where the evidences of progress are steady and substantial; and there can be no doubt that one of the most marked results of this progress will be the importance which the Holy Land is destined to assume in the event of the Eastern question being reopened, for there is no province in the empire upon which political and religious interests of so varied and universal a nature are concentrated.

19

THE RECENT DISCOVERY OF GEZER.

JERUSALEM, June 23.—I was much struck on my way from Jaffa to this place the other day by contrasting the different systems which are resorted to by the varied races of foreigners who are invading Palestine. There is the Jew, with curling ear-locks and greasy gaberdine, and wallet slung over his shoulder, trudging painfully along the dusty road. He has had hard work to slip into the country at all, and has only succeeded probably by means of backshish and a false passport. He has undergone discomfort and privations innumerable to win the privilege, which, to judge by his wan and sickly face, is not likely long to be denied him, of dying in Jerusalem.

As he plods on, leaning wearily on his long staff, he is almost run over by a bright yellow barouche dashing along the road, with four horses, in a style which shows how rapidly Western civilization is striding into the East. It is an English duke "doing" Palestine. He is followed by a motley group of his own country men and women, mounted on horses and donkeys, the women for the most part apparently old maids in straw hats, green spectacles, and veils, while a large proportion of the men are evidently parsons, who wear clerical coats and waistcoats and unclerical pith hats and jack boots. The whole party, consisting of about thirty persons, white with dust, are preceded by an elaborately attired dragoman, whom they are about to follow over the country like a flock of sheep, for they are the last batch of the season of Cook's tourists.

But they were not to be compared for picturesqueness or singularity of appearance with the next *cortège* which I overtook, and the aspect of which, from a distance, puzzled me excessively. There appeared in front of me a large object of some sort, which was being slowly dragged along by a crowd of people who were evidently not natives of the country. On reaching it I found that it was a huge bell, weighing seven or eight tons, most elaborately ornamented with scriptural and sacred designs in *basso-rilievo*, and which, placed on a truck with low wheels, was being hauled by about eighty Russian peasants, more than half of whom were women. Looking on this singular group of rugged-featured people, with their light hair and Kalmuck countenances, one felt suddenly transported from the hills of Palestine to the steppes of Southern Russia. The men wore high boots, baggy trousers, long full-skirted coats, tight at the waist, and flat caps, and the women the sombre and dowdy habiliments common to the Russian peasant class. They were all yoked by the breast with ropes to the truck, tugging it slowly but cheerfully along, and when I stopped and tried to stammer out the few words of Russian which I still remembered, they greeted my attempts with loud shouts of laughter, and made explanations which my knowledge of the language was too limited to enable me to comprehend. But my curiosity was destined to be satisfied at a later period on the arrival of this precious burden at Jerusalem. Meantime I could not but regard with interest the eager devotion of these poor people, and especially of the women, who were thus satisfying a religious instinct by exercising the functions of draught animals, and toiling up the road they deemed so sacred to the holy city, which is invested with a higher sanctity to the adherents of the Greek rite than to those of any other Christian communion. I found afterwards that it took them just a week to drag their bell up to Jerusalem, many falling ill by the way, and one dying, and reinforcements had to be sent from Jerusalem to assist them.

Had it not been for the various houses which have been built for the accommodation of travellers the mortality would probably have been greater, but the increase of travel along this road has multiplied the number of rest-houses, and there are now four or five of various degrees of excellence, to say nothing of Greek and Catholic convents, more or less far from the road, to which pilgrims can resort. The new hotel which has just been put up by a German colonist at Ramleh is among the most conspicuous of these improve-

ments; and here, as the place is one of some archæological
interest, and I thought the enterprise of my host deserved to
be encouraged, I stayed to pass the night.

In the centuries immediately subsequent to the crusades,
Ramleh is often mentioned by the old chroniclers, for it was
then, as now, a favorite resting-place for travellers and pilgrims on their way between Jaffa and Jerusalem. But it
gradually fell into decay, and three hundred years ago, when
the traveller Belon was there, he found it almost deserted,
scarcely twelve houses being inhabited, and the fields mostly
untilled. It is now one of the most go-ahead places in
Palestine, containing a population of at least five thousand,
and is surrounded by extensive gardens and olive groves,
above which the lofty tower erected by the Sultan Bibars,
in the thirteenth century, conspicuously rears its graceful
proportions.

By far the most interesting spot, however, in the whole of
this section of country lies about two miles to the right of
the road from Ramleh to Jerusalem, an hour after leaving
the former place, which places it as much out of the track
of tourists as if it were a day's journey. It is a mound called
Tell el-Gezer, at the village of Abu Shusheh. This village is
the property of a Mr. Bergheim, a Jew banker of Jerusalem,
who owns an estate here of about five thousand acres, from
which I may say, *en passant*, that he derives a very large
revenue.* Apart from the interest of the fact of a Jew being so large a landed proprietor in Palestine, Abu Shusheh
has claims upon our notice which have only recently been
discovered, and which to those who have been bitten with
the enthusiasm of elucidating the ancient topography of
Palestine, and identifying its antique sites, is replete with
the highest importance.

Among those who have devoted themselves to the study
of Palestine geography and antiquarian research the French
savant Monsieur Clermont Ganneau ranks second to none.
One of the problems which has for many years excited the
interest and curiosity of Palestine explorers was the where-

---

* Since the above was written Mr. Bergheim has been brutally murdered
by the peasants on his estate.

abouts of the ancient city of Gezer. We gather from the
Biblical record that this was an important town prior to the
arrival and settlement of the Israelites in the country. In
the book of Joshua it is classed among the royal cities of
Canaan. Its king, Horam, was defeated by Joshua while attempting to relieve Lachish, which was besieged by the Israelites. Later it was included in the territory of the tribe
of Ephraim, and assigned to the Levitical family of Kohath.
It is mentioned several times during the wars between David
and the Philistines, and during Solomon's reign one of the
Pharaohs made an expedition against it, which resulted in
the capture and burning of the town. It afterwards became
part of the dowry of Pharaoh's daughter when she became
Solomon's wife, and he rebuilt it. The last we hear of it
was in the wars of the Maccabees, when it reappears under
the name of Gazara. Taken by assault in the first instance
by the Jews, it passed successively into the hands of the two
contending parties, who attached equal importance to its
possession. John Hyrcanus, the Jewish commander, made
it his military residence.

It was during his study of the old Arab geographers that
M. Clermont Ganneau came upon the name Tell el-Gezer, and
finding that it met all the topographical requirements of
the Bible, he went in search of it at Abu Shusheh. Here he
found that a mound on Mr. Bergheim's property was known
to the natives by that name, though it was too insignificant
ever to have figured on any map. On making minute investigation, he discovered, to his delight, a bilingual inscription; the first word, in Greek characters of the classical epoch,
was the name of a man, "Alkio," immediately followed by
Hebrew letters of ancient square form, the translation of
which was "limit of Gezer." This settled the question, and
the English Palestine Exploration Fund at once sent a special mission to verify Monsieur Ganneau's discoveries. This
they did most completely, finding four other inscriptions,
besides making a most complete survey of the place. As is
not uncommon with such very ancient remains, the first aspect of the spot is disappointing. There are, in fact, no
ruins visible, with the exception of a few terraces on the
Tell, consisting of large blocks of unhewn stone. The Tell

itself, on which part of the city appears to have stood, is a sort of ridge about six hundred yards long, one hundred across, and two hundred and fifty feet above the surrounding rocky valleys. The foundations of the ancient houses may be traced possibly in the numerous rock-cuttings with which the place abounds, but it is difficult to distinguish them from cuttings for quarrying stone on the old method, and certainly many of the cuttings were those of quarriers. There are the remains of what was apparently an old fortress at the eastern end of the Tell, but the most remarkable features are the numerous wine-presses, which number about thirty, some of them in an excellent state of preservation. There are also some tombs, but these are rare and scattered, which is to be accounted for by the fact that this was a Levitical city, within the limits of which no interment was allowed. There are numerous chips of stone, some apparently basaltic, and much broken pottery all over the Tell, and many flints, some of which were worked, have been discovered. While he was building his house, which is just under the Tell, Mr. Bergheim found a deep cistern about forty feet square, lined with small stones and covered with two coats of cement, which was hard and white; the walls were about two feet thick, and it seemed to have a niche in its eastern wall, as though it had at one time been used as a chapel. In the niche a cross was found, painted red, and beneath it a stone altar, which has been removed; but all this points to an early Christian occupation. Mr. Bergheim has since converted the cistern to its original use. He also found a curious idol in hard red pottery. The fellahin say that many of these "dolls," as they call them, used to be picked up, and were given to the children as playthings. Flint instruments, earthenware weights, and rubbers in composition, for use in cementing cisterns, have been found in ploughing on the Tell, and near its southwest extremity a number of skeletons were discovered, apparently of persons slain in battle; one had a sword-cut on the skull. An aqueduct cut in the rock is also traceable along the hillside.

Altogether the place is a good deal more interesting than it looks at first sight, and had its owner been an antiquary he would doubtless have had splendid opportunities of making a valuable collection. That the spot has always had a semi-sacred character in the eyes of the country people is evident from the traditions which attach to it. One is that the city of Noah stood upon the hill here, and that the deluge came from a place called Et Tannur, which is a cavity with an old well on the east slope of the hill. The modern name Abu Shusheh, or "Father of the Topknot," is said to be derived from a dervish who prayed for rain in time of drought, and was told by a sand diviner that he would perish if it came. The water came out of the earth and formed a pool, into which he stepped and was drowned. The people, seeing only his topknot left, cried, "Ya Abu Shusheh" (O Father of the Topknot).

It is a pity that, with the exception of the one deciphered by Monsieur Ganneau, the inscriptions are so much effaced that, although certain characters can be made out, they have hitherto defied translation. Some of them appear to approach to the later Hebrew forms, while others bear some resemblance to Cufic.

There are other sites of interest which lie more or less distant from the road from Jaffa to Jerusalem, but I had not time to visit them, though the comparatively more advanced state of civilization of this province and the good accommodation to be found on the road would facilitate the explorer's task. On the other hand, the examination of this part of the country has been so thorough that he cannot hope for the rich rewards that are to be found in more inaccessible districts.

Haifa, July 20.—It is a melancholy reflection, and one by no means creditable to the Christianity which prevailed in the fourth century after Christ, that the Jerusalem of the present day, the Holy City of the world par excellence, should contain within its walls more sacred shams and impostures than any other city in the world. The responsibility for the gross superstition which prevails in regard to sites and localities mainly rests with the fourth century, and chiefly with the Empress Helena, who was principally instrumental in inventing them, and the Christian churches, especially the Greek and Latin, find it in their interest to foster these transparent frauds, for the enormous pecuniary advantages which accrue from them.

The extraordinary amount of research and investigation of which Jerusalem has been the subject during the last twenty years, the extent of the excavations which have been made, involving an expenditure of about $100,000, and the conscientious impartiality and profound acquirements of the explorers, have demolished the whole superstructure which early and mediæval Christianity had reared upon the credulity of its votaries; and which the churches of the present day, despite all the evidences to the contrary, find it in their interest to perpetuate. Thus it has now been proved to demonstration that, wherever the tomb in which Christ was laid after his crucifixion may have been, it could not have been in the cave over which the gorgeous edifice called the Church of the Holy Sepulchre now stands; for we now know by recent examination the position of the walls which enclosed the city in the time of Christ, though some still deny the correctness of the latest conclusions which have been arrived at. We also know that Calvary, or Golgotha, where he was crucified, was "nigh at hand" to the sepulchre; that Golgotha was "nigh to the city," and not in it, and that Jesus "suffered without the gate," and that all tombs, saving those of David and Huldah and eight Jewish kings, were without the walls, while the cave over which the Church of the Holy Sepulchre is built is within them. As, however, even the churches do not go so far as to maintain that any tradition had been preserved among Christians during the first three centuries after the death of Christ of his place of burial, they have had to resort to inspiration as the means of its discovery. Some of the early writers maintain that it was the Emperor Constantine himself who was divinely inspired to find it ; others that it was his mother, the Empress Helena. This is a trifling discrepancy. Whichever it was, the fact of the inspiration remains, and scientific investigation has, ever since the days of Galileo, been bound to give way before ecclesiastical inspiration and infallibility. So, no matter whatever evidences exist to the contrary, crowds of pilgrims will continue to crawl over those sanctified stones, wearing them hollow with their kisses, as long as the sacerdotal organization of which it is the representative remains to impose upon them its authority.

With considerate ingenuity, and possibly with a view to lightening the labors of the pilgrims as much as possible, the early Church crowded as many sacred stones together under the roof of the holy edifice as it could with decency. Thus we have the Stone of Unction, on which Christ's body was laid for anointing, but it was getting so worn that the real stone lies below the marble slab, which, however, answers the purpose for the pilgrims. Close by is the Circular Stone, where the Virgin stood while the body was being anointed ; also the stone on which Jesus stood when he appeared to Mary Magdalene, and the stone on which she stood, and the column to which he was bound when scourged ; and your devout guide will show you, if you have the patience to attend to him, the exact place where Jesus was stripped by the soldiers, the place where the purple robe was put on him, the place where the soldiers cast lots for his raiment, the rent in the rock made by the earthquake, the place where his body was wrapped in linen cloths, the place where he indicated with his own hand the centre of the world, and so on, *ad nauseam.*

Sometimes another Church commits a burglary and steals some of these stones. The Armenians have been especially guilty in this respect. They have stolen from the holy sepulchre the stone on which the angel sat, that had been rolled away from the door of the sepulchre, which they now display in the chapel of the Palace of Caiaphas; also a piece of the true cross, which was originally discovered under inspiration by Helena, as well as that of the penitent thief, who is now canonized under the name of Dimas. I don't know what authority they have for calling him Dimas, whose reputed birthplace is, for political reasons, going to be converted into another holy place. There is something rather appropriate in the idea of the power that is waiting for a chance to despoil the Turkish empire of Syria erecting a shrine in worship of the penitent thief.

The most remarkable sites are those which illustrate the parables. Thus, pilgrims are shown the window which was the post of observation of Dives, and the stone, now worn by the kisses of the faithful, where Lazarus sat when the dog licked his sores. I asked my guide where the dog was, but he said he was dead, and added, with a smile, "I don't believe any of these things."

I asked him why not.

"Oh," he replied, "I'm a Jew."

After that the glibness with which he pattered off all the Christian traditions was very edifying until my patience was exhausted, and I said, "Well, supposing, as we neither of us believe in any of these invented sites, we go and try and find something that is real."

He had been in the service of some of the recent Jerusalem explorers, and I afterwards found him an intelligent companion.

It is a striking illustration of Moslem religious toleration, as compared with that shown by Christians in Jerusalem towards Jews, that while this man could accompany me into the Mosque of Omar, that most beautiful and sacred of Mohammedan temples, he was not allowed even to enter the street in which stands the Christian Church of the Holy Sepulchre.

So far as Christian rites are concerned, it may, then, be

taken as a fact that the interest which attaches to Jerusalem has but a very slender relation to them. The great natural features, of course, must always remain. Bethlehem, Bethany, and the Mount of Olives are as they ever were, but there are two Gardens of Gethsemane, one claimed by the Latins and one by the Greeks. When we descend to more minute details they are either purely mythical or at best only matters of vague conjecture. One of the best illustrations of the purely mythical is Christ's footprint on the rock from which he ascended into heaven, which is a good deal smaller than that of Buddha, which I have also seen on the top of Adam's Peak in Ceylon, or of Jethro, which the Druses showed me in the Neby Schaib.

Among those open to conjecture, the position of Calvary and the tomb of Joseph of Arimathea are points upon which research may still throw light. Every indication goes to show that Golgotha, or Calvary, was a knoll outside the Damascus gate, exactly in the opposite direction to that affixed by Christian tradition, and which would do away with the Via Dolorosa as a sacred thoroughfare, the street shown as that along which Christ bore his cross on his way to execution. It is only probable that Calvary was the ordinary execution ground of Jerusalem, which is called in the Talmud "the House of Stoning" about A.D. 150, and which current tradition among the Jews identifies with this knoll, a tradition borne out by the account of it contained in the Mishnah, or text of the Talmud, which describes a cliff over which the condemned was thrown by the first witness. If he was not killed by the fall, the second witness cast a stone on him, and the crowd on the cliff or beneath it completed his execution. It was outside the gate, at some distance from the Judgment Hall. The knoll in question is just outside the gate, with a cliff about fifty feet high. Moreover, we are informed that sometimes "they sunk a beam in the ground, and a crossbeam extended from it, and they bound his hands, one over the other, and hung him up." (Sanhedrim vi. 4.) Thus the House of Stoning was a recognized place of crucifixion. It is curious that an early Christian tradition pointed to this site as the place of stoning of Stephen, the proto-martyr. The vicinity has apparently always been considered unlucky. An Arab writer in the Middle Ages pronounces a barren tract adjoining accursed and haunted, so that the traveller should not pass it at night.

The Valley of Judgment (or Jehosaphat), which the Arab calls the Valley of Hell, passes not far east of the knoll, the Arab name of which is Heirimayeh, probably from a cave in the knoll called Jeremiah's grotto. The idea that this was in fact the Place of the Skull was warmly adopted by the late heroic defender of Khartoum, General Gordon, who spent the year before he went on his fatal mission to the Soudan in investigating points bearing on these subjects as tending to uphold theories which he held in regard to them, and which he explained to me at great length. Before leaving England he sent some notes on these to the Palestine Exploration Fund, and in their last quarterly statement these are published. They are full of pathetic interest now. In regard to the Place of the Skull, General Gordon says that "the mention of the Place of the Skull in each of the four Gospels is a call to attention. Whenever a mention of any particular is made frequently we may rely there is something in it. If the skull is mentioned four times, one naturally looks for the body, and if you take Warren's or other contours, with the earth or rubbish removed, showing the natural state of the land, you cannot help seeing that there is a body, that the conduit (discovered by Shick) is the œsophagus, that the quarries are the chest, and if you are venturesome you will carry out the analogy further. You find in the verse in the Psalms, 'Zion on the sides of the North,' the word 'pleura,' the same as they 'pierced his pleuron, and there came forth blood and water.' God took a pleuron from the side of Adam and made woman. Now the Church of Christ is made up of or came from his pleura. The stones of the Temple came from the quarries, or chest of the figure, and so on. So that fixed the figure of the body to the skull."

This theory led to Gordon's forming a singular and mystical conception of the emblematic character of the city as typifying in actual configuration the New Jerusalem, the divine bride.

The most interesting fact, however, in connection with this knoll is the recent discovery upon it of a tomb, which has excited considerable interest as being, from its position, more likely to be the tomb of Joseph of Arimathea, in which never man had been laid before Christ, than any hitherto known. From the knowledge we have now acquired of rock-cut tombs in Palestine we are able to judge from its appearance and construction its probable date, and these all go to prove that it belongs to the later Jewish period, or that which terminated with the destruction of Jerusalem. The appearance of this tomb so near the old place of execution, and so far from the other tombs in the old cemeteries of the city, is very remarkable. A careful plan of the site and tomb has been made by Lieutenant Mantell, R. E., and sent to England, where the subject has lately afforded matter for discussion. The reason why the tomb was not found by the early Christians in their search for it at the time of Constantine is easy to be accounted for by the fact that, about ten years after the crucifixion, the "Women's Towers" were built by Agrippa upon the rock over the tomb, and it must have been hidden beneath or within the new building. Under these circumstances the sepulchre could no longer be visited, and in course of time its existence was forgotten, until the Empress Helena destroyed the temple to Venus which the Romans had built on the present site of the Holy Sepulchre Church, and "beyond all hope" (as Eusebius words it), discovered the rock-cut Jewish tomb, which the faithful accepted as the tomb of Christ.

A peculiar interest does nevertheless attach to these extremely ancient tombs in the Holy Sepulchre Church, one of which is now appropriated to Nicodemus, the nature of which I will discuss in my next letter. It is extremely probable that either Constantine or Helena heard that tombs of a high sanctity stood beneath the Venus temple, and they thought they could not do better than take the most sacred tomb to which tradition of any sort attached, and call it the holy sepulchre. Modern iconoclasticism and love of truth have, however, proved too strong for fourteen hundred years of unfounded tradition. If the

churches had only taken half as much trouble to preserve
the moral truths which are to be found in the teachings
of Christ, as they have to preserve a cave in which he was
never buried, the world would have been so much the better instead of so much the worse for their exertions.

HAIFA, August 3.—The discoveries which have been made in Jerusalem during the last few years, and the conclusions at which those who have most deeply studied the subject have arrived in consequence, render it extremely desirable that a new or revised description of the Holy City should be inserted in the tourists' hand-books for Syria and Palestine. Travellers should be warned against dragomans who waste their time taking them to see Christian sites which have no relation to the facts they are supposed to commemorate, and possess no interest of any kind beyond the philosophical one that they illustrate the extraordinary credulity and superstitions which exist among the professors of Christianity in the nineteenth century, and which are certainly not exceeded, even if they are paralleled, by those of any heathen religion.

A Jerusalem hand-book, to be of any interest, should deal with the conclusions resulting from the excavations and researches of Sir Charles Wilson, Sir Charles Warren, Captain Conder, M. Clermont Ganneau, and others, during the last twenty years, and leave the traditions of the Latin and Greek churches almost out of the question altogether. Their researches have settled nearly all the topographical questions connected with ancient Jerusalem, which had previously been the subject of so much controversy and error, the doubts and difficulties connected with them arising from the fact that the city had been more or less destroyed and built over so many times that the original foundations of its walls and Temple could only be determined by extensive and laborious excavations; and in the course of these many collateral discoveries were made.

We learn from the publications of the Palestine Exploration Fund that these excavations were carried on under difficulties of every kind, in face of the opposition of the local government and in spite of continued fevers and lack of funds. The mines were driven to extraordinary depths; one at the southeast angle of the Haram being eighty feet deep, and another, near the northeast angle, being one hundred and twenty feet beneath the surface, where it reaches the solid rock. In consequence of the great depths, the scarcity of the mining frames, and the treacherous character of the débris through which the shafts and galleries were driven, the work was one of unusual danger and difficulty, requiring much courage and determination. Sir Charles Warren and the non-commissioned officers of his staff worked constantly with their lives in their hands, and often undertook operations from which the native workmen recoiled. The prudence and discipline of the party, however, secured valuable discoveries without an accident; and it is generally acknowledged that the results are of an importance which fully repays the labor and difficulty of the operations.

Sir Charles Warren was the officer who so courageously entered the desert of Sinai after the late Egyptian war, when he succeeded in capturing the murderers of Professor Palmer, Captain Gill, and Lieutenant Sharrington, and bringing them to justice. The result of his labors in Jerusalem, and that of his fellow-explorers, is a magnificent atlas, published last year by the Palestine Exploration Fund, containing a most elaborate series of maps, plans, elevations, and engravings, which reproduce the sacred city in all its most striking features, accompanied by a handsome volume of descriptive matter. We are thus able to base an account of the ancient topography of the city on data more exact than any previously acquired, and to read the ancient historic accounts by the light of ascertained facts, instead of guessing at probabilities by the aid of descriptions, which, however carefully written, are still, as all descriptions must be, vague where the student requires most exactitude, and deficient where he most wishes for details.

With the assistance of these publications a guide-book might be compiled which would enable the tourist to order his dragoman to take him straight to the places worth seeing, instead of—following on the track of exploded tradition—going with him like a sheep to those that are not. Much could be done to clear away existing confusion and prevent the perpetuation of error by a change in the received nomenclature, whereby things should be called by their right names so far as they are known, instead of by misleading appellations, derived from the records of early pilgrims or the later crusaders. I will take a few examples as illustrations. Not far from the Church of the Holy Sepulchre the guide shows the traveller an immense reservoir, now being filled up. This, he says, is the Pool of Bethesda, but it has only been thus designated since the fourteenth century. In the twelfth this pool was supposed to be a cistern near the Church of St. Anne, and in the fourth the site of Bethesda was shown at the twin pools, northwest of Antonia. The fact is that there are only two sites which may be regarded as possible for Bethesda, one being the spring of En-Rogel, which has an intermittent ebb and flow, and which is still frequented by the Jews, who bathe in it to cure various diseases. The other is the curious well immediately west of the Temple enclosure, now called Hamman Esh-Shefa, or the Healing Spring, a long reservoir reached by a shaft nearly one hundred feet deep. None of the pools which have at various times been selected by tradition have any supply of living water, and none can well be supposed to have any intermittent rise and fall, such as we understand by the moving of the waters.

Again, take the tombs of Absalom and St. James. There is nothing whatever to connect the first with Absalom. The singular style of its architecture shows that it cannot be the pillar "Absalom reared up for himself during his lifetime in the king's dale." M. Clermont Ganneau has made excavations uncovering the bases and pedestals of the columns, all of which are purely Greek. Indeed, it is only since the twelfth century that it was called the tomb of Absalom at all. The author of the Jerusalem Itinerary calls it the tomb of Hezekiah, and Adamanus, in the seventh century, calls it the tomb of Jehoshaphat. It is possibly the monument of Alexander Jannæus spoken of by Josephus. So, too, the tomb of St. James has nothing to do with St. James; for

20

there has lately been discovered on the façade an inscription
in square Hebrew in so inaccessible a position as to have
been only probably cut before the façade was completed,
which mentions that the family of the Beni Hezir are buried
there. This family of priests is mentioned in the Bible
(1 Chron. xxiv. 15). The inscription seems to date from
the first century before Christ.

The so-called tomb of David is a vault over which has
been built a room, called the chamber in which the Feast of
the Passover prior to the crucifixion is supposed to have
taken place. Close to it is the Palace of Caiaphas, and in it
is shown the spot where Peter stood when he denied his
Master. Near it is the rock upon which the cock roosted when
he crew. The "rock," the "spot," the "palace," the "Cæ-
naculum," and the "tomb" all rest upon equally invalid authority. As regards the tomb of David, we know that it was
within the walls, together with those of eight other Jewish
kings. That the place was apparently well known as late as
the time of Christ we gather both from the Acts and
Josephus. It is remarkable that one undisputed Jewish
tomb still exists in such a position as to have been certainly
within the city of David. This is the so-called tomb of
Nicodemus, and it is yet more remarkable that in its original
condition, before it was partly destroyed, this tomb must
have been just made to contain nine bodies, placed in kokim,
or graves cut according to the oldest arrangement employed
by the Jews. Josephus mentions as a peculiarity of the
tombs of the kings that some of the coffins were buried beneath the surface, so as to be unseen even to those standing
within the monument. Just such an arrangement exists in
the tomb under consideration, the floor of which is sunk so
that the graves on one side are on a lower tier. It seems,
therefore, quite possible that the Church of the Holy Sepulchre preserves the monument of the nine chief kings of
Jerusalem. Of course, tradition, with its usual ignorance,
places "the tombs of the kings" on the hill of the upper
city, where your guide takes you to see them, and where
there are no ancient tombs at all, the tombs there being of
a date not earlier than the first century before Christ. A
fine sarcophagus, with an Aramaic inscription, stating that

it held the body of a certain Queen Sara, was discovered in them. Though called by a wrong name, they are, nevertheless, well worth visiting. As it is supposed by some authorities that Helena, Queen of Adiabene, was also buried here, they might more properly be called the tombs of the queens.

But the really great work which recent investigation has accomplished has mainly reference, not so much to such details as these, which must always remain more or less matters of speculation, as to the settlement of controversies affecting the topographical questions connected with ancient Jerusalem. First, in regard to points upon which all are now agreed. There is no doubt about the Mount of Olives and the brook Kedron. It is agreed that the Temple stood on the spur immediately west of the Kedron, and that the southern tongue of this spur was called Ophel. It is also agreed that the flat valley west of this spur is that to which Josephus applies the name Tyropœan, though there was a diversity as to the exact course of the valley, which has now been set at rest by the collection of the rock levels within the city. It is also agreed by all authorities that the high southwestern hill, to which the name of Sion has been applied since the fourth century, is that which Josephus calls the upper city, or upper Market Place. The site of the Pool of Siloam is also undisputed, and certain natural features have been determined, which serve as data on which to construct the walls of the ancient city and fix the site and area of the Temple enclosure in the time of Herod. There is still some controversy in regard to the exact position and course of the city walls prior to its destruction by Titus, but this is chiefly maintained by those who are fatally affected in their religious sentiments. There is also a difference of opinion in regard to the area of the Temple building. Practically, however, this point has been settled by the great weight of authority on one side, which affirms that the present Haram enclosure, in which are situated the mosque of Omar, and the sacred stone, represent the area of Herod's Temple, only one or two standing out for a restriction of this area. If the Turkish government would only allow explorations to be made under the platform of the dome of the rock, the very rock upon which Abraham is supposed to have been ordered to sacrifice Isaac, and if the examination of the closed chambers known to exist on the north and east sides of this platform could be carried out, the controversy might be set at rest by actual discovery. Of the Temple of Solomon little is known, though it is possible that the great scarps in the present British cemetery may be as old as the time of David, or the eleventh century before Christ. They are, without doubt, the oldest existing remains in Jerusalem, and formed part of the ramparts of the upper city. Meantime, the most interesting spot which it contains, whether for Jew, Christian, or Mohammedan, is that mysterious dome of the rock, with its gorgeous mosque covering the sacred stone, which Christ himself must have regarded with as much veneration in his day as the adherents of the two other religions, so widely opposed to the one of which he was the founder, do now.

PROGRESS IN JERUSALEM.

Haifa, August 10.—There is probably no city in the dominions of the sultan which has undergone more change during the last few years than Jerusalem, and as any change which implies progress, implies also the increase of foreign influence, and is always viewed with suspicion by the Porte, the march of events in Palestine is watched by Turkish statesmen with a jealousy which finds its expression in a persistent effort to oppose it. As, however, the basis of the movement to which Jerusalem owes its increase during recent years is a religious one, and is founded upon a sentiment which proverbially thrives by opposition, all efforts to retard the influx of population and capital into the Holy City have proved unavailing. Owing to increased facilities of travel, the pilgrimages both of the Greek and Latin churches have been more numerous. A new feature is that some of the richer pilgrims from time to time establish themselves here. This is especially the case with the Russian members of the Greek Church. The influx of Jews has also been increasing to a remarkable extent. The Protestant sects are constantly enlarging the field of their operations, and new charitable and educational establishments are springing up from year to year. An American society of Second Adventists has been resident here for some years, while isolated religious cranks find in the Holy City an appropriate dwelling-place, for reasons known only to themselves.

The result of all this is that whereas when I was last here, six years ago, only a very few houses had been built on the Jaffa road outside the walls of the town, now there is an extensive and constantly increasing Frank suburb. The price of land has risen fifty per cent., and is still constantly rising. New hotels and shops have been opened to meet the increasing demand. Within the last twenty years the population of the Holy City has certainly doubled, the increase consisting entirely of Jews and Christians. Apart from its sacred associations the city has no attractions as a residence of any kind, but quite the reverse. This fact possesses a highly important political significance, because it is evident that in the degree in which the vested interests of rival sects and religions accumulate upon this spot is it destined some day to become a bone of contention between them. It is probably the only city in the world where the same amount of capital and enterprise is expended on objects which are in no sense remunerative, while in proportion to its size there is none where a larger sum is annually given away, either in the form of charitable or religious donations. Nothing strikes one more than the proportion of buildings having some sort of public character or other to private dwellings, and these buildings are constantly increasing. This year the estimated expenditure of the Greek and Latin churches will be over $600,000 for building purposes alone. The number of Russian pilgrims who visit Jerusalem annually is about five thousand, and it is constantly increasing. They are all accommodated in the extensive premises belonging to the Russian government, in the centre of which the Russian consulate is situated, and which forms a sort of Russian suburb to the Holy City. Here one feels transported for the time to the dominions of the czar, as he hears on all sides the Slav tongue, and finds himself jostled by men and women in the peasant costume of their own country, chaffering over wares which the more enterprising of their number have imported to sell to their own country people, while they squat in stalls and booths which they have roughly extemporized for the purpose.

When you consider the amount of foreign money which is annually expended in Jerusalem by these hosts of pilgrims —those of the Latin Church, however, do not equal in number those of the Greek—by the tourists and general influx of sightseers who flock here during Easter week, and by the churches and societies in building operations, you cannot wonder that many persons have of late years become wealthy, and that many natives of Syria and the Levant are attracted to the town in the hope of becoming so. The tide having thus set in, it goes on increasing, and the rivalry of the Latin and Greek churches imparts, as it were, a stimulus to the whole jumble of creeds and nationalities which cluster round the sacred shrines.

Among the latest and most interesting arrivals are a number of Jews from Yemen. Hitherto these little-known people had only been heard of, or at most seen, by one or two enterprising travellers who have penetrated from Aden into the southern deserts of Arabia Felix. I was told that they consider themselves as belonging to the tribe of Dan. They have lately arrived as refugees in Jerusalem from Yemen, where they have suffered great misery during the recent wars between the Arab tribes which inhabit that province and the Turkish troops. Finding themselves ultimately reduced to starvation by the plunder of which they were the victims from both sides, they determined to seek shelter in the Holy City, where they arrived in rags in a starving and destitute condition. They have since been provided for by subscriptions among their co-religionists raised in Europe. I met some of them one afternoon, down at the Place of Wailing, and was much struck by the mild and gentle expression of their countenances. They are reputed to be well versed in their own religious lore, and to be devout without being hypocritical, which is more than can be said for Palestinian Jews generally. Although they were themselves engaged in sedentary and commercial pursuits in Sana and other towns in the fertile oases of southern Arabia, they report that among the nomads of these deserts are wandering tribes in no wise, so far as their external appearance goes, to be distinguished from Arabs, but who are nevertheless purely Jewish.

I also met while in Jerusalem a black Jew from Cochin in India, where Jews have been established from time immemorial, but he seemed somewhat vague as to his ancestry.

Among all these different nationalities and sects, which as a rule hold each other in holy abhorrence, it is singular that they all have one view in common, or rather, perhaps, it should be said that they all seem to labour under one impression, or presentiment, and that is that before very long

the Holy City will undergo a change of some sort. The
nature of this change naturally takes the form peculiar to
the national or religious tendency of thought. With the
Russians and French it is reduced to a very simple political
expression, which may be summed up in the word annexation. This idea is more firmly fixed among the Russians
than the French. Indeed, the Holy City plays a greater
part in the Greek religion than it does in the Latin, and the
affections of the orthodox are centred on these shrines to a
degree unknown among Christians of any other denomina-
tion. There is hardly a village in Russia in which there is
not to be found a bottle of Jordan water, and the devotional
instincts of the peasantry, which are very strong, are directed
by the Church, which is in Russia synonymous with the government, upon the holy places in Palestine, as shrines which
have a spiritual value not recognized by other churches to
the same extent, and which, therefore, when the day comes,
should entitle it to their temporal and territorial proprietorship. In other words, there is not a Russian pilgrim who
visits Jerusalem who does not hope that he may live to see
the day when it will become a Russian city, and who does
not long for the call to a holy war, the object of which
should be the exclusive possession by Russia of the Church
of the Holy Sepulchre and of the city in which it stands.*

In France there is no such religious enthusiasm, except
with a section of society, and, although the conquest of Syria

---

* RUSSIA IN PALESTINE. — The St. Petersburg correspondent of the *Daily
News* says, " In Palestine, the orthodox religion and Russian influence seem
to be increasing. Some days ago ' The Orthodox Palestine Society ' celebrated
its anniversary. It was made known on this occasion that the society—which
is protected by the government, and which has one of the emperor's uncles,
the Grand Duke Nicholas Nicolaievitch, as president—numbers already six
hundred and fifteen members, and that its reserve capital amounts to about
90,000 roubles. The society has constructed a church at Nazareth, is constructing a church at Mudshile, and has bought a piece of ground at Jerusalem. The leaders of the Palestine Society assert that their researches have
proved in ' the most indubitable ' manner that Christ, on his way to Golgotha,
' passed just over the ground which has been bought by the society.' One of
the society's tasks is to facilitate Russian pilgrimage to the Holy Land. The
emperor has recently given his sanction to the establishment of branches of
this society in all cities of the Russian Empire."

and Palestine enters into the programme of the government, and their religious protectorate over the Latin Church and its interests gives them a strong point of departure, it is weakened by the fact that the government is professedly anti-Catholic, and that, even were it not so, the sentiment for the holy places is not so strong among the Latins as among the Greeks. With the Protestants there is a large class who base their belief in an immediately pending altera- tion in the political conditions under which Jerusalem now exists, upon their interpretation of prophecy. They profess to find it clearly indicated in Ezekiel, Daniel, Revelations, and elsewhere in the Bible, that the protectorate of Pales- tine is to be vested in England. Among the Jews there are many also, though they interpret the prophetic writings in a totally different sense, who believe that the fulfilment of the prophecy which is to restore to them their ancient coun- try, with its sacred city, is at hand, and all Moslem tradition points to the present time as one critical to the fortunes of Islam, with which the fate of Jerusalem, which is to them also a holy city, is inextricably interwoven.

Whether we have any sympathy with any of these views or not, the mere fact that so many nations and races of di- verse religions, from one point of view or another, centre their political and religious aspirations upon this spot, makes it the most interesting city upon the earth's surface, because there is none other which, when its possession comes to be disputed, will excite such powerful or such conflicting ambi- tions, superstitions, and passions. These considerations be- come doubly interesting when we connect them with the events which are now transpiring in the East.

One day while I was in Jerusalem the huge bell which I had seen dragged by Russian pilgrims along the road from Jaffa arrived. It was destined for a new Russian church which has lately been built upon the Mount of Olives. Anxious to witness the ceremony of its reception, I set out for the Mount and reached the summit just in time to see the bronze monster, which I calculated weighed about eight tons, arrive at its destination. A large crowd of Russian men and women, headed by two priests of the Greek Church in full canonicals, and chanting sacred songs, were dragging it to the platform from which it was to be finally elevated into the belfry prepared for it. When, after much pulling and hauling, it was at last placed upon the platform, a solemn religious service took place. Every individual man and woman in the crowd pressed forward to kiss the uplifted crucifix which the priest presented for their adoration, crossing and prostrating themselves, and crowding also around the bell to kiss the various sacred groups of figures represented upon it in *basso-rilievo*. At last, after a final melodious chant in which all joined with great earnestness, the officiating priest gave the signal for three cheers, which was responded to with heartiness, and the ceremony was over.

I now went to examine the interior of the new church which it was intended to decorate, and was glad to find that the accident which had led me to come here to witness the arrival of the bell was the means of introducing me to a new and interesting discovery of recent date. The Russians, in excavating for the foundations of their new church, came upon the pavement and other remains of an ancient building, which they have been careful to preserve. Many of the most interesting objects found are placed in a cabinet. In the hall of the priest's house adjoining the church is a beautiful tessellated pavement, representing animals, fish, apples, and geometrical patterns, with an inscription in Armenian formed of colored tesserae. East of the gate into the garden, and close to the house, is a rock-cut chamber, with a vault of modern masonry. It measures about twenty-four feet by fourteen, and contains sixteen sarcophagi, arranged in groups of four, with a passage between. These were closed by slabs, and on three inscriptions were dimly discernible. North of this were the foundations of a building, apparently a chapel, with a tessellated floor and a row of piers about two feet square. Near by is a cave with a modern vaulted chamber, and an iron door which has apparently been placed there to protect a long inscription in old Armenian characters, formed also of colored tesserae, but I have no means of knowing what it signifies. Beneath the floor of the house are said to be other tombs, which can be reached through a masonry trap-door. It is not unlikely that all these remains belong to an Armenian mediæval monastery. The site, which has recently been acquired by the Russians, is some hundreds of yards distant from the highest part of Olivet, where the Latin chapel stands, usually visited by tourists who go there to see Christ's footprint. It commands a magnificent view, and the new Russian edifice will make an important addition to their rapidly growing collection of sacred buildings.

Nothing is more aggravating to the members of either the Greek or Latin churches than to find the rival sect in solitary possession of a holy place. It is the immediate signal for the purchase of another site as near as possible to the one already occupied, and the erection upon it of an opposition building. No greater piece of luck can befall the owner of a piece of land than to stumble upon remains which show that it had been in the occupation of the early Christians. He can then name his own price, and, like the fortunate proprietor of the land on which St. Stephen's Church is now about to be built by the French, may get a thousand napoleons for what he had a very short while before only paid fifty.

Before bidding adieu to Jerusalem, it may be interesting to my readers that I should notice some of the more important discoveries that have been made there within the last year or two, and which are not, therefore, to be found in any guide-book. For many of the details I am indebted to the Palestine Exploration Fund publications. Among these have been many tombs, some of them of much interest, but none equal to that to which I have already alluded, as being the most likely of any which have yet been discovered, to be the tomb of Christ. I have given at length the reasons in a former letter in support of this presumption. It is approached by a court cut in the rock seven feet square, and two stones in this are so placed as to give the idea that they may have held in place a rolling stone before the door. On the right is a side entrance leading into a chamber with a single loculus, and thence into a cave eight feet by ten. If, instead of turning into this, we go straight on, we descend two steps into a chamber six feet by nine; from either side wall, and in the back wall of this chamber, are three low passages; they lead into three other small chambers, each about seven feet long by six wide, and on each side of each are stone benches on which bodies could be placed, with a narrow passage between them ; so that, in fact, the whole tomb could contain six bodies. Whether it be the real Holy Sepulchre or not, it is interesting from the fact that it is the only Jewish tomb that has ever been found so close to the ramparts of the modern city on the north, and to the spot which may, with comparative certainty, be identified with Calvary. It stands not very far distant from a piece of land which a man bought a year or so ago for fifty napoleons. On beginning to excavate for the foundations of his house he came upon some tessellated pavement, carvings, and all the evidences of remains of some importance. He lost no time in making his discovery known, and, finding that it stood upon what must have been the site of the early Christian Church of St. Stephen, to commemorate the spot of his martyrdom, the Roman Catholics gave the man a thousand napoleons for his land, and have laid bare the remains with a view to building another church over them. I examined them with some interest, as it was such a recent discovery, though the historical interest only dates back to the year A.D. 460, when it was built by the Empress Eudoxia. The crusaders found it in ruins, since which time it had become buried, and its site lost. The whole plan of the church can now be distinctly traced, its pavements in many places remaining perfect, with the foundations of its side walls, fragments of columns, etc. The two most interesting features in connection with it, however, are a slab of fine limestone on which are the figures of the twelve apostles, each surrounded by a sort of canopy. They stand six each side of a central figure of a throned Christ. The figures are rather stiffly drawn and have long robes; although they were very distinct when first discovered, instead of moving the slab under shelter, it has been left exposed to the storms of winter; the result is that the outlines, which were in colour, can now scarcely be distinguished, and another year will completely efface them; besides this there is an inscription which has so far puzzled experts, though it is in Greek characters, but a good deal of it is effaced. There are also tombs in the vicinity, but though rock-cut they are evidently Christian.

Recent excavations within the city have also exposed a vast area, depressed considerably below the present level of the surface, which once formed the extensive establishment of the Knights Hospitallers, or Knights of St. John. It was given some time ago by the Turkish government to the Crown-Prince of Germany; since then the whole place has been cleared out with a view to its restoration on a grand scale, and it will doubtless form, when completed, one of the finest architectural monuments of modern date in Jerusalem. Several very deep and finely-vaulted cisterns, with arches fifty feet high, have been brought to light, besides cloisters, corridors, and vaulted chambers hitherto unknown. Some idea of the scale of the establishment which these celebrated knights possessed in Jerusalem may be gathered from the character and extent of the ruins, which cover an area of one hundred and seventy square yards, of which only half, unfortunately, belongs to the German government.

But the latest discovery, which has excited the greatest interest, is that of the inscription in the tunnel which connects the Virgin's Fount with the Pool of Siloam. The exploration of this tunnel, which is about six hundred yards long, involved great danger and difficulty. Colonel, now Sir Charles Warren, gives a most graphic picture of the horrors of his experience. For some distance the passage was only one foot four inches high, and as there was one foot of water, the explorers, who were crawling on their stomachs, naked, were submerged to their chins, having only four inches of breathing-room, with the additional danger of being drowned by the rising of the waters, which does not take place regularly. Often their mouths were under water, and a breath of air could only be obtained by twisting their faces up. To keep a light burning, to take measurements, and make observations under these circumstances was a work of no little difficulty; and yet, after crawling through mud and water for four hours, the honour of finding the inscription was reserved for a naked urchin of the town, who, some years after, announced he had seen writing on the wall. Whereupon Professor Sayce, and Herr Schick, and Doctor Guthe plunge naked into the muddy tunnel with acid solutions, and blotting-paper, and everything necessary to make squeezes, and emerge shivering and triumphant with the most interesting Hebrew inscription that has ever been found in Palestine, about which pamphlets and articles have been written, and scholars have wrangled, but which is now admitted to be as old as the time of Solomon, and it is agreed on all hands that the interpretation thereof is as follows:

" Behold the excavation. Now this is the history of the Tunnel. While the excavators were still lifting up the Pick towards each other, and while there were yet three cubits to be broken through, the voice of one called to his neighbour, for there was an excess in the rock on the right. They rose up. They struck on the west of the excavation. They struck, each to meet the other, pick to pick. And there flowed the waters from their outlet to the Pool, for a thousand two hundred cubits, and . . . of a cubit was the height of the rock over the heads of the excavators." From this it will appear that there were two working-parties, working from opposite ends, and the indefatigable explorers have actually discovered the spot where the " excess " in the rock occurred and where they probably met. Most people who have not got Palestine exploration on the brain will, however, be content to take their word for it without going to see for themselves. Still it cannot be denied that an engineering work, executed in the time of Solomon, and an inscription describing it, is of the greatest interest. The date of the inscription can be determined with tolerable accuracy by a comparison of the letters with those on the Moabite stone and other of the most ancient inscriptions known.

THE THREE JERICHOS.

HAIFA, Sept. 2.—The signs of progress to which I have alluded in former letters as being manifest in Judea are not confined to Jaffa and Jerusalem. The contemplated carriage-road to Jericho will be an immense boon to the crowds of pilgrims who flock annually to the Jordan. The first evidence of activity in this direction was at the Khan el-Ahmah. Here are the ruins of an old building. Fragments of walls and broken arches remain, and a deep well indicates that in former days it was inhabited—probably as a half-way house of entertainment. Whether this be so or not, I was glad to see a large force of stone-masons and builders actively engaged, under the superintendence of a European, in erecting a handsome khan or rest-house, which, considering that there is not at present a single habitation between Jerusalem and Jericho, with the exception of Bethany, distant only two miles from the former city, is much needed.

This place has always had an evil reputation for thieves since the days when the Good Samaritan performed his charitable offices to the plundered and beaten wayfarer. Indeed, it is at this very place that the spot is shown to the credulous pilgrim where the incident in the parable is said to have occurred, and the guide-books solemnly warn the tourist that he must be careful to be provided with an escort, because an English traveller, Sir Frederick Henniker, was attacked here by Bedouins, stripped, wounded, and left for dead in 1820. This is imputing stagnation to the Turkish government with a vengeance. It moves slowly, it is true, but the state of security has improved somewhat in sixty-five years. Six years ago I rode alone with a friend from Jericho to Jerusalem with no thought of danger. The Bedouins find it to their interest to keep up the traditions of the guide-books, and travellers continue to pay Bedouin

sheiks blackmail which they might with perfect confidence
keep in their pockets. I consider the road from Jerusalem
to Jericho in the present day as safe as Broadway, at all
events in the daytime.

It might not be safe to venture along it quite alone at
night, but the same might be said of roads in other far more
civilized countries. Nevertheless, the road in places is so
wild and desolate that it may well appal the imagination of
the timid traveller, notably so where it enters the Wady Kelt,
a deep, narrow gorge, flanked by precipitous cliffs, honeycombed with caverns, above which rise white chalk hills,
presenting a tangled network of narrow water-worn torrent
beds with knife-like ridges between. Hundreds of feet below
the path rushes a mountain torrent, which is none other than
the traditional brook Cheritt. Here, if we leave the regular
track, and make up our minds to follow a dizzy path cut out
of the precipitous cliff, which winds back up the gorge, soon
disappearing in the depth of its gloomy recesses, we plunge
into one of the wildest and weirdest scenes that the ingenuity of nature has conceived in any country, so fantastic are
the crags and so labyrinthine the gorges. The only travellers who ever thus diverge from the beaten route are Russian pilgrims, whose devotional instincts lead them to pay
their homage to every accessible shrine, and to the credit of
the Greek Church it must be said that it has contrived to
perch shrines on spots which nature only intended for eagles.

One of the most notable of these is the monastery which
commemorates the cave, to which the path we are now
following will lead us, in which Elijah is said to have been
fed by the ravens. The monastery is literally hung on to
the face of the precipice, and consists of a series of cells, and
a hall supported on vaults through which lies the entrance.
A few Greek monks live, like birds perched on the edge of
a nest, in this singular abode, to which a chapel pinnacled on
a rock is attached, dating, if we may judge from the character
of the masonry, from about the twelfth century. Perhaps
the little side chapel, with rock-cut chambers, and the vault
containing ancient bones, to which a corridor covered with
frescoes representing the Last Judgment leads, is the oldest
part of these buildings, which were apparently constructed

at three different epochs, as two layers of frescoes cover the wall, while the newest is in its turn covered by the piers supporting the ribs of the roof. Numerous caves, now inaccessible, are visible in the face of the cliff, which for a distance of about thirty yards is covered with frescoes now almost entirely defaced. In front of one of the cells is a heavy iron bar, from which, no doubt, in former days a ladder depended, the only means of access when these caves, now almost deserted, contained quite a population of hermits. This curious place is well worth a visit, and though lying so close to the tourist's route, I have not seen it described in any guide-book.

On reaching the base of the hills where the Wady Kelt debouches into the Jordan Valley, we find ourselves in the immediate presence of four ancient sites. Three of these are the sites of three different Jerichos, and one is the site of Gilgal. It is certain that the Jewish, the Roman, and the Byzantine Crusaders' Jericho occupied three different positions. The first has been identified with tolerable certainty as having existed where mounds of rubble mark its site, near the spring called in old times the Fountain of Elijah, and known now as the Ain es-Sultan. This was the Jericho of Joshua, and these mounds of rubble may contain the débris of the identical walls which fell to the sound of his trumpet. We pitched our tents at the beautiful and copious spring which must have supplied the old town with water, so as to have an opportunity of examining the neighbourhood at our leisure. The spring comes out beneath the mound on the east, and has on the west a wall of small masonry in hard cement. In this wall there is a small semicircular niche, probably intended to hold a statue of the genius of the spring. The reservoir from which the water gushes forth is about twenty by forty feet, and, though shallow, forms a delightful bath, with temperature slightly tepid. The high tumuli behind had been excavated by Sir Charles Warren, and I examined the traces of his cuttings. The mounds are formed for the most part of a light yellow clay, which, on being touched, crumbles into an impalpable powder. In some cases no strata could be discerned in the clay, in others, layers of brick, stone, and mortar were clearly visible. In another

21

large mound, a little to the south, graves were found six feet
below the surface. All these except one were of sun-dried
brick. Bones appeared to have been thrown into these after
the decomposition of the bodies. Altogether Sir Charles
Warren dug trenches through no fewer than eight of the
mounds, which form a conspicuous feature in the plain in
which the ancient cities of Jericho were situated, as they
stand to a height of about sixty feet above it; and the result at which he arrived was that they are formed by the
gradual crumbling away of great towers or castles of sun-
burned brick. Although in some cases shafts were sunk to
a depth of forty feet, nothing was found except pottery jars,
stone mortars for grinding corn, and broken glass. In one
were found, eight feet below the surface, the remains of a
large amphora, the neck, handles, and base of which were entire, and which must have stood about five feet high. Sir
Charles Warren's working party consisted of one hundred
and seventy-four men, and he thoroughly exhausted the subject.

Near the spring is a ruin which may have been that of a
small Roman temple, a portion of an aqueduct, for the waters
of the spring evidently irrigated a large extent of the plain,
and near by traces of ruins, apparently Byzantine. Here are
pillar-shafts, cornices, capitals, and other indications of a city
of later date than those we have been considering.

The site of the Jericho of Herod, which existed at the
time of Christ, was at the mouth of the Wady Kelt, deriving its water supply from that stream, and more than a mile
from Ain es-Sultan. Here there are the remains of a bridge,
foundations of buildings which were evidently Roman work,
and two large artificial mounds, in one of which was found
a rectangular chamber, the outer wall built of sun-dried
bricks, and the interior of undressed stones cemented over.

The site of the third, or Crusading Jericho, was probably
identical with that on which the modern village of Jericho
now stands; but no ruins of importance remain there, though
the whole surface of the plain between the sites of the three
Jerichos is covered with remains which attest the denseness
of the population which once inhabited it. That this should
once have been a large inhabited centre must ever appear an

astounding fact to the modern traveller who has suffered from the heat of the plain. Except during the winter months all this region is not only unbearably hot, but most insalubrious. The very Arabs desert it for the hillsides. It is possible that neglect and inattention to irrigation works may make the climate much less healthy than it was in former times, but nothing can be changed in the matter of temperature, and either the population must have deserted it for the mountains during summer or they must have been far better able to bear heat than their degenerate descendants. Sunk nearly twelve hundred feet below the level of the sea, and shut in from all breeze by lofty ranges of barren mountains on both sides, Jericho in summer must be one of the hottest places on the earth's surface. Even Jerusalem, which is four thousand feet above it, is pretty warm. On the other hand, Josephus vaunts the wonderful fertility of the place, and calls it "a region fit for the gods."

Its magnificent and extensive palm groves were celebrated, but these have disappeared since the eighth century, and there is only one date-tree left. Still the abundance of the water, the richness of the soil, and the warmth of the climate, wonderfully adapt it to the growth of all tropical produce. · All kinds of vegetables are in season all the year round. Grapes, which are trellised on high poles, as in Italy, grow to enormous size; indigo, cotton, and sugar would all flourish, but there are no people to cultivate them.

The remains of the old aqueducts testify to the skilful manner in which the ancients used their abundant water supply for the irrigation of this extensive plain. I counted altogether nine different ancient aqueducts. One or two of these are still utilized, and of late years a handsome bridge has been built in connection with one of them, but the engineering skill of the ancients holds its own with our more modern constructions. Many of the bridges by which these aqueducts span the ravines are very handsome. Some are on two tiers of arches, one above another. In places they are tunnelled through the hills. One bridge of massive masonry of large stones is one hundred and twenty feet long and thirty-five feet high, with pointed arches. There is one aqueduct eight miles long, consisting of a cemented channel two feet broad, and terminating in a handsome cemented cistern. It is carried over several bridges, one fifty feet long and thirty feet high.

I mention this system of aqueducts because I have never seen any account of Jericho in the records of travellers or in guide-books which does justice to them. They are important as showing how much money must have been spent in developing the resources of this plain, and what a garden it must have been in old times. So late as the thirteenth century we hear that the sugar-cane was cultivated around Jericho, and I believe that at this day there are few spots on the earth's surface which could be turned to more profitable account. Here all the products of the tropics could be raised without having to go to the tropics for them, and many fruits could be conveyed from here to a European market, which it would be impossible to preserve for the length of time which is now required to transport them from the tropics. At a comparatively small expense the ancient system of aqueducts could be repaired and the abundant water supply utilized, which is now left to stagnate in marshes and breed fever and pestilence. It is, in fact, impossible to appreciate the magnificent capabilities which this plain possesses and not feel convinced that in these days of civilized enterprise the question of their development is only one of time.

JERICHO—A NEW WINTER RESORT.

HAIFA, Sept. 15.—When I last visited Jericho, six years ago, it consisted of a miserable village of mud huts, containing a population of mixed negroes and Bedouins, amounting at most to three hundred souls. I was astonished now to find that, of all places in the world, it was going ahead. There was a sort of boom going on; a very minute boom, it is true, but still it was progress, and there is no saying what it may lead to.

It is due entirely to the Russians, and I think that a progressive Jericho, owing to Russian enterprise, is a phenomenon worthy of remark. Indirectly it may be attributed to the passion Russian pilgrims have for bathing in the Jordan and carrying away bottles full of the water of that sacred stream. This passion for holy ablutions is one which a wise and far-seeing government has turned to profitable political account. It was only in obedience to the most ordinary instincts of humanity that some sort of accommodation should be provided for the pious crowds, consisting largely of old and frail women, who trudge thirty miles in a broiling sun to bathe in the Jordan, and who could not find a roof to shelter them, or a place in which to be fed, until they got back to Jerusalem. So a large, handsome, red-stone building, not unlike a state lunatic asylum, has been erected for their accommodation at Jericho. Here not only the Russian pilgrim, but the ordinary travelling lunatic, can find first-class accommodation.

The protection which so handsome an establishment afforded was all that was required to give a start to the place. Devout Russians, always acting under the auspices of a pious, intelligent, and paternal government, are beginning gradually to make Jericho a place of winter resort. They build little cottages there, surround them with gardens which supply them with most delicious fruit and vegetables, spend their summers in Jerusalem, and come down here in the winter and bathe in the Jordan to their hearts' content. In other words, in a religious and quite unostentatious way, Russia is quietly colonizing Jericho. The obnoxious word colony, so hateful to Turkish ears, is never pronounced, but I counted no fewer than twelve neat little whitewashed cottages, where a few years ago there was not one.

One of my travelling companions, who was an English medical man of some eminence, was so much struck with the climatic advantages of the place as a winter resort for consumptive patients that, now that good accommodation is to be found there, he has decided to advise invalids to try the effects of its air. Hitherto when one told a person "to go to Jericho" it was a polite way of intimating to him that he might go somewhere else, Jericho being the next hottest place known to that more distant region; but now we may tell our friends to go to Jericho in a spirit of benevolence, in the hope that it may restore them to health. What an unbearable place, by the way, Jericho would be if all the bores who have been metaphorically sent there had literally gone. As it is, I cannot imagine a more agreeable place for a person not absolutely dependent upon society to go to and spend a month or two in winter.

There is a peculiar softness and balminess in the air, not to be found elsewhere in the world, for there is no other place in the world eleven hundred feet below the sea-line. There is a wide, level, open plain to scamper across on horseback in all directions; there are thickets of tamarisk and nebk and bamboo swarming with wild boar, deer, gazelle, and other animals, some of them not to be found elsewhere, to delight the sportsman. There is the Jordan handy, with first-rate fishing to satisfy the most ardent angler; there is the Dead Sea to bathe in and boat on (only there are no boats) for persons whose tastes are aquatic. There is a flora which would be a source of never-ending interest to the botanist, for it is peculiar to this region; and the same remark applies, to some extent, to its ornithology and entomology. There are ancient ruins in all directions to satisfy the most inveterate archæologist, while the explorer has only

to cross the Jordan, and in a few hours he will find himself
in a region almost untrodden by the foot of the tourist, with
all manner of interesting discoveries awaiting him. Then
he is still comparatively in the world, for a smart ride of five
hours will take him back to Jerusalem, and he need not be
afraid of having to suffer hardship, for the fare in the Russian hospice is reported excellent, especially in the matter of
milk and vegetables. My advice, then, to the invalid, the
sportsman, the man of natural history, and the antiquarian,
who may be looking out for a new winter resort, is, " Go to
Jericho !" There is no particular reason that I can see why
the Russians should have a monopoly of this charming spot,
though we should be very much obliged to them for making
it habitable. No doubt when the partition of "the sick
man's" property, for which they have been waiting so long,
takes place, they will put in a claim for Jericho.

Meantime I am glad to see that the government seem to
be put upon their mettle. Not only have they built a handsome aqueduct across the ravine on which the modern village stands, but they have cleared a large expanse of the
plain on the other side with a view of bringing it into cultivation and irrigating it by means of the said aqueduct.
This plain extends in an unbroken level to the Dead Sea,
and affords a pleasant six-miles scamper. It is the grazing-
ground generally of large herds of camels, and on a hot
and thirsty day they come in very opportunely. They are
ever-ready if not ever-willing fountains, and there is nothing
more refreshing than a drink of warm camels' milk. It is
not easy to milk them, as they don't like strangers, and one
is apt to get charged by a savage mother who mistakes one's
intentions. Moreover, it requires some dexterity to milk a
camel into a tumbler. In fact, this is difficult with any
animal. I have had a battle with a nanny-goat on a bare
Palestine hillside when I was thirsty, which ended in my
utter discomfiture. The only plan is to backshish the
goatherd or camelherd. It is an odd sight to see a young
camel tugging away at one side of its mother and the camelherd tugging away at the other, and the resigned old female
chewing her cud between them; it suggested to me a design
for a picture which I sent to an artist friend, to be called

" The Rivals." With the Dead Sea and the burning hills of Moab for a background, I think it would make rather an effective picture.

However often I might visit the Dead Sea, I would always bathe in it, in spite of its stickiness afterwards. The sensation of floating without the slightest effort for an indefinite time when one is hot and tired is infinitely soothing.

The government intend building a bridge over the Jordan, and on my way back from visiting its proposed site I passed the much-disputed position of Gilgal, where the Israelites made their first camp in the Promised Land. This has but recently been identified by the ever-to-be-lamented Palestine explorer, Mr. Tyrwhitt Drake, who fell a victim to his zeal in the Jordan valley. Nothing is to be seen there now but some mounds, in which have been found pottery, broken glass, and tesseræ. It was for long the resting-place of the Ark and the Tabernacle. It was somewhere on this plain that Sodom and Gomorrah, "the Cities of the Plain," were situated, and not to the south of the Dead Sea, as was formerly supposed, but their sites have been looked for in vain.

The great events of which the plain of Jericho had in early times been the scene, together with its traditional connection with the temptation of Christ on the Mount, which rises abruptly behind the Spring of Ain-es-Sultan, and actual interest with regard to his baptism in the Jordan and other events, attracted the Christians of a very early age to this part of the country. Hence from Justinian's time the plain began to be covered with monastic edifices, and the gorges and precipices of the enclosing mountains to be burrowed with hermit's caves and sacred shrines and chapels.

There is a tendency, on the part especially of the Greek and Armenian churches, to reoccupy some of these. Certainly of all the uncomfortable and dreary and broiling monasteries I ever saw, that of Kusr Hajlah, near the Dead Sea, now inhabited by half a dozen monks, claims pre-eminence. It is placed just on the edge of the saline plain, which exhales in summer a pungent heat that must render life almost insupportable. Nevertheless, it bears all the marks of having been an important mediæval monastery. The old walls still exist on three sides, and measure about forty yards by sixty. These contained two chapels above ground and one beneath in the vaults. The walls are still covered with frescoes, the designs of which are distinctly visible, as well as the inscriptions in Greek beneath them. They are evidently of Crusading times. There is a large cistern here, thirty feet by ten and twenty-four deep, which is in good preservation. So is another at the monastery of El-Yahud, thirty feet deep, with piers and arches also almost perfect. This monastery is distant about half an hour from the Jordan, and dates from the twelfth century. It stands on the site of one which was called the Monastery of St. John on the Jordan, but which was destroyed by an earthquake. The interest attaching to these monasteries, however, is comparatively slight. Upon archæological grounds they exhibit no very striking features, while from a religious point of view they are significant chiefly as showing how soon the religion of Christ became degraded into a system of useless asceticism, and, considering the tendency which is exhibited to return to it, the lamentable reflection is forced upon one that the true spirit of Christianity is as little understood now as it was in those days.

The monks who inhabit these buildings are in one sense as interesting as the buildings themselves, for one has only to converse with them to be transported to the Middle Ages. They are probably the only class of men who have remained absolutely unaffected by nineteenth-century civilization or modes of thought. They are like the toads that have been locked up for centuries in stone, and might in so far as their religious views are concerned be the identical individuals who, in the time of the crusaders, used to inhabit the cells they now occupy. From a psychological point of view, then, it is curious to converse with them on matters of faith and religion, for unless one has had personal experience of the degree of ignorance and superstition which are still to be found in a recluse of the Armenian Church, for instance, one could not credit the fact that such a being exists; and still represents a considerable class in the days in which we live.

The Arabs around Jericho are of a tribe called Abou

Nuseir. They venerate a place called "The Place of Sepulchre of Dawar." This personage was their ancestor, and the Abou Nuseir bury their dead in the tombs of the Dawar people. Arabs of any other tribe passing this spot make use of the expression, "Permission, oh, Dawar," and the valley is sacred, and ploughs, grain, and other articles are deposited here for safety. The usual votive offerings—sticks, rags, bracelets—are found near the tombs. This tribe is scattered about in tents among the thorny bushes that cover the plain, amid which their flocks find good pasture. They are reputed to have a bad character, but we made great friends with them, owing to a circumstance which secured their gratitude.

While sitting by the fountain one afternoon we saw a number of Arabs carrying a man on a litter. This excited our doctor's curiosity, and we immediately hailed the procession. They told us they had a wounded man, and we replied we had a doctor, and they waited till we came up. In fact, an elderly man had just received a bullet in the leg from a friend with whom he had had a quarrel, which splintered the bone a little below the knee. The ball was still lodged in the leg. The doctor, who had made five military campaigns, and had probably dressed as many gunshot wounds as any man alive, was in his element. Instantly the man was taken to the nearest tents, splints of bamboo and bandages of flour and the white of an egg were speedily extemporized, while a large audience of wild-looking men, women, children, and dogs crowded around to watch operations.

The ball was probed for, not with any surgical instrument, for we were unprepared for any such emergency, but with the finger. The only instruments forthcoming were a penknife and a razor. The question was how to get the ball out with such appliances. The occasion was one which called for a display of genius, but the demand was not made in vain; with that simplicity which is its most marked characteristic, the doctor cut into the opposite side of the leg with the razor, and then pushed the ball clean through with his finger. The astonishment of the audience was excessive at the appearance of the crushed bullet, and the wounded man, a weather-beaten old Semite, who had

bellowed lustily while the operation was going on, kissed
the doctor's hand effusively, and consoled himself with
coffee and cigarettes, in which we joined, while the band-
aging and splinting was in progress. For a couple of days
after this the doctor visited his patient twice a day amid the
warmest expressions of gratitude on the part of the tribe,
who forthwith brought all their sick to be cured, and the
blessings which were invoked upon us echoed in our ears
when we took our departure, till they died away in the distance.

A SHORT CUT OVER AN UNKNOWN COUNTRY.

HAIFA, Oct. 1.—About half a mile in rear of our camp, at Ain-es-Sultan, rose a precipice a thousand feet high, which culminated in the lofty crest of a mountain called Quarantul. It derives its name from a tradition which identifies it with the mount upon which Christ was tempted for forty days in the wilderness. Of course, it is not the mountain at all, or, at all events, there is not the smallest particle of evidence to prove that it is, but that is a trifle where sacred sites are concerned. The face of this precipitous cliff is honeycombed with the black mouths of caverns. Sitting round our camp-fire at night we observed lights gleaming from the sheer side of the rock. Otherwise there was nothing to lead us to suppose that any of these caverns could be occupied by human beings. But these fires excited our curiosity, and we determined to pay the cave-dwellers perched so high above our heads a visit.

The operation turned out a more dizzy one than I had anticipated. No guide was necessary, for we could see the track winding like a thread up the face of the precipice. For the first three hundred feet or so it was all plain sailing, but then the ledge became horribly narrow. Occasionally the path was so steep that it dwindled into rock-cut steps. A false step would have sent you thundering hundreds of feet down into the abyss. At one place the height was so dizzy, the foothold so slight, that my nerve, which for this sort of work is not what it once was, began to give way, and I ignominiously squatted down, with my face turned to the rock, and tried to steady myself by forgetting that six inches behind me was a yawning chasm, from which a pebble might have been dropped plumb to the bottom. Retreat was as bad as advance, and more humiliating. For the rest of the way I went on my hands and knees, to the amusement of my

companion, whose brain was not similarly affected. I don't
know anything more disagreeable than the irresistible im-
pulse which overtakes one sometimes to pitch one's self headlong over a precipice of this kind.

At last, to my inexpressible relief, I reached the mouth of
a cave, into which I sprawled, panting, with thankfulness,
but oppressed nevertheless with the horrible consciousness
that I had the return voyage still to make. However, I dismissed this painful consideration for the moment, and applied myself to the examination of the curious grotto which
we had reached. It was a sort of ante-chamber to a tunnel
in the rock, passing through which we came upon some
dreadful steps cut on the face of the rock; but here there
was a slight, rickety balustrade of wood, and at the top stood
a greasy old monk, a sight which, under the circumstances,
produced a more soothing effect upon my mind than such a
sight usually does. This ecclesiastical worthy received us
with gracious smiles, and led us through another tunnel into
a sort of vestibule, which opened into a chapel which had been
constructed at the mouth of a cave, so that the front facing
the precipice was of masonry. Looking out of the window
which had been constructed in this wall, a stone might have
been dropped at least five hundred feet without touching
anything till it reached the bottom. This chapel was gorgeously fitted up, thanks to the contributions of pilgrims
whose heads must have been steadier than mine was. It
had a handsomely decorated screen covered with sacred
designs richly gilt. The apse was six feet in diameter, and
the total length from the inside of the apse to the back of
the cave about twenty-five feet, the breadth being about
twenty. A door led out of this chapel into a narrow passage and up two or three steps into another cave, or niche,
where there was a figure of a saint.

As far as I could understand from the monk, who spoke
Greek, and very bad Italian, somewhere here was the spot
where Christ stood when he was tempted. The walls of the
chapel were covered with frescoes. The large, cavernous
vestibule was the dwelling-place of the monk, with whom
was associated a younger sort of acolyte, who lived in a cave
overhead, which was reached by a flight of stone-cut steps

from the back of the vestibule. There was also a small inner cave, fitted with a door, in which they kept their stores. The old man told me he had lived here like an eagle in an eyrie for ten years without even descending to the plain below. I wondered how he kept his health without taking exercise. All hermits who live on the sides of precipices should, I think, have treadwheels of some kind fitted up for them, or rotating cages like those in which Italian white mice take their exercise. I don't think our old friend, however, led a very ascetic life, so far as eating and drinking are concerned. He insisted on our staying to drink some excellent coffee, after which he produced a bottle of very good mastic, or spirit made from corn and flavored with anise-seed. I observed some fresh green salad and cauliflower on his side-table, which the Arabs bring him from their gardens at the foot of the hill. He had also an abundant supply of good Arab bread. His water is supplied from a cistern, of which there are several attached to the caves. He told me that eight of these were at present inhabited, but most of them were higher up. He was the spiritual superior of them all, and although there was another chapel in ruins, his was the only one in which service was performed. He invited me to continue my explorations to the caves higher up, but my mind was so much occupied with thinking how I was to get down as to exclude from it any idea of going higher up. Altogether this hermit was a jolly, hospitable old fellow, and it would be as cruel to pick him out of his hole and drop him into the busy world as it is to pick a periwinkle out of his shell with a pin.

Partially shutting my eyes and presenting my rear to the enemy, I crawled backwards down the giddy steps, and just at an uncomfortable corner came upon a jet-black man in a sort of priestly garb, who turned out to be an Abyssinian hermit. He has no connection with the establishment I had been visiting, having his own cell and his own church all to himself. His bosom was stuffed with manuscripts in Ethiopian characters. Under any other circumstances I would have endeavored to converse with so rare a specimen of ecclesiastical humanity; but how can a man engage in a theological discussion in an unknown tongue, hanging be-

tween earth and heaven on six inches of slippery rock? I
felt rather inclined to say *vade retro Satanas*—not an inappropriate remark, considering the mountain I was on; and
yet the poor man meant well, and, indeed, gave me an arm.
He does not stick to his perch, however, like the old raven I
had been visiting above, but usually resides in Jerusalem,
visiting his cave during the forty days of Lent and at other
stated periods.

We now determined to bid adieu to Jericho and the Mount
of the Temptation and to strike across country into Samaria.
This would take us over an unbeaten track and show us a
country very imperfectly known. We trusted to finding our
way by asking it, or by picking up local guides when we
were utterly at a loss. By this means, although one runs a
considerable risk of being benighted, or of having to scramble over almost impracticable mountain paths, you get a better chance of stumbling upon objects of interest than by following a more trodden route. For more than two miles we
skirted in a northeasterly direction the base of the lofty cliffs
of the Jebel Quarantul. On our right a copious steam, which
has its rise in a fountain called Ain Duk, irrigated an extensive tract of land, which was green and well cultivated. . If
there had only been population enough to develop it properly it would be a most productive region. There were all the
evidences that in ancient times its resources were not thus
neglected. Everywhere the remains of stone watercourses
and aqueducts were visible, one bridge in particular having
no fewer than three tiers of arches one above another. The
construction was ingenious and peculiar. At the bottom or
narrowest part of the ravine which it spanned was one huge
pointed arch. Immediately over this were four pointed
arches, while at the side of them was a fifth, double the
height of the others, the foundations of which were in the
steep side of the ravine. Above these again were six more
pointed arches which supported the aqueduct. Thus there
were altogether twelve arches, and of these only two were
the same size. The old Roman masonry of which they were
composed was still in a very good state of preservation.
Near this aqueduct were also the substantial remains of an
old Roman road.

We now crossed, for about three miles, a fine undulating country covered with rich herbage, upon which large herds of cattle were feeding, and followed most of the way an ancient cemented channel, about four feet wide, which had formerly conveyed the waters of another stream to swell those which had their origin at Ain Duk, and all of which were carried over the aforementioned high level bridge. The stream which we were now approaching was also surrounded by cultivated and irrigated land. The whole of this plain in its richness and wealth of water far surpassed anything my expectations had led me to anticipate. Near the base of the mountains from which this fine stream issues are the remains of an ancient fortress situated on a high mound or tell, called Khurbet el Aujeh. The stream bears the same name. This is the sixth large stream which I have counted gushing from these mountains in a distance of about eight miles. My compass now told me that I must get up into the mountains if I intended to strike the Jerusalem and Samaria road at the point which I proposed. From information which I had taken before starting I expected to find the track in question ascending the valley from which the Aujeh issues, but we looked in vain for signs of any such track. Indeed, on forcing our way up it a little distance, we found that its precipitous sides closed in on us in a manner which effectually barred all further progress. We were wondering what to do in our dilemma, when, fortunately, we observed some peasants making some irrigating channels, and from them, after much chaffering, we obtained a guide. It is a singular thing that these poor peasantry, whose day's labor in the fields cannot be worth more than ten cents to them, will refuse fifty rather than leave what they are about and act as guides. On this occasion it was with great difficulty that I bribed a man with a dollar. To our surprise he took us straight to the base of an apparently impracticable cliff and proceeded to climb up it. As my experience of Palestine horses has convinced me that they can go almost wherever a man can, provided you leave them to find their own way, we proceeded to breast the limestone crags without misgiving, the only hardship being that the day was hot and we had to climb them on foot. To scramble up a thousand feet on a stretch by a path which was generally quite invisible is no slight operation, and one which, in this instance, it would have been impossible to perform without a guide, such impassable barriers did the rocks seem to present until the guide showed us the way to circumvent them. When we did reach what we fondly hoped was the summit, it was only to find a barren, undulating wilderness stretching before us, every now and then involving more climbing, for the elevation at which we were destined to arrive before the end of our day's journey was more than four thousand feet higher than the level from which we started.

If the scenery by which we now found ourselves surrounded was rugged, it was wild and grand in the extreme. Gloomy and precipitous gorges intersect these mountains in every direction. Not a sign of a habitation is visible anywhere, and with the exception of a single goatherd we did not meet a human being for hours. The vegetation was also very sparse, relieved, however, by great quantities of the fragrant white broom in flower, and cyclamen and scarlet anemones. Even in the days of the ancients it must have been a barren, uncultivated tract, but I was repaid for the scramble across it by one or two evidences of extreme antiquity of the greatest interest. The first of these consisted of four huge prostrate slabs of stone. They were evidently the blocks which had once formed a dolmen that had been overturned. Now, the interest of this lies in the fact that no dolmen, or signs of a dolmen, has ever yet been discovered in Judea, though eagerly searched for. There is only one doubtful one in Galilee, but they are abundant to the east of the Jordan. The reason assigned for this is that the tribes to the east of the Jordan did not obey the command, when they entered the land of Canaan, to "overturn the tables of stone," to destroy the Canaanitish altars, and to break or smash their pillars; while the tribes to the west, especially Judah and Benjamin, were very particular in this regard.

Here, I think, is the only evidence which has yet been found in Judea of this interesting fact. This region was apparently one much dedicated to Baal worship. I saw many stone circles and one or two alignments of large stones, but the most curious was an enclosure about twenty-

22

four yards square, formed of rough, unhewn stones, each
weighing a ton or more, piled to a height of two or three
upon each other. In the centre was a circle, eight feet in
diameter, of large stones, with a single stone in the middle of
it. This was a monument which evidently existed from pre-
Judaic times; but, although I attempted hurriedly to take its
bearings, I am afraid that in that wilderness of stone I should
never be able to find it again.

We were pretty well worn out when we reached at last the
village of Mugheir, the first inhabited place we had seen
since leaving our camp near Jericho, and where we proposed
to call a halt for the refreshment of man and beast. Meantime, as our tents and baggage had been sent by another
road, we began to feel extremely doubtful as to when we
should ever see them again.

Haifa, Oct. 7.—The village of Mugheir, where we halted to rest after our long and weary scramble from the Jordan valley, is one of the most out-of-the-way places to be found in Palestine. It is not on the way anywhere, but a sort of *Ultima Thule*—the last spot where ground fit for cultivation is to be found. It stands on the margin of a charming little plain, where there is a fine olive grove. Indeed, looking westward, the prospect is cheery enough, but eastward it is wild rock, black, gloomy gorges, or less precipitous but equally barren valleys. The sheik received us with great cordiality, albeit quite unused to the visits of travellers, and spread before us such fare as he could, flat Arab bread, roasted eggs, curdled goat's milk, and figs, butter, and honey. I mention the last three together because you eat them together. You first dip your dried fig into the butter, you then dip it into the honey, and then put it into your mouth. I never tried the combination before, but it is not bad. He also gave us a hot compound of flour and sugar boiled together, which he seemed to think a great deal of, but, beyond being sweet and sticky, it had no especial merit. His wife was the fairest woman I ever saw for a pure-blooded fellahah peasant. In fact, she could not have been fairer had she been a blue-eyed, light-haired Swede or German.

After satisfying my hunger I went to look for antiquities, and found several rock-cut tombs and cisterns, a fine rock-hewn wine-press, and four towers all in a good state of preservation, and three of them inhabited. They measured thirty feet square and as many in height. The basement stones were massive enough to be the masonry of a former period, but exactly of what date I am unable to say, possibly not earlier than the crusades; though I found some foundations of walls which I am inclined to ascribe to a much older date. There has been probably a town or village here from time immemorial, though I am unable to identify it with any Biblical site.

The sheik insisted upon accompanying us himself as guide to a place called Singil, which we had fixed upon as our night quarters. Our way led us through a small, depressed plain. After passing some remains of no special interest we reached a very remarkable ruin, called El-Habs. It is a tower on a rocky scarp, with walls built partly of masonry, partly of rock, which measure about sixty feet by thirty. The stones of which these walls are composed are of immense size, measuring from twelve feet up to eighteen feet in length, with a height of from three to four feet each. The masonry is thus quite equal to the average size of the temple stones in Jerusalem. The tower has two entrances. Near it are the remains of another large building of about one hundred feet square outside measurement, and with walls six feet thick. Its interior is divided into four parallel chambers, running east and west, of various breadth. One of the partition walls has archways through it, with piers between. All round these buildings are the foundations of ancient walls and houses and bell-mouthed cisterns. The whole place bears the marks of extreme antiquity. It has been examined by the officers of the Palestine Survey, but is not mentioned in any guide-book, and I am unable to form any conjecture in regard to it.

Our road now lay through a fertile plain, called The Meadow of the Feast, possibly in some connection with the yearly feast which used to be held by the Jews in old times at Shiloh, from which historical site we were not far distant. It is a comfort now and then to come upon a Biblical site about the identity of which there is not the slightest doubt, and such is the case with Seilun, the modern name for Shiloh. It stands in an extremely retired valley, and on our way to it we put up the third batch of gazelles we had started in one day. This was the spot where the Tabernacle was first permanently set up in Canaan, and where the Israelites assembled to allot the Promised Land. They were probably encamped hard by on The Meadow of the Feast, across which we had just been riding, and it was probably on this meadow, while the maidens were dancing at the festival in honour of the ark, that the remnant of the Benjamites concealed themselves among the vineyards on the hillsides and carried off two hundred maidens. At present it is impossible to be certain whether any of the remains now visible existed at the time when the Tabernacle was there. The ruins which first strike the eye on the hillside are evidently those of a comparatively modern village, with here and there fragments of masonry which may date back to Crusading times. Then there is a low, square building supported by two rows of columns, which has been used as a mosque, but in early times may have been a Christian church; but the most remarkable monument is a square building of which only the walls remain. It is apparently of three architectural periods, and it is just possible that the oldest may have been Jewish. The original walls have been added to by a sloping scarp having been built against them, so that the wall, which is about fourteen feet high, is nine feet thick at the bottom, and about three feet thick at the top. Inside are some fragments of columns, capitals, and a door lintel, which has recently fallen from the principal entrance, on which are carved two wreaths, flanked by two double-handled pitchers, and in the centre an amphora.

There are no inhabitants at Shiloh now, so we pushed on to Singil, a village situated about three thousand feet above the sea-level, and commanding a most magnificent view. The villagers here showed me some foundations of what they said had been an old castle built by a certain King Sinbil, but I strongly suspect that they substituted the b for a g, as the village takes its name from a certain Crusading hero, who was afterwards canonized and became St. Gilles, and that here he built himself a castle. The natives also sent me into a cave on a wild goose chase after an inscription, which, after much scrambling with lighted tapers, I failed to find.

We had now left Judea, and were entering ancient Samaria, which is governed, not from Jerusalem, but Damascus, the seat of government being Nablous, a large town of about twenty thousand inhabitants, whose principal industry is the manufacture of soap, with which they supply al-

most the whole country. The town is squeezed in between
the lofty hills of Ebal and Gerizim, both of which are over
three thousand feet above the sea-level. This is the valley
of Shechem. Nothing can exceed in picturesqueness the
situation of this place and the beauty of its surroundings,
especially when the almond and peach trees are in bloom in
the valley. The steep hillsides seem to be a mass of huge
cactuses; these are used to line the terraces of the vineyards
as hedges, but as they are great absorbers of vitality from
the soil, I should think they must impoverish the land. In
the autumn these ungainly plants are thickly covered with
fruit about the size of a large fig, when ripe of a bright red.
They are full of small seeds, but sweet and refreshing. The
natives gorge themselves upon them, as they are esteemed
wholesome, but they are traps to the unwary and inexpe-
rienced of the most painful kind, being covered outside with
diminutive and almost invisible prickly hairs. The first time
I ever tried to eat one I filled my mouth with these unpleasant little spikes, and spent half an hour with my tongue out,
while a friend was engaged with a pair of tweezers extracting each individual irritant, but then he only partially succeeded, and for the rest of the day I felt as if I had tried to
swallow half a chopped-up hair-brush. The natives pick
the fruit by digging a pronged iron into them, with which
they twitch them off the stalk; they then roll them on the
ground, so as to get the hairy prickles off, and then carefully peel them. The great green leaves have spikes like
pins half an inch long upon them, which inflict a most vi-
cious and poisonous prick. I once tumbled into a cactus
bush, and really suffered severely for many hours. Under
these circumstances it is something amazing to see camels
munching these leaves, prickles and all, with apparent relish;
a donkey eating thistles is a joke to it.

Nablous is also surrounded by extensive olive groves, and
the oil is celebrated throughout Palestine; it also exports
cotton of native growth. In fact, for a Moslem city, it may
be considered an enterprising and go-ahead place. At present it lacks the prime necessity of a carriage road to the sea-
coast. All its exports and imports have to be conveyed on
the backs of camels. If the long-projected railway from

Haifa to Damascus could ever be consummated, a wagon road could easily be constructed in connection with it, and Haifa would then become the port of Nablous, instead of Jaffa, which is slightly nearer to it. With the exception of the long central street, which forms the principal bazaar, the streets as a rule are more gloomy and tunnel-like than most Oriental towns, though there are many handsome stone houses, and the building of new ones afforded evidence of the growing wealth of the inhabitants. The consequence is an improvement in the reputation of the population, who have in former times been notorious for their turbulent fanaticism, but of late years the Turkish government has succeeded in establishing its authority on a firmer foundation and making its exercise felt. Indeed, the superficial traveller in the Turkish empire, who only sees the defects of the existing system of administration, is hardly a fair judge of the progress that has been made in a certain direction unless he is able to compare it with what has been.

There can be no doubt that during the last twenty years a great change has been worked in the establishment of law and order and in the security of life and property. If oppression has the disadvantage of grinding the people and making their lives miserable, it, at all events, has the merit of intimidating them and restraining them from acts of violence and crime. If the unjust judge and extortionate tax-gatherer are taking the heart out of the people, they are taking the pluck out of them, too, and one result is that the stranger can now travel in safety through regions where he was once sure of being plundered and possibly murdered, and walk unmolested through Moslem crowds, where formerly he might have been subjected to insult. Nor is this due to the direct action of any foreign power or to the exercise of any diplomatic pressure in favor of reform. On the contrary, the influence of foreign powers was never so low as it is at present, and I am convinced that all attempts on the part of foreign powers to enforce reforms on Turkey only hinder them. The influence of the sultan and his government is not to be maintained throughout Islam by any action in obedience to the dictates of Christian powers. They resent it, just as the South used to resent the inter-

ference of the North in the matter of slavery; but this does
not prevent their being alive to any advantages which accrue to the empire by enforcing, as far as may be, a respect
for law and order; and, so far as it is possible, to develop
its resources without being beholden to foreign capital, or
increasing the power and influence of the native Christian
population. The difficulty is that the instinct of the Moslem is not in favor of progress, and that he is always out-
stripped in the race by his Christian neighbour.

Again, the country can only be developed through the
education and enlightenment of the people; but where an
administrative system is in itself corrupt and unenlightened,
the education and illumination of the masses means their
endowment with the faculty of perceiving abuses, and possibly with a determination to resist them; and this danger
is so great that it must be averted, even at the cost of the
national prosperity. For this reason the government sets
its face against the education of Moslems in Christian
schools, not because they are afraid of the Moslems being
converted to Christianity—there is not the slightest danger
of that—but because they are afraid of their imbibing Western ideas of social and political life, which are opposed to
the conditions which characterize the existing administration of affairs. In fact they are not opposed to reform, but
it must be a reform not suggested from without, nor imposed upon them from within; it must neither be in obedience to diplomatic pressure nor to popular clamour; it must
be a reform of their own initiative, and as any such reform,
to be effectual, must begin by the authorities with whom it
is to originate reforming themselves, the process seems almost hopeless. Still, as I have already remarked, there has
distinctly been change, and change for the better, so far as
security for life and property and the extension and en-
forcement of official authority are concerned, during the
last twenty years—security of property to the people, be it
understood, from their own mutual plundering propensities.
Whether this security extends to the demands of the tax-
gatherer, and how far it has conduced to their own material
welfare and happiness, is quite another question.

SACRED SAMARITAN RECORDS.

HAIFA, Oct. 15.—The chief interest connected with Nablous lies in the fact that it is the residence of the remnant of those Samaritans who were colonized here by Shalmaneser, King of Assyria, when he carried away the children of Israel captive. From the Biblical record (2 Kings xvii.), it would appear that the new settlers were drawn from mixed nationalities and various cities within his dominions. Some came from Babylon itself, some from Hamath, a town between Damascus and Aleppo, and others from Cuthah—probably the Kutha of Arabian geographers, a town and district between the Tigris and Euphrates—some from Ava, which has been identified with the modern Hit, and some from Sepharvaim, once the famous city of Sippara, both cities on the Euphrates, in lower Mesopotamia.

We are also told that the new colonists petitioned the King of Assyria to be taught the religion of the Jews, and that he sent them a Jewish priest to teach it to them, and that they added it on, after a curious fashion, to the various forms of idolatry which they had imported from their different localities, and hence established a mongrel sort of worship, which became afterwards purified, but which nevertheless rendered them especially obnoxious to the Jews of Judea, all the more so because they intermarried with the remnant of the tribes of Israel which had escaped the captivity, thus forming a race as mongrel as their religion. It is about twenty-six hundred years since this event took place, but the ancient worship of the Samaritans exists to this day; so also does the bitter antagonism which they and the Jews entertain for each other.

This is the oldest national feud, probably, in existence, but is as fresh as if it only originated yesterday. Like the Jews, the Samaritans have managed to survive all the vicissitudes of fate, but with the difference that a small remnant has clung through them all to the locality in which they were originally established, though they have dwindled in numbers to one hundred and sixty souls. As an ethnological fraction of antiquity they are, perhaps, the most interesting group of people extant. The first one I ever made acquaintance with was a young man who called upon me in a mysterious manner one day in Haifa. He handed me a document in Arabic, in which, after stating that for certain reasons, which he implied were by no means discreditable to him (he was an outcast from his own people), he implored charity, and requested me "to cast upon him a regard of compassion and benevolence." The document further said:

"All that I have inherited from my parents and ancestors is a manuscript written in ancient Hebrew, nine hundred years old, containing two chapters of the Bible, including the commandments, which I beg to offer you, in the hope that you will recompense me in return by a sum which will relieve my distress."

He signed himself "Shellabi, the son of Jacob, the Samaritan." Now, I knew that Jacob es Shellabi was once the spiritual head of the sect, for he had been in London under the title of "The Prince of the Samaritans," and the romance which attended his style and dignity had, it was reported, even captivated a fair Englishwoman, who was willing to become a Samaritan for his sake. Fortunately for her "the Prince" was already married, a fact which I believe he only divulged on his return to his native land.

Anyhow, here was the son of a prince in distress, and here was an extremely ancient and curious manuscript for sale. The youth looked such a scamp, however, that he did not enlist my sympathies. I suspected that he had lost his money by gambling, which proved afterwards to be the case; so when he said he considered the manuscript worth ten dollars I offered him one dollar, on which he retired indignantly. A few days later, however, he reappeared, took his dollar thankfully, and I retain possession of the manuscript. It is on coarse parchment of a yellowish-brown color, two feet six long, and fifteen inches wide. It was evidently originally longer, but has been torn off. One edge has been subjected to the action of fire. The writing is in transverse columns, each column thirteen inches long by five wide, and containing from sixty to seventy lines. The characters are of the old Samaritan type, small, rude, and irregular, differing in many important respects from the ancient Hebrew, and illegible to a good modern Hebrew scholar to whom I have shown it. I have no doubt, however, that it could be deciphered by an expert in such matters, who would also be able to establish from the formation of the characters its antiquity.*

This incident excited my interest in the Samaritan question, and when I was at Nablous I visited the synagogue, examined the ancient Thorah, or book of the law, and have since looked into the subject generally. The ancient synagogue was appropriated by the Moslems some centuries ago. The modern building is a small, unpretentious, oblong structure. The walls are rough and whitewashed, and the roof is vaulted with two little domes in the centre. The mizbah, or altar, is about five feet square, covered with a veil of yellow silk. Within are receptacles for the sacred books. Of these the most valuable are never shown to strangers. One or two persons have, however, seen the most ancient, which the Samaritans claim to have been written by Abishua, the son of Phinehas, thirty-five hundred years ago. It is only seen by the congregation once a year, when elevated above the priest's head on the Day of Atonement.

The Thorah was rolled round a cylinder of wood similar to those used in ordinary Jewish synagogues, and I was gratified to observe that it exactly resembled the fragment in my possession. It was evidently very ancient. The priest who showed me the synagogue was a remarkably handsome, dignified-looking man about forty years old. I asked him whether he was the chief priest. He said he was, and that Jacob Shellabi no longer had any position among them. I then said I had obtained a piece of manuscript from his son, to which he made no reply, but at once turned the subject. I suspect the youth was a *mauvais sujet*, who committed an act of sacrilegious theft before leaving the paternal mansion, and who did not, therefore, deserve more than he got.

* This MS. has since been examined, and is pronounced to be part of the Pentateuch in Samaritan characters of the fifteenth century.

Now, with regard to the sacred books which I did not see:
They are in some respects in the highest degree interesting,
as throwing light upon the Biblical record. In the first
place, from what is known of the most ancient version,
claiming to be by Abishua, Gesenius and other great scholars have given it as their opinion that if it could be col-
lated, it would be found in many cases to preserve the sense,
which has been lost in the Jewish version. This opinion is
founded upon the results of such collation as has been possible with Samaritan texts which have fallen into the hands
of scholars.

Besides the most ancient roll there are three other books
known to be in the possession of the Samaritans.* These are
the Samaritan book of Joshua, the Samaritan Chronicle, and
the so-called "Fire-tried Manuscript." The Samaritan book
of Joshua probably dates from the thirteenth century. It
was published at Leyden about forty years ago from an
Arabic manuscript in Samaritan character, and is thought to
have been compiled from an early Samaritan and three later
Arabic chronicles. It is invested with a peculiar interest
from the fact that it helps to supply a remarkable lacuna in
the Biblical record, which does not appear to have received
the attention it deserves from Biblical students. It is, in
fact, evident that a large portion of the present book of
Joshua is missing. That book purports to be an account of
the conquest of Canaan and its allotment among the twelve
tribes. Under these circumstances it is most remarkable that
we have no account of the conquest of Samaria, though the
campaigns in the south, including the siege and taking of
seven cities, and the invasion of Galilee, and the defeat of
the league of six kings of Northern Palestine, are fully described. Then we have no list of royal Samaritan cities,
though all of them in the other parts of the country are
carefully enumerated. We have no description of the bound-
aries of the two tribes to which Samaria was allotted, nor
any list of the cities awarded to them. Some of the Levitical
towns mentioned in Chronicles as belonging to Samaria are
not to be found in Joshua. It will be found also that, taken

---

* I am indebted to the researches of the Palestine Exploration Fund for
these details.

as a whole, there are only about forty Samaritan places noted out of some four or five hundred places in Western Palestine.

The Jewish hatred of the Samaritans rose in the early Christian period to so great a pitch that the Mishnic doctors avoided even mentioning the name of Samaria. Thus, in the Talmud only some half-dozen Samaritan towns are noticed. In describing Palestine the Mishna divides it into Judea, Galilee, and Perea, leaving out all mention of Samaria. It is just possible that long before this an omission may have been purposely made by the early transcribers of the Biblical book of Joshua in regard to Samaria. At all events, the meagre record which it contains is richly supplemented by the Samaritan book of Joshua, which brings down the history of Israel from the date of the conquest to the time of Samuel, whose predecessor, Eli, was, from a Samaritan point of view, the earliest schismatic, and the founder of a new and heretical temple at Shiloh in opposition to that built by Joshua on Mount Gerizim. The divine glory rested upon Gerizim for two hundred and sixty years, or during the reign of nine successors of Joshua, the schism between the children of Judah and the orthodox, as the Samaritans' call themselves, dating from the time of Sin, after the death of Samson.

The book opens much in accordance with the Biblical narrative, but no less than four chapters are devoted to the history of Balaam and his death, being an enlargement of one Biblical verse. The conquest of Shechem by Joshua contains an account of the miraculous discomfiture of the enemy, and of a letter sent by him announcing it to Eleazar, the priest, fastened to the wings of a dove. It contains also the account of a new league against the children of Israel under a king called Sanbac, in conjunction with the kings of five other towns, which can all now be identified. A thrilling narrative of the battle which takes place between Joshua and these kings at El-Lejjun, on the ancient Megiddo (Armageddon), is also given. With this episode the history of the war ends. The chief value of the book lies, however, in the light it throws upon the ancient geography of Samaria. Out of a total of thirty-one places mentioned in it, thirteen are within the confines of Samaria, and most of these are not to be found in the Bible.

The Samaritan chronicle goes back to the beginning and gives the astronomical reckoning from Adam. Some of its topographical details are of much value. Thus it contains a list of twenty-two towns where the high-priest who succeeded Tobiah resided, all being apparently in Samaria as far as they can be identified. It is known that in the second and third centuries the Samaritans were in a very flourishing condition, and had colonies in Egypt, and even a synagogue in Rome. The chronicle gives their possessions in Palestine as allotted by the High-Priest Baba the Great, about one hundred and sixty years after the destruction of Jerusalem. This description is interesting, as it seems to include all Palestine, with the exception of Judea proper, to the mountains of which the Jews are confined.

At a later period the chronicle gives a list of those towns which were inhabited by the Samaritans after the Hegira. This is a period when very little is known of this nation. The places mentioned extend nearly over the whole of Palestine outside of Judea, and colonies are also mentioned in Damascus, Cairo, and Baalbek. There is a ruin about five miles from Haifa called Kefr Samir, or the town of the Samaritans, which I occasionally visit to grub for inscriptions, which was one of their colonies. Those at Gerar and Gaza lasted till the present century, but none are to be found now outside of Nablous. It is only to be expected that the chronicle should centre all the holy places of the Samaritans at Shechem or Nablous.

The fifth article of the Samaritan creed was the assertion that Gerizim was the chosen abode of God upon earth. Here Adam and Seth raised altars; here Melchisedec, servant of the Most High God, was met by Abraham—for Gerizim the Samaritans hold to the present day is the highest mountain in the world, the only one not covered by the flood. Here Abraham offered up Isaac, the very spot being shown on the eastern brow of the mountain; and, indeed, as Dean Stanley has argued, it is as likely to be here as at Jerusalem, as Josephus and the Talmudists affirm. Gerizim was also the site of Jacob's vision, and, finally, it was on

Gerizim, and not on Ebal, just opposite, as stated in the Bible, that, according to the Samaritans, Joshua erected, first an altar, afterwards the tabernacle, and lastly a temple.

The fourth and last of the known ancient sacred books of the Samaritans is the fire-tried manuscript. It consists of two hundred and seventeen leaves, containing the law from the twenty-ninth verse of the first chapter of Genesis to the blessing of Moses in Deuteronomy. It is much worn; the letters are not so small as those of Abishua's roll, nor as large as those of the later roll. The hand is steady and uniform, and the character of the letters indicates that it is of very ancient date. A note at the end of the book of Numbers connects the manuscript with a story in the Samaritan book of Joshua. It runs:

"It came out from the fire by the power of the Lord to the hand of the King of Babel in the presence of Zerubbabel the Jew, and was not burned. Thanks be to the Lord for the law of Moses."

HAIFA, Oct. 25.—In my last letter I gave some account of the ancient literature of the Samaritans, which is still extant and in their possession. The people themselves, however, are such an interesting ethnological fragment of a remote past that there are many points connected with their origin and history which are worthy of consideration, the more especially as they bear upon a problem which has, of late years, exercised a singular species of fascination over a certain class of minds. I refer to the so-called "lost" ten tribes. It may be a disappointment to the Anglo-Israelites to suggest that they are more likely to be found in the neighbourhood of the country they were carried from than in England; but, under the circumstances, it is certainly a more rational and less strained hypothesis, as I think may be clearly shown by a reference to existing traditions, facts, and records.

It would appear from the recently discovered cuneiform tablets which are now under the investigation of Assyrian scholars, that, while they substantially afford a remarkable confirmation of Biblical history, there are certain discrepancies in regard to the capture of Samaria and the carrying away of the Israelites into captivity, which make it somewhat difficult to determine the exact date and nature of that event. The complete recovery of the records of Shalmaneser (IV.), who no doubt did besiege Samaria, will clear this up, and throw light upon the records of his successor, Sargon, who seems to have succeeded to the throne about the time of the capture of the city, after a three years' siege, and who in that case would be the monarch who actually carried off the Israelites. If this were so, then, according to the date of his accession, the captivity must have occurred before the invitation which Hezekiah sent out through the

country of Ephraim and Manasseh inviting Israelites to the
Passover at Jerusalem, where we are informed that large
numbers attended it (2 Chron. xxx. 18) ; and it would put
beyond a doubt, what is in fact most probable, that Sargon,
in carrying away the Israelites captive, did exactly what
Nebuchadnezzar also did not long afterwards, when he carried off the tribes of Judah and Benjamin, and left a large
population of the poorer classes behind, who were not worth
taking.

Indeed, when one comes to consider the population which
we know to have inhabited Samaria and Galilee at this time,
it seems incredible that any conqueror would have burdened
himself with a host which must have numbered at the lowest estimate over a million souls and probably a great many
more; and this conjecture is borne out by the fact that we
read, in Jeremiah xli. 5, that a deputation of fourscore Israelites came to Jerusalem after its destruction, or more than a
hundred years after the captivity of the Israelites. That
the Israelites thus left intermarried with the colonists sent
from Assyria on the adoption by these latter of the Jewish
religion, under the instruction of a priest sent for the purpose, is extremely probable. The Samaritans themselves,
however, deny all intermixture with the colonists, and maintain they are pure-blooded Israelites ; and in confirmation of
this we may mention their marked Jewish type of countenance, their possession of an ancient text of the books of
Moses, and their observance of the Jewish Passover according to the most ancient forms of that rite.

The Samaritan account of their origin and composition is,
as may be supposed, diametrically opposed to that contained
in the books of Ezra and Nehemiah. They assert that at
the time when the two tribes returned from the captivity
a large number of the ten tribes also returned to Samaria
under Sanballat, called by Nehemiah a Horonite, but the
Samaritans call him a Levite. The Samaritan account goes
on to state that while the two tribes under Zerubbabel repaired to Jerusalem, the rest of the congregation, three hundred thousand in all, besides youth, women, children, and
strangers, were led to Gerizim, where they established the
Temple. Then came the quarrels between the Jews at Jeru-

23

salem and the Israelites at Samaria about the building of the Temple; and the accounts contained in the books of Ezra and Nehemiah and the Samaritan records are not very discordant. Making allowance always for the fact that the Biblical books do not admit that the Samaritans were Israelites at all, though they admit that Sanballat's son was married to the daughter of Eliashib, the Jewish high-priest, while this latter is stated to have allied himself with Tobiah, who was a Samaritan priest. This caused great displeasure to Nehemiah, and increased the schism, but it goes, too, far to confirm the supposition that Sanballat and Tobiah were Israelites.

The Samaritans are, indeed, in the peculiarities of their doctrine, almost identical with the original Jewish party—the Karaite and Sadducean sects. They are even called Sadducees in Jewish writings, and their denial of the resurrection was, like that of the Sadducees, based on the declaration that nothing was to be found in the law of Moses on the subject. Again, their version of the law is closely similar to that of the Septuagint, which was a translation authorized by a Sadducean high-priest from a text differing from that finally established by the Pharisees. It is often supposed that the Samaritans borrowed their doctrine from the Sadducees, but it seems more rational to admit that they were a sect originally identical, because originally Israelite. The animosity of Josephus, who was a Pharisee; the fierce denunciation of the Talmud, written by Pharisees; the destruction of the Gerizim temple by Hyrcanus, also a Pharisee—all combine to indicate that the Jewish hatred had nothing to do with any foreign origin of the race, but was rather roused by the religious differences of a people whom they knew to be their own kith and kin.

If we adopt this theory the fate of the ten tribes is no longer a mystery. As we know that before the captivity they were addicted to strange gods and strange marriages, it is not improbable that a large proportion lost their tribal identity while in captivity by intermarrying with the people by whom they were surrounded, and became merged with them. It is also probable that a certain number, according to the Samaritan chronicle three hundred thousand (but it need not be so large a number), returned from their captivity at the time when the two tribes received permission from Cyrus to return. It is also likely that others who still retained their religion did not return, and are the ancestors of certain Hebrew nomads still wandering in the desert. The Jews from Yemen, for instance, assert that they are of the tribe of Dan, while there are Jewish shepherds in Mesopotamia whose ancestry seems not distinctly traceable to the two tribes.

The fact that those who returned to Palestine have dwindled numerically to so small a number is no reason why they should not have been at one time a considerable nation, as indeed we know they were from their subsequent history. They made serious revolts against the Romans in the time of Pilate, and again during the reigns of Vespasian and Severus, but under Hadrian they assisted the Romans against the Pharisees. In the sixth century they attacked the Christians and put the Bishop of Nablous (or, as it was then called, Neapolis) to death, being at that time spread over Egypt and the whole of Palestine, except the hills of Judea. Clinging to the unity of God, they hold Moses to be the one messenger of God, and Gerizim to be the earth's centre, as it is the shrine of their faith. In this they are supported by the fact that while blessings and curses are invoked on the two Samaritan mountains in the books of Moses, there is no mention in those books of Jerusalem.

They also believe in a state of future retribution, and of angels and devils as ministers of God in the unseen world. They look for a Messiah who is to be of the sons of Joseph, and they hold that he is now on earth, though not yet declared. His name is to begin with the letter M. His titles are Taheb, "the restorer," and El-Mahdi, "the guide." Under his direction the congregation will repair to Gerizim. Under the famous twelve stones they will find the ten commandments, and under the stone of Bethel the golden vessels of the Temple and the manna. After one hundred and ten years the Prophet, who is considered inferior to Moses, is to die, and be buried beside Joseph, whose tomb they show in the valley. Soon after, on the conclusion of seven thousand years from its creation, the world is to come to an end.

The Samaritans keep the Feast of the Passover on Gerizim, near the ruins of the ancient temple; here they pitch
their tents, and at sunset they slay sheep and bake them for
several hours in a huge oven in the ground, which is lined
with stone. The men are girded with ropes, with staves in
their hands and shoes on their feet, as though prepared for
a journey. They generally eat standing or walking. After
the women have eaten, the scraps are burned and a bonfire
kindled and fed with the fat. The rest of the night is spent
in prayer, and the following day in rejoicing. Besides this,
the Feast of Tabernacles is also held on the mountain, where
they construct arbors of arbutus branches. The Feasts of
Pentecost and of Purim and the Day of Atonement are also
observed.

The mountain is very barren, rising abruptly to a height
of one thousand feet above the valley in which the town is
situated. The ruins which are to be found upon it are described in the guide-books, so I shall only allude to what is
new in regard to them. Considerable excavation was carried out here by Captain Anderson under the auspices of
the Palestine Exploration Fund, and plans made of what
remains of the Fortress of Justinian, which is one of the
most valuable monuments of Byzantine art in Palestine, and
of the church said to have been built by Zeno. The twelve
stones, traditionally said to have come from the Jordan,
were also excavated, and found to be large, unhewn masses
of rock placed upon two other courses of stone rudely dressed
and not squared. Some paved platforms were also laid bare.
These, together with the twelve stones, may possibly have
formed part of the temple built by Sanballat on Gerizim.
Curiously enough, there is a sacred rock here, with a cave
under it, not very unlike the rock and cave over which the
Mosque of Omar is built in the Haram at Jerusalem, and
with the same traditions attached to them. There is also a
large ruin on Mount Ebal, enclosing an area ninety-two feet
square, with walls twenty feet thick; but the excavations
which were made here were attended with no result, and
conjecture is at fault as to what it may have been.

Perhaps the most interesting spots at Nablous are Jacob's
well and Joseph's tomb, but this from the point of view

purely of association. Where sites which can be identified with any certainty are so rare, these two spots stand out pre-eminently as places about which there is a unanimity of agreement and force of tradition which go far to confirm their authenticity. They are venerated by the members of every religious community in Palestine. Here also we may look with almost positive certainty upon the position taken up by the Israelites when they stood "half over against Geri-zim" and "half over against Ebal," to listen to the reading of the law. Great pains have also been taken to discover the position of "the great stone" which Joshua "set up under an oak that was by the sanctuary of the Lord" when he made his covenant with the people in Shechem imme-diately before his death, and not altogether without success. The exactitude with which the tombs of Joshua, Eleazar, and Phinehas are described in the sacred record enables us to regard the ancient sepulchres which are still pointed out as theirs with far less skepticism than usually accompanies our notice of such memorials of the dead.

Altogether, the extreme antiquity of Shechem as a site, and the important events of which it was the scene in the earliest period of Jewish history, invest it with an interest denied to every other locality in Palestine, excepting Jeru-salem itself, while the well of Jacob must ever be memo-rable—if, as was most likely, it was the spot where Christ met the woman of Samaria—for perhaps the most remarkable of all his utterances. When we remember the religious fanaticism which characterized both Jew and Samaritan, and the bigoted prejudice which envenomed the inveterate hatred they felt for each other, and which turned principally upon the rival claims for sanctity of Jerusalem and Gerizim, it seems almost incredible that a Jew could have been found, and he a carpenter, gifted with such lofty courage and such high spiritual intuition that he should dare to say: "Woman, believe me, the hour cometh when ye shall neither on this mountain, nor at Jerusalem, worship the Father. They that worship him must worship him in spirit and in truth."

HAIFA, Nov. 3.—While at Nablous I received information that a large piece of ancient sculpture had been discovered by a man in excavating some foundations. I procured a guide, and proceeded to his dwelling. It was evidently the residence of a man of means, and stood in a large courtyard, at the entrance to which I knocked for admittance. After hammering for some time a voice from within asked who I was and what I wanted. On my shouting a reply, I was abruptly told to go away, and all was silent. Now, the accounts I had heard of this antiquity stimulated my curiosity to such a degree that, in addition to the indignation I felt at this treatment, my desire to see the relic overcame my forbearance, and, seizing a stone, while I ordered my attendant to take another, we made the quarter ring with our blows. After a time the voice was heard again : " Why don't you go away. I won't open the door."

"I won't go away, and I will break open the door if you don't open it," I shouted.

" But I am the chief of the police."

" I don't care who you are; open the door," and bang went a stone against it.

There was silence for a moment, and then another and a milder voice: " Wait a moment. I will let you in," and the door opened and revealed an empty courtyard and a youth.

" My father was angry because you disturbed him so early," he remarked, apologetically, and I then observed many signs betokening a recent rapid evacuation on the part of the female members of the family.

Now that I was in, with a large fragment of a beautifully carved frieze staring me in the face, I could afford to be civil. I was profuse in my apologies, and promised to disturb no one if I were only shown the antiquities. But I was destined to experience another reaction of disappointment when the mild youth informed me that this was all there was left. The others had been sent to the museum at Constantinople. Fortunately antiquities, especially when they are massive, travel slowly in this country, and as I had an opportunity of seeing these before they left Haifa, and made such careful copies of them as time permitted, I will describe them.

The peculiar interest which attaches to these remains, which evidently belong to the Græco-Roman period, arises from the fact that they may possibly have formed part of the great pagan temple which is represented on the Greek imperial coins of the ancient Acropolis. The main objection to this theory is that the temple, it is supposed, was erected on Mount Gerizim, and the coins show that it was approached by a handsome flight of steps, whereas these remains were found not far from the base of the mountain, though sufficiently on its slope to warrant the approach of a flight of steps. The fact that the subjects of the tableaux are all taken from Greek mythology would indicate that there must have been a large population in Samaria in those days, who, so far as their worship was concerned, were not Samaritans.

Besides two draped figures, unfortunately without their heads, one life-size and one fifty inches in height, there was a pedestal forty inches high, triangular in shape, and on each face were two tableaux in bas-relief, making six carved representations in all, in a very perfect state of preservation, with inscriptions in Greek above them, of which, however, I have only been able to make out the general tenor in some cases. Besides copying the inscriptions, I made such sketches as I was able of the tableaux. Where many figures are crowded together this is a very difficult operation. The first scene represents a chariot drawn by serpents, in which is a robed female, while on the left a woman is crouched down under a tree. The second consists of Artemis, Apollo, and Leto, with their names inscribed above them, while on the right is the serpent Python, his head pierced by an arrow. The third represented an infant struggling with a serpent between two draped female figures, evidently Hercules strangling the serpents sent against him by Hera; for above were the words, " *Trophoi Erakles.*" These formed the upper tableaux. Below them were three other tableaux, illustrating the legend of Theseus, the inscription being " *Theseus gnorismata,*" above a tableau in which he is represented raising a stone under which are hidden the sword and shoes of his father Aigeus. In the second he is kneeling on one knee in a struggle with the Minotaur, while behind him are a group of boys whom he came to save. In the third he has slain the robber, who is lying prostrate at his feet. Theseus is nude and leaning on his club, with three other persons all robed standing by him.

There can be little doubt that had any one been present when this discovery was made, a fuller excavation would have been amply repaid, and that the house of the ill-tempered old Moslem stands on a site of the highest interest. I have carefully noted its position, in the hope that at some future day conditions may exist which would render possible an examination of his garden, which is now surrounded by a high wall. It would require little digging to determine whether this was the site of the celebrated temple or not.

I now left Nablous for the purpose of visiting the ruins of the ancient city of Samaria, distant about five miles, and formerly the political capital of the country. It is placed in a most commanding position, and, from a strategical point of view, was well chosen. Nothing can exceed the beauty of the prospect of the surrounding country which is obtained from it. We first inspect the Crusading church of St. John the Baptist, which must have been a beautiful edifice in its day. The walls alone are now standing. In an underground crypt, now held sacred by the Moslem peasantry, the saint is supposed to have been beheaded. The tradition, though erroneous, is ancient, and existed in 380 A.D. It has some colour, from the fact that the wilderness in which John preached is near this, and not near Jericho, as is generally supposed. It can be pretty well identified by the description " Onon, near to Salem," where John was baptizing, " because there was much water there." Both these places retain their names, and there is an abundant supply of water, which flows hence into the Jordan. The fact that Bethabara must be placed much higher up the Jordan valley than the position usually assigned to it by tradition makes it pretty certain that the Wady Far'ah, the head of which is near Samaria, in which are Onon and Salem, and which flows into the Jordan not far from the probable position of Bethabara, was the scene of John's ministrations.

The most interesting ruins, however, are those of Herod's Colonnade, to the west of the modern village. It seems to have run round the hill on a flat terrace, in the middle of which rises a rounded knoll, on which the temple dedicated to Augustus, and stated by Josephus to be in the middle of the town, presumably stood. The remains are most perfect on the south, where some eighty columns are standing. These are mainly monolithic. The width of the cloister was sixty feet, and the pillars are sixteen feet high and six feet apart. The whole length of what must have been a most imposing colonnade was about two thousand yards, or nearly a mile and a quarter. Josephus makes it nearly two miles, but this is exaggerated. There is another street of columns at the bottom of the hill running in a line oblique to the sides of the upper colonnade. The colonnade was entered by a gateway, flanked by small towers, the scarps of which still remain.

Samaria is not to be compared in antiquity with Shechem, its most flourishing time being, probably, during the reign of Herod, when, in fact, all Palestine enjoyed a period of architectural magnificence greater than anything it had previously known. If, instead of following the ordinary road from Samaria, we ascend, from the large village of Burka, a steep hill, we burst upon a view which is well worth the climb, which has also the advantage of being a short cut. We look down into a fertile basin covered with olive groves and villages, and in the distance can see a considerable extent of coast line near Cæsarea, while the familiar outline of Carmel to the northwest closes the prospect. Then we plunge down into the gardens of the village of Fendakumiyeh, where there is a sacred cave worth visiting, contain-

ing two recesses, before which there is a detached block of
stone like an altar. It may probably have been an ancient
rock-cut chapel. Close to this village is another called Zeba,
which I was sorely tempted to visit, as I had received an invitation to do so from the sheik who lives here, and who is
one of the richest and most powerful sheiks in the country.
He had already called upon me in Haifa, and represents the
great family of Jerrar, who once exercised an almost independent rule in this district, setting the Turkish government at defiance, and levying blackmail on the inhabitants,
while they were in perpetual feud with rival families who
claimed a like local supremacy in other parts of the country.
The whole of this system was broken down during the
Egyptian occupation of the country by Ibrahim Pasha.
When, by British intervention, it was handed back to the
Turkish government, the latter succeeded in preventing its
recurrence—not, however, without the application of force.
More than one of these local sheiks can point out to you a
hole in the wall of his house which was made by a Turkish
cannon-ball. They are by degrees submitting to the influence of civilization, and, finding that it is no longer possible
to compete successfully with the officials in plundering the
peasantry, are making friends with these latter, so as either
to go shares with them, or to obtain their favor and assistance in their own agricultural operations, and thus avoid
being robbed themselves.

Thus in the immediate neighbourhood of this village
there is a plain called the Drowned Meadow, from the fact
that during a great part of the year it is a marsh, and
therefore unavailable for crops. Could it be drained it
would add some thousands of acres of arable land to the
village to which it belonged. Not long ago I was consulted
in regard to the possibility of its being drained, and an engineer even went so far as to make an estimate of the probable cost of the operation. Although the sum charged was
very moderate, it was more than the capitalists could venture upon, but the very fact that they could entertain such
an idea was a marked evidence of progress on the part of
men whose only notion of drainage heretofore had been confined to their neighbours' pockets.

Although probably I should have seen a splendid specimen of a native magnate's establishment, I found that a halt
at Zeba would have lost me a day, and I therefore pushed
on without allowing the sheik to suspect my proximity to
his hospitable abode, still keeping to bypaths instead of
following the beaten track to Jenin, the ancient Engannin,
or Spring of Gardens. From thence, in a day's journey
across the plain of Esdrælon, I reached Haifa.

A DRUSE FATHER'S VENGEANCE.

DALIET - EL - CARMEL, Nov. 7. — An incident so highly characteristic of Druse life and manners has just occurred here that it seems worthy of narration. About three months ago I was invited to be present at the ceremony of the betrothal of the son of the richest man in the village, by name Sheik Saleh, with the daughter of a neighbour called Kara, whose wife was a sister of Sheik Saleh. The affair came off in the house of the former, a small mud-built cottage situated in a court, with the usual arched roof, and floor of a rough kind of cement, on which were spread rugs and mats for the guests who crowded in to witness the ceremony. This took place at nine o'clock at night, and was performed by the khateeb, or spiritual sheik. It consisted in his joining the hands of the future bridegroom and bride's father— the bride herself was not present—and in his repeating several formulas in Arabic, among which I detected some of the verses of the Koran. A small sum of money was then paid over to the family of the bride, the khateeb took his fee out of it, refreshments were brought in, and the rite was over.

It was a relatively tame performance, and not to be compared with an actual wedding of another couple which took place shortly afterwards, when the festivities lasted three days and nights, during which time the bride, loaded with her dowry, which consisted chiefly of silver coins formed into a head-dress and breastplate, danced incessantly in the centre of admiring circles of girls who danced round her, while the men were also making the night resound with their discordant clamour to the utter destruction of slumber, firing off guns, making bonfires, and singing. In fact, at the end of the three days the whole village, but especially the bride, were utterly exhausted by their protracted gaieties. At the end of this time she was put upon a horse and marched in solemn procession to the door of every house in the village, followed by a bevy of damsels screaming and clapping their hands. Each house was expected to contribute a small sum —make a wedding-present, in fact, to the newly-married couple. In this way she was finally conducted to the bridegroom's house, where he was waiting for her with a capacious mantle, in which, on her arrival, he enveloped her, and then carried her into his house triumphant.

To go back to the episode of the betrothal. It is the Druse custom for the father of the bridegroom to pay a sum of money to the bride's family—in other words, he buys his son a wife. Now, in this case, although I saw some money pass on the occasion, it was a mere formality. The father of the bride had, in a fit of generosity, probably interested, refused a sum of 2000 piastres, or about $75 for his daughter. He proposed instead that he should form a partnership for agricultural operations with Sheik Saleh, who, being rich, would be an advantageous partner. This Sheik Saleh agreed to, and the arrangement was completed, when it was objected to by Sheik Saleh's wife, who, being a woman of character and resolution, induced her husband to break it off. This made Kara furious. He is a man of ungovernable temper, and he determined that his daughter should never wed Sheik Saleh's son. But a betrothal of the kind I had witnessed is a very solemn ceremony, and the only person who can break it is the betrothed bridegroom. The girl and her family are powerless in the matter. Kara was so maddened by what had occurred that, rather than let his daughter marry the son of the man by whom he felt himself to have been outraged, he determined to kill her. This was an odd resolution to arrive at. One would have thought he might have gratified his vengeance better by killing Sheik Saleh or his son. Druse passion, however, runs in curious channels, and he appears to have been exasperated because his daughter did not share in his fury against her cousin.

So he led her out to slaughter, riding his horse and armed with his gun, and driving the poor girl, who was weeping and wailing bitterly, before him. Many of the villagers saw him, and were well aware of his intention, but shrank from interfering. The place which he had selected for the execution was just at the bottom of the hill upon which my house is situated, and the hour at which he was bent upon this bloody errand was eight in the evening. Now, it so happened that I have a Druse servant who has been with me for more than a year, a powerful man, a splendid sportsman, a most courageous fellow, and, what perhaps was of more importance, a near relation of Kara's. He chanced to be passing at the time, and knowing his relative's furious temper, and perceiving that he really intended to murder his daughter, he interfered at the risk of his own life, and succeeded in rescuing the girl. Kara, however, was still too angry to be reasonable. He returned to his house foaming with passion, and finding his wife—who had lived with him for many years—weeping bitterly over the whole occurrence, he accused her of sympathy with her brother's family, and in the heat of the moment pronounced the fatal words which, according to Druse custom, constitute a divorce.

The trouble about a Druse divorce is, that the sentence which bids a woman return to her family, once pronounced by her husband, is irrevocable. Not only can he never take her back again as his wife, but he can never, in this life, so much as even speak to her again. If he sees her at the other end of the street he must turn away to avoid meeting her. Nor may he enter a house in which he has reason to think that she is. A man may, therefore, in a moment of passion ruin his own happiness for life, and this is what Kara did. The whole occurrence only happened two days ago, and Kara has been in the deepest distress ever since. Had he killed his daughter, he said, it would not have mattered. He would scarcely have missed her, and if she were to marry Sheik Saleh's son she would be dead to him any way; but to be deprived of a wife, against whom he had never had a complaint to make, who had loved him and served him faithfully all these years—this was a loss that nothing could replace.

When I heard that he had spoken in this cold-blooded way about his daughter, and had alluded to the intention, which he admitted he had entertained, of killing her, without a shadow of compunction, I half regretted that he had not

been allowed to die the other day of a leech which he had
in his throat. He sent word that he was dying, and a medical friend who is staying with me went to see him, and
found him in the last stages of exhaustion from a leech
which had been sixteen days fastened too far down his throat
to be liberated. These cases are not uncommon, and are due
to the water of some of the springs in the neighbourhood.
We have had five cases this year, but none so bad as Kara's,
which was the first. Salt and all the usual means were tried
in vain, and, as the doctor was anxious to get some leeches
to experiment with, Kara's wife and daughter, who both exhibited the greatest distress, were despatched to a spring
three miles off to get them. The alacrity they displayed
in his service were ill requited by his subsequent conduct
towards them. Here I may remark that large doses of tur-
pentine, taken internally, proved completely successful.
There is little doubt that, had the leech not succumbed to
this treatment, in two days more Kara must have succumbed
to the leech.

The daring with which Druses resort to acts of violence
is to be accounted for by the fact that they can always
escape justice. The moment a Druse commits a crime he
flies to the Hauran, which he can reach with hard travel in
eight-and-forty hours. Here he takes refuge among his
coreligionaries of the Jebel Druse Mountain, over whom the
Turkish government exercises only a nominal authority, and
where pursuit is impossible for any Ottoman official.

Meantime there is to be a great gathering of the village
elders to consider whether it is possible to arrange the feud
between Sheik Saleh and Kara. One of the uses to which
Druse Khalwès, or places of worship, is put, is to discuss
every question which is of interest to the village. For instance, should I desire to buy a tract of land from the village held by many proprietors, they would hold a secret
council in the Khalwè to discuss the best method of cheat-
ing me. What passes at these meetings is considered absolutely secret, and the minority are bound to accept the
opinion of the majority, and afterwards to act with it. This
imparts a wonderful unanimity to all their proceedings with
outsiders, though they quarrel very much among themselves,

and these Khalwè meetings sometimes lead to serious feuds and bloodshed. It seems likely to do so in this case, for it has been reported to me that Kara announced that if the decision of the meeting went against him, he would commit such an act as should prevent it—in other words, murder either his own daughter or her betrothed.

I was considering how I could best interfere to prevent such a catastrophe, when I received a few hours ago a visit from Kara himself. The purport of it, as usual, was to borrow money. I told him I could not possibly lend money to a man who first decided to kill his own daughter, and then for no cause divorced his wife. He replied that when he had committed these acts he was possessed of the devil and unconscious of what he was doing. I told him that to lend money to a man who was subject to such demoniac possession was like lending money to the devil himself, and this I declined to do. He assured me that the devil had left him so completely that there was no fear of his getting hold of it. I said I required proof of this, and he could furnish me with it by assuring me of his readiness to allow his daughter to marry her betrothed. He said that was a matter in the hands of Allah. "Then," I said, "under these circumstances you are prepared, I presume, to accept the decision of the village as the decision of Allah."

"Yes," he replied, "if they decide also that Sheik Saleh is to pay me fifty Turkish pounds for my daughter."

"I am sorry," I remarked, "that Allah has just decided that I am not to lend you the money you want to borrow from me, and it will depend entirely upon the extent to which you allow the devil to influence you against the will of Allah how I treat you for the future."

With that he took his departure; but I saw enough of his cowed temper for the present to hope that the matter may be arranged with a little judicious financial management. It does not give an encouraging view of human nature to discover how potent a factor money is in its affairs, even in a primitive Druse village.

In many respects Kara is a superior man, decidedly better than his enemy, Sheik Saleh, who will also have to be dealt with, and who behaved badly in backing out of an arrangement which had already been concluded, for no valid reason. Owing, however, to the position which I occupy financially to the village, they are all more or less under control, and I have it in my power to exercise a pressure which even the Khalwè would find it difficult to resist.

Unfortunately, I shall be obliged to leave instructions with regard to this delicate matter, as my stay in Palestine for the present is about to draw to a close, and with it must terminate this record of my experiences in a country which, in spite of its many drawbacks, possesses in my eyes superior attractions as a residence to any other in which my lot has been cast.

24

THE END.

CATALOGUE

OF

MESSRS BLACKWOOD & SONS'

PUBLICATIONS.

CATALOGUE

OF

MESSRS BLACKWOOD & SONS'

PUBLICATIONS.

✦

ALISON. History of Europe. By Sir ARCHIBALD ALISON, Bart., D.C.L.

1. From the Commencement of the French Revolution to the Battle of Waterloo.
   LIBRARY EDITION, 14 vols., with Portraits. Demy 8vo, £10, 10s.
   ANOTHER EDITION, in 20 vols. crown 8vo, £6.
   PEOPLE'S EDITION, 13 vols. crown 8vo, £2, 11s.

2. Continuation to the Accession of Louis Napoleon.
   LIBRARY EDITION, 8 vols. 8vo, £6, 7s. 6d.
   PEOPLE'S EDITION, 8 vols. crown 8vo, 34s.

3. Epitome of Alison's History of Europe. Twenty-ninth Thousand, 7s. 6d.

4. Atlas to Alison's History of Europe. By A. Keith Johnston.
   LIBRARY EDITION, demy 4to, £3, 3s.
   PEOPLE'S EDITION, 31s. 6d.

—— Life of John Duke of Marlborough. With some Account of his Contemporaries, and of the War of the Succession. Third Edition, 2 vols. 8vo. Portraits and Maps, 30s.

—— Essays: Historical, Political, and Miscellaneous. 3 vols. demy 8vo, 45s.

AIRD. Poetical Works of Thomas Aird. Fifth Edition, with Memoir of the Author by the Rev. JARDINE WALLACE, and Portrait. Crown 8vo, 7s. 6d.

ALLARDYCE. The City of Sunshine. By ALEXANDER ALLARDYCE. Three vols. post 8vo, £1, 5s. 6d.

—— Memoir of the Honourable George Keith Elphinstone, K.B., Viscount Keith of Stonehaven Marischal, Admiral of the Red. One vol. 8vo, with Portrait, Illustrations, and Maps. 21s.

ALMOND. Sermons by a Lay Head-master. By HELY HUTCHINSON ALMOND, M.A. Oxon., Head-master of Loretto School. Crown 8vo, 5s.

ANCIENT CLASSICS FOR ENGLISH READERS. Edited by

Rev. W. LUCAS COLLINS, M.A. Complete in 28 vols., cloth, 2s. 6d. each; or in 14 vols., tastefully bound, with calf or vellum back, £3, 10s.

Contents of the Series.

HOMER : THE ILIAD. By the Editor.
HOMER : THE ODYSSEY. By the Editor.
HERODOTUS. By George C. Swayne, M.A.
XENOPHON. By Sir Alexander Grant, Bart., LL.D.
EURIPIDES. By W. B. Donne.
ARISTOPHANES. By the Editor.
PLATO. By Clifton W. Collins, M.A.
LUCIAN. By the Editor.
ÆSCHYLUS. By the Right Rev. the Bishop of Colombo.
SOPHOCLES. By Clifton W. Collins, M.A.
HESIOD AND THEOGNIS. By the Rev. J. Davies, M.A.
GREEK ANTHOLOGY. By Lord Neaves.
VIRGIL. By the Editor.
HORACE. By Sir Theodore Martin, K.C.B.
JUVENAL. By Edward Walford, M.A.

PLAUTUS AND TERENCE. By the Editor.
THE COMMENTARIES OF CÆSAR. By Anthony Trollope.
TACITUS. By W. B. Donne.
CICERO. By the Editor.
PLINY'S LETTERS. By the Rev. Alfred Church, M.A., and the Rev. W. J. Brodribb, M.A.
LIVY. By the Editor.
OVID. By the Rev. A. Church, M.A.
CATULLUS, TIBULLUS, AND PROPERTIUS. By the Rev. Jas. Davies, M.A.
DEMOSTHENES. By the Rev. W. J. Brodribb, M.A.
ARISTOTLE. By Sir Alexander Grant, Bart., LL.D.
THUCYDIDES. By the Editor.
LUCRETIUS. By W. H. Mallock, M.A.
PINDAR. By the Rev. F. D. Morice, M.A.

AYLWARD. The Transvaal of To-day : War, Witchcraft, Sports, and Spoils in South Africa. By ALFRED AYLWARD, Commandant, Transvaal Republic. Second Edition. Crown 8vo, 6s.

AYTOUN. Lays of the Scottish Cavaliers, and other Poems. By W. EDMONDSTOUNE AYTOUN, D.C.L., Professor of Rhetoric and Belles-Lettres in the University of Edinburgh. Cheap Edition, printed from a new type, and tastefully bound. Fcap. 8vo, 3s. 6d.
Another Edition, being the Thirtieth. Fcap. 8vo, cloth extra, 7s. 6d.

——— An Illustrated Edition of the Lays of the Scottish Cavaliers. From designs by Sir NOEL PATON. Small 4to, 21s., in gilt cloth.

——— Bothwell : a Poem. Third Edition. Fcap., 7s. 6d.

——— Poems and Ballads of Goethe. Translated by Professor AYTOUN and Sir THEODORE MARTIN, K.C.B. Third Edition. Fcap., 6s.

——— Bon Gaultier's Book of Ballads. By the SAME. Fourteenth and Cheaper Edition. With Illustrations by Doyle, Leech, and Crowquill. Fcap. 8vo, 5s.

——— The Ballads of Scotland. Edited by Professor AYTOUN. Fourth Edition. 2 vols. fcap. 8vo, 12s.

——— Memoir of William E. Aytoun, D.C.L. By Sir THEODORE MARTIN, K.C.B. With Portrait. Post 8vo, 12s.

BACH. On Musical Education and Vocal Culture. By ALBERT B. BACH. Fourth Edition. 8vo, 7s. 6d.

——— The Principles of Singing. A Practical Guide for Vocalists and Teachers. With Course of Vocal Exercises. Crown 8vo, 6s.

——— The Art of Singing. With Musical Exercises for Young People. Crown 8vo, 3s.

BALCH. Zorah : A Love-Tale of Modern Egypt. By ELISABETH BALCH (D.T.S.) Post 8vo, 7s. 6d.

BALLADS AND POEMS. By MEMBERS OF THE GLASGOW BALLAD CLUB. Crown 8vo, 7s. 6d.

BEDFORD. The Regulations of the Old Hospital of the Knights of St John at Valetta. From a Copy Printed at Rome, and preserved in the Archives of Malta; with a Translation, Introduction, and Notes Explanatory of the Hospital Work of the Order By the Rev. W. K. R. BEDFORD, one of the Chaplains of the Order of St John in England. Royal 8vo, with Frontispiece, Plans, &c., 7s. 6d.

BELLAIRS. The Transvaal War, 1880-81. Edited by Lady BEL-
LAIRS. With a Frontispiece and Map. 8vo, 15s.

BESANT. The Revolt of Man. By WALTER BESANT, M.A.
Eighth Edition. Crown 8vo, 3s. 6d.

—— Readings in Rabelais. Crown 8vo, 7s. 6d.

BEVERIDGE. Culross and Tulliallan; or Perthshire on Forth. Its
History and Antiquities. With Elucidations of Scottish Life and Character
from the Burgh and Kirk-Session Records of that District. By DAVID
BEVERIDGE. 2 vols. 8vo, with Illustrations, 42s.

BLACKIE. Lays and Legends of Ancient Greece. By JOHN
STUART BLACKIE, Emeritus Professor of Greek in the University of Edinburgh. Second Edition. Fcap. 8vo. 5s.

—— The Wisdom of Goethe. Fcap. 8vo. Cloth, extra gilt, 6s.

BLACKWOOD'S MAGAZINE, from Commencement in 1817 to
December 1886. Nos. 1 to 854, forming 139 Volumes.

—— Index to Blackwood's Magazine. Vols. 1 to 50. 8vo, 15s.

—— Tales from Blackwood. Forming Twelve Volumes of
Interesting and Amusing Railway Reading. Price One Shilling each in Paper
Cover. Sold separately at all Railway Bookstalls.
They may also be had bound in cloth, 18s., and in half calf, richly gilt, 30s.
Or 12 volumes in 6, Roxburghe, 21s., and half red morocco, 28s.

—— Tales from Blackwood. New Series. Complete in Twenty-
four Shilling Parts. Handsomely bound in 12 vols., cloth, 30s. In leather
back, Roxburghe style, 37s. 6d. In half calf, gilt, 52s. 6d. In half morocco, 55s.

—— Standard Novels. Uniform in size and legibly Printed.
Each Novel complete in one volume.

Florin Series, Illustrated Boards.

TOM CRINGLE'S LOG. By Michael Scott.
THE CRUISE OF THE MIDGE. By the Same.
CYRIL THORNTON. By Captain Hamilton.
ANNALS OF THE PARISH. By John Galt.
THE PROVOST, &c. By John Galt.
SIR ANDREW WYLIE. By John Galt.
THE ENTAIL. By John Galt.
MISS MOLLY. By Beatrice May Butt.
REGINALD DALTON. By J. G. Lockhart.

PEN OWEN. By Dean Hook.
ADAM BLAIR. By J. G. Lockhart.
LADY LEE'S WIDOWHOOD. By General
Sir E. B. Hamley.
SALEM CHAPEL. By Mrs Oliphant.
THE PERPETUAL CURATE. By Mrs Oli-
phant.
MISS MARJORIBANKS. By Mrs Oliphant.
JOHN: A Love Story. By Mrs Oliphant.

Or in Cloth Boards, 2s. 6d.

Shilling Series, Illustrated Cover.

THE RECTOR, and THE DOCTOR'S FAMILY.
By Mrs Oliphant.
THE LIFE OF MANSIE WAUCH. By D. M.
Moir.
PENINSULAR SCENES AND SKETCHES. By
F. Hardman.

SIR FRIZZLE PUMPKIN, NIGHTS AT MESS,
&c.
THE SUBALTERN.
LIFE IN THE FAR WEST. By G. F. Ruxton.
VALERIUS: A Roman Story. By J. G.
Lockhart.

Or in Cloth Boards, 1s. 6d.

BLACKMORE. The Maid of Sker. By R. D. BLACKMORE, Author
of 'Lorna Doone,' &c. New Edition. Crown 8vo, 6s.

BOSCOBEL TRACTS. Relating to the Escape of Charles the
Second after the Battle of Worcester, and his subsequent Adventures. Edited
by J. Hughes, Esq., A.M. A New Edition, with additional Notes and Illustrations, including Communications from the Rev. R. H. Barham, Author of
the 'Ingoldsby Legends.' 8vo, with Engravings, 16s.

BROADLEY. Tunis, Past and Present. With a Narrative of the
French Conquest of the Regency. By A. M. BROADLEY. With numerous
Illustrations and Maps. 2 vols. post 8vo. 25s.

BROOKE, Life of Sir James, Rajah of Sarāwak. From his Personal
Papers and Correspondence. By SPENSER ST JOHN, H.M.'s Minister-Resident
and Consul-General Peruvian Republic; formerly Secretary to the Rajah.
With Portrait and a Map. Post 8vo, 12s. 6d.

BROUGHAM. Memoirs of the Life and Times of Henry Lord Brougham. Written by HIMSELF. 3 vols. 8vo, £2, 8s. The Volumes are sold separately, price 16s. each.

BROWN. The Forester: A Practical Treatise on the Planting, Rearing, and General Management of Forest-trees. By JAMES BROWN, LL.D., Inspector of and Reporter on Woods and Forests, Belmore House, Port Elgin, Ontario. Fifth Edition, revised and enlarged. Royal 8vo, with Engravings. 36s.

BROWN. The Ethics of George Eliot's Works. By JOHN CROMBIE BROWN. Fourth Edition. Crown 8vo, 2s. 6d.

BROWN. A Manual of Botany, Anatomical and Physiological. For the Use of Students. By ROBERT BROWN, M.A., Ph.D. Crown 8vo, with numerous Illustrations, 12s. 6d.

BUCHAN. Introductory Text-Book of Meteorology. By ALEXANDER BUCHAN, M.A., F.R.S.E., Secretary of the Scottish Meteorological Society, &c. Crown 8vo, with 8 Coloured Charts and other Engravings, pp. 218. 4s. 6d.

BUCHANAN. The Shirè Highlands (East Central Africa). By JOHN BUCHANAN, Planter at Zomba. Crown 8vo, 5s.

BURBIDGE. Domestic Floriculture, Window Gardening, and Floral Decorations. Being practical directions for the Propagation, Culture, and Arrangement of Plants and Flowers as Domestic Ornaments. By F. W. BURBIDGE. Second Edition. Crown 8vo, with numerous Illustrations, 7s. 6d.

—— Cultivated Plants: Their Propagation and Improvement. Including Natural and Artificial Hybridisation, Raising from Seed, Cuttings, and Layers, Grafting and Budding, as applied to the Families and Genera in Cultivation. Crown 8vo, with numerous Illustrations, 12s. 6d.

BURTON. The History of Scotland: From Agricola's Invasion to the Extinction of the last Jacobite Insurrection. By JOHN HILL BURTON, D.C.L., Historiographer-Royal for Scotland. New and Enlarged Edition, 8 vols., and Index. Crown 8vo, £3, 3s.

—— History of the British Empire during the Reign of Queen Anne. In 3 vols. 8vo. 36s.

—— The Scot Abroad. Third Edition. Crown 8vo, 10s. 6d.

—— The Book-Hunter. New Edition. Crown 8vo, 7s. 6d.

BUTE. The Roman Breviary: Reformed by Order of the Holy Œcumenical Council of Trent; Published by Order of Pope St Pius V.; and Revised by Clement VIII. and Urban VIII.; together with the Offices since granted. Translated out of Latin into English by JOHN, Marquess of Bute, K.T. In 2 vols. crown 8vo, cloth boards, edges uncut. £2, 2s.

—— The Altus of St Columba. With a Prose Paraphrase and Notes. In paper cover, 2s. 6d.

BUTLER. Pompeii: Descriptive and Picturesque. By W. BUTLER. Post 8vo, 5s.

BUTT. Miss Molly. By BEATRICE MAY BUTT. Cheap Edition, 2s.

—— Alison. 3 vols. crown 8vo, 25s. 6d.

—— Lesterre Durant. 2 vols. crown 8vo, 17s.

—— Eugenie. Crown 8vo, 6s. 6d.

CAIRD. Sermons. By JOHN CAIRD, D.D., Principal of the University of Glasgow. Sixteenth Thousand. Fcap. 8vo, 5s.

—— Religion in Common Life. A Sermon preached in Crathie Church, October 14, 1855, before Her Majesty the Queen and Prince Albert. Published by Her Majesty's Command. Cheap Edition, 3d.

CAMPBELL. Sermons Preached before the Queen at Balmoral. By the Rev A. A. CAMPBELL, Minister of Crathie. Published by Command of Her Majesty. Crown 8vo, 4s. 6d.

CAMPBELL. Records of Argyll. Legends, Traditions, and Recollections of Argyllshire Highlanders, collected chiefly from the Gaelic. With Notes on the Antiquity of the Dress, Clan Colours or Tartans of the Highlanders. By LORD ARCHIBALD CAMPBELL. Illustrated with Nineteen full-page Etchings. 4to, printed on hand-made paper, £3, 3s.

CAPPON. Victor Hugo. A Memoir and a Study. By JAMES CAPPON, M.A. Post 8vo, 10s. 6d.

CARRICK. Koumiss ; or, Fermented Mare's Milk : and its Uses in the Treatment and Cure of Pulmonary Consumption, and other Wasting Diseases. With an Appendix on the best Methods of Fermenting Cow's Milk. By GEORGE L. CARRICK, M.D., L.R.C.S.E. and L.R.C.P.E., Physician to the British Embassy, St Petersburg, &c. Crown 8vo, 10s. 6d.

CAUVIN. A Treasury of the English and German Languages. Compiled from the best Authors and Lexicographers in both Languages. Adapted to the Use of Schools, Students, Travellers, and Men of Business; and forming a Companion to all German-English Dictionaries. By JOSEPH CAUVIN, LL.D. & Ph.D., of the University of Göttingen, &c. Crown 8vo, 7s. 6d.

CAVE-BROWN. Lambeth Palace and its Associations. By J. CAVE-BROWN, M.A., Vicar of Detling, Kent, and for many years Curate of Lambeth Parish Church. With an Introduction by the Archbishop of Canterbury. Second Edition, containing an additional Chapter on Medieval Life in the Old Palaces. 8vo, with Illustrations, 21s.

CHARTERIS. Canonicity; or, Early Testimonies to the Existence and Use of the Books of the New Testament. Based on Kirchhoffer's 'Quellensammlung.' Edited by A. H. CHARTERIS, D.D., Professor of Biblical Criticism in the University of Edinburgh. 8vo, 18s.

CHRISTISON. Life of Sir Robert Christison, Bart., M.D., D.C.L. Oxon., Professor of Medical Jurisprudence in the University of Edinburgh. Edited by his Sons. In two vols. 8vo. Vol. I.—Autobiography. 16s. Vol. II. —Memoirs. 16s.

CHURCH SERVICE SOCIETY. A Book on Common Order : Being Forms of Worship issued by the Church Service Society. Fifth Edition, 6s.

CLELAND. True to a Type. By R. CLELAND. In 2 vols., post 8vo, 17s.

CLOUSTON. Popular Tales and Fictions : their Migrations and Transformations. By W. A. CLOUSTON, Editor of 'Arabian Poetry for English Readers,' 'The Book of Sindibad,' &c. 2 vols. post 8vo, roxburghe binding, 25s.

COCHRAN. A Handy Text-Book of Military Law. Compiled chiefly to assist Officers preparing for Examination; also for all Officers of the Regular and Auxiliary Forces. Specially arranged according to the Syllabus of Subjects of Examination for Promotion, Queen's Regulations, 1883. Comprising also a Synopsis of part of the Army Act. By MAJOR F. COCHRAN, Hampshire Regiment, Garrison Instructor, North British District. Crown 8vo, 7s. 6d.

COLLIER. Babel. By the Hon. MARGARET COLLIER (Madame GALLETTI DI CADILHAC). Author of 'Our Home by the Adriatic.' 2 vols. post 8vo, 17s.

COLQUHOUN. The Moor and the Loch. Containing Minute Instructions in all Highland Sports, with Wanderings over Crag and Corrie, Flood and Fell. By JOHN COLQUHOUN. Sixth Edition, greatly enlarged. With Illustrations. 2 vols. post 8vo, 26s.

CONGREVE. Tales of Country Life in La Gruyère. From the French of Pierre Sciobéret. By L. DORA CONGREVE. Crown 8vo, 7s. 6d.

COTTERILL. The Genesis of the Church. By the Right. Rev. HENRY COTTERILL, D.D., Bishop of Edinburgh. Demy 8vo, 16s.

COTTERILL. Suggested Reforms in Public Schools. By C. C. COTTERILL, M.A., Assistant Master at Fettes College, Edin. Crown 8vo, 3s. 6d.

COX. The Opening of the Line: A Strange Story of Dogs and their Doings. By POSSONBY COX. Profusely Illustrated by J. H. O. BROWN. 4to, 1s.

CRANSTOUN. The Elegies of Albius Tibullus. Translated into English Verse, with Life of the Poet, and Illustrative Notes. By JAMES CRAN-STOUN, LL.D., Author of a Translation of 'Catullus.' Crown 8vo, 6s. 6d.

—— The Elegies of Sextus Propertius. Translated into English Verse, with Life of the Poet, and Illustrative Notes. Crown 8vo, 7s. 6d.

CRAWFORD. Saracinesca. By F. MARION CRAWFORD, Author of 'Mr Isaacs,' 'Dr Claudius,' 'Zoroaster,' &c. &c. 3 vols. post 8vo, 25s. 6d.

CRAWFORD. The Doctrine of Holy Scripture respecting the Atonement. By the late THOMAS J. CRAWFORD, D.D., Professor of Divinity in the University of Edinburgh. Fourth Edition. 8vo, 12s.

—— The Fatherhood of God, Considered in its General and Special Aspects, and particularly in relation to the Atonement, with a Review of Recent Speculations on the Subject. Third Edition, Revised and Enlarged. 8vo, 9s.

—— The Preaching of the Cross, and other Sermons. 8vo, 7s. 6d.

—— The Mysteries of Christianity. Crown 8vo, 7s. 6d.

DAVIES. A Book of Thoughts for every Day in the Year. Selected from the Writings of the Rev. J. LLEWELLYN DAVIES, M.A. By Two CLERGYMEN. Fcap. 8vo, 3s. 6d.

DAVIES. Norfolk Broads and Rivers; or, The Waterways, Lagoons, and Decoys of East Anglia. By G. CHRISTOPHER DAVIES, Author of 'The Swan and her Crew.' Illustrated with Seven full-page Plates. New and Cheaper Edition. Crown 8vo, 6s.

DAYNE. In the Name of the Tzar. A Novel. By J. BELFORD DAYNE. Crown 8vo, 6s.

DESCARTES. The Method, Meditations, and Principles of Philosophy of Descartes. Translated from the Original French and Latin. With a New Introductory Essay, Historical and Critical, on the Cartesian Philosophy. By JOHN VEITCH, LL.D., Professor of Logic and Rhetoric in the University of Glasgow. A New Edition, being the Eighth. Price 6s. 6d.

DOGS, OUR DOMESTICATED: Their Treatment in reference to Food, Diseases, Habits, Punishment, Accomplishments. By 'MAGENTA.' Crown 8vo, 2s. 6d.

DU CANE. The Odyssey of Homer, Books I.-XII. Translated into English Verse. By Sir CHARLES DU CANE, K.C.M.G. 8vo, 10s. 6d.

DUDGEON. History of the Edinburgh or Queen's Regiment Light Infantry Militia, now 3rd Battalion The Royal Scots; with an Account of the Origin and Progress of the Militia, and a Brief Sketch of the old Royal Scots. By Major R. C. DUDGEON, Adjutant 3rd Battalion The Royal Scots. Post 8vo, with Illustrations, 10s. 6d.

DUNCAN. Manual of the General Acts of Parliament relating to the Salmon Fisheries of Scotland from 1828 to 1882. By J. BARKER DUNCAN. Crown 8vo, 5s.

DUNSMORE. Manual of the Law of Scotland, as to the Relations between Agricultural Tenants and their Landlords, Servants, Merchants, and Bowers. By W. DUNSMORE. 8vo, 7s. 6d.

DUPRÉ. Thoughts on Art, and Autobiographical Memoirs of Giovanni Dupré. Translated from the Italian by E. M. PERUZZI, with the permission of the Author. New Edition. With an Introduction by W. W. Story. Crown 8vo, 10s. 6d.

ELIOT. George Eliot's Life, Related in her Letters and Journals. Arranged and Edited by her husband, J. W. CROSS. With Portrait and other Illustrations. Third Edition. 3 vols. post 8vo, 42s.

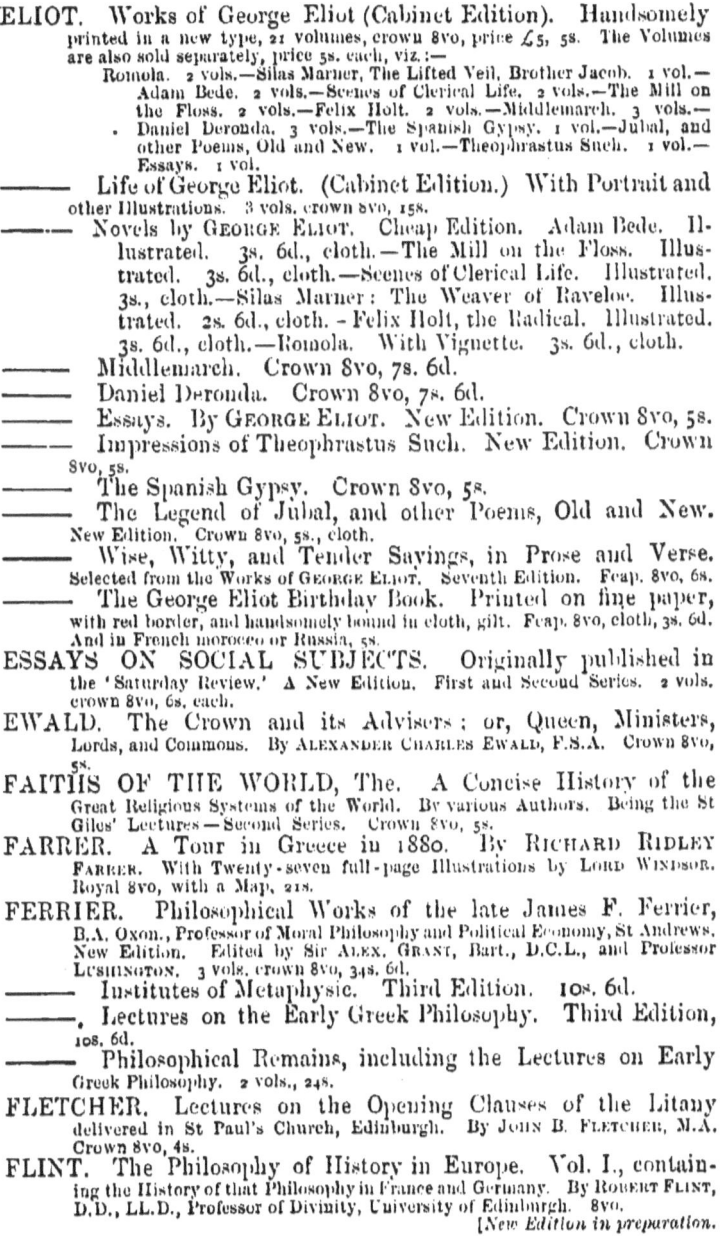

ELIOT. Works of George Eliot (Cabinet Edition). Handsomely printed in a new type, 21 volumes, crown 8vo, price £5, 5s. The Volumes are also sold separately, price 5s. each, viz. :—

Romola. 2 vols.—Silas Marner, The Lifted Veil, Brother Jacob. 1 vol.— Adam Bede. 2 vols.—Scenes of Clerical Life. 2 vols.—The Mill on the Floss. 2 vols.—Felix Holt. 2 vols.—Middlemarch. 3 vols.— Daniel Deronda. 3 vols.—The Spanish Gypsy. 1 vol.—Jubal, and other Poems, Old and New. 1 vol.—Theophrastus Such. 1 vol.— Essays. 1 vol.

——— Life of George Eliot. (Cabinet Edition.) With Portrait and other Illustrations. 3 vols. crown 8vo, 15s.

——— Novels by GEORGE ELIOT. Cheap Edition. Adam Bede. Illustrated. 3s. 6d., cloth.—The Mill on the Floss. Illustrated. 3s. 6d., cloth.—Scenes of Clerical Life. Illustrated. 3s., cloth.—Silas Marner: The Weaver of Raveloe. Illustrated. 2s. 6d., cloth. - Felix Holt, the Radical. Illustrated. 3s. 6d., cloth.—Romola. With Vignette. 3s. 6d., cloth.

——— Middlemarch. Crown 8vo, 7s. 6d.

——— Daniel Deronda. Crown 8vo, 7s. 6d.

——— Essays. By GEORGE ELIOT. New Edition. Crown 8vo, 5s.

——— Impressions of Theophrastus Such. New Edition. Crown 8vo, 5s.

——— The Spanish Gypsy. Crown 8vo, 5s.

——— The Legend of Jubal, and other Poems, Old and New. New Edition. Crown 8vo, 5s., cloth.

——— Wise, Witty, and Tender Sayings, in Prose and Verse. Selected from the Works of GEORGE ELIOT. Seventh Edition. Feap. 8vo, 6s.

——— The George Eliot Birthday Book. Printed on fine paper, with red border, and handsomely bound in cloth, gilt. Feap. 8vo, cloth, 3s. 6d. And in French morocco or Russia, 5s.

ESSAYS ON SOCIAL SUBJECTS. Originally published in the 'Saturday Review.' A New Edition. First and Second Series. 2 vols. crown 8vo, 6s. each.

EWALD. The Crown and its Advisers : or, Queen, Ministers, Lords, and Commons. By ALEXANDER CHARLES EWALD, F.S.A. Crown 8vo, 5s.

FAITHS OF THE WORLD, The. A Concise History of the Great Religious Systems of the World. By various Authors. Being the St Giles' Lectures—Second Series. Crown 8vo, 5s.

FARRER. A Tour in Greece in 1880. By RICHARD RIDLEY FARRER. With Twenty-seven full-page Illustrations by LORD WINDSOR. Royal 8vo, with a Map, 21s.

FERRIER. Philosophical Works of the late James F. Ferrier, B.A. Oxon., Professor of Moral Philosophy and Political Economy, St Andrews. New Edition. Edited by Sir ALEX. GRANT, Bart., D.C.L., and Professor LUSHINGTON. 3 vols. crown 8vo, 34s. 6d.

——— Institutes of Metaphysic. Third Edition. 10s. 6d.

———. Lectures on the Early Greek Philosophy. Third Edition, 10s. 6d.

——— Philosophical Remains, including the Lectures on Early Greek Philosophy. 2 vols., 24s.

FLETCHER. Lectures on the Opening Clauses of the Litany delivered in St Paul's Church, Edinburgh. By JOHN B. FLETCHER, M.A. Crown 8vo, 4s.

FLINT. The Philosophy of History in Europe. Vol. I., containing the History of that Philosophy in France and Germany. By ROBERT FLINT, D.D., LL.D., Professor of Divinity, University of Edinburgh. 8vo.

[New Edition in preparation.

FLINT. Theism. Being the Baird Lecture for 1876. By ROBERT FLINT, D.D., LL.D., Professor of Divinity, University of Edinburgh. Fifth Edition. Crown 8vo, 7s. 6d.

———— Anti-Theistic Theories. Being the Baird Lecture for 1877. Third Edition. Crown 8vo, 10s. 6d.

FORBES. The Campaign of Garibaldi in the Two Sicilies : A Personal Narrative. By CHARLES STUART FORBES, Commander, R.N. Post 8vo, with Portraits. 12s.

FOREIGN CLASSICS FOR ENGLISH READERS. Edited by Mrs OLIPHANT. Price 2s. 6d. *For List of Volumes published, see p. 2.*

FRANZOS. The Jews of Barnow. Stories by KARL EMIL FRANZOS. Translated by M. W. MACDOWALL. Crown 8vo, 6s.

GALT. Annals of the Parish. By JOHN GALT. Fcap. 8vo, 2s.

———— The Provost. Fcap. 8vo, 2s.

———— Sir Andrew Wylie. Fcap. 8vo, 2s.

———— The Entail ; or, The Laird of Grippy. Fcap. 8vo, 2s.

GENERAL ASSEMBLY OF THE CHURCH OF SCOTLAND.

———— Family Prayers. Authorised by the General Assembly of the Church of Scotland. A New Edition, crown 8vo, in large type, 4s. 6d. Another Edition, crown 8vo, 2s.

———— Prayers for Social and Family Worship. For the Use of Soldiers, Sailors, Colonists, and Sojourners in India, and other Persons, at home and abroad, who are deprived of the ordinary services of a Christian Ministry. Cheap Edition, 1s. 6d.

———— The Scottish Hymnal. Hymns for Public Worship. Published for Use in Churches by Authority of the General Assembly. Various sizes—viz.: 1. Large type, for Pulpit use, cloth, 3s. 6d. 2. Longprimer type, cloth, red edges, 1s. 6d. ; French morocco, 2s. 6d. ; calf, 6s. 3. Bourgeois type, cloth, red edges, 1s. ; French morocco, 2s. 4. Minion type, French morocco, 1s. 6d. 5. School Edition, in paper cover, 2d. 6. Children's Hymnal, paper cover, 1d. No. 2, bound with the Psalms and Paraphrases, cloth, 3s. ; French morocco, 4s. 6d. ; calf, 7s. 6d. No. 3, bound with the Psalms and Paraphrases, cloth, 2s. ; French morocco, 3s.

———— The Scottish Hymnal, with Music. Selected by the Committees on Hymns and on Psalmody. The harmonies arranged by W. H. Monk. Cloth, 1s. 6d.; French morocco, 3s. 6d. The same in the Tonic Sol-fa Notation, 1s. 6d. and 3s. 6d.

———— The Scottish Hymnal, with Fixed Tune for each Hymn. Longprimer type, 3s. 6d.

———— The Scottish Hymnal Appendix. 1. Longprimer type, 1s. 2. Nonpareil type, cloth limp, 4d.; paper cover, 2d.

———— Scottish Hymnal with Appendix Incorporated. Bourgeois type, limp cloth, 1s. Large type, cloth, red edges, 2s. 6d. Nonpareil type, paper covers, 3d. ; cloth, red edges, 6d.

GERARD. Reata: What's in a Name. By E. D. GERARD. New Edition. Crown 8vo, 6s.

———— Beggar my Neighbour. New Edition. Crown 8vo, 6s.

———— The Waters of Hercules. New Edition. Crown 8vo, 6s.

GERARD. Stonyhurst Latin Grammar. By Rev. JOHN GERARD. Fcap. 8vo, 3s.

GILL. Free Trade : an Inquiry into the Nature of its Operation. By RICHARD GILL. In 1 vol. crown 8vo. [*In the press.*

GOETHE'S FAUST. Part I. Translated into English Verse by Sir THEODORE MARTIN, K.C.B. Second Edition, post 8vo, 6s. Eighth Edition, fcap., 3s. 6d.

———— Part II. Translated into English Verse by Sir THEODORE MARTIN, K.C.B. Second Edition, revised. Fcap 8vo, 6s.

GOETHE. Poems and Ballads of Goethe. Translated by Professor AYTOUN and Sir THEODORE MARTIN, K.C.B. Third Edition, fcap. 8vo, 6s.

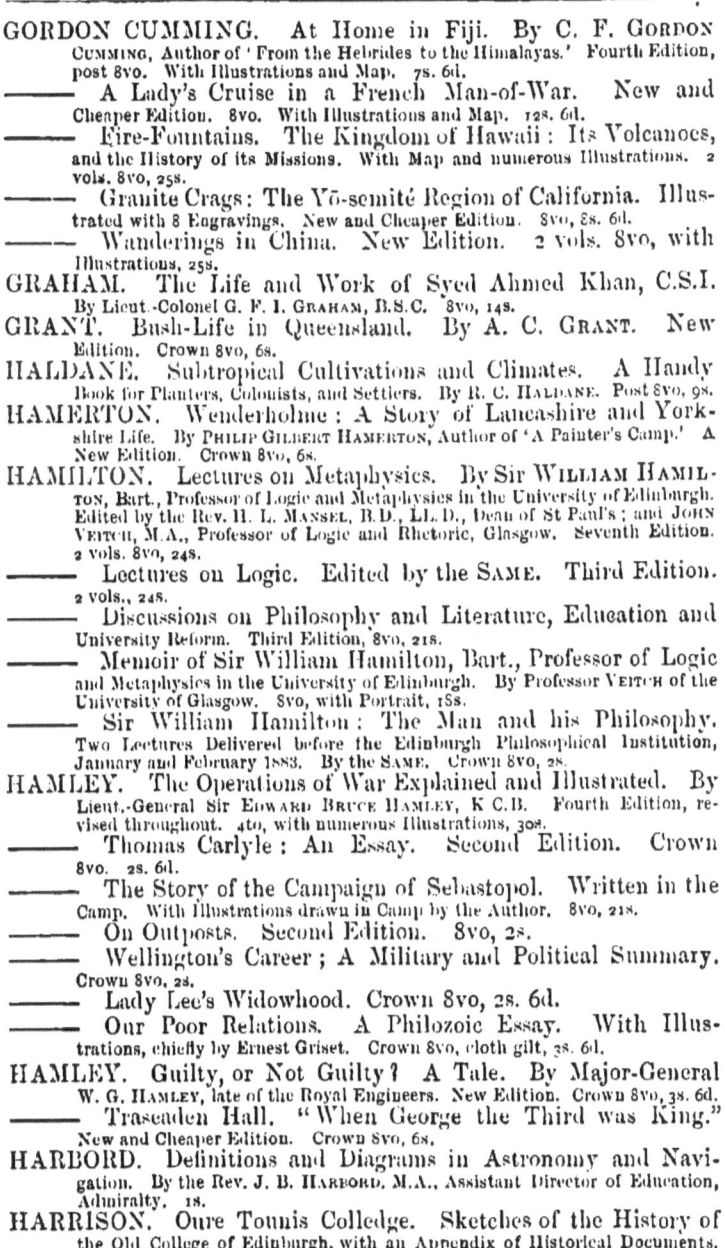

GORDON CUMMING. At Home in Fiji. By C. F. GORDON
CUMMING, Author of ' From the Hebrides to the Himalayas.' Fourth Edition,
post 8vo. With Illustrations and Map. 7s. 6d.

—— A Lady's Cruise in a French Man-of-War. New and
Cheaper Edition. 8vo. With Illustrations and Map. 12s. 6d.

—— Fire-Fountains. The Kingdom of Hawaii : Its Volcanoes,
and the History of its Missions. With Map and numerous Illustrations. 2
vols. 8vo, 25s.

—— Granite Crags: The Yō-semité Region of California. Illustrated with 8 Engravings. New and Cheaper Edition. 8vo, 8s. 6d.

—— Wanderings in China. New Edition. 2 vols. 8vo, with
Illustrations, 25s.

GRAHAM. The Life and Work of Syed Ahmed Khan, C.S.I.
By Lieut.-Colonel G. F. I. GRAHAM, B.S.C. 8vo, 14s.

GRANT. Bush-Life in Queensland. By A. C. GRANT. New
Edition. Crown 8vo, 6s.

HALDANE. Subtropical Cultivations and Climates. A Handy
Book for Planters, Colonists, and Settlers. By R. C. HALDANE. Post 8vo, 9s.

HAMERTON. Wenderholme : A Story of Lancashire and York-
shire Life. By PHILIP GILBERT HAMERTON, Author of 'A Painter's Camp.' A
New Edition. Crown 8vo, 6s.

HAMILTON. Lectures on Metaphysics. By Sir WILLIAM HAMIL-
TON, Bart., Professor of Logic and Metaphysics in the University of Edinburgh.
Edited by the Rev. H. L. MANSEL, B.D., LL.D., Dean of St Paul's ; and JOHN
VEITCH, M.A., Professor of Logic and Rhetoric, Glasgow. Seventh Edition.
2 vols. 8vo, 24s.

—— Lectures on Logic. Edited by the SAME. Third Edition.
2 vols., 24s.

—— Discussions on Philosophy and Literature, Education and
University Reform. Third Edition, 8vo, 21s.

—— Memoir of Sir William Hamilton, Bart., Professor of Logic
and Metaphysics in the University of Edinburgh. By Professor VEITCH of the
University of Glasgow. 8vo, with Portrait, 18s.

—— Sir William Hamilton : The Man and his Philosophy.
Two Lectures Delivered before the Edinburgh Philosophical Institution,
January and February 1883. By the SAME. Crown 8vo, 2s.

HAMLEY. The Operations of War Explained and Illustrated. By
Lieut.-General Sir EDWARD BRUCE HAMLEY, K C.B. Fourth Edition, revised throughout. 4to, with numerous Illustrations, 30s.

—— Thomas Carlyle : An Essay. Second Edition. Crown
8vo. 2s. 6d.

—— The Story of the Campaign of Sebastopol. Written in the
Camp. With Illustrations drawn in Camp by the Author. 8vo, 21s.

—— On Outposts. Second Edition. 8vo, 2s.

—— Wellington's Career ; A Military and Political Summary.
Crown 8vo, 2s.

—— Lady Lee's Widowhood. Crown 8vo, 2s. 6d.

—— Our Poor Relations. A Philozoic Essay. With Illustrations, chiefly by Ernest Griset. Crown 8vo, cloth gilt, 3s. 6d.

HAMLEY. Guilty, or Not Guilty? A Tale. By Major-General
W. G. HAMLEY, late of the Royal Engineers. New Edition. Crown 8vo, 3s. 6d.

—— Traseaden Hall. "When George the Third was King."
New and Cheaper Edition. Crown 8vo, 6s.

HARBORD. Definitions and Diagrams in Astronomy and Navi-
gation. By the Rev. J. B. HARBORD, M.A., Assistant Director of Education,
Admiralty. 1s.

HARRISON. Oure Tounis Colledge. Sketches of the History of
the Old College of Edinburgh, with an Appendix of Historical Documents.
By JOHN HARRISON. Crown 8vo, 5s.

HASELL. Bible Partings. By E. J. HASELL. Crown 8vo, 6s.
———— Short Family Prayers. By Miss HASELL. Cloth, 1s.

HAY. The Works of the Right Rev. Dr George Hay, Bishop of
Edinburgh. Edited under the Supervision of the Right Rev. Bishop STRAIN.
With Memoir and Portrait of the Author. 5 vols. crown 8vo, bound in extra
cloth, £1, 1s. Or, sold separately—viz.:
The Sincere Christian Instructed in the Faith of Christ from the Written Word.
2 vols., 8s.—The Devout Christian Instructed in the Law of Christ from the Written
Word. 2 vols., 8s.—The Pious Christian Instructed in the Nature and Practice of the
Principal Exercises of Piety. 1 vol., 4s.

HEATLEY. The Horse-Owner's Safeguard. A Handy Medical
Guide for every Man who owns a Horse. By G. S. HEATLEY, M.R.C.V.S.
Crown 8vo, 5s.
———— The Stock-Owner's Guide. A Handy Medical Treatise for
every Man who owns an Ox or a Cow. Crown 8vo, 4s. 6d.

HEMANS. The Poetical Works of Mrs Hemans. Copyright Edi-
tions.—One Volume, royal 8vo, 5s.—The Same, with Illustrations engraved on
Steel, bound in cloth, gilt edges, 7s. 6d.—Six Volumes in Three, fcap., 12s. 6d.
SELECT POEMS of MRS HEMANS. Fcap., cloth, gilt edges, 3s.

HOLE. A Book about Roses: How to Grow and Show Them. By
the Rev. Canon HOLE. Ninth Edition, revised. Crown 8vo, 3s. 6d.

HOME PRAYERS. By Ministers of the Church of Scotland and
Members of the Church Service Society. Second Edition. Fcap. 8vo, 3s.

HOMER. The Odyssey. Translated into English Verse in the
Spenserian Stanza. By PHILIP STANHOPE WORSLEY. Third Edition, 2 vols.
fcap., 12s.
———— The Iliad. Translated by P. S. WORSLEY and Professor
CONINGTON. 2 vols. crown 8vo, 21s.

HOSACK. Mary Queen of Scots and Her Accusers. Containing a
Variety of Documents never before published. By JOHN HOSACK, Barrister-
at-Law. A New and Enlarged Edition, with a Photograph from the Bust on
the Tomb in Westminster Abbey. 2 vols. 8vo, £1, 1s.

HUTCHINSON. Hints on the Game of Golf. By HORACE G.
HUTCHINSON. Second Edition. Fcap. 8vo, cloth, 1s. 6d.

HYDE. The Royal Mail; its Curiosities and Romance. By JAMES
WILSON HYDE, Superintendent in the General Post Office, Edinburgh. Second
Edition, enlarged. Crown 8vo, with Illustrations, 6s.

INDEX GEOGRAPHICUS: Being a List, alphabetically arranged,
of the Principal Places on the Globe, with the Countries and Subdivisions of
the Countries in which they are situated, and their Latitudes and Longitudes.
Applicable to all Modern Atlases and Maps. Imperial 8vo, pp. 676, 21s.

JAMIESON. Discussions on the Atonement: Is it Vicarious?
By the Rev. GEORGE JAMIESON, A.M., B.D., D.D., Author of 'Profound Problems in Philosophy and Theology.' 8vo, 16s.

JEAN JAMBON. Our Trip to Blunderland; or, Grand Excursion
to Blundertown and Back. By JEAN JAMBON. With Sixty Illustrations
designed by CHARLES DOYLE, engraved by DALZIEL. Fourth Thousand.
Handsomely bound in cloth, gilt edges, 6s. 6d. Cheap Edition, cloth, 3s. 6d.
In boards, 2s. 6d.

JENNINGS. Mr Gladstone: A Study. By LOUIS J. JENNINGS,
M.P., Author of 'Republican Government in the United States,' 'The Croker
Memoirs,' &c. Third Edition. Crown 8vo, 5s.

JERNINGHAM. Reminiscences of an Attaché. By HUBERT
E. H. JERNINGHAM. Second Edition. Crown 8vo, 5s.

JOHNSON. The Scots Musical Museum. Consisting of upwards
of Six Hundred Songs, with proper Basses for the Pianoforte. Originally pub-
lished by JAMES JOHNSON; and now accompanied with Copious Notes and
Illustrations of the Lyric Poetry and Music of Scotland, by the late WILLIAM
STENHOUSE; with additional Notes and Illustrations, by DAVID LAING and
C. K. SHARPE. 4 vols. 8vo, Roxburghe binding.

JOHNSTON. The Chemistry of Common Life. By Professor J. F. W. JOHNSTON. New Edition, Revised, and brought down to date. By ARTHUR HERBERT CHURCH, M.A. Oxon.; Author of 'Food: its Sources, Constituents, and Uses;' 'The Laboratory Guide for Agricultural Students;' 'Plain Words about Water,' &c. Illustrated with Maps and 102 Engravings on Wood. Complete in one volume, crown 8vo, pp. 618, 7s. 6d.

——— Elements of Agricultural Chemistry and Geology. Fourteenth Edition, Revised, and brought down to date. By Sir CHARLES A. CAMERON, M.D., F.R.C.S.I., &c. Fcap. 8vo, 6s. 6d.

——— Catechism of Agricultural Chemistry and Geology. An entirely New Edition, revised and enlarged, by Sir CHARLES A. CAMERON, M.D., F.R.C.S.I. &c. Eighty-sixth Thousand, with numerous Illustrations, 1s.

JOHNSTON. Patrick Hamilton: a Tragedy of the Reformation in Scotland, 1528. By T. P. JOHNSTON. Crown 8vo, with Two Etchings by the Author, 5s.

KENNEDY. Sport, Travel, and Adventures in Newfoundland and the West Indies. By Captain W. R. KENNEDY, R.N. With Illustrations by the Author. Post 8vo, 14s.

KING. The Metamorphoses of Ovid. Translated in English Blank Verse. By HENRY KING, M.A., Fellow of Wadham College, Oxford, and of the Inner Temple, Barrister-at-Law. Crown 8vo, 10s. 6d.

KINGLAKE. History of the Invasion of the Crimea. By A. W. KINGLAKE. Cabinet Edition. Seven Volumes, illustrated with maps and plans, crown 8vo, at 6s. each. The Volumes respectively contain:—
    I. THE ORIGIN OF THE WAR between the Czar and the Sultan. II. RUSSIA MET AND INVADED. III. THE BATTLE OF THE ALMA. IV. SEBASTOPOL AT BAY. V. THE BATTLE OF BALACLAVA. VI. THE BATTLE OF INKERMAN. VII. WINTER TROUBLES.

——— History of the Invasion of the Crimea. Vol. VI. Winter Troubles. Demy 8vo, with a Map, 16s.

——— History of the Invasion of the Crimea. Vol. VII. Demy 8vo. [In preparation.

——— Eothen. A New Edition, uniform with the Cabinet Edition of the 'History of the Invasion of the Crimea,' price 6s.

KNOLLYS. The Elements of Field-Artillery. Designed for the Use of Infantry and Cavalry Officers. By HENRY KNOLLYS, Captain Royal Artillery; Author of 'From Sedan to Saarbrück,' Editor of 'Incidents in the Sepoy War,' &c. With Engravings. Crown 8vo, 7s. 6d.

LAING. Select Remains of the Ancient Popular and Romance Poetry of Scotland. Originally Collected and Edited by DAVID LAING, LL.D. Re-edited, with Memorial-Introduction, by JOHN SMALL, M.A. With a Portrait of Dr Laing. 4to, 25s.

LAVERGNE. The Rural Economy of England, Scotland, and Ireland. By LEONCE DE LAVERGNE. Translated from the French. With Notes by a Scottish Farmer. 8vo, 12s.

LAWLESS. Hurrish: a Study. By the Hon. EMILY LAWLESS, Author of 'A Chelsea Householder,' 'A Millionaire's Cousin.' Third and cheaper Edition, crown 8vo, 6s.

LEE. A Phantom Lover: A Fantastic Story. By VERNON LEE. Crown 8vo, 1s.

LEE. Glimpses in the Twilight. Being various Notes, Records, and Examples of the Supernatural. By the Rev. GEORGE F. LEE, D.C.L. Crown 8vo. 8s. 6d.

LEE-HAMILTON. Poems and Transcripts. By EUGENE LEE-HAMILTON. Crown 8vo, 6s.

LEES. A Handbook of Sheriff Court Styles. By J. M. LEES, M.A., LL.B., Advocate, Sheriff-Substitute of Lanarkshire. New Ed., 8vo, 21s.

——— A Handbook of the Sheriff and Justice of Peace Small Debt Courts. 8vo, 7s. 6d.

LETTERS FROM THE HIGHLANDS. Reprinted from 'The Times.' Fcap. 8vo, 4s. 6d.

LINDAU. The Philosopher's Pendulum, and other Stories. By RUDOLPH LINDAU. Crown 8vo, 7s. 6d.

LITTLE. Madagascar: Its History and People. By the Rev. HENRY W. LITTLE, some years Missionary in East Madagascar. Post 8vo, 10s. 6d.

LOCKHART. Doubles and Quits. By LAURENCE W. M. LOCKHART. With Twelve Illustrations. Fourth Edition. Crown 8vo, 6s.

—— Fair to See: a Novel. Eighth Edition. Crown 8vo, 6s.

—— Mine is Thine : a Novel. Eighth Edition. Crown 8vo, 6s.

LORIMER. The Institutes of Law : A Treatise of the Principles of Jurisprudence as determined by Nature. By JAMES LORIMER, Regius Professor of Public Law and of the Law of Nature and Nations in the University of Edinburgh. New Edition, revised throughout, and much enlarged. 8vo, 18s.

—— The Institutes of the Law of Nations. A Treatise of the Jural Relation of Separate Political Communities. In 2 vols. 8vo. Volume I., price 16s. Volume II., price 20s.

M'COMBIE. Cattle and Cattle-Breeders. By WILLIAM M'COMBIE, Tillyfour. New Edition, enlarged, with Memoir of the Author. By JAMES MACDONALD, Editor of the 'Live-Stock Journal.' Crown 8vo, 3s. 6d.

MACRAE. A Handbook of Deer-Stalking. By ALEXANDER MACRAE, late Forester to Lord Henry Bentinck. With Introduction by HORATIO ROSS, Esq. Fcap. 8vo, with two Photographs from Life. 3s. 6d.

M'CRIE. Works of the Rev. Thomas M'Crie, D.D. Uniform Edition. Four vols. crown 8vo, 24s.

—— Life of John Knox. Containing Illustrations of the History of the Reformation in Scotland. Crown 8vo, 6s. Another Edition, 3s. 6d.

—— Life of Andrew Melville. Containing Illustrations of the Ecclesiastical and Literary History of Scotland in the Sixteenth and Seventeenth Centuries. Crown 8vo, 6s.

—— History of the Progress and Suppression of the Reformation in Italy in the Sixteenth Century. Crown 8vo, 4s.

—— History of the Progress and Suppression of the Reformation in Spain in the Sixteenth Century. Crown 8vo, 3s. 6d.

—— Lectures on the Book of Esther. Fcap. 8vo, 5s.

MACDONALD. The Flower and the Spirit. By FREDERIKA MACDONALD, Author of 'Nathaniel Vaughan,' 'Iliad of the East,' &c. 2 vols. post 8vo, 17s.

M'INTOSH. The Book of the Garden. By CHARLES M'INTOSH, formerly Curator of the Royal Gardens of his Majesty the King of the Belgians, and lately of those of his Grace the Duke of Buccleuch, K.G., at Dalkeith Palace. Two large vols. royal 8vo, embellished with 1350 Engravings. £4, 7s. 6d. Vol. I. On the Formation of Gardens and Construction of Garden Edifices. 776 pages, and 1073 Engravings, £2, 10s. Vol. II. Practical Gardening. 868 pages, and 279 Engravings, £1, 17s. 6d.

MACKAY. A Manual of Modern Geography ; Mathematical, Physical, and Political. By the Rev. ALEXANDER MACKAY, LL.D., F.R.G.S. 11th Thousand, revised to the present time. Crown 8vo, pp. 688. 7s. 6d.

—— Elements of Modern Geography. 51st Thousand, revised to the present time. Crown 8vo, pp. 300, 3s.

—— The Intermediate Geography. Intended as an Intermediate Book between the Author's 'Outlines of Geography' and 'Elements of Geography.' Eleventh Edition, revised. Crown 8vo, pp. 238, 2s.

—— Outlines of Modern Geography. 175th Thousand, revised to the present time. 18mo, pp. 118, 1s.

—— First Steps in Geography. 86th Thousand. 18mo, pp. 56. Sewed, 4d. ; cloth, 6d.

MACKAY. Elements of Physiography and Physical Geography. With Express Reference to the Instructions recently issued by the Science and Art Department. By the Rev. ALEXANDER MACKAY, LL.D., F.R.G.S. 25th Thousand, revised. Crown 8vo, 1s. 6d.

—— Facts and Dates; or, the Leading Events in Sacred and Profane History, and the Principal Facts in the various Physical Sciences. The Memory being aided throughout by a Simple and Natural Method. For Schools and Private Reference. New Edition. Crown 8vo, 3s. 6d.

MACKAY. An Old Scots Brigade. Being the History of Mackay's Regiment, now incorporated with the Royal Scots. With an Appendix containing many Original Documents connected with the History of the Regiment. By JOHN MACKAY (late) OF HERRIESDALE. Crown 8vo, 5s.

MACKAY. The Founders of the American Republic. A History of Washington, Adams, Jefferson, Franklin, and Madison. With a Supplementary Chapter on the Inherent Causes of the Ultimate Failure of American Democracy. By CHARLES MACKAY, LL.D. Post 8vo, 10s. 6d.

MACKELLAR. More Leaves from the Journal of a Life in the Highlands, from 1862 to 1882. Translated into Gaelic by Mrs MARY MACKELLAR. By command of Her Majesty the Queen. Crown 8vo, with Illustrations. 10s. 6d.

MACKENZIE. Studies in Roman Law. With Comparative Views of the Laws of France, England, and Scotland. By LORD MACKENZIE, one of the Judges of the Court of Session in Scotland. Sixth Edition, Edited by JOHN KIRKPATRICK, Esq., M.A. Cantab.; Dr Jur. Heidelb.; LL.B. Edin.; Advocate. 8vo, 12s.

MAIN. Three Hundred English Sonnets. Chosen and Edited by DAVID M. MAIN. Fcap. 8vo, 6s.

MAIR. A Digest of Laws and Decisions, Ecclesiastical and Civil. Relating to the Constitution, Practice, and Affairs of the Church of Scotland. With Notes and Forms of Procedure. By the Rev. WILLIAM MAIR, D.D., Minister of the Parish of Earlston. In 1 vol. crown 8vo, [Immediately.

MAITLAND. Parva. By E. FULLER MAITLAND (E. F. M.) Fcap. 8vo, 5s.

MANNERS. Notes of an Irish Tour in 1846. By Lord JOHN MANNERS, M.P., G.C.B. New Edition Crown 8vo, 2s. 6d.

MANNERS. Gems of German Poetry. Translated by Lady JOHN MANNERS. Small quarto, 3s. 6d.

—— Impressions of Bad-Homburg. Comprising a Short Account of the Women's Associations of Germany under the Red Cross. By Lady JOHN MANNERS. Crown 8vo, 1s. 6d.

—— Some Personal Recollections of the Later Years of the Earl of Beaconsfield, K.G. Sixth Edition, 6d.

—— Employment of Women in the Public Service. 6d.

—— Some of the Advantages of Easily Accessible Reading and Recreation Rooms, and Free Libraries. With Remarks on Starting and Maintaining Them. Second Edition, crown 8vo, 1s.

—— A Sequel to Rich Men's Dwellings, and other Occasional Papers. Crown 8vo, 2s. 6d.

—— Encouraging Experiences of Reading and Recreation Rooms. Aims of Guilds, Nottingham Social Guild, Existing Institutions, &c., &c. Crown 8vo, 1s.

MARMORNE. The Story is told by ADOLPHUS SEGRAVE, the youngest of three Brothers. Third Edition. Crown 8vo, 6s.

MARSHALL. French Home Life. By FREDERIC MARSHALL. Second Edition. 5s.

MARSHMAN. History of India. From the Earliest Period to the Close of the India Company's Government; with an Epitome of Subsequent Events. By JOHN CLARK MARSHMAN, C.S.I. Abridged from the Author's larger work. Second Edition, revised. Crown 8vo, with Map, 6s. 6d.

MARTIN. Goethe's Faust. Part I. Translated by Sir THEODORE
MARTIN, K.C.B. Second Edition, crown 8vo, 6s. Eighth Edition, fcap.
8vo, 3s. 6d.
—— Goethe's Faust. Part II. Translated into English Verse.
Second Edition, revised. Fcap. 8vo, 6s.
—— The Works of Horace. Translated into English Verse,
with Life and Notes. In 2 vols. crown 8vo, printed on hand-made
paper, 21s.
—— Poems and Ballads of Heinrich Heine. Done into Eng-
lish Verse. Second Edition. Printed on papier vergé, crown 8vo, 8s.
—— Catullus. With Life and Notes. Second Edition, post 8vo,
7s. 6d.
—— The Vita Nuova of Dante. With an Introduction and
Notes. Second Edition, crown 8vo, 5s.
—— Aladdin : A Dramatic Poem. By ADAM OEHLENSCHLAE-
GER. Fcap. 8vo, 5s.
—— Correggio : A Tragedy. By OEHLENSCHLAEGER. With
Notes. Fcap. 8vo, 3s.
—— King Rene's Daughter : A Danish Lyrical Drama. By
HENRIK HERTZ. Second Edition, fcap., 2s. 6d.
MARTIN. On some of Shakespeare's Female Characters. In a
Series of Letters. By HELENA FAUCIT, LADY MARTIN. Dedicated by per-
mission to Her Most Gracious Majesty the Queen. New Edition. Royal 8vo,
with Portrait. 9s.
MATHESON. Can the Old Faith Live with the New? or the
Problem of Evolution and Revelation. By the Rev. GEORGE MATHESON, D.D.
Second Edition. Crown 8vo, 7s. 6d.
MEIKLEJOHN. An Old Educational Reformer—Dr Bell. By
J. M. D. MEIKLEJOHN, M.A., Professor of the Theory, History, and Practice
of Education in the University of St Andrews. Crown 8vo, 3s. 6d.
—— The Golden Primer. With Coloured Illustrations by Wal-
ter Crane. Small 4to, boards, 5s.
—— The English Language : Its Grammar, History, and Litera-
ture. With Chapters on Versification, Paraphrasing, and Punctuation.
Crown 8vo, 4s. 6d.
MICHEL. A Critical Inquiry into the Scottish Language. With
the view of Illustrating the Rise and Progress of Civilisation in Scotland. By
FRANCISQUE-MICHEL, F.S.A. Lond. and Scot., Correspondant de l'Institut de
France, &c. In One handsome Quarto Volume, printed on hand-made paper,
and appropriately bound in Roxburghe style. Price 66s.
MICHIE. The Larch : Being a Practical Treatise on its Culture
and General Management. By CHRISTOPHER Y. MICHIE, Forester, Cullen House.
Crown 8vo, with Illustrations. New and Cheaper Edition, enlarged, 5s.
MILNE. The Problem of the Churchless and Poor in our Large
Towns. With special reference to the Home Mission Work of the Church
of Scotland. By the Rev. ROBT. MILNE, M.A., D.D., Ardler. Crown 8vo, 5s.
MINTO. A Manual of English Prose Literature, Biographical
and Critical : designed mainly to show Characteristics of Style. By W. MINTO,
M.A., Professor of Logic in the University of Aberdeen. Third Edition,
revised. Crown 8vo, 7s. 6d.
—— Characteristics of English Poets, from Chaucer to Shirley.
New Edition, revised. Crown 8vo, 7s. 6d.
—— The Crack of Doom. 3 vols. post 8vo, 25s. 6d.
MITCHELL. Biographies of Eminent Soldiers of the last Four
Centuries. By Major-General JOHN MITCHELL, Author of 'Life of Wallenstein.'
With a Memoir of the Author. 8vo, 9s.
MOIR. Life of Mansie Wauch, Tailor in Dalkeith. With 8
Illustrations on Steel, by the late GEORGE CRUIKSHANK. Crown 8vo, 3s. 6d.
Another Edition, fcap. 8vo, 1s. 6d.

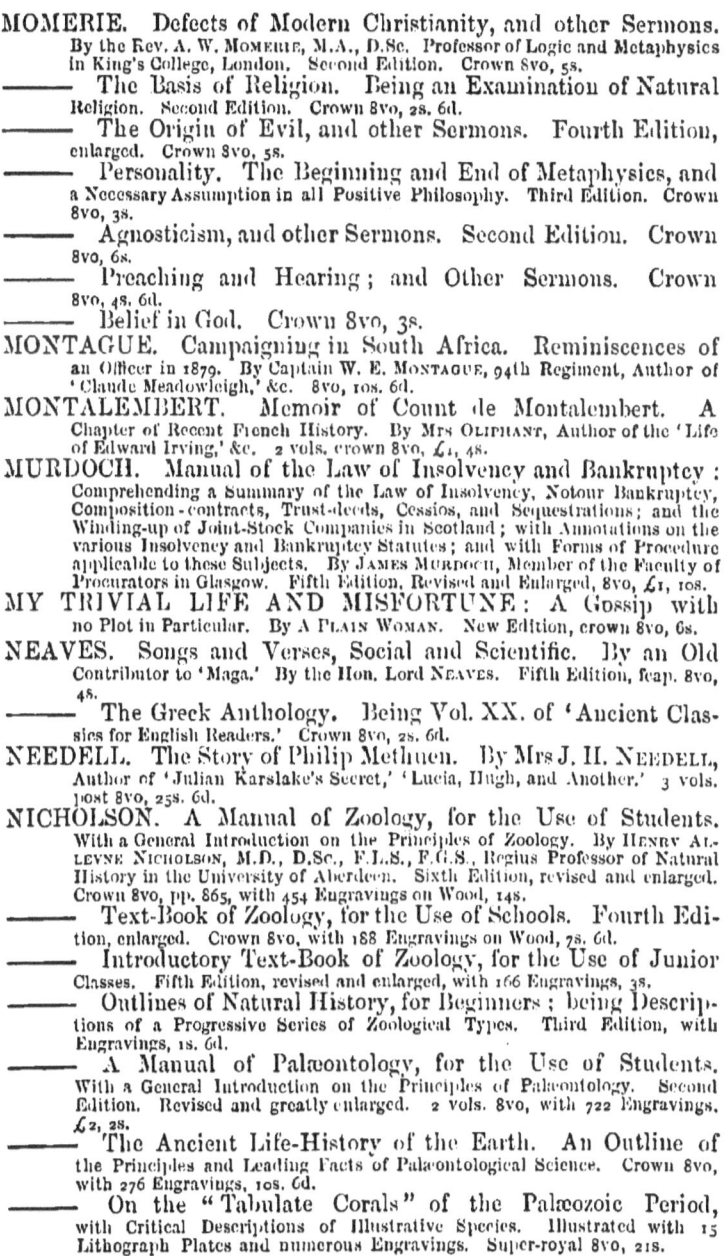

MOMERIE. Defects of Modern Christianity, and other Sermons. By the Rev. A. W. MOMERIE, M.A., D.Sc. Professor of Logic and Metaphysics in King's College, London. Second Edition. Crown 8vo, 5s.

—— The Basis of Religion. Being an Examination of Natural Religion. Second Edition. Crown 8vo, 2s. 6d.

—— The Origin of Evil, and other Sermons. Fourth Edition, enlarged. Crown 8vo, 5s.

—— Personality. The Beginning and End of Metaphysics, and a Necessary Assumption in all Positive Philosophy. Third Edition. Crown 8vo, 3s.

—— Agnosticism, and other Sermons. Second Edition. Crown 8vo, 6s.

—— Preaching and Hearing ; and Other Sermons. Crown 8vo, 4s. 6d.

—— Belief in God. Crown 8vo, 3s.

MONTAGUE. Campaigning in South Africa. Reminiscences of an Officer in 1879. By Captain W. E. MONTAGUE, 94th Regiment, Author of ' Claude Meadowleigh,' &c. 8vo, 10s. 6d.

MONTALEMBERT. Memoir of Count de Montalembert. A Chapter of Recent French History. By Mrs OLIPHANT, Author of the ' Life of Edward Irving,' &c. 2 vols. crown 8vo, £1, 4s.

MURDOCH. Manual of the Law of Insolvency and Bankruptcy : Comprehending a Summary of the Law of Insolvency, Notour Bankruptcy, Composition - contracts, Trust-deeds, Cessios, and Sequestrations; and the Winding-up of Joint-Stock Companies in Scotland ; with Annotations on the various Insolvency and Bankruptcy Statutes; and with Forms of Procedure applicable to these Subjects. By JAMES MURDOCH, Member of the Faculty of Procurators in Glasgow. Fifth Edition, Revised and Enlarged, 8vo, £1, 10s.

**MY TRIVIAL LIFE AND MISFORTUNE : A Gossip with no Plot in Particular. By A PLAIN WOMAN. New Edition, crown 8vo, 6s.

NEAVES. Songs and Verses, Social and Scientific. By an Old Contributor to 'Maga.' By the Hon. Lord NEAVES. Fifth Edition, fcap. 8vo, 4s.

—— The Greek Anthology. Being Vol. XX. of 'Ancient Classics for English Readers.' Crown 8vo, 2s. 6d.

NEEDELL. The Story of Philip Methuen. By Mrs J. H. NEEDELL, Author of ' Julian Karslake's Secret,' ' Lucia, Hugh, and Another.' 3 vols. post 8vo, 25s. 6d.

NICHOLSON. A Manual of Zoology, for the Use of Students. With a General Introduction on the Principles of Zoology. By HENRY ALLEYNE NICHOLSON, M.D., D.Sc., F.L.S., F.G.S., Regius Professor of Natural History in the University of Aberdeen. Sixth Edition, revised and enlarged. Crown 8vo, pp. 865, with 454 Engravings on Wood, 14s.

—— Text-Book of Zoology, for the Use of Schools. Fourth Edition, enlarged. Crown 8vo, with 188 Engravings on Wood, 7s. 6d.

—— Introductory Text-Book of Zoology, for the Use of Junior Classes. Fifth Edition, revised and enlarged, with 166 Engravings, 3s.

—— Outlines of Natural History, for Beginners ; being Descriptions of a Progressive Series of Zoological Types. Third Edition, with Engravings, 1s. 6d.

—— A Manual of Palæontology, for the Use of Students. With a General Introduction on the Principles of Palæontology. Second Edition. Revised and greatly enlarged. 2 vols. 8vo, with 722 Engravings. £2, 2s.

—— The Ancient Life-History of the Earth. An Outline of the Principles and Leading Facts of Palæontological Science. Crown 8vo, with 276 Engravings, 6d.

—— On the "Tabulate Corals" of the Palæozoic Period, with Critical Descriptions of Illustrative Species. Illustrated with 15 Lithograph Plates and numerous Engravings. Super-royal 8vo, 21s.

NICHOLSON.   On the Structure and Affinities of the Genus Mon-
ticulipora and its Sub-Genera, with Critical Descriptions of Illustrative
Species.   By HENRY ALLEYNE NICHOLSON, M.D., D.Sc., F.L.S., F.G.S.,
Regius Professor of Natural History in the University of Aberdeen.   Illustrated with numerous Engravings on wood and lithographed Plates.   Super-
royal 8vo, 18s.

—— Synopsis of the Classification of the Animal Kingdom. 8vo, with 106 Illustrations, 6s.

NICHOLSON.   Communion with Heaven, and other Sermons.
By the late MAXWELL NICHOLSON, D.D., Minister of St Stephen's, Edinburgh.
Crown 8vo, 5s. 6d.

—— Rest in Jesus.   Sixth Edition.   Fcap. 8vo, 4s. 6d.

OLIPHANT.   Masollam: a Problem of the Period.   A Novel.
By LAURENCE OLIPHANT.   3 vols. post 8vo, 25s. 6d.

—— Altiora Peto.   Eighth Edition, Illustrated.   Crown 8vo, 6s.

—— Piccadilly: A Fragment of Contemporary Biography.   With
Eight Illustrations by Richard Doyle.   Eighth Edition, 4s. 6d.   Cheap Edition,
in paper cover, 2s. 6d.

—— Traits and Travesties; Social and Political.   Post 8vo, 10s. 6d.

—— The Land of Gilead.   With Excursions in the Lebanon.
With Illustrations and Maps.   Demy 8vo, 21s.

—— The Land of Khemi.   Post 8vo, with Illustrations, 10s. 6d.

—— Sympneumata: or, Evolutionary Functions now Active in
Man.   Edited by LAURENCE OLIPHANT.   Post 8vo, 10s. 6d.

—— Haifa: Life in Modern Palestine.   8vo, 7s. 6d.

—— Fashionable Philosophy, and other Sketches.   In paper
cover, 1s.

OLIPHANT.   The Story of Valentine; and his Brother.   By Mrs
OLIPHANT.   5s., cloth.

—— Katie Stewart.   2s. 6d.

—— A House Divided against Itself.   3 vols. post 8vo, 25s. 6d.

OSBORN.   Narratives of Voyage and Adventure.   By Admiral
SHERARD OSBORN, C.B.   3 vols. crown 8vo, 12s.

OSSIAN.   The Poems of Ossian in the Original Gaelic.   With a
Literal Translation into English, and a Dissertation on the Authenticity of the
Poems.   By the Rev. ARCHIBALD CLERK.   2 vols. imperial 8vo, £1, 11s. 6d.

OSWALD.   By Fell and Fjord; or, Scenes and Studies in Iceland.
By E. J. OSWALD.   Post 8vo, with Illustrations.   7s. 6d.

OUR OWN POMPEII.   A Romance of To-morrow.   2 vols. crown
8vo, 17s.

OUTRAM.   Lyrics: Legal and Miscellaneous.   By the late GEORGE
OUTRAM, Esq., Advocate.   New Edition, Revised.   In 1 vol. small quarto,
with Illustrations.   [Immediately.

PAGE.   Introductory Text-Book of Geology.   By DAVID PAGE,
LL.D., Professor of Geology in the Durham University of Physical Science,
Newcastle.   With Engravings on Wood and Glossarial Index.   Twelfth
Edition.   [In the press.

—— Advanced Text-Book of Geology, Descriptive and Indus-
trial.   With Engravings, and Glossary of Scientific Terms.   Sixth Edition, revised and enlarged, 7s. 6d.

—— Introductory Text-Book of Physical Geography.   With
Sketch-Maps and Illustrations.   Edited by CHARLES LAPWORTH, F.G.S., &c.,
Professor of Geology and Mineralogy in the Mason Science College, Birming-
ham.   12th Edition.   [In preparation.

—— Advanced Text-Book of Physical Geography.   Third
Edition, Revised and Enlarged by Professor LAPWORTH.   With Engravings.
5s.

PATON.   Spindrift.   By Sir J. NOEL PATON.   Fcap., cloth, 5s.

PATON. Poems by a Painter. By Sir J. NOEL PATON. Fcap.,
cloth, 5s.

PATTERSON. Essays in History and Art. By R. HOGARTH
PATTERSON. 8vo, 12s.

—— The New Golden Age, and Influence of the Precious
Metals upon the World. 2 vols. 8vo, 31s. 6d.

PAUL. History of the Royal Company of Archers, the Queen's
Body-Guard for Scotland. By JAMES BALFOUR PAUL, Advocate of the Scottish
Bar. Crown 4to, with Portraits and other Illustrations. £2, 2s.

PAUL. Analysis and Critical Interpretation of the Hebrew Text of
the Book of Genesis. Preceded by a Hebrew Grammar, and Dissertations on
the Genuineness of the Pentateuch, and on the Structure of the Hebrew Language. By the Rev. WILLIAM PAUL, A.M. 8vo, 18s.

PEILE. Lawn Tennis as a Game of Skill. With latest revised
Laws as played by the Best Clubs. By Captain S. C. F. PEILE, B.S.C. Third
Edition, fcap. cloth, 1s. 6d.

PETTIGREW. The Handy Book of Bees, and their Profitable
Management. By A. PETTIGREW. Fourth Edition, Enlarged, with Engravings. Crown 8vo, 3s. 6d.

PHILOSOPHICAL CLASSICS FOR ENGLISH READERS.
Companion Series to Ancient and Foreign Classics for English Readers.
Edited by WILLIAM KNIGHT, LL.D., Professor of Moral Philosophy, Uni-
versity of St Andrews. In crown 8vo volumes, with portraits, price 3s. 6d.

1. DESCARTES. By Professor Mahaffy, Dublin.
2. BUTLER. By the Rev. W. Lucas Collins, M.A.
3. BERKELEY. By Professor A. Campbell Fraser, Edinburgh.
4. FICHTE. By Professor Adamson, Manchester.
5. KANT. By Professor Wallace, Oxford.
6. HAMILTON. By Professor Veitch, Glasgow.
7. HEGEL. By Professor Edward Caird, Glasgow.
8. LEIBNIZ. By J. Theodore Merz.
9. VICO. By Professor Flint, Edinburgh.
10. HOBBES. By Professor Croom Robertson, London.
11. HUME. By the Editor.

POLLOK. The Course of Time : A Poem. By ROBERT POLLOK,
A.M. Small fcap. 8vo, cloth gilt, 2s. 6d. The Cottage Edition, 32mo, sewed,
8d. The Same, cloth, gilt edges, 1s. 6d. Another Edition, with Illustrations
by Birket Foster and others, fcap., gilt cloth, 3s. 6d., or with edges gilt, 4s.

PORT ROYAL LOGIC. Translated from the French : with Introduction, Notes, and Appendix. By THOMAS SPENCER BAYNES, LL.D., Professor in the University of St Andrews. Eighth Edition, 12mo, 4s.

POTTS AND DARNELL. Aditus Faciliores : An easy Latin Con-
struing Book, with Complete Vocabulary. By A. W. POTTS, M.A., LL.D.,
Head-Master of the Fettes College, Edinburgh, and sometime Fellow of St
John's College, Cambridge; and the Rev. C. DARNELL, M.A., Head-Master of
Cargilfield Preparatory School, Edinburgh, and late Scholar of Pembroke and
Downing Colleges, Cambridge. Ninth Edition, fcap. 8vo, 3s. 6d.

—— Aditus Faciliores Graeci. An easy Greek Construing Book,
with Complete Vocabulary. Fourth Edition, fcap. 8vo, 3s.

PRINGLE. The Live-Stock of the Farm. By ROBERT O. PRINGLE.
Third Edition. Revised and Edited by JAMES MACDONALD, Editor of the
'Live-Stock Journal,' &c. Crown 8vo, 7s. 6d.

PRINGLE. A Journey in East Africa. By Mrs PRINGLE of
Whytbank, Yair. With a Map, 8vo, 5s.

PUBLIC GENERAL STATUTES AFFECTING SCOTLAND,
from 1707 to 1847, with Chronological Table and Index. 3 vols. large 8vo, £3, 3s.

PUBLIC GENERAL STATUTES AFFECTING SCOTLAND,
COLLECTION OF. Published Annually with General Index.

RAMSAY. Rough Recollections of Military Service and Society.
By Lieut.-Col. BALCARRES D. WARDLAW RAMSAY. Two vols. post 8vo, 21s.

RAMSAY. Scotland and Scotsmen in the Eighteenth Century. From
the MSS. of JOHN RAMSAY, Esq. of Ochtertyre. In two vols. 8vo. [In the press.

RANKINE. A Treatise on the Rights and Burdens incident to the Ownership of Lands and other Heritages in Scotland. By JOHN RANKINE M.A., Advocate. Second Edition, Revised and Enlarged. 8vo, 45s.

RECORDS OF THE TERCENTENARY FESTIVAL OF THE UNIVERSITY OF EDINBURGH. Celebrated in April 1884. Published under the Sanction of the Senatus Academicus. Large 4to, £2, 12s. 6d.

RICE. Reminiscences of Abraham Lincoln. By Distinguished Men of his Time. Collected and Edited by ALLEN THORNDIKE RICE, Editor of the 'North American Review.' Large 8vo, with Portraits, 21s.

RIMMER. The Early Homes of Prince Albert. By ALFRED RIMMER, Author of 'Our Old Country Towns,' &c. Beautifully Illustrated with Tinted Plates and numerous Engravings on Wood. 8vo, 10s. 6d.

ROBERTSON. Orellana, and other Poems. By J. LOGIE ROBERTSON, M.A. Fcap. 8vo. Printed on hand-made paper. 6s.

—— The White Angel of the Polly Ann, and other Stories. A Book of Fables and Fancies. Fcap. 8vo, 3s. 6d.

—— Our Holiday Among the Hills. By JAMES and JANET LOGIE ROBERTSON. Fcap. 8vo, 3s. 6d.

ROSCOE. Rambles with a Fishing-rod. By E. S. ROSCOE. Crown 8vo, 4s. 6d.

ROSS. Old Scottish Regimental Colours. By ANDREW ROSS, S.S.C., Hon. Secretary Old Scottish Regimental Colours Committee. Dedicated by Special Permission to Her Majesty the Queen. Folio, handsomely bound in cloth, £2, 12s. 6d.

RUSSELL. The Haigs of Bemersyde. A Family History. By JOHN RUSSELL. Large 8vo, with Illustrations. 21s.

RUSTOW. The War for the Rhine Frontier, 1870 : Its Political and Military History. By Col. W. RUSTOW. Translated from the German, by JOHN LAYLAND NEEDHAM, Lieutenant R.M. Artillery. 3 vols. 8vo, with Maps and Plans, £1, 11s. 6d.

SCOTCH LOCH FISHING. By "Black Palmer." Crown 8vo, interleaved with blank pages. 4s.

SCOTTISH METAPHYSICS. Reconstructed in accordance with the Principles of Physical Science. By the Writer of 'Free Notes on Herbert Spencer's First Principles.' Crown 8vo, 5s.

SELLER AND STEPHENS. Physiology at the Farm ; in Aid of Rearing and Feeding the Live Stock. By WILLIAM SELLER, M.D., F.R.S.E., Fellow of the Royal College of Physicians, Edinburgh, formerly Lecturer on Materia Medica and Dietetics ; and HENRY STEPHENS, F.R.S.E., Author of 'The Book of the Farm,' &c. Post 8vo, with Engravings, 16s.

SETH. Scottish Philosophy. A Comparison of the Scottish and German Answers to Hume. Balfour Philosophical Lectures, University of Edinburgh. By ANDREW SETH, M.A., Professor of Logic and Philosophy in the University College of South Wales and Monmouthshire. Crown 8vo, 5s.

SETON. A Budget of Anecdotes. Chiefly relating to the Current Century. Compiled and Arranged by GEORGE SETON, Advocate, M.A. Oxon. fcap. 8vo., 3s. 6d.

SHADWELL. The Life of Colin Campbell, Lord Clyde. Illustrated by Extracts from his Diary and Correspondence. By Lieutenant-General SHADWELL, C.B. 2 vols. 8vo. With Portrait, Maps, and Plans. 36s.

SHAND. Fortune's Wheel. By ALEX. INNES SHAND, Author of 'Against Time,' &c. 3 vols. post 8vo, 25s. 6d.

—— Letters from the West of Ireland. Reprinted from the 'Times.' Crown 8vo, 5s.

SHARPE. The Correspondence of Charles Kirkpatrick Sharpe. With a Memoir. In two vols. 8vo. Illustrated with Etchings and other Engravings.   [In the press.

SIM. Margaret Sim's Cookery. With an Introduction by L. B. WALFORD, Author of 'Mr Smith : A Part of His Life,' &c. Crown 8vo, 5s.

SIMPSON. Dogs of other Days : Nelson and Puck. By EVE BLANTYRE SIMPSON. Fcap. 8vo, with Illustrations, 2s. 6d.

SMITH. Italian Irrigation : A Report on the Agricultural Canals of Piedmont and Lombardy, addressed to the Hon. the Directors of the East India Company ; with an Appendix, containing a Sketch of the Irrigation System of Northern and Central India. By Lieut.-Col. R. BAIRD SMITH, F.G.S., Bengal Engineers. Second Edition. 2 vols. 8vo, with Atlas, 30s.

SMITH. Thorndale ; or, The Conflict of Opinions. By WILLIAM SMITH, Author of 'A Discourse on Ethics,' &c. A New Edition. Crown 8vo, 10s. 6d.

—— Gravenhurst ; or, Thoughts on Good and Evil. Second Edition, with Memoir of the Author. Crown 8vo, 8s.

SMITH. Greek Testament Lessons for Colleges, Schools, and Private Students, consisting chiefly of the Sermon on the Mount and the Parables of our Lord. With Notes and Essays. By the Rev. J. HUNTER SMITH, M.A., King Edward's School, Birmingham. Crown 8vo, 6s.

SMITH. Writings by the Way. By JOHN CAMPBELL SMITH, M.A., Sheriff-Substitute. Crown 8vo, 9s.

SMITH. The Secretary for Scotland. Being a Statement of the Powers and Duties of the new Scottish Office. With a Short Historical Introduction and numerous references to important Administrative Documents. By W. C. SMITH, LL.B., Advocate. 8vo, 6s.

SOLTERA. A Lady's Ride Across Spanish Honduras. By MARIA SOLTERA. With Illustrations. Post 8vo, 12s. 6d.

SORLEY. The Ethics of Naturalism. Being the Shaw Fellowship Lectures, 1884. By W. R. Sorley, M.A , Fellow of Trinity College, Cambridge, and Examiner in Philosophy in the University of Edinburgh. Crown 8vo, 6s.

SPEEDY. Sport in the Highlands and Lowlands of Scotland with Rod and Gun. By TOM SPEEDY. Second Edition, Revised and Enlarged. With Illustrations by Lieut.-General Hope Crealocke, C.B., C.M.G., and others. 8vo, 15s.

SPROTT. The Worship and Offices of the Church of Scotland ; or, the Celebration of Public Worship, the Administration of the Sacraments, and other Divine Offices, according to the Order of the Church of Scotland. By GEORGE W. SPROTT, D.D., Minister of North Berwick. Crown 8vo, 6s.

STARFORTH. Villa Residences and Farm Architecture : A Series of Designs. By JOHN STARFORTH, Architect. 102 Engravings. Second Edition, medium 4to, £2, 17s. 6d.

STATISTICAL ACCOUNT OF SCOTLAND. Complete, with Index, 15 vols. 8vo, £16, 16s. Each County sold separately, with Title, Index, and Map, neatly bound in cloth, forming a very valuable Manual to the Landowner, the Tenant, the Manufacturer, the Naturalist, the Tourist, &c.

STEPHENS. The Book of the Farm ; detailing the Labours of the Farmer, Farm-Steward, Ploughman, Shepherd, Hedger, Farm-Labourer, Field-Worker, and Cattleman. By HENRY STEPHENS, F.R.S.E. Illustrated with Portraits of Animals painted from the life ; and with 557 Engravings on Wood, representing the principal Field Operations, Implements, and Animals treated of in the Work. A New and Revised Edition, the third, in great part Re-written. 2 vols. large 8vo, £2, 10s.

—— The Book of Farm Buildings ; their Arrangement and Construction. By HENRY STEPHENS, F.R.S.E., Author of 'The Book of the Farm ;' and ROBERT SCOTT BURN. Illustrated with 1045 Plates and Engravings. Large 8vo, uniform with 'The Book of the Farm,' £1, 11s. 6d.

—— The Book of Farm Implements and Machines. By J. SLIGHT and R. SCOTT BURN, Engineers. Edited by HENRY STEPHENS. Large 8vo, uniform with 'The Book of the Farm,' £2, 2s.

—— Catechism of Practical Agriculture. With Engravings. 1s.

STEVENSON. British Fungi. (Hymenomycetes.) By Rev. JOHN STEVENSON, Author of 'Mycologia Scotia,' Hon. Sec. Cryptogamic Society of Scotland. 2 vols. post 8vo, with Illustrations, price 12s. 6d. each. Vol. I. AGARICUS—BOLBITIUS. Vol. II. CORTINARIUS—DACRYMYCES.

STEWART. Advice to Purchasers of Horses. By JOHN STEWART, V.S., Author of 'Stable Economy.' 2s. 6d.

—— Stable Economy. A Treatise on the Management of Horses in relation to Stabling, Grooming, Feeding, Watering, and Working. By JOHN STEWART, V.S. Seventh Edition, fcap. 8vo, 6s. 6d.

STORMONTH. Etymological and Pronouncing Dictionary of the English Language. Including a very Copious Selection of Scientific Terms. For Use in Schools and Colleges, and as a Book of General Reference. By the Rev. JAMES STORMONTH. The Pronunciation carefully Revised by the Rev. P. H. PHELP, M.A. Cantab. Ninth Edition, Revised throughout. Crown 8vo, pp. 800. 7s. 6d.

—— Dictionary of the English Language. Pronouncing, Etymological, and Explanatory. Revised by the Rev. P. H. PHELP. Library Edition. Imperial 8vo, handsomely bound in half morocco, 31s. 6d.

—— The School Etymological Dictionary and Word-Book. Combining the advantages of an ordinary pronouncing School Dictionary and an Etymological Spelling-book. Fcap. 8vo, pp. 254. 2s.

STORY. Nero; A Historical Play. By W. W. STORY, Author of 'Roba di Roma.' Fcap. 8vo, 6s.

—— Vallombrosa. Post 8vo, 5s.

—— He and She; or, A Poet's Portfolio. Fcap. 8vo, in parchment, 3s. 6d.

—— Poems. 2 vols., fcap., 7s. 6d.

—— Fiammetta. A Summer Idyl. Crown 8vo, 7s. 6d.

STRICKLAND. Life of Agnes Strickland. By her SISTER. Post 8vo, with Portrait engraved on Steel, 12s. 6d.

STURGIS. John-a-Dreams. A Tale. By JULIAN STURGIS. New Edition, crown 8vo, 3s. 6d.

—— Little Comedies, Old and New. Crown 8vo, 7s. 6d.

SUTHERLAND. Handbook of Hardy Herbaceous and Alpine Flowers, for general Garden Decoration. Containing Descriptions, in Plain Language, of upwards of 1000 Species of Ornamental Hardy Perennial and Alpine Plants, adapted to all classes of Flower-Gardens, Rockwork, and Waters; along with Concise and Plain Instructions for their Propagation and Culture. By WILLIAM SUTHERLAND, Gardener to the Earl of Minto; formerly Manager of the Herbaceous Department at Kew. Crown 8vo, 7s. 6d.

TAYLOR. The Story of My Life. By the late Colonel MEADOWS TAYLOR, Author of 'The Confessions of a Thug,' &c. &c. Edited by his Daughter. New and cheaper Edition, being the Fourth. Crown 8vo, 6s.

TEMPLE. Lancelot Ward, M.P. A Love-Story. By GEORGE TEMPLE. Crown 8vo, 7s. 6d.

THOLUCK. Hours of Christian Devotion. Translated from the German of A. Tholuck, D.D., Professor of Theology in the University of Halle. By the Rev. ROBERT MENZIES, D.D. With a Preface written for this Translation by the Author. Second Edition, crown 8vo, 7s. 6d.

THOMSON. Handy Book of the Flower-Garden: being Practical Directions for the Propagation, Culture, and Arrangement of Plants in Flower-Gardens all the year round. Embracing all classes of Gardens, from the largest to the smallest. With Engraved Plans, illustrative of the various systems of Grouping in Beds and Borders. By DAVID THOMSON, Gardener to his Grace the Duke of Buccleuch, K.G., at Drumlanrig. Fourth and Cheaper Edition, crown 8vo.

—— The Handy Book of Fruit-Culture under Glass: being a series of Elaborate Practical Treatises on the Cultivation and Forcing of Pines, Vines, Peaches, Figs, Melons, Strawberries, and Cucumbers. With Engravings of Hothouses, &c., most suitable for the Cultivation and Forcing of these Fruits. Second Edition. Crown 8vo, with Engravings, 7s. 6d.

THOMSON. A Practical Treatise on the Cultivation of the Grape-Vine. By WILLIAM THOMSON, Tweed Vineyards. Tenth Edition, 8vo, 5s.

THOMSON. Cookery for the Sick and Convalescent. With Directions for the Preparation of Poultices, Fomentations, &c. By BARBARA THOMSON. Fcap. 8vo, 1s. 6d.

TOM CRINGLE'S LOG. A New Edition, with Illustrations. Crown 8vo, cloth gilt, 5s. Cheap Edition, 2s.

TRANSACTIONS OF THE HIGHLAND AND AGRICUL-TURAL SOCIETY OF SCOTLAND. Published annually, price 5s.

TULLOCH. Rational Theology and Christian Philosophy in England in the Seventeenth Century. By JOHN TULLOCH, D.D., Principal of St Mary's College in the University of St Andrews; and one of her Majesty's Chaplains in Ordinary in Scotland. Second Edition. 2 vols. 8vo, 16s.

—— Modern Theories in Philosophy and Religion. 8vo, 15s.

—— Theism. The Witness of Reason and Nature to an All-Wise and Beneficent Creator. 8vo, 10s. 6d.

—— Luther, and other Leaders of the Reformation. Third Edition, enlarged. Crown 8vo, 3s. 6d.

TWO STORIES OF THE SEEN AND THE UNSEEN. 'THE OPEN DOOR,' 'OLD LADY MARY.' Crown 8vo, cloth, 2s. 6d.

VEITCH. Institutes of Logic. By JOHN VEITCH, LL.D., Professor of Logic and Rhetoric in the University of Glasgow. Post 8vo, 12s. 6d.

—— The Feeling for Nature in Scottish Poetry. From the Earliest Times to the Present Day. In 2 vols., fcap. 8vo. [In the press.

VIRGIL. The Æneid of Virgil. Translated in English Blank Verse by G. K. RICKARDS, M.A., and Lord RAVENSWORTH. 2 vols. fcap. 8vo, 10s.

WALFORD. The Novels of L. B. WALFORD. New and Uniform Edition. Crown 8vo, each 5s.

MR SMITH : A PART OF HIS LIFE.	TROUBLESOME DAUGHTERS.
COUSINS.	DICK NETHERBY.
PAULINE.	THE BABY'S GRANDMOTHER.
HISTORY OF A WEEK.	

—— Nan, and other Stories. 2 vols. crown 8vo, 12s.

WARDEN. Poems. By FRANCIS HEYWOOD WARDEN. With a Notice by Dr Vanroth. Crown 8vo, 5s.

WARREN'S (SAMUEL) WORKS. People's Edition, 4 vols. crown 8vo, cloth, 15s. 6d. Or separately :—
Diary of a Late Physician. Cloth, 2s. 6d.; boards, 2s.
Ten Thousand A-Year. Cloth, 3s. 6d.; boards, 2s. 6d.
Now and Then. The Lily and the Bee. Intellectual and Moral Development of the Present Age. 4s. 6d.
Essays : Critical, Imaginative, and Juridical. 5s.

WARREN. The Five Books of the Psalms. With Marginal Notes. By Rev. SAMUEL L. WARREN, Rector of Esher, Surrey ; late Fellow, Dean, and Divinity Lecturer, Wadham College, Oxford. Crown 8vo, 5s.

WATSON. Christ's Authority ; and other Sermons. By the late ARCHIBALD WATSON, D.D., Minister of the Parish of Dundee, and one of Her Majesty's Chaplains for Scotland. With Introduction by the Very Rev. PRINCIPAL CAIRD, Glasgow. Crown 8vo, 7s. 6d.

WEBSTER. The Angler and the Loop-Rod. By DAVID WEBSTER. Crown 8vo, with Illustrations, 7s. 6d.

WELLINGTON. Wellington Prize Essays on "the System of Field Manœuvres best adapted for enabling our Troops to meet a Continental Army." Edited by Lieut.-General Sir EDWARD BRUCE HAMLEY, K.C.B. 8vo, 12s. 6d.

WESTMINSTER ASSEMBLY. Minutes of the Westminster Assembly, while engaged in preparing their Directory for Church Government, Confession of Faith, and Catechisms (November 1644 to March 1649). Edited by the Rev. Professor ALEX. T. MITCHELL, of St Andrews, and the Rev. JOHN STRUTHERS, LL.D. With a Historical and Critical Introduction by Professor Mitchell. 8vo, 15s.

WHITE. The Eighteen Christian Centuries. By the Rev. JAMES WHITE. Seventh Edition, post 8vo, with Index, 6s.

——— History of France, from the Earliest Times. Sixth Thousand, post 8vo, with Index, 6s.

WHITE. Archæological Sketches in Scotland—Kintyre and Knapdale. By Colonel T. P. WHITE, R.E., of the Ordnance Survey. With numerous Illustrations. 2 vols. folio, £4, 4s. Vol. I., Kintyre, sold separately, £2, 2s.

——— The Ordnance Survey of the United Kingdom. A Popular Account. Crown 8vo, 5s.

WILLS AND GREENE. Drawing-room Dramas for Children. By W. G. WILLS and the Hon. Mrs GREENE. Crown 8vo, 6s.

WILSON. Works of Professor Wilson. Edited by his Son-in-Law, Professor FERRIER. 12 vols. crown 8vo, £2, 8s.

——— Christopher in his Sporting-Jacket. 2 vols., 8s.

——— Isle of Palms, City of the Plague, and other Poems. 4s.

——— Lights and Shadows of Scottish Life, and other Tales. 4s.

——— Essays, Critical and Imaginative. 4 vols., 16s.

——— The Noctes Ambrosianæ. 4 vols., 16s.

——— The Comedy of the Noctes Ambrosianæ. By CHRISTOPHER NORTH. Edited by JOHN SKELTON, Advocate. With a Portrait of Professor Wilson and of the Ettrick Shepherd, engraved on Steel. Crown 8vo, 7s. 6d.

——— Homer and his Translators, and the Greek Drama. Crown 8vo, 4s.

WILSON. From Korti to Khartum : A Journal of the Desert March from Korti to Gubat, and of the Ascent of the Nile in General Gordon's Steamers. By Colonel Sir CHARLES W. WILSON, K.C.B., K.C.M.G., R.E. Seventh Edition. Crown 8vo, 2s. 6d.

WINGATE. Annie Weir, and other Poems. By DAVID WINGATE. Fcap. 8vo, 5s.

——— Lily Neil. A Poem. Crown 8vo, 4s. 6d.

WORDSWORTH. The Historical Plays of Shakspeare. With Introductions and Notes. By CHARLES WORDSWORTH, D.C.L., Bishop of S. Andrews. 3 vols. post 8vo, each price 7s. 6d.

WORSLEY. Poems and Translations. By PHILIP STANHOPE WORSLEY, M.A. Edited by EDWARD WORSLEY. Second Edition, enlarged. Fcap. 8vo, 6s.

YATE. England and Russia Face to Face in Asia. A Record of Travel with the Afghan Boundary Commission. By Lieutenant A. C. YATE, Bombay Staff Corps, Special Correspondent of the 'Pioneer,' 'Daily Telegraph,' &c., &c., with the Afghan Boundary Commission. 8vo, with Maps and Illustrations, 21s.

YOUNG. Songs of Béranger done into English Verse. By WILLIAM YOUNG. New Edition, revised. Fcap. 8vo, 4s. 6d.

YULE. Fortification : for the Use of Officers in the Army, and Readers of Military History. By Col. YULE, Bengal Engineers. 8vo, with numerous Illustrations, 10s. 6d.

ZIT AND XOE : Their Early Experiences. Reprinted from 'Blackwood's Magazine.' Crown 8vo, paper cover, 1s.

4/87.

www.ingramcontent.com/pod-product-compliance
Lightning Source LLC
Chambersburg PA
CBHW032002120726
47898CB00005BA/1454